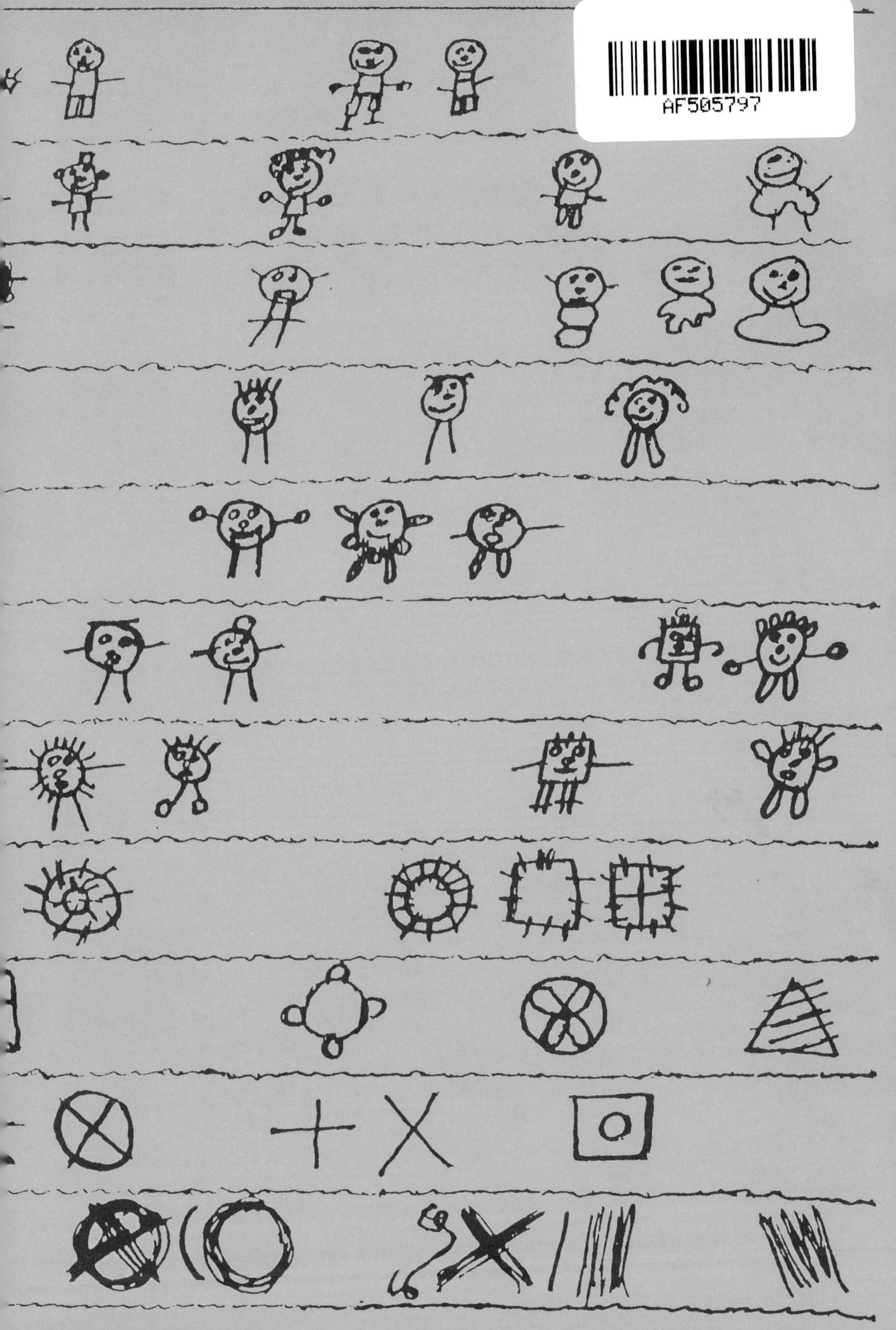

To Begin Again

To Begin Again: Artists and Childhood

Jeffrey De Blois and Ruth Erickson
Institute of Contemporary Art/Boston and
DelMonico Books • D.A.P., New York

Foreword

Childhood is a time of life experienced by us all. Given this universal truth, the complexities, layers, and differences of individual experiences are rich and textured areas for exploration and understanding. This original, profound, and exciting exhibition, organized by Ruth Erickson, the ICA's Mannion Family Senior Curator, with Jeffrey De Blois, Associate Curator and Publications Manager, does just that. *To Begin Again: Artists and Childhood* investigates the agency of children and the influence of their art, language, gestures, needs, power, and vulnerability on visual artists since the early twentieth century. This careful selection and presentation of more than seventy-five works by a diverse array of artists spans time, geography, generations, and cultures to craft a narrative about modernism, labor, innocence, and the institutional structures surrounding childhood.

My father often repeated the quote from Maria Montessori that "play is the work of children." Through works of photography, painting, sculpture, and installation in *To Begin Again*, we see children at play and at work, capturing both the joys and the dangers of young lives entering and inhabiting the world. They are depicted in the many precarious situations and the societal structures that inflict isolation, loneliness, difference, and persecution, but we also see them through the fantasies, books, and objects they imbue with fun and creativity. Art by children—its scribbles, stick figures, games, and storytelling—is a gateway to inspire open expression for artists and a tool for pedagogy. Childhood emerges in this exhibition as myriad experiences; as an intellectual query into language, learning, and meaning; and as strong, vibrant works of art by and about children.

On behalf of the ICA, I extend our gratitude to Ruth Erickson and Jeffrey De Blois for organizing this ambitious and timely exhibition and publication. We appreciate all the institutions and individuals who generously lent works, the contributors to this book, and the donors who made it possible to share this endeavor with our audiences. Thanks are due to the Radcliffe exploratory seminar participants—Brian Belott, Robin Bernstein, Allison Curseen, Michelle Millar Fisher, Marah Gubar, Anne Higonnet, Catherine Huang, Francie Latour, Robin Meisner, Camille Owens, Liz Phipps-Soeiro, Vivian Poey, Siddhartha V. Shah, Rachel Tang, Vita Weinstein, and Ellen Winner—for their ideas and help in shaping themes and related programs. To the entire ICA staff and boards, I applaud your talent, efforts, commitment, and generosity.

Time spent with children is a constant and necessary reminder of the fullness of their minds and imaginations. *To Begin Again* is an equally urgent reminder of our responsibility as adults for their care, development, support, learning, and access to opportunities.

Jill Medvedow
Ellen Matilda Poss Director
ICA/Boston

Introduction

"Children are the ways the world begins again and again."
—June Jordan, *The Voice of the Children*

Childhood is a subject of universal significance, and of personal experience; everyone was once a child. Even so, there are many competing ideas about childhood that play out in the world of adults, and the child remains a marginalized and vulnerable figure. Artists have long been inspired by children—by their imagination, creativity, and unique ways of seeing and being in the world. For many artists, it is the subject to which their work most frequently returns. *To Begin Again: Artists and Childhood* surveys how artists have reflected on and contributed to notions of childhood at different moments from the early twentieth century to the present. These works may depict children or involve them as collaborators, represent or mimic their ways of drawing or telling stories, highlight their unique cultures, or negotiate ideas of innocence and spontaneity closely associated with young people. Artists have challenged problematic ideals of childhood as often as they have perpetuated them. Still, the works in *To Begin Again* offer distinctive viewpoints revealing how time and place, race, gender, class, and aesthetics fundamentally shape how we experience and understand childhood.

This catalogue follows the exhibition it accompanies in endeavoring to orchestrate conversations and encounters between artworks from disparate times and places in order to complicate common assumptions about childhood and to think deeply about both the sense of possibility embodied in childhood and its inherent risks. Introductions to the exhibition's six thematic sections highlight what has been most resonant for artists in the many differing approaches to childhood as a subject, while reproductions of every artwork invite readers to explore their own connections between the gathered works. The catalogue's contributors offer a diverse array of expansive and richly detailed views. For the artist Anna Craycroft, "when artists personify children and childhood in their work, a deeper social imaginary is revealed." Craycroft refers to this as "childishism," an artistic methodology that forms the basis of her experimental visual essay, which maps an associative history between artistic representations of the childish in the form of an imagined search engine's algorithmically organized results according to a set of search terms. Jeffrey De Blois considers the formative role children's art played in twentieth-century art, as one of the emblematic "others" that was central to modernism's self-construction. Joshua Bennett's autotheoretical text considers the role of folk heroes in the Black aesthetic tradition, looking specifically at how Malcolm X has figured in his own life and in the Black cultural imaginary more broadly. Ruth Erickson focuses on the specters of power and agency in the contours of childhood, exploring how artworks in the exhibition give form to the negotiation of care and constraint in the experiences of children from different identity positions. Anne Higonnet examines how the problematic of childhood innocence, whose construction was the subject of one of her books, animates works in the exhibition. An excerpt from Valeria Luiselli's *Tell Me How It Ends: An Essay in Forty Questions* (2017), a book structured around the questions she translates and asks undocumented Latin American children facing deportation, is reprinted for the ways in which it interweaves individual stories with broader questions of ethics and power, institutions and survival. Naima J. Keith and exhibiting artists Oscar Murillo and Sable Elyse Smith discuss childhood and its relationships to institutions such as schools and prisons in a conversation focused on the larger ramifications of their projects. The volume concludes with a conversation between exhibiting artists Mierle Laderman Ukeles and Carmen Winant, who discuss labor, lineages of parent-child collaboration, and gestures of care in a continuation of their long-term correspondence. *To Begin Again* underscores that while there is no single, uniform idea of childhood, it is nevertheless the ground upon which so much of society is built, negotiated, and imagined.

Jeffrey De Blois
Ruth Erickson

Childishism

Spiritual–Child

Spiritual Child · 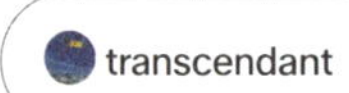 transcendant · 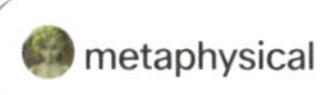 metaphysical · 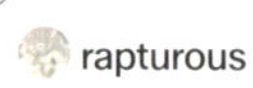 rapturous · 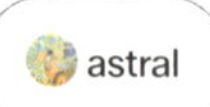 astral · 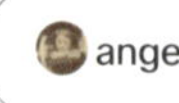 angel

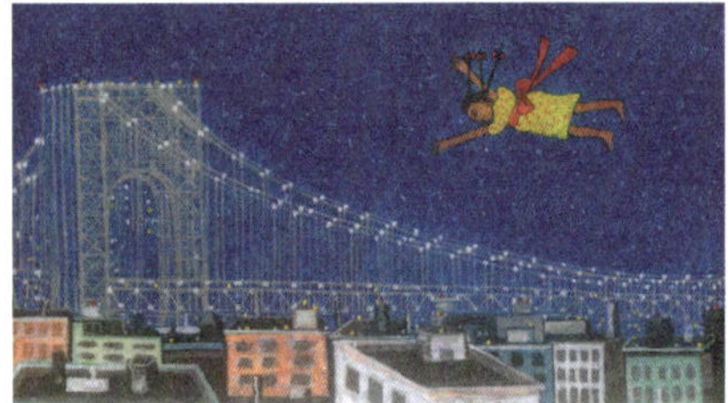

Faith Ringgold, Tar Beach 2 (Quilt Detail)

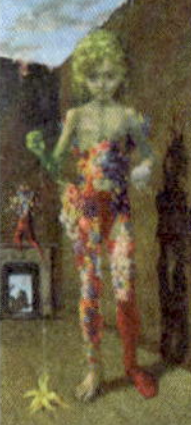

Dorothea ...

William Blake, Ga...

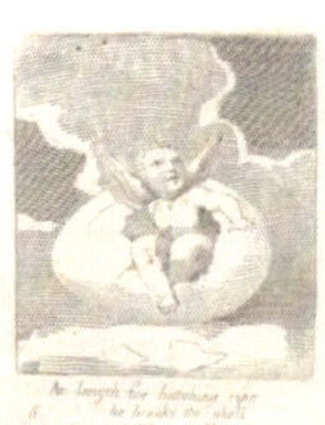

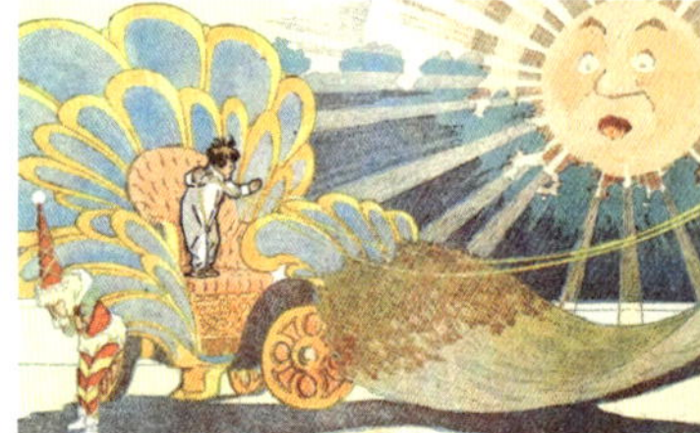

Windsor McCay, Little Nemo

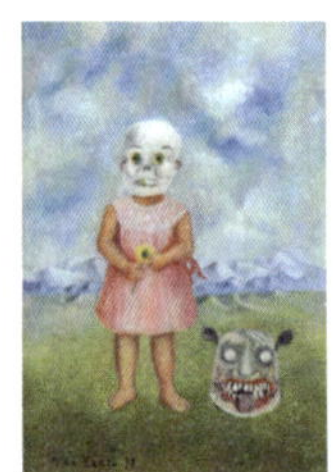

Frida Kahlo, Girl ...

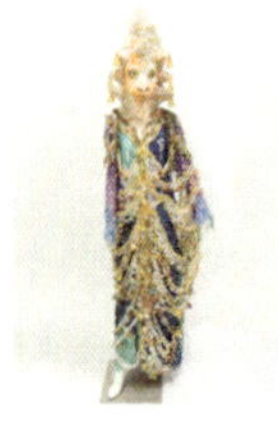

Raúl de Nieves...

Other Types

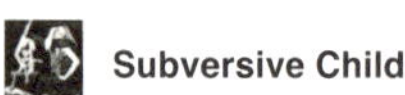 Subversive Child

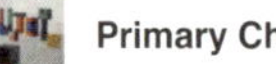 Primary Child

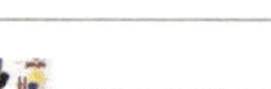 Revolutionary Child

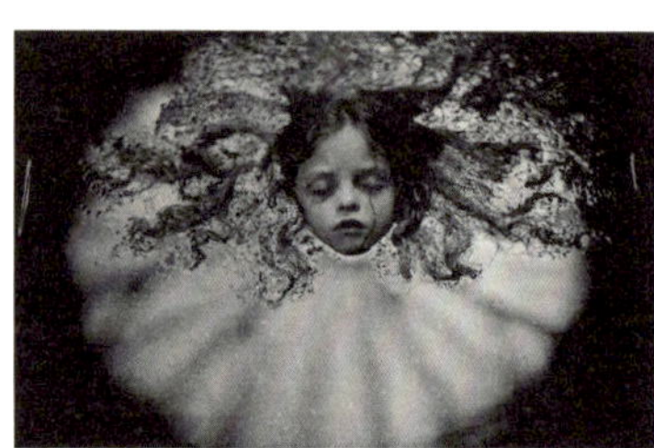

Sally Mann, At Warm Springs

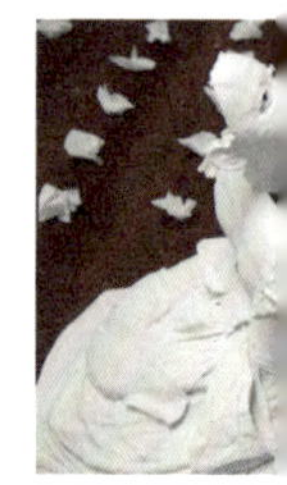

Karon Davis, N

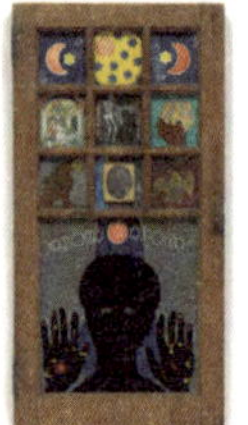

Betye Saar ...

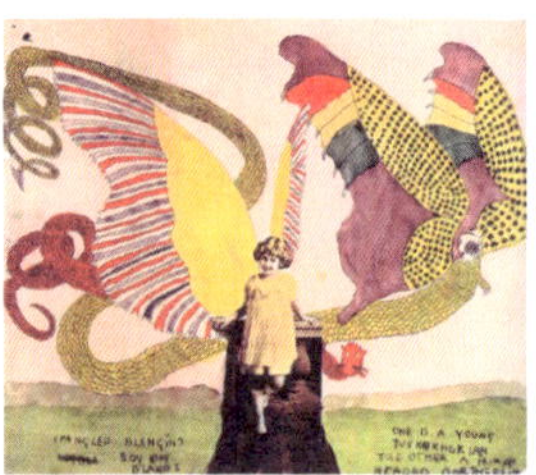

Henry Darger, Spangled Ble ...

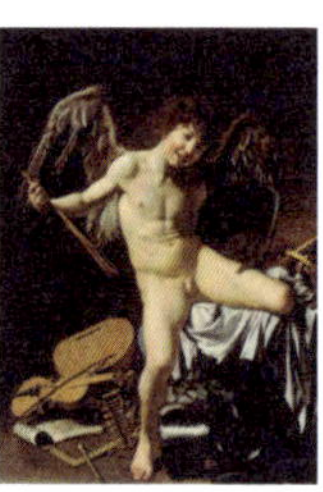

Caravaggio, Am...

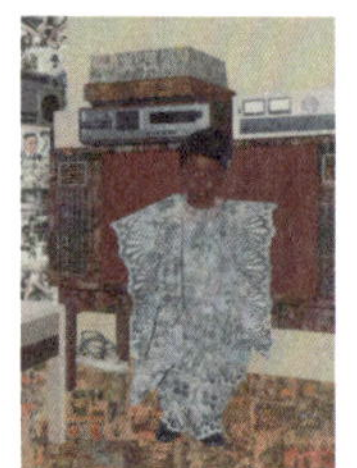

Njideka Akunyili ...

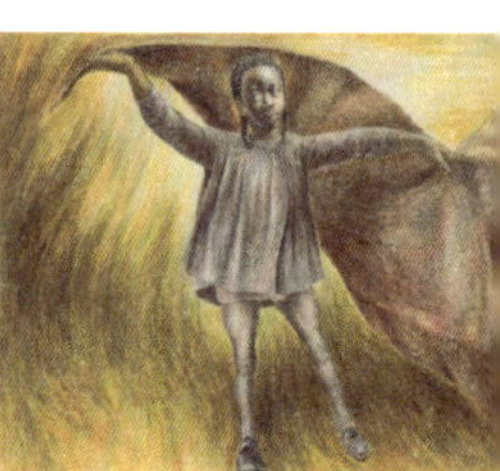

Charles White, Sometimes I

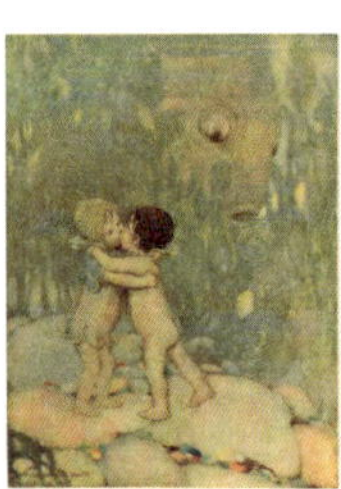

Jesse Wilcox Sm...

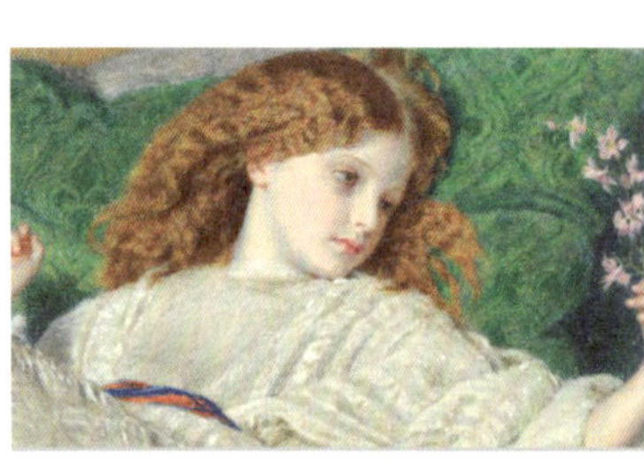

Frederick William Burton, Dreams

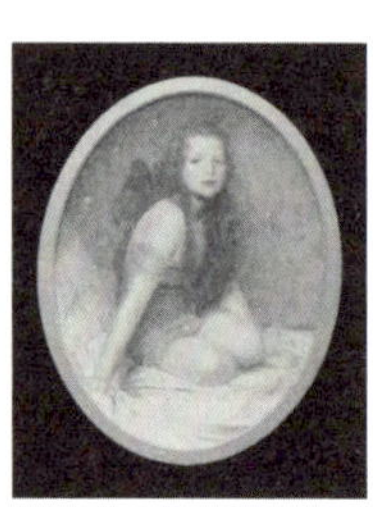

William Sergeant ...

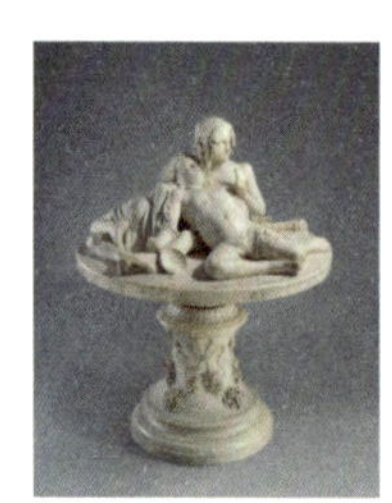

Lorenzo Bartolini ...

GCC, Positiv

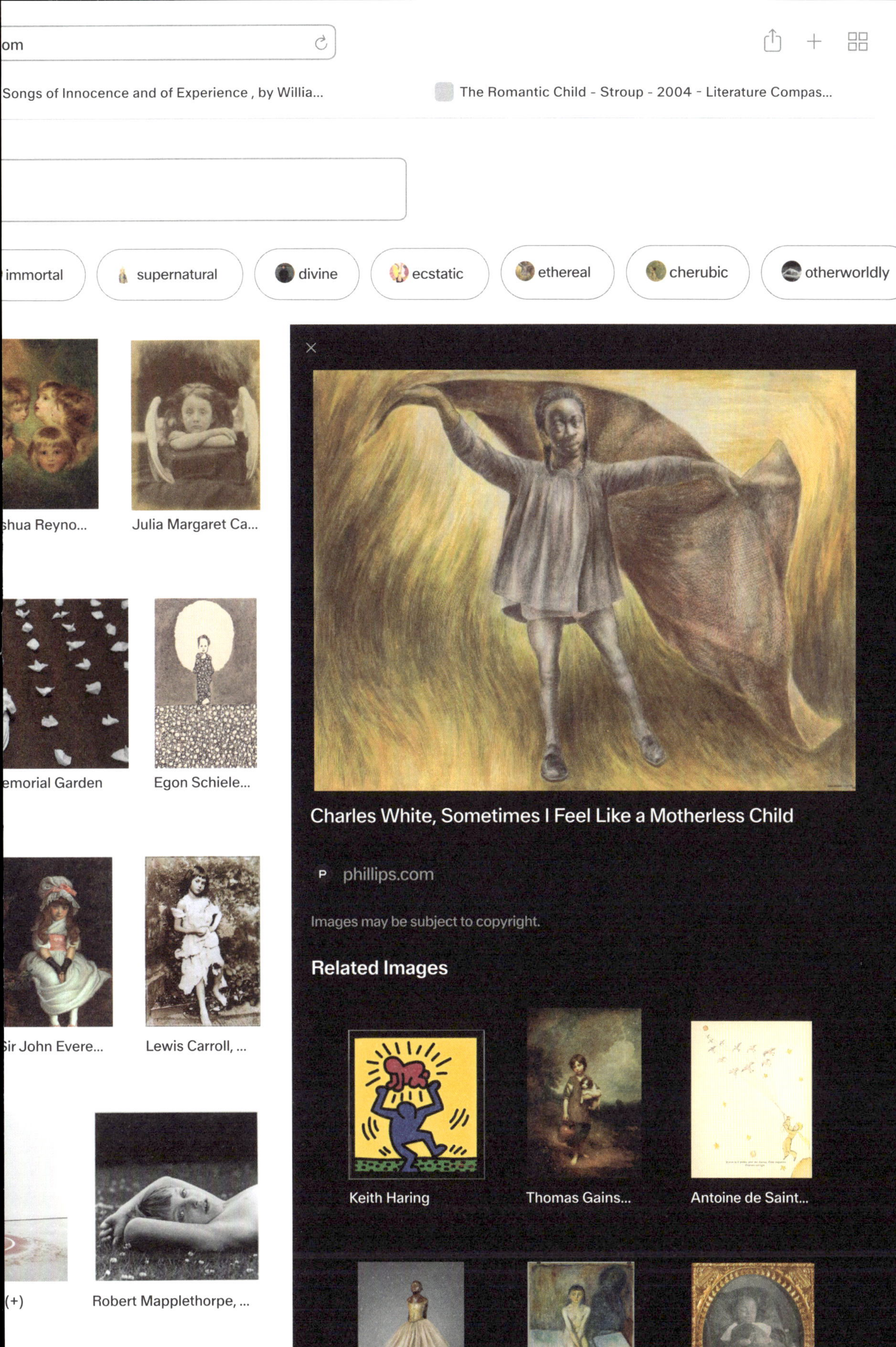

Childishism

Natural-Child

Natural Child 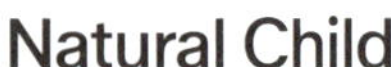 unrefined 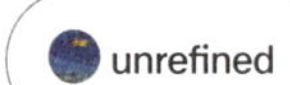 natural 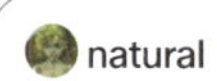 originality 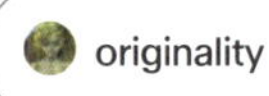 spontaneous 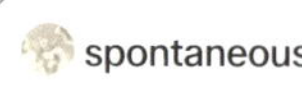 primitiv

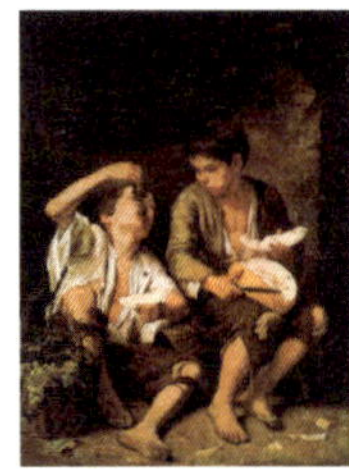

Bartolomé Esteb...

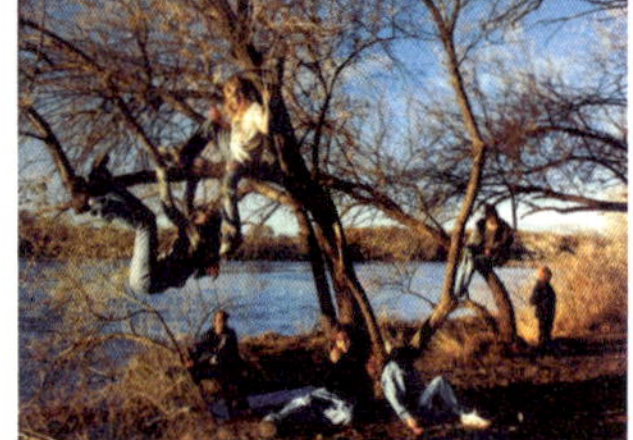

Justine Kurland, Always plenty...

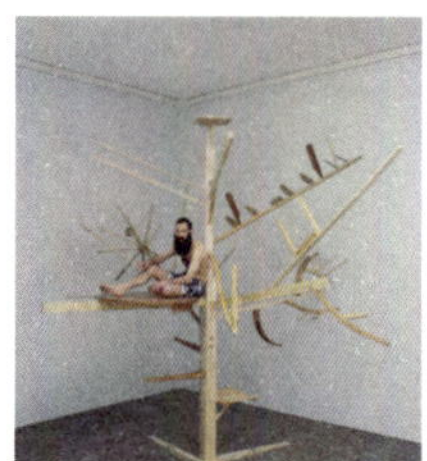

Guy Ben-Ner, Tree...

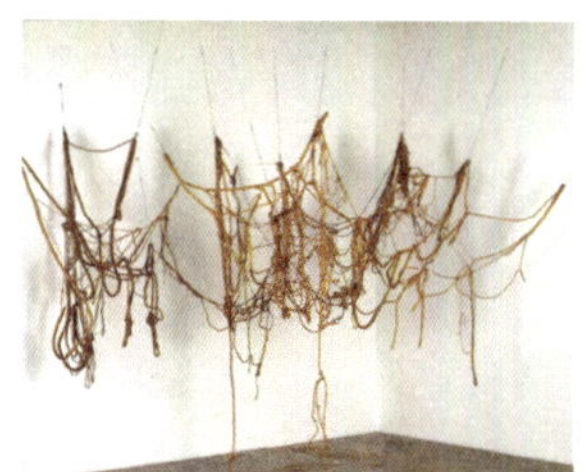

Eva Hesse, No Title

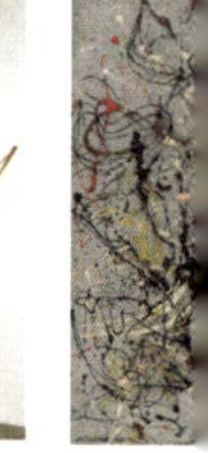

Jackso

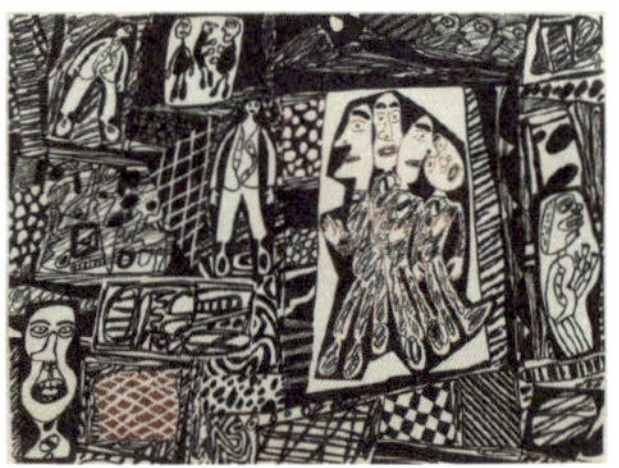

Jean Dubuffet, Untitled 1978

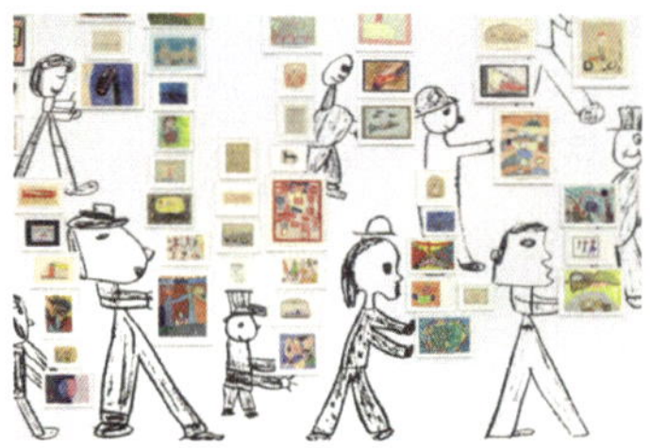

Brian Belott, Dr. Kid President Jr. 2 (4)

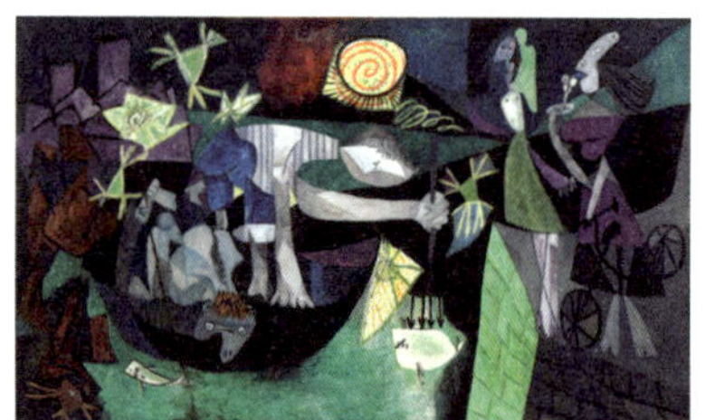

Pablo Picasso, Night Fishing at Antibes

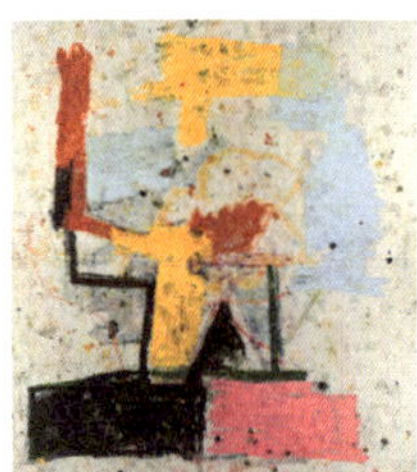

Bradley, Big Boy

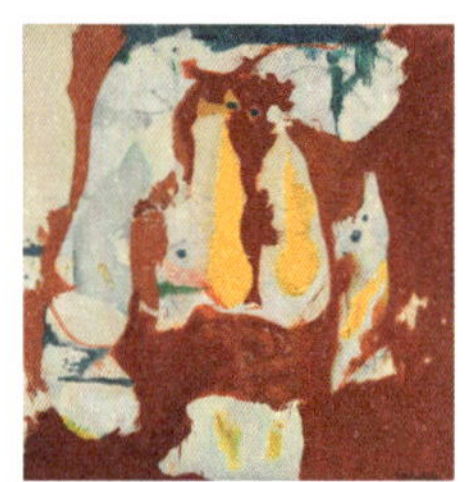

Helen Frankenthaler,...

Other Types

Revolutionary Child

Primary Child

Regressive Child

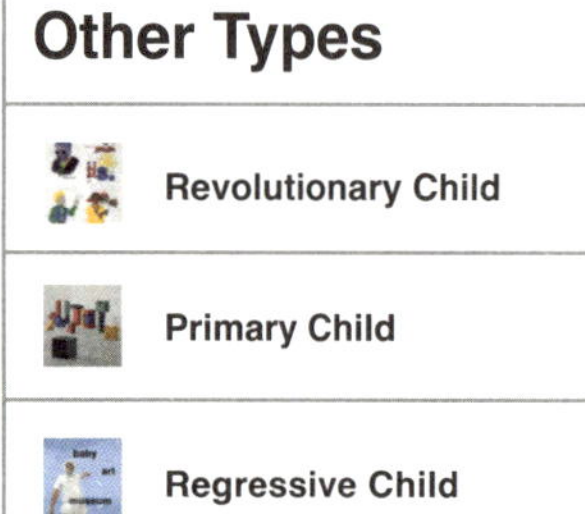

Ree Morton, Ring

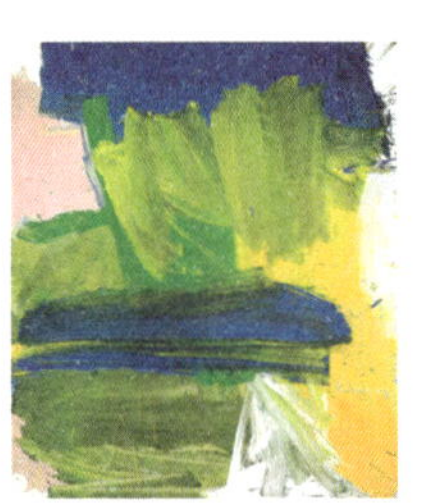

Willem de Kooning...

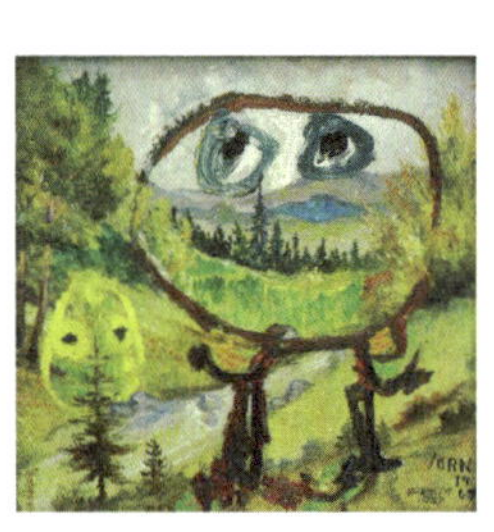

Asger Jorn, Enticement

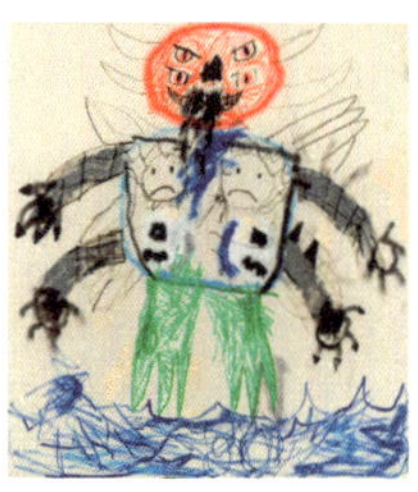

Robert Nava, Devou...

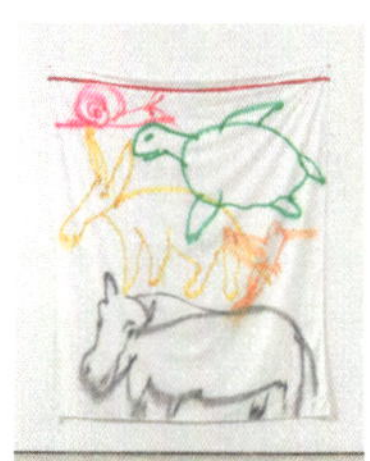

Polly Apfelbaum,...

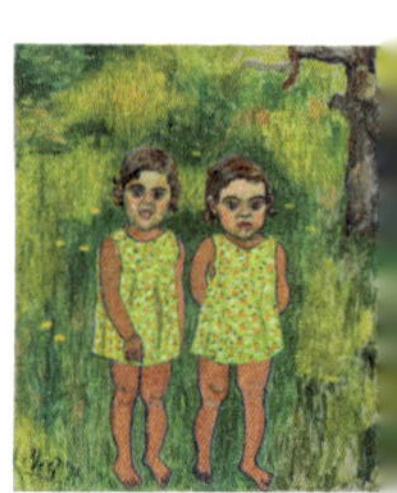

Alice Neel, Antonia...

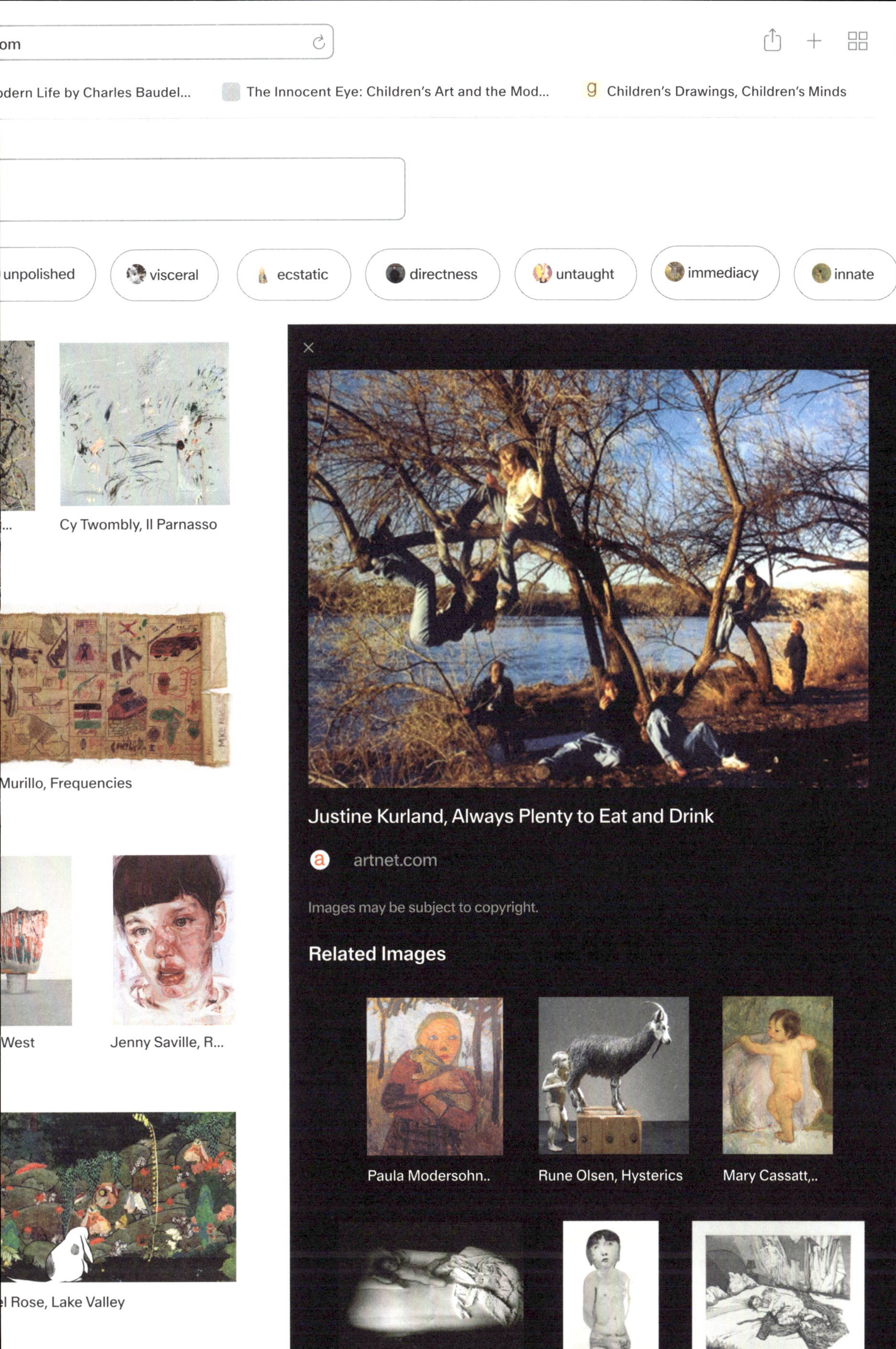
om
Modern Life by Charles Baudel...
The Innocent Eye: Children's Art and the Mod...
Children's Drawings, Children's Minds
unpolished
visceral
ecstatic
directness
untaught
immediacy
innate
Cy Twombly, Il Parnasso
Murillo, Frequencies
West
Jenny Saville, R...
Rose, Lake Valley
Justine Kurland, Always Plenty to Eat and Drink
artnet.com
Images may be subject to copyright.
Related Images
Paula Modersohn..
Rune Olsen, Hysterics
Mary Cassatt,..

Childishism

Primary-Child

Primary Child   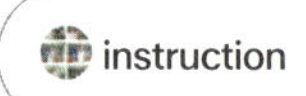 instruction   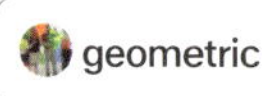 geometric   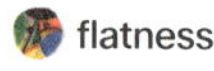 flatness   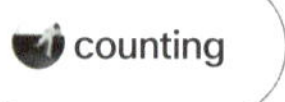 counting   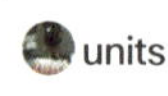 units

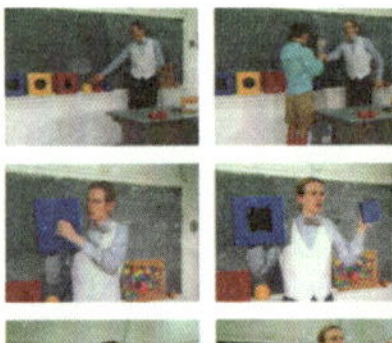

Ericka Beckman, Blin...

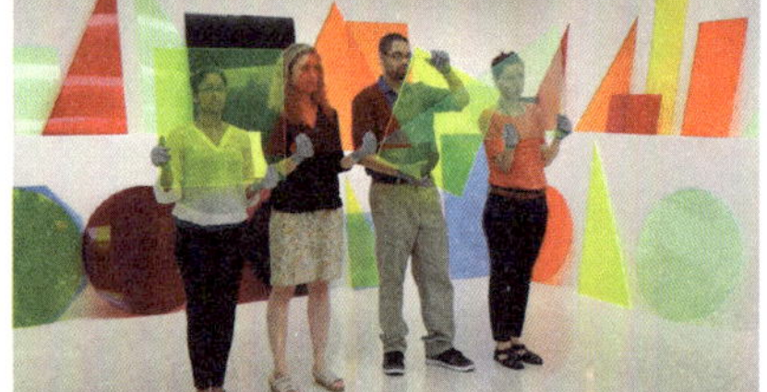

Amalia Pica, A ∩B ∩C

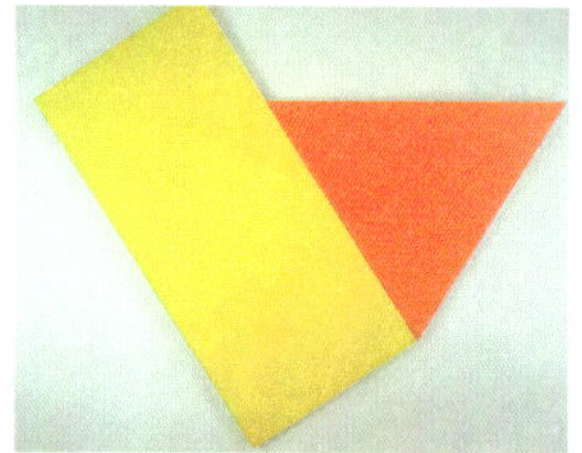

Ellsworth Kelly, Yellow with R...

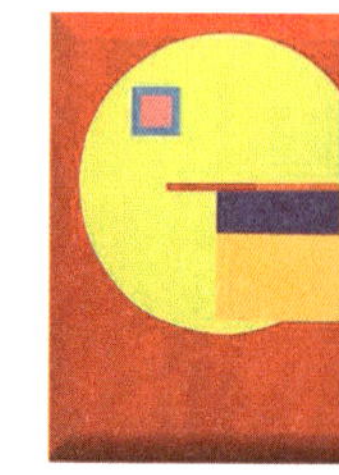

Daniel LaRue Joh...

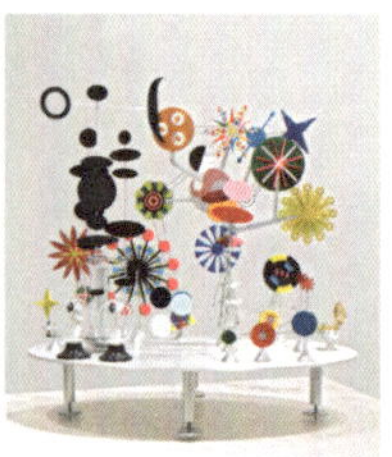

Edgar Orlaineta, Sol...

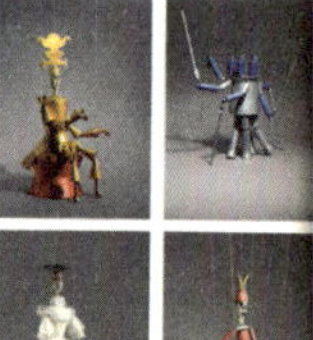

Sophie Taeuber...

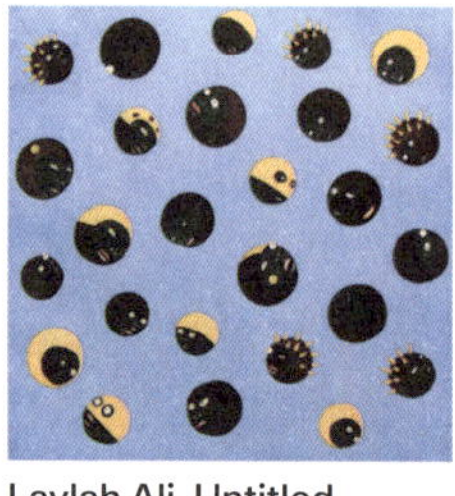

Laylah Ali, Untitled

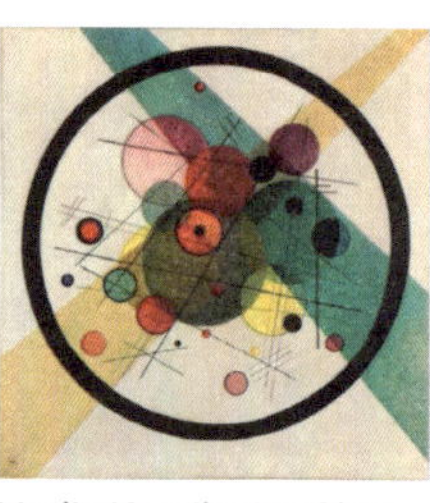

Vasily Kandinsky, Circl...

Other Types

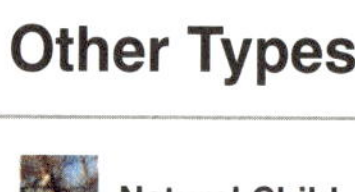 **Natural Child**

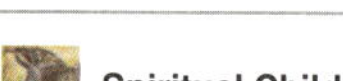 **Spiritual Child**

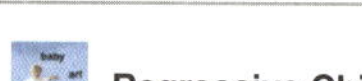 **Regressive Child**

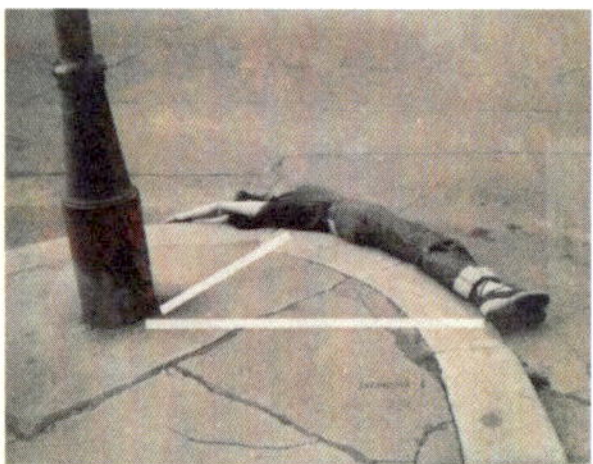

Valie Export, Abrundung II (Rou...

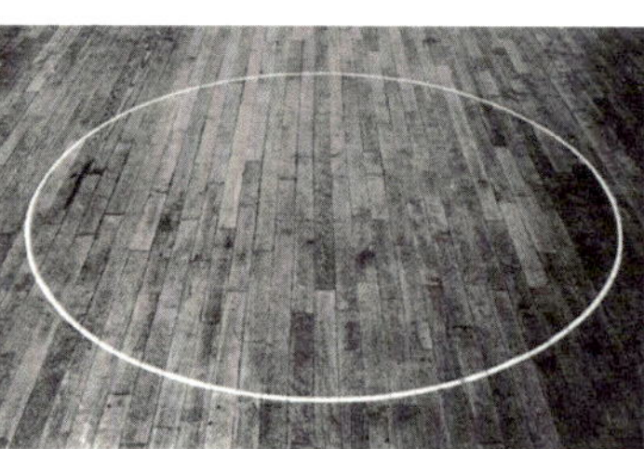

Ian Wilson, Circle on the floor

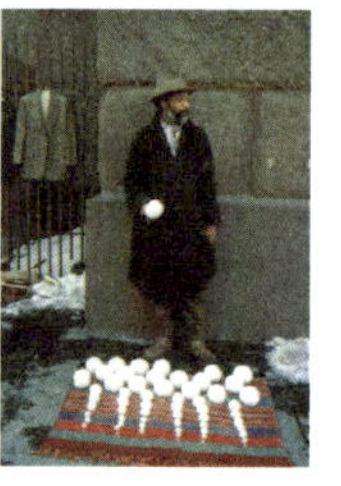

David Hammon...

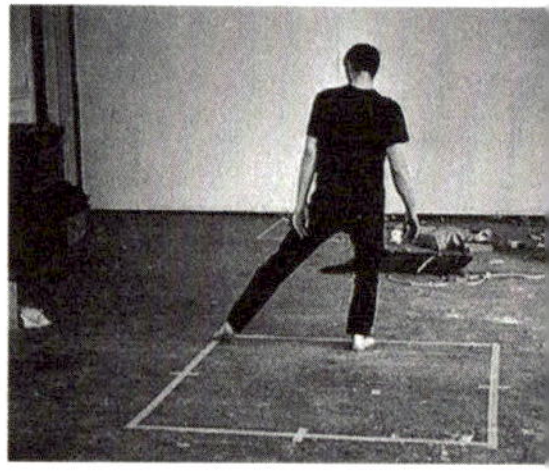

Bruce Nauman, Dance or Exerc...

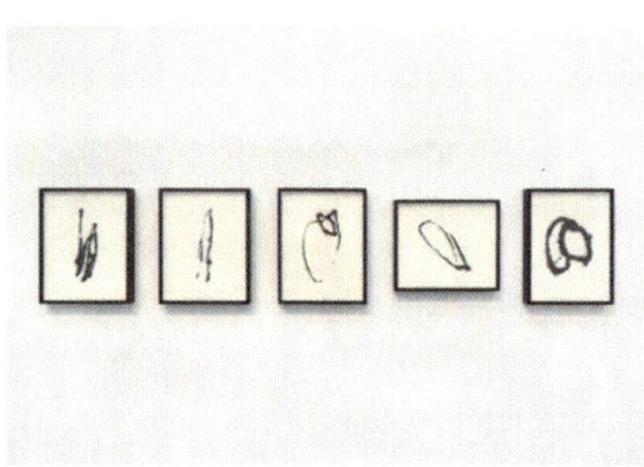

Allan McCollum, Traces: Past and P...

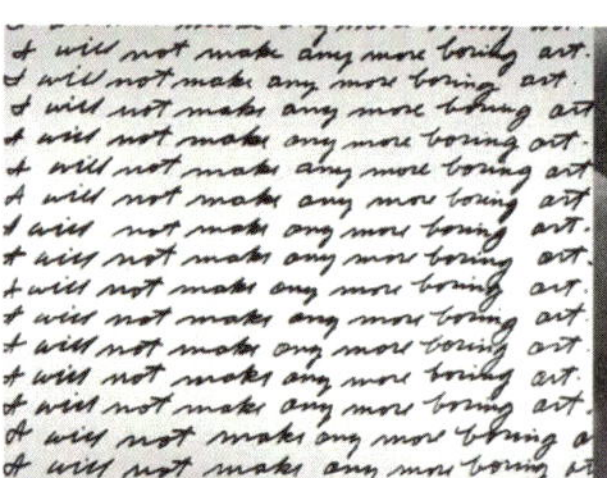

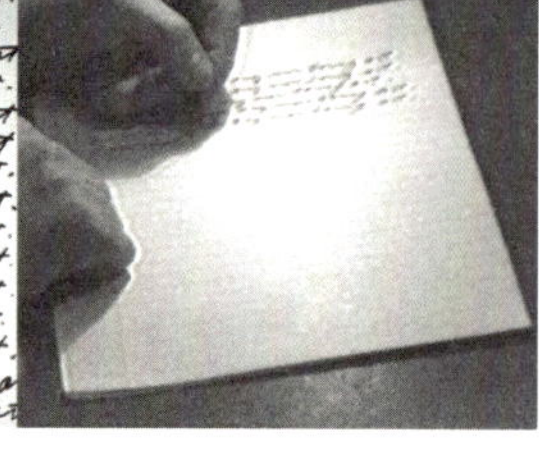

John Baldessari, I Will Not Make Any More Boring Art

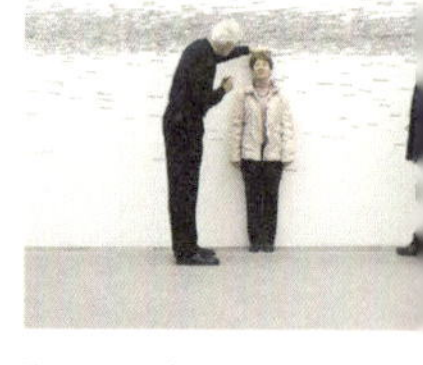

Roman Ondak, Measur...

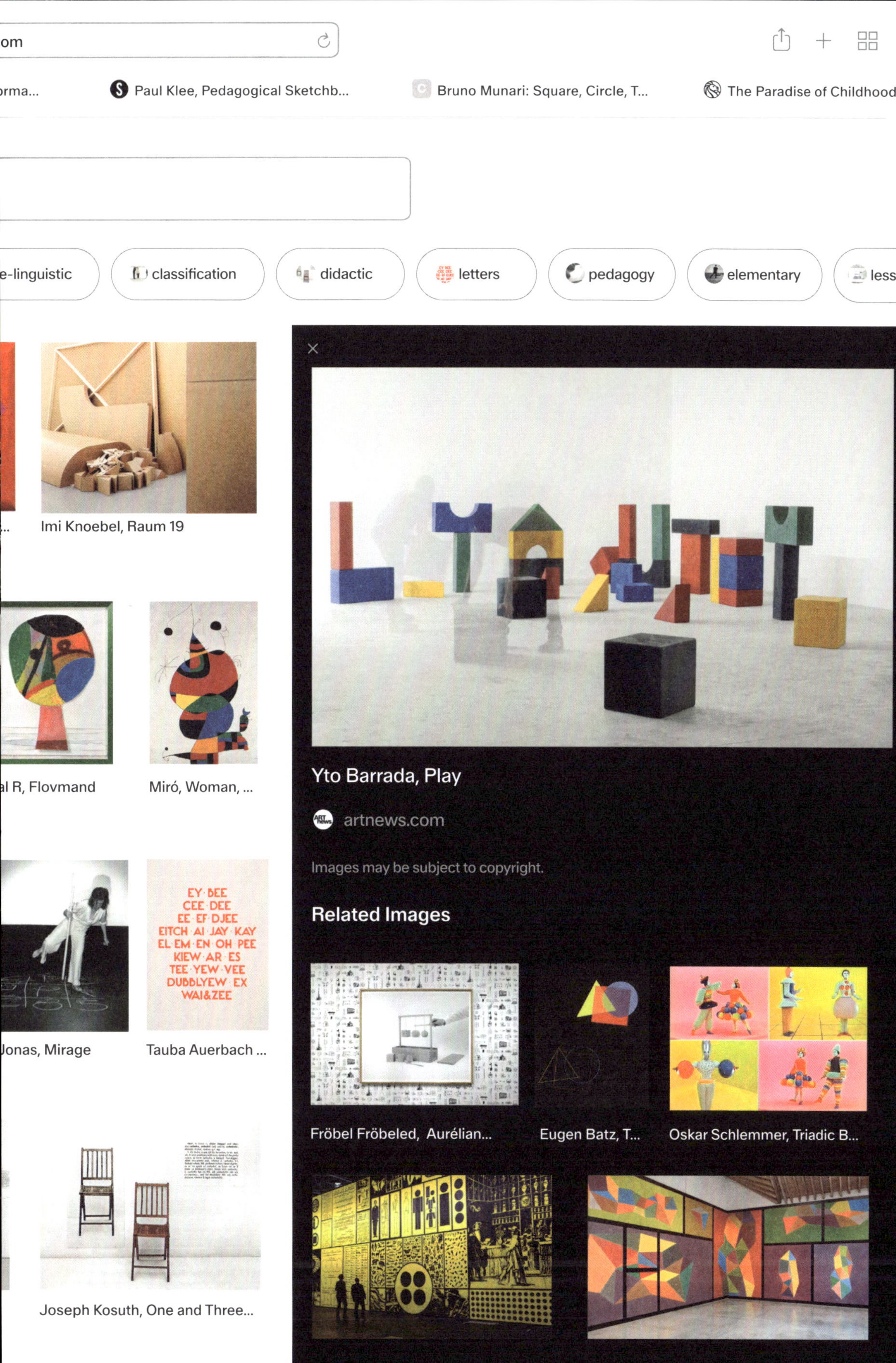
om
orma...
Paul Klee, Pedagogical Sketchb...
Bruno Munari: Square, Circle, T...
The Paradise of Childhood:
e-linguistic
classification
didactic
letters
pedagogy
elementary
lesso
Imi Knoebel, Raum 19
R, Flovmand
Miró, Woman, ...
EY · BEE
CEE · DEE
EE · EF DJEE
EITCH · AI JAY KAY
EL · EM · EN OH PEE
KIEW · AR ES
TEE · YEW VEE
DUBBLYEW · EX
WAI&ZEE
Jonas, Mirage
Tauba Auerbach ...
Joseph Kosuth, One and Three...
Yto Barrada, Play
artnews.com
Images may be subject to copyright.
Related Images
Fröbel Fröbeled, Aurélian...
Eugen Batz, T...
Oskar Schlemmer, Triadic B...

Childishism

Regressive-Child

Regressive Child   ⬡ tantrum   ⬡ catharsis   ⬡ unmoored   ⬡ raw   ⬡ abject

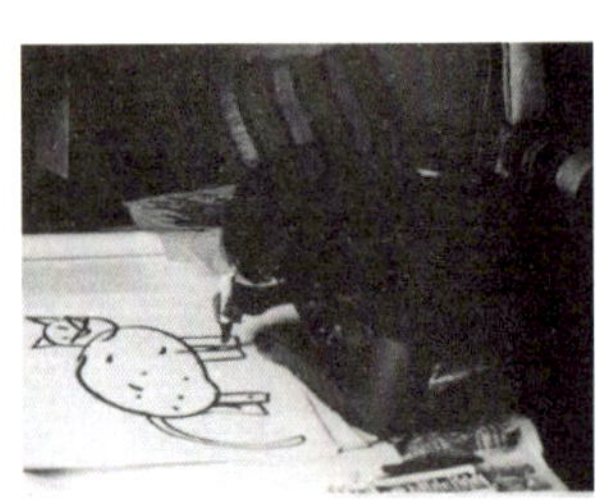

Matt Mullican, Drawing While…

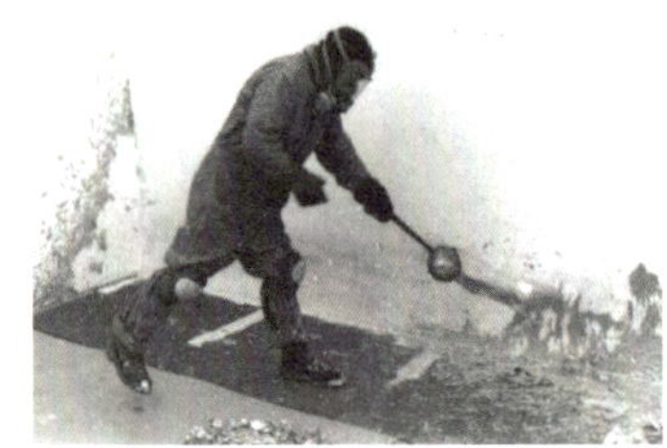

Richard Serra, Throwing Lead

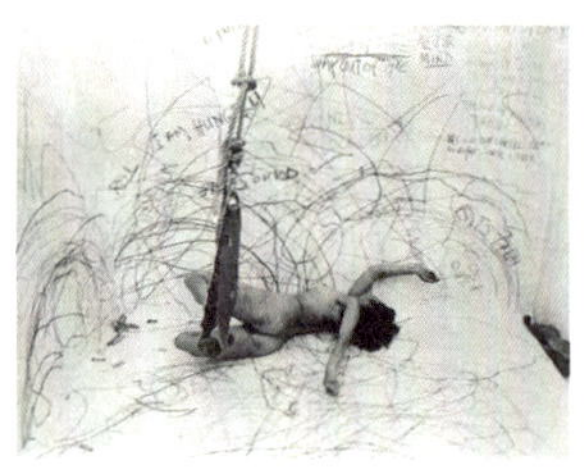

Carolee Schneemann, Up to …

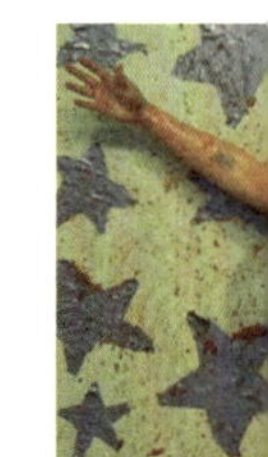

Kate Gilmor

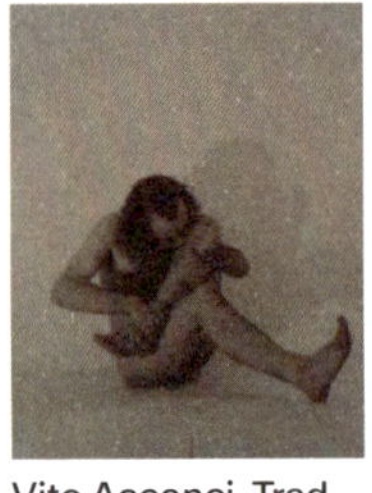

Vito Acconci, Trad…

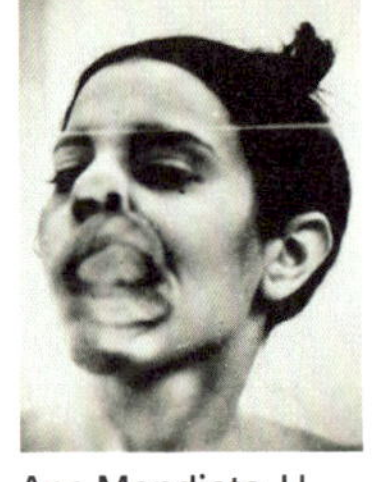

Ana Mendieta, U…

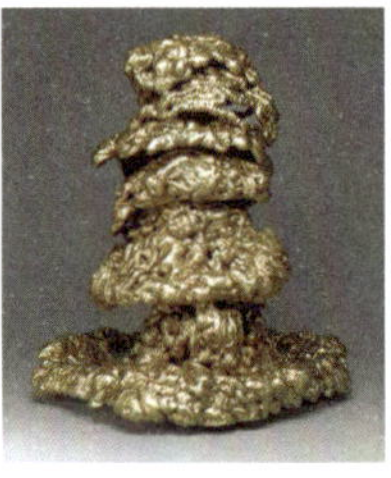

Lynda Benglis, Sum…

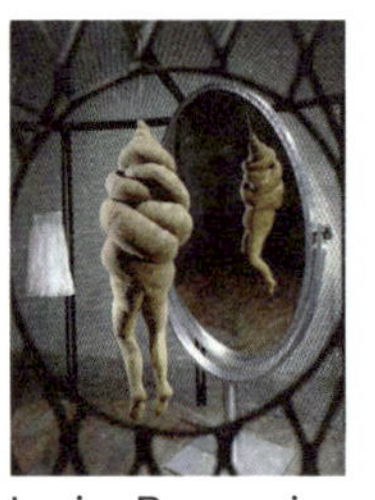

Louise Bourgeoi…

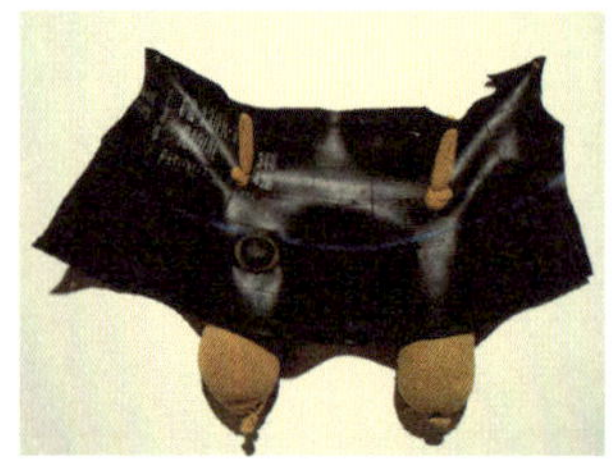

Senga Nengudi, Rubber Maid

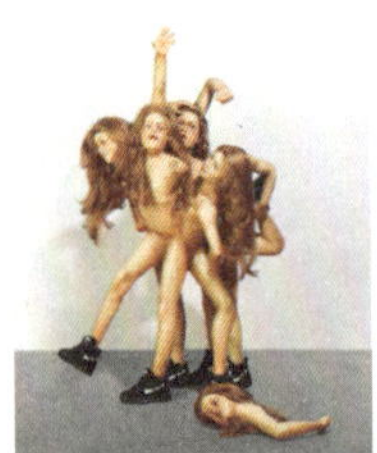

Jake and Dinos C…

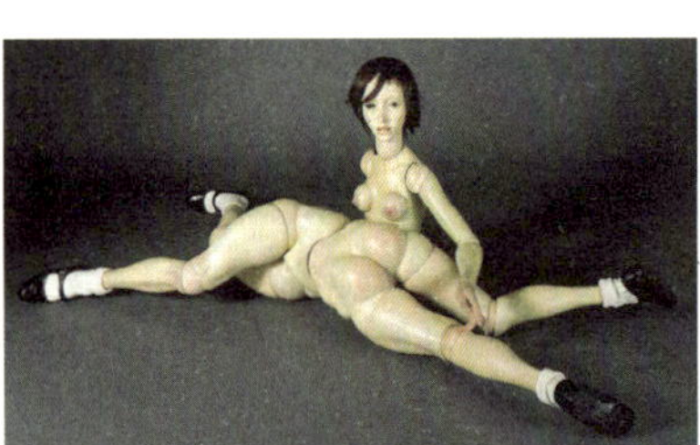

Hans Bellmer, La Poupée

Other Types

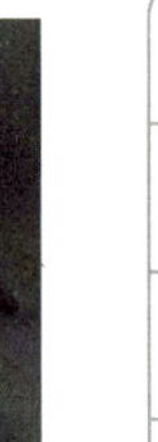 **Natural Child**

Primary Child

Spiritual Child

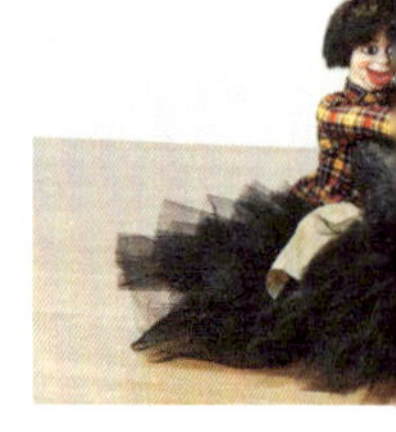

Annette Messager, L

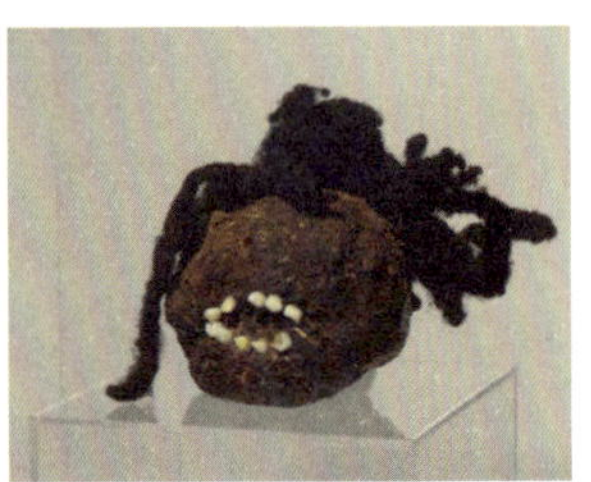

Chris Ofili, Shithead

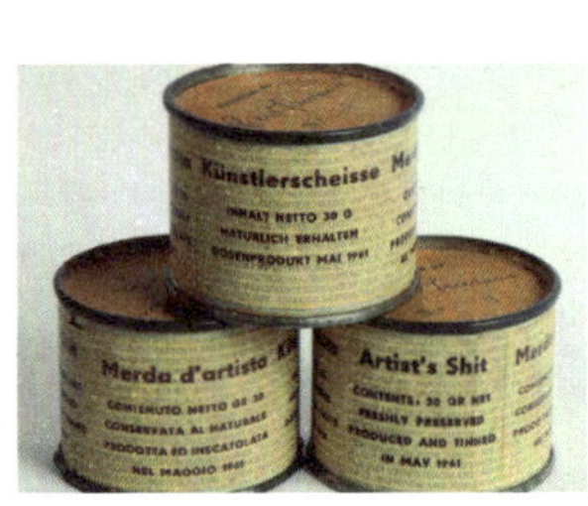

Piero Manzoni, Artist's Shit

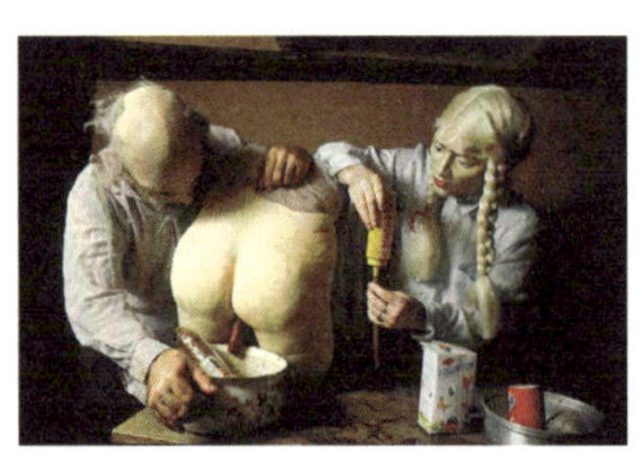

Mike Kelley and Paul McCarthy, Hei…

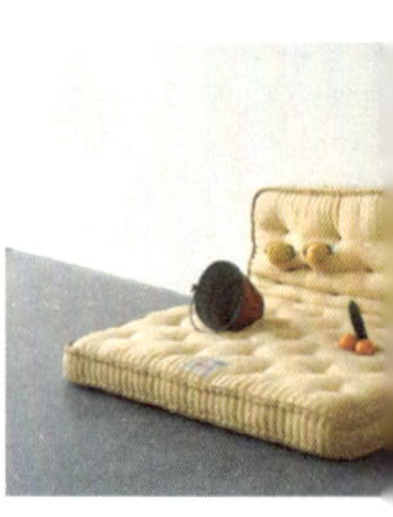

Sarah Lucas, Au Natu

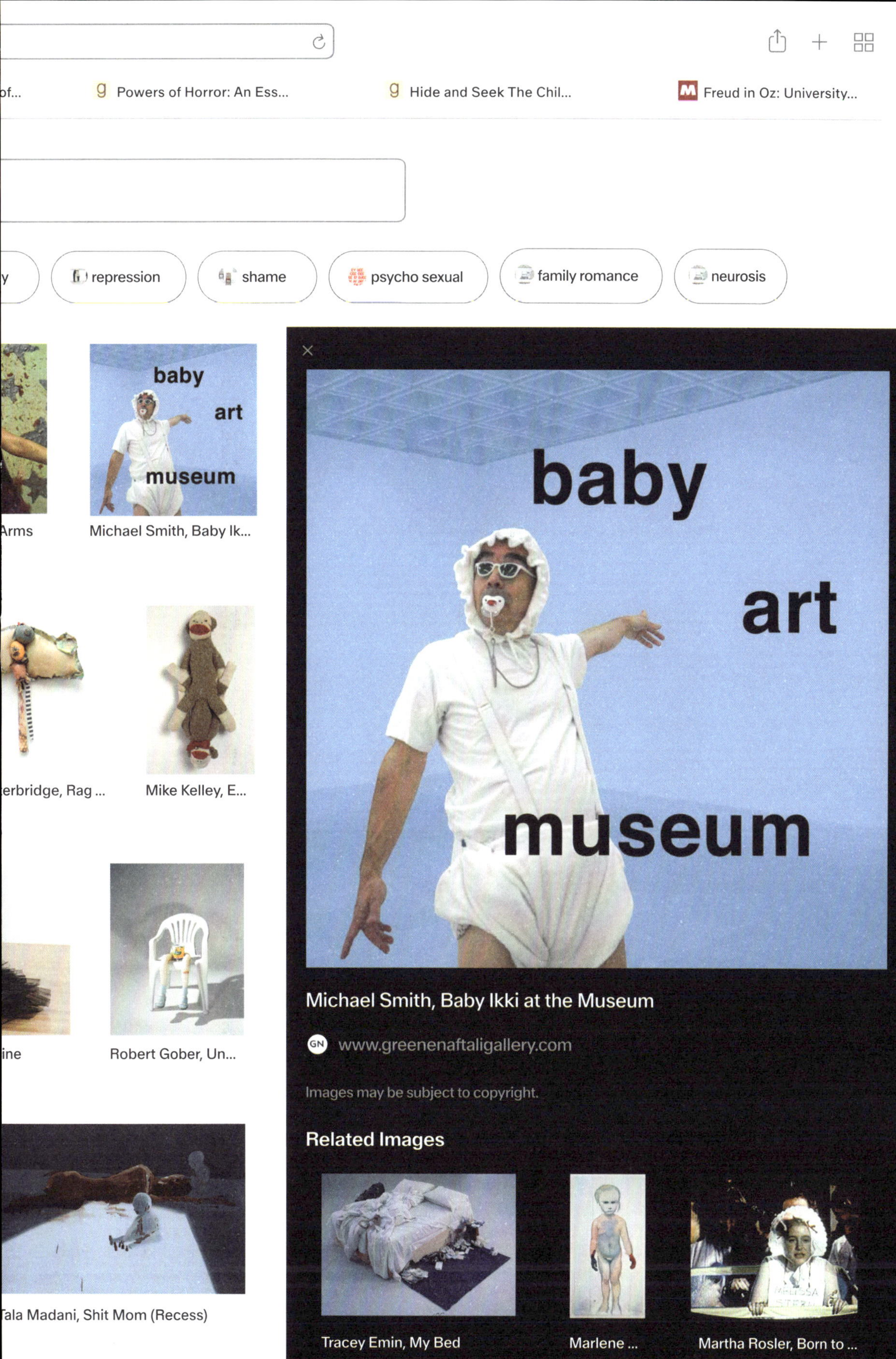
Powers of Horror: An Ess...
Hide and Seek The Chil...
Freud in Oz: University...
repression
shame
psycho sexual
family romance
neurosis
baby
art
museum
Michael Smith, Baby Ik...
Arms
erbridge, Rag ...
Mike Kelley, E...
Robert Gober, Un...
ine
Tala Madani, Shit Mom (Recess)
baby
art
museum
Michael Smith, Baby Ikki at the Museum
www.greenenaftaligallery.com
Images may be subject to copyright.
Related Images
Tracey Emin, My Bed
Marlene ...
Martha Rosler, Born to ...

Childishism

Subversive-Child

Subversive Child 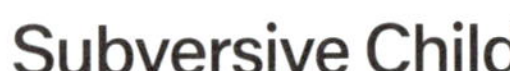   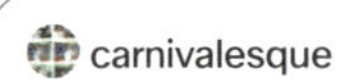 carnivalesque   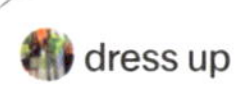 dress up   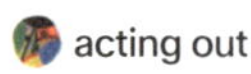 acting out   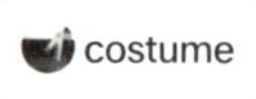 costume

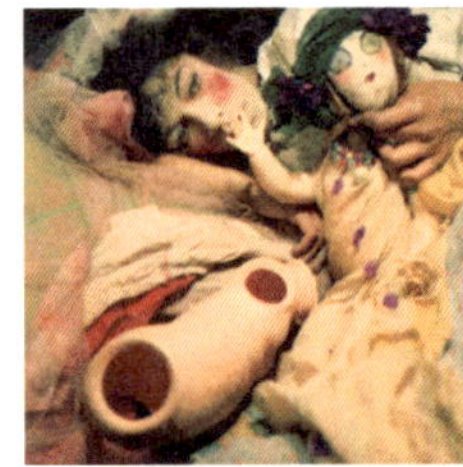

Jack Smith, Early Color...

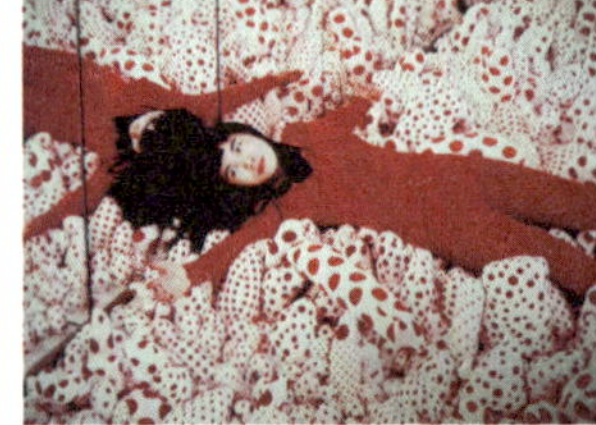

Yayoi Kusama, Infinity Mirror R...

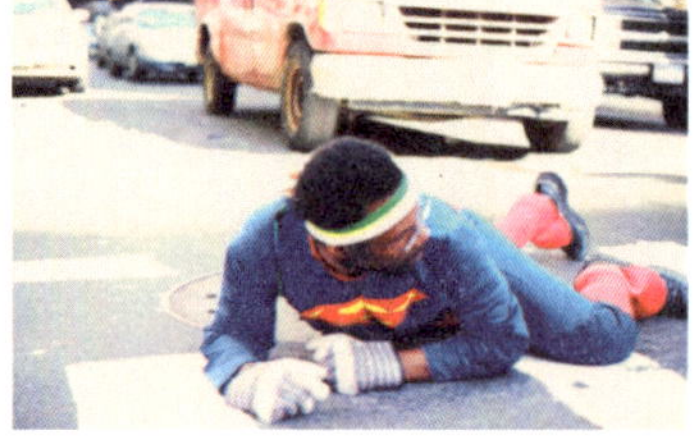

Pope.L, The Great White Way...

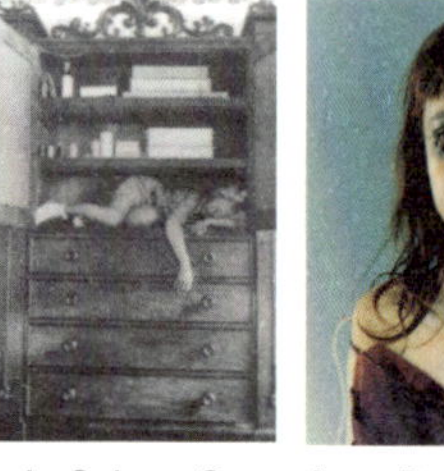

Claude Cahun, S...   Aura Ros...

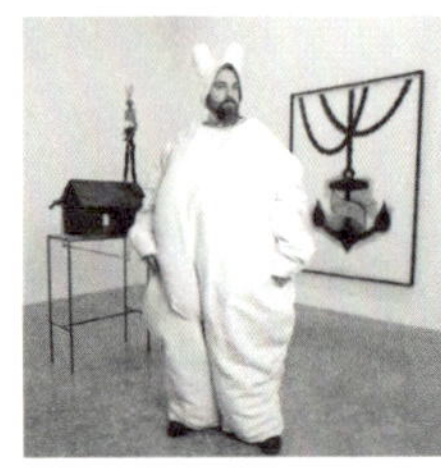

Nayland Blake, Start...

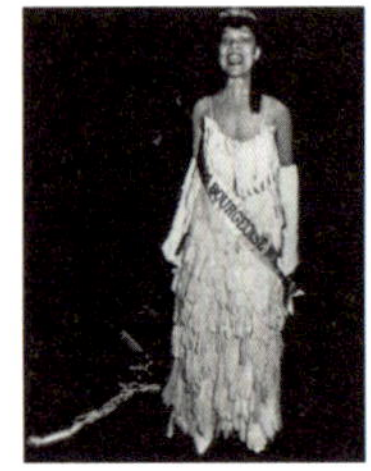

Lorraine O'Grady...

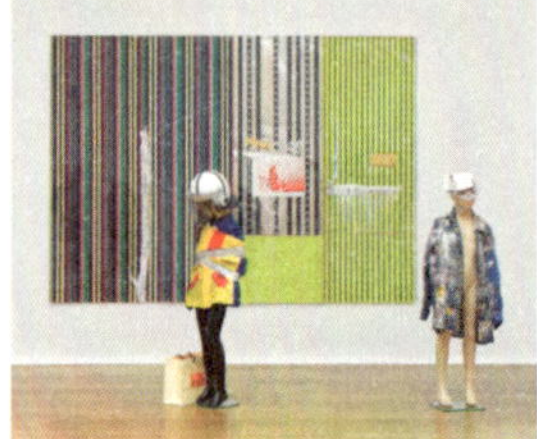

Isa Genzken, Installation V...

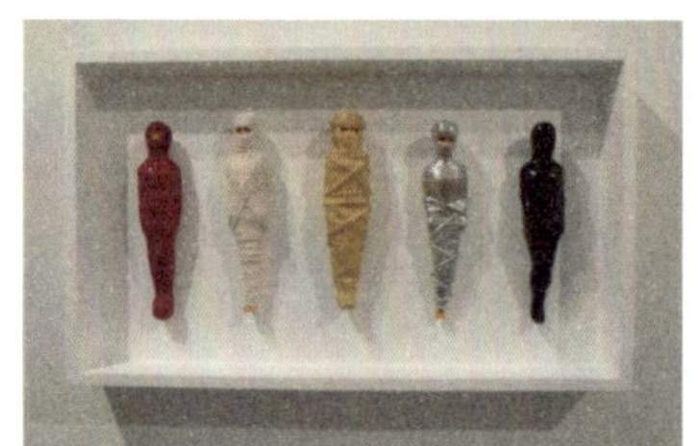

E.V. Day, Mummified Barbies

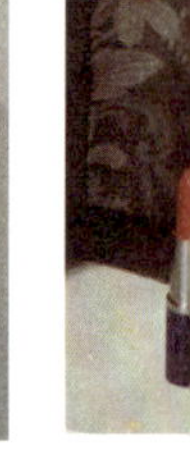

Laurie S...

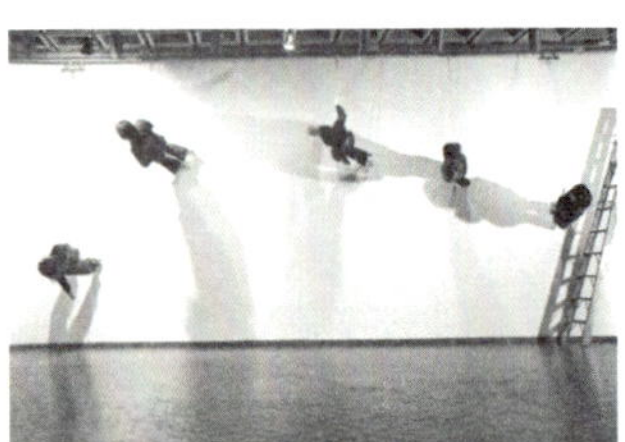

Trisha Brown, Walking on the Wall

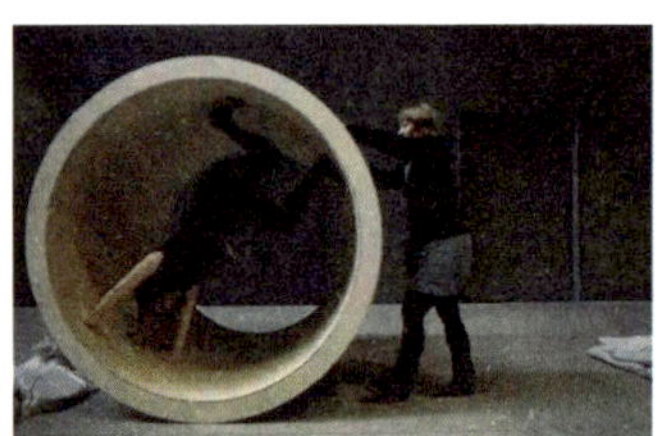

Robert Morris, Bodyspacemotion...

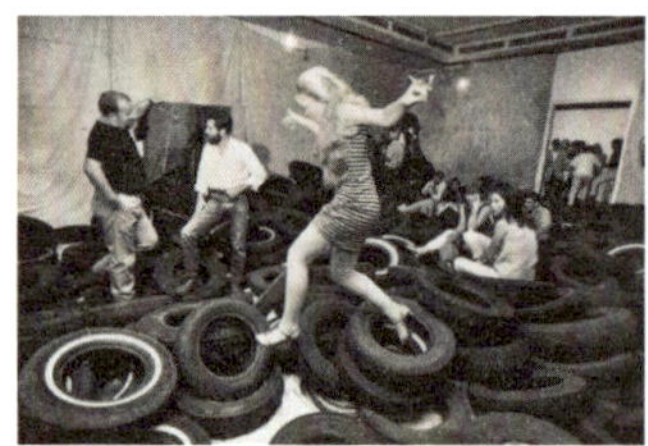

Allan Kaprow, Yard

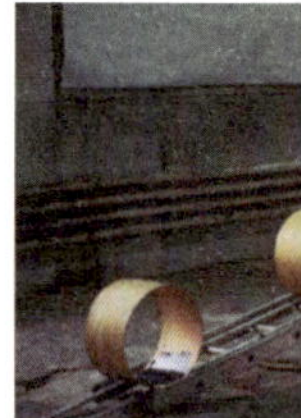

Peter Fischli & D...

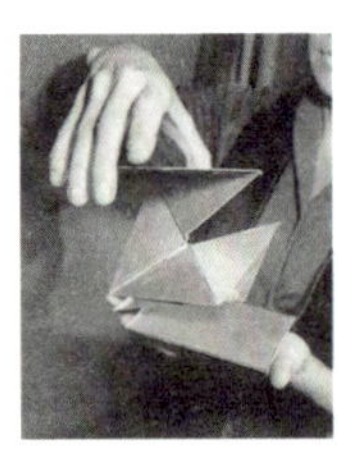

Lygia Clark, Bic...

Other Types

Natural Child

Primary Child

Spiritual Child

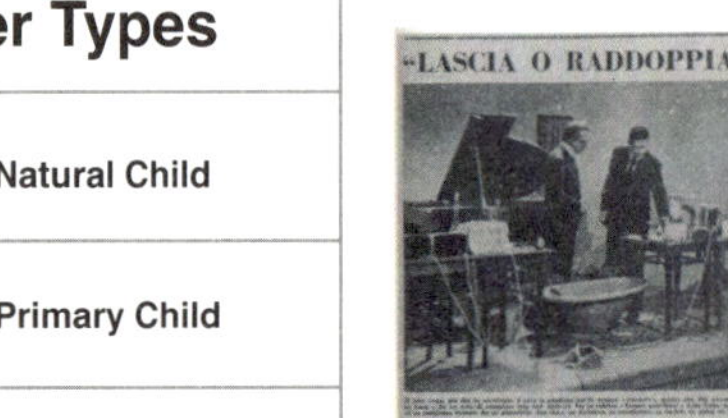

John Cage, Lascia...

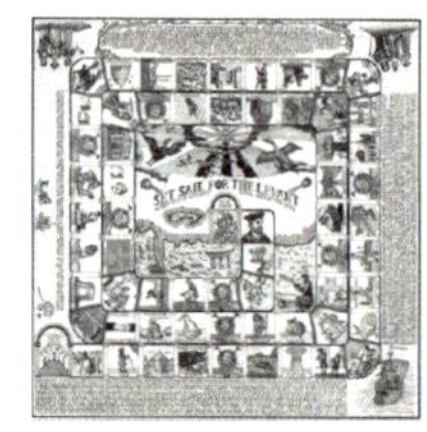

Olivia Plender, Set S...

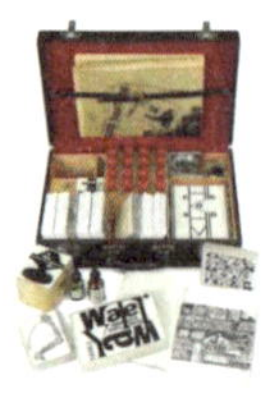

George Maci...

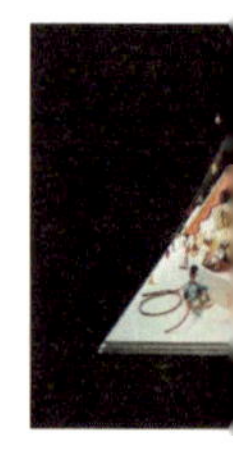

Alexander C...

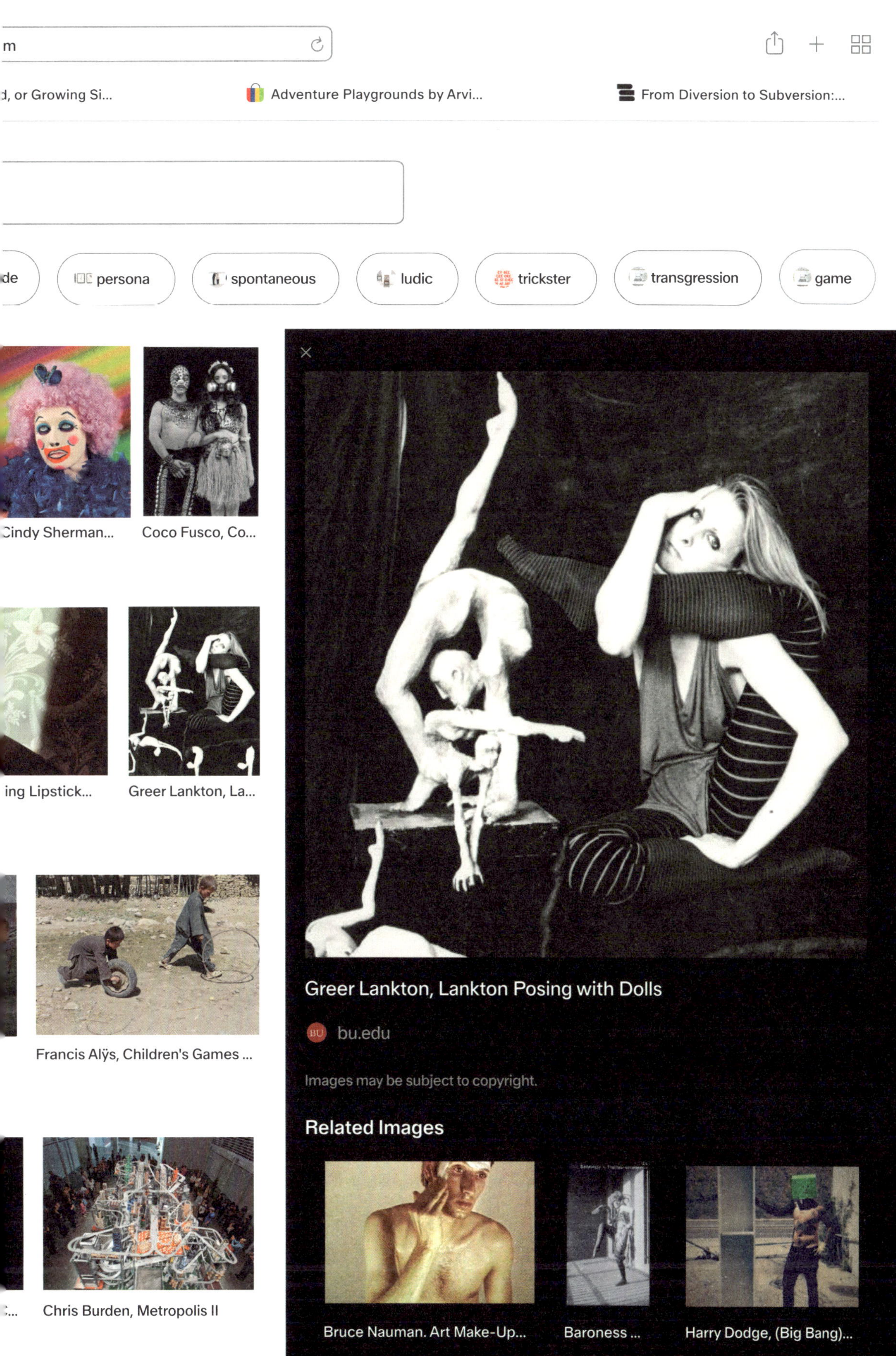
m
d, or Growing Si...
Adventure Playgrounds by Arvi...
From Diversion to Subversion:...
persona
spontaneous
ludic
trickster
transgression
game
Cindy Sherman...
Coco Fusco, Co...
ing Lipstick...
Greer Lankton, La...
Francis Alÿs, Children's Games ...
Chris Burden, Metropolis II
Greer Lankton, Lankton Posing with Dolls
bu.edu
Images may be subject to copyright.
Related Images
Bruce Nauman. Art Make-Up...
Baroness ...
Harry Dodge, (Big Bang)...

Childishism

Revolutionary-Child

Revolutionary Child 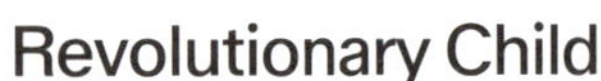 · revolutionary · 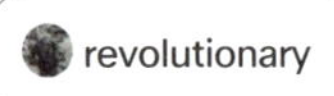 rebellious · 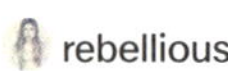 rabble rouser · 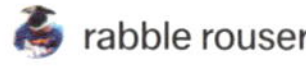 oppres...

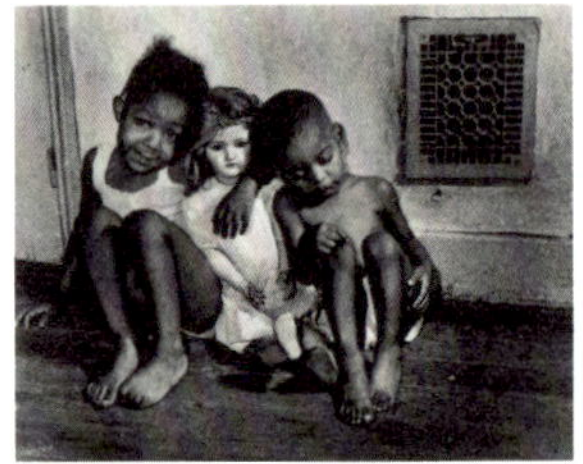

Gordon Parks, Children with ...

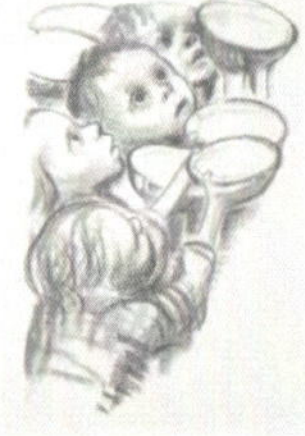

Käthe Kollwitz, ...

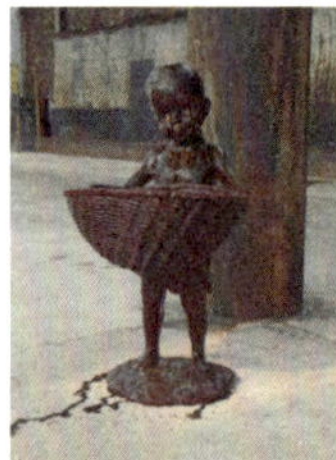

Kara Walker, Afri...

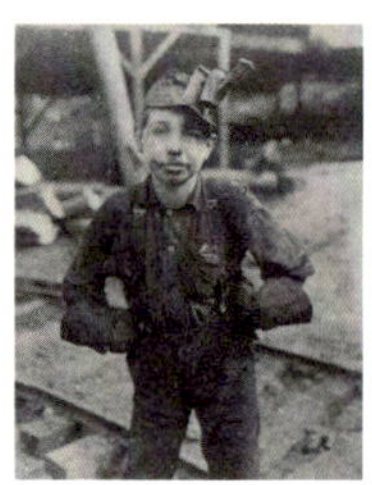

Lewis Hine, Youn...

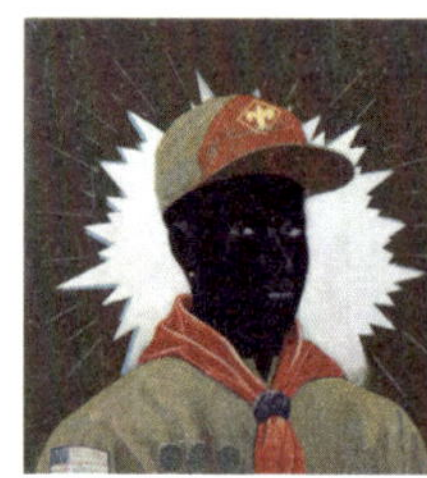

Kerry James Marshall, ..

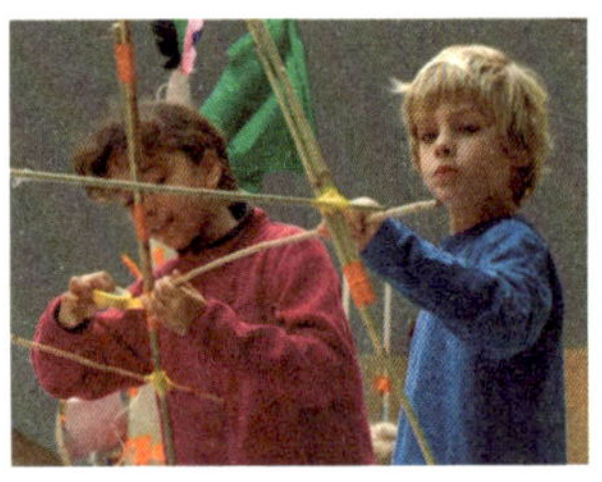

Adelita Husni-Bey, Postcards ...

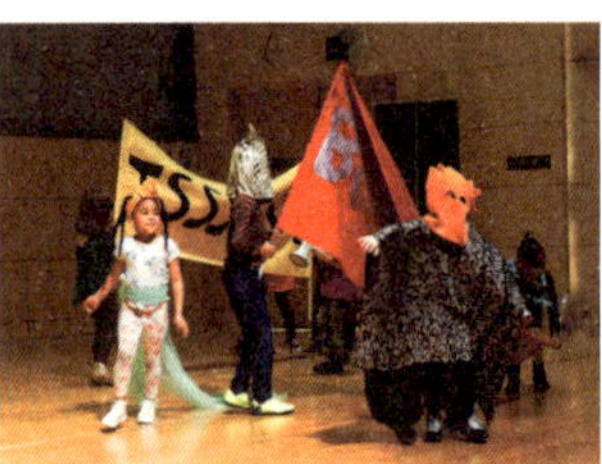

Gabo Camnitzer, We Are Animals

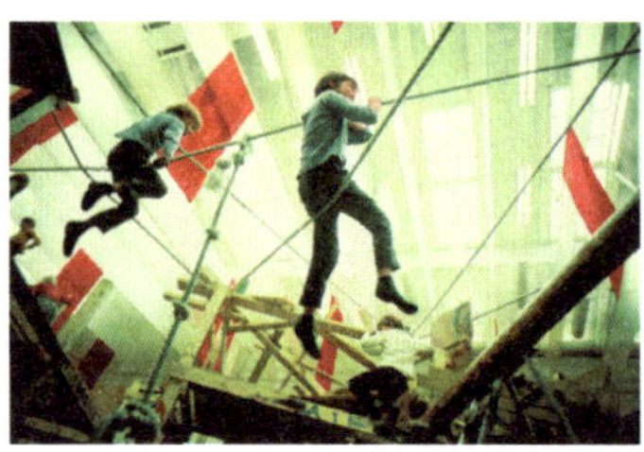

Palle Nielsen, The Model - A Model ...

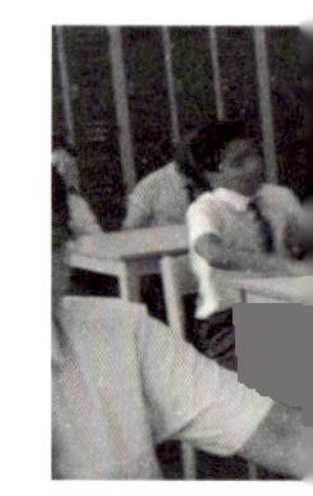

Eglė Budvytytė

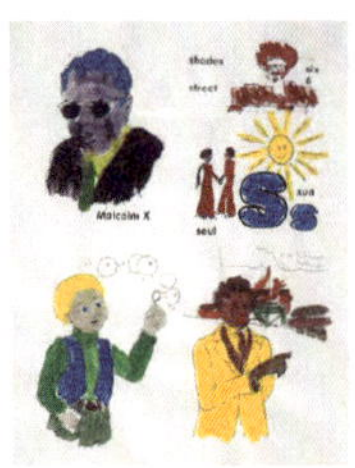

Glenn Ligon, Mal...

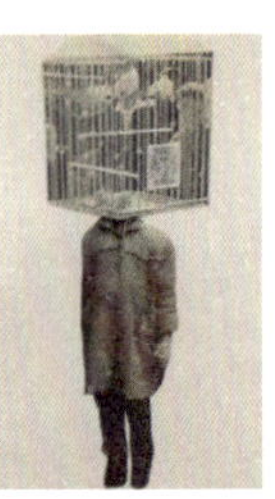

Eva Kot'átkov...

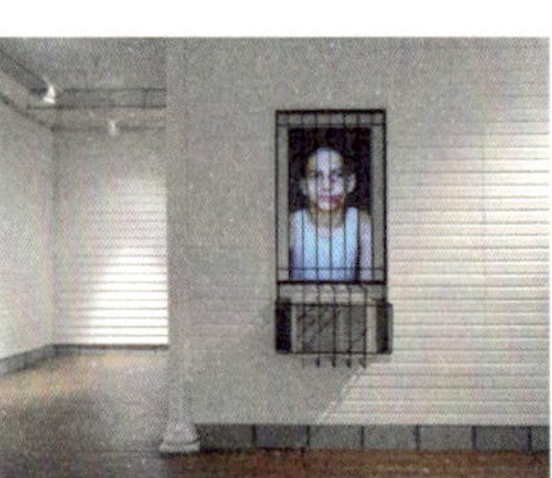

Pepón Osorio, Todo O Nada

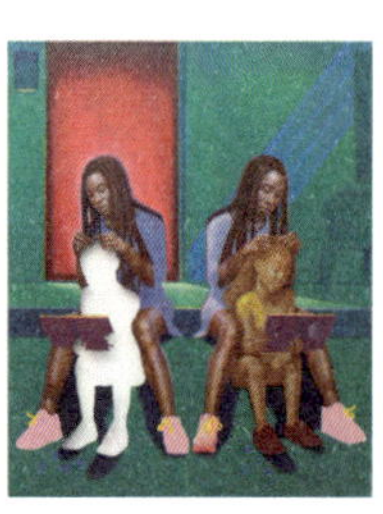

Titus Kaphar, Brai...

Other Types

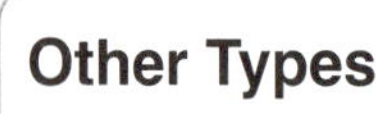 **Regressive Ch...**

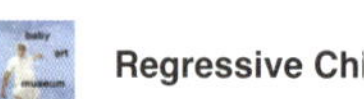 **Natural Child**

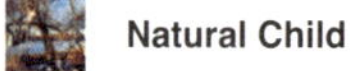 **Primary Child**

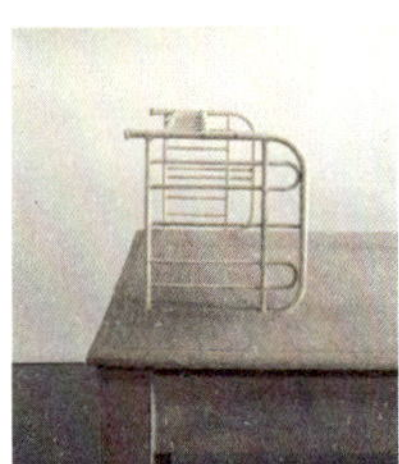

Doris Salcedo, Unt...

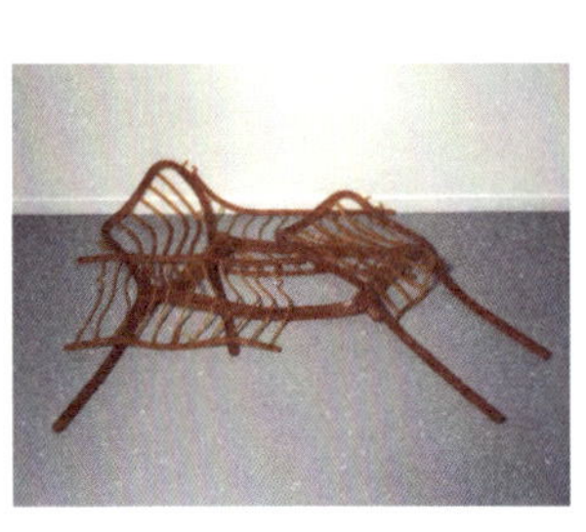

Mona Hatoum, Marrow

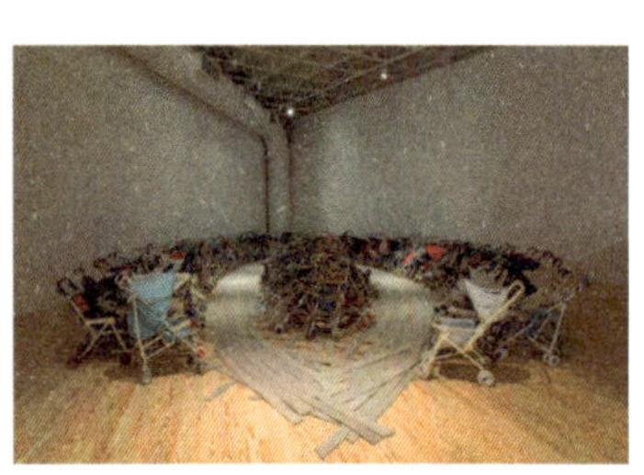

Nari Ward, Amazing Grace

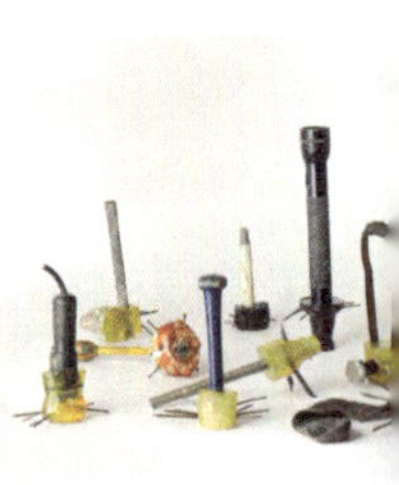

Harry Dodge, Emergen...

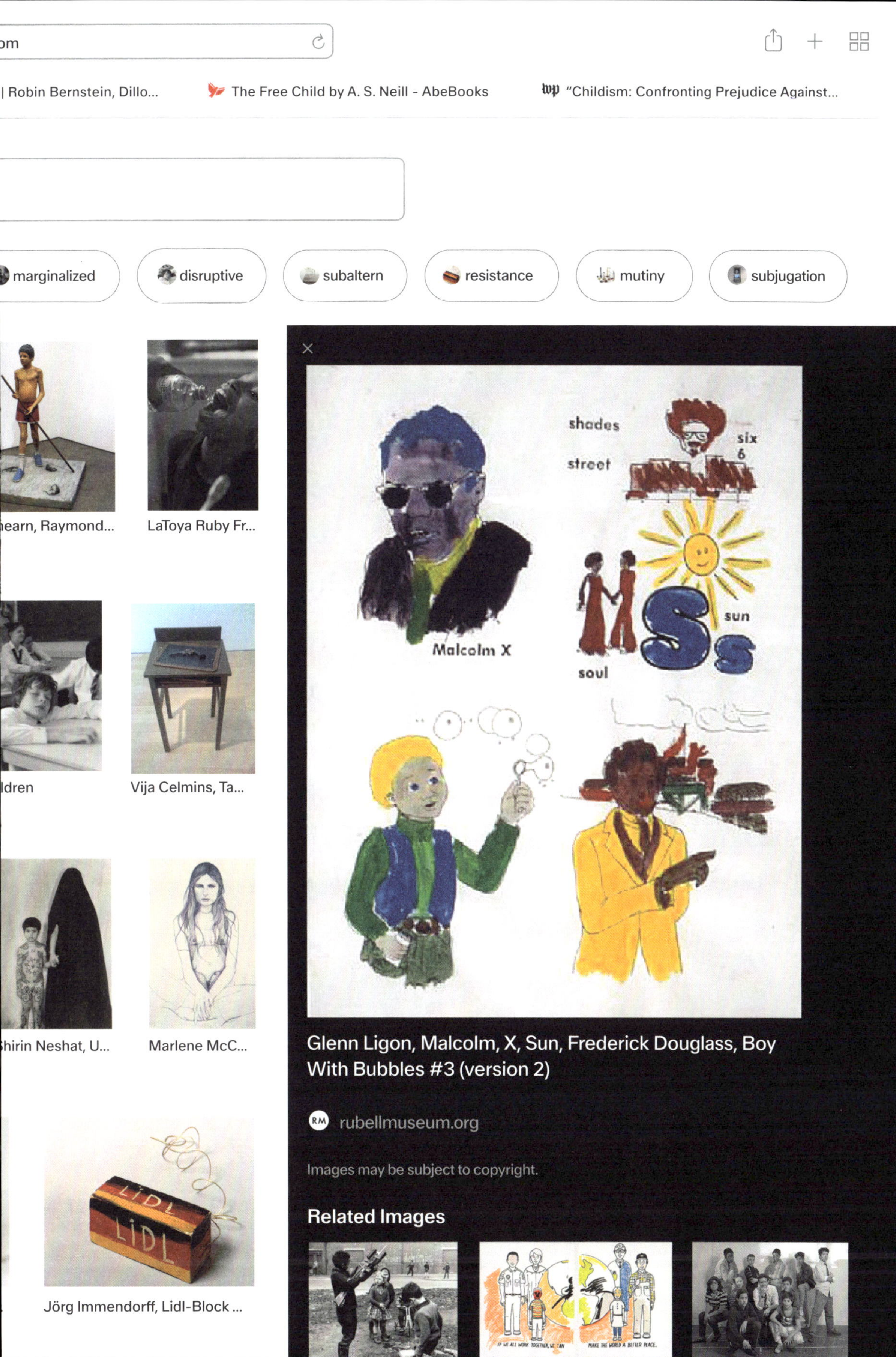
om
Robin Bernstein, Dillo...
The Free Child by A. S. Neill - AbeBooks
"Childism: Confronting Prejudice Against...
marginalized
disruptive
subaltern
resistance
mutiny
subjugation
hearn, Raymond...
LaToya Ruby Fr...
Idren
Vija Celmins, Ta...
Shirin Neshat, U...
Marlene McC...
Jörg Immendorff, Lidl-Block ...
shades
street
six
6
Malcolm X
soul
sun
Ss
Glenn Ligon, Malcolm, X, Sun, Frederick Douglass, Boy
With Bubbles #3 (version 2)
rubellmuseum.org
Images may be subject to copyright.
Related Images

Childishism

Consumer-Child

Consumer Child   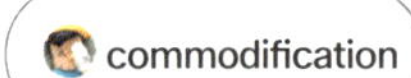 commodification   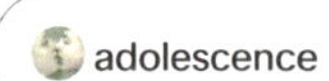 adolescence   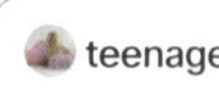 teenage   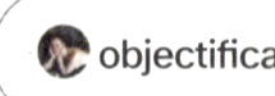 objectificati

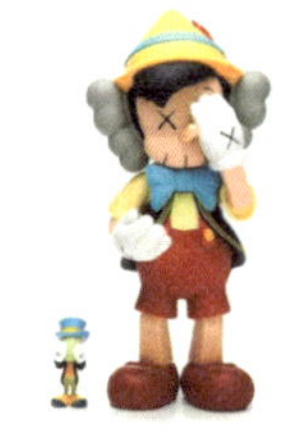
KAWS, Pinocchio...

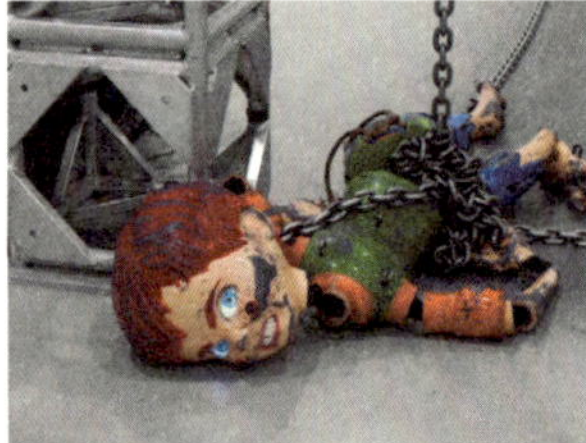
Jordan Wolfson, Colored Sculp...

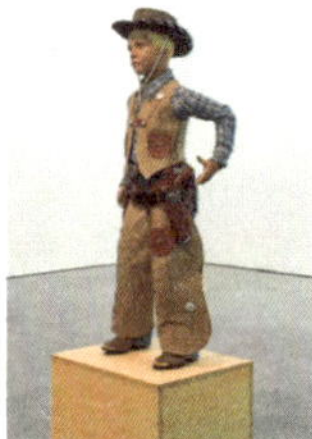
Richard Prince ...

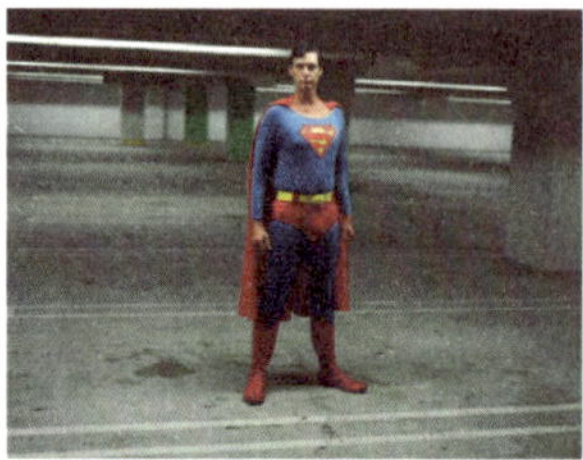
Siri Kaur, This Kind of Face (ser...

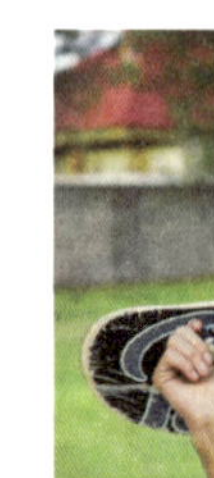
Larry Clar

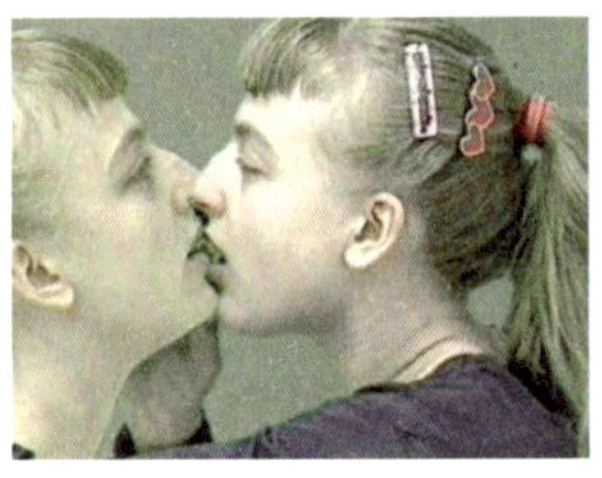
Sue de Beer, Making Out with...

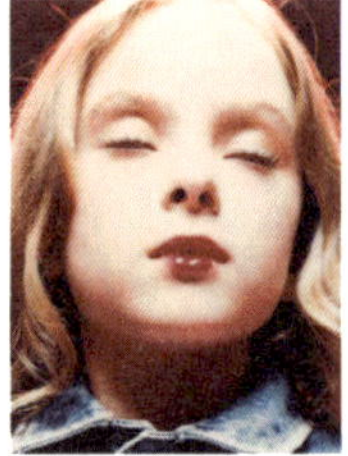
Inez van Lamswe...

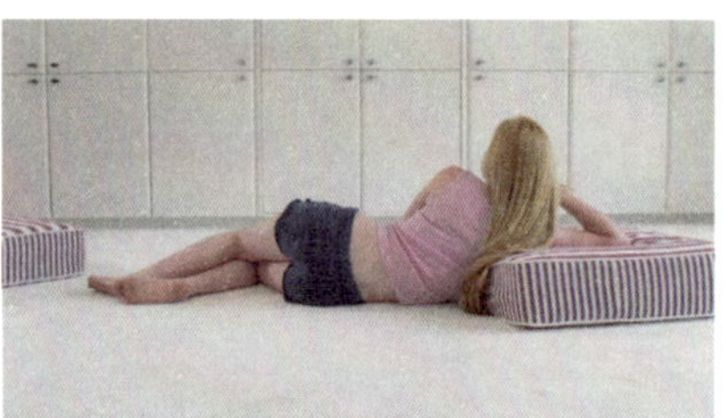
Charlie White, American Minor

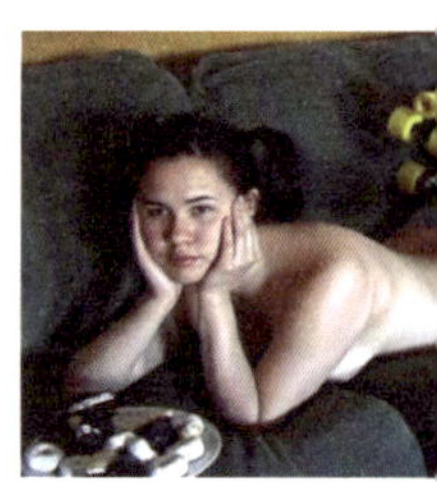
Laurel Nakadate, Good

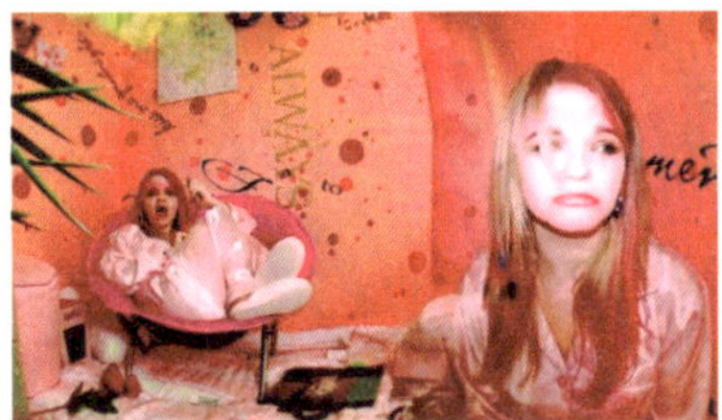
Ryan Trecartin, The Re'Search (Re'Searc...

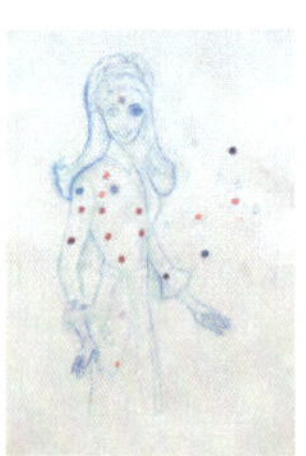
Ellen Cantor...

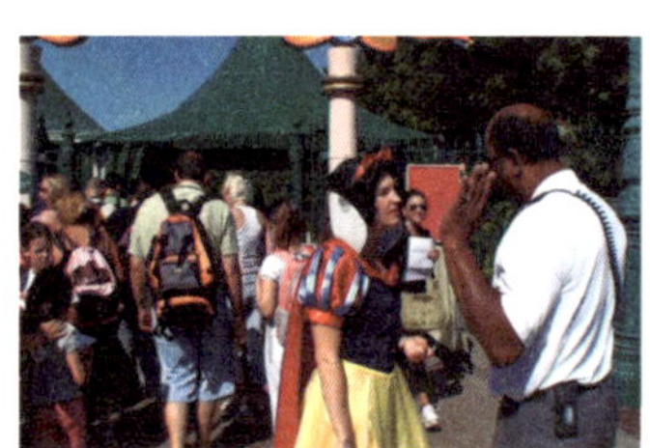
Pilvi Takala, Real Snow White

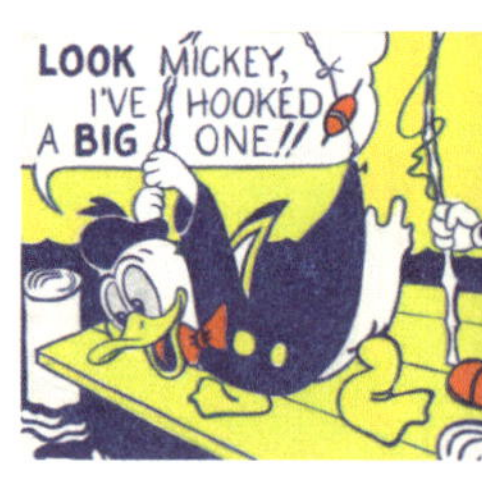

Roy Lichtenstein, Look Mic

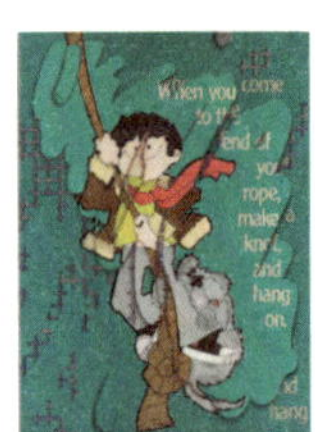
Laura Owens, ...

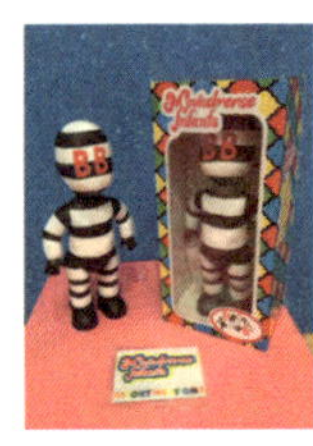
Trenton Doyle ...

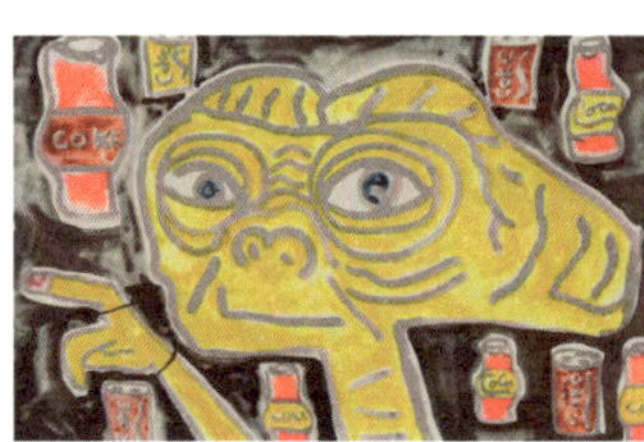
Katherine Bernhardt, ET Phone Ho...

Other Types

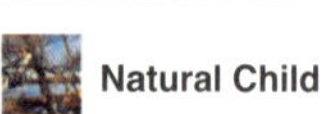
Natural Child

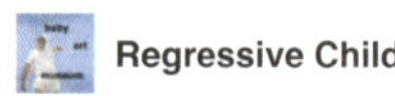
Regressive Child

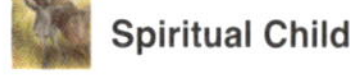
Spiritual Child

Taka

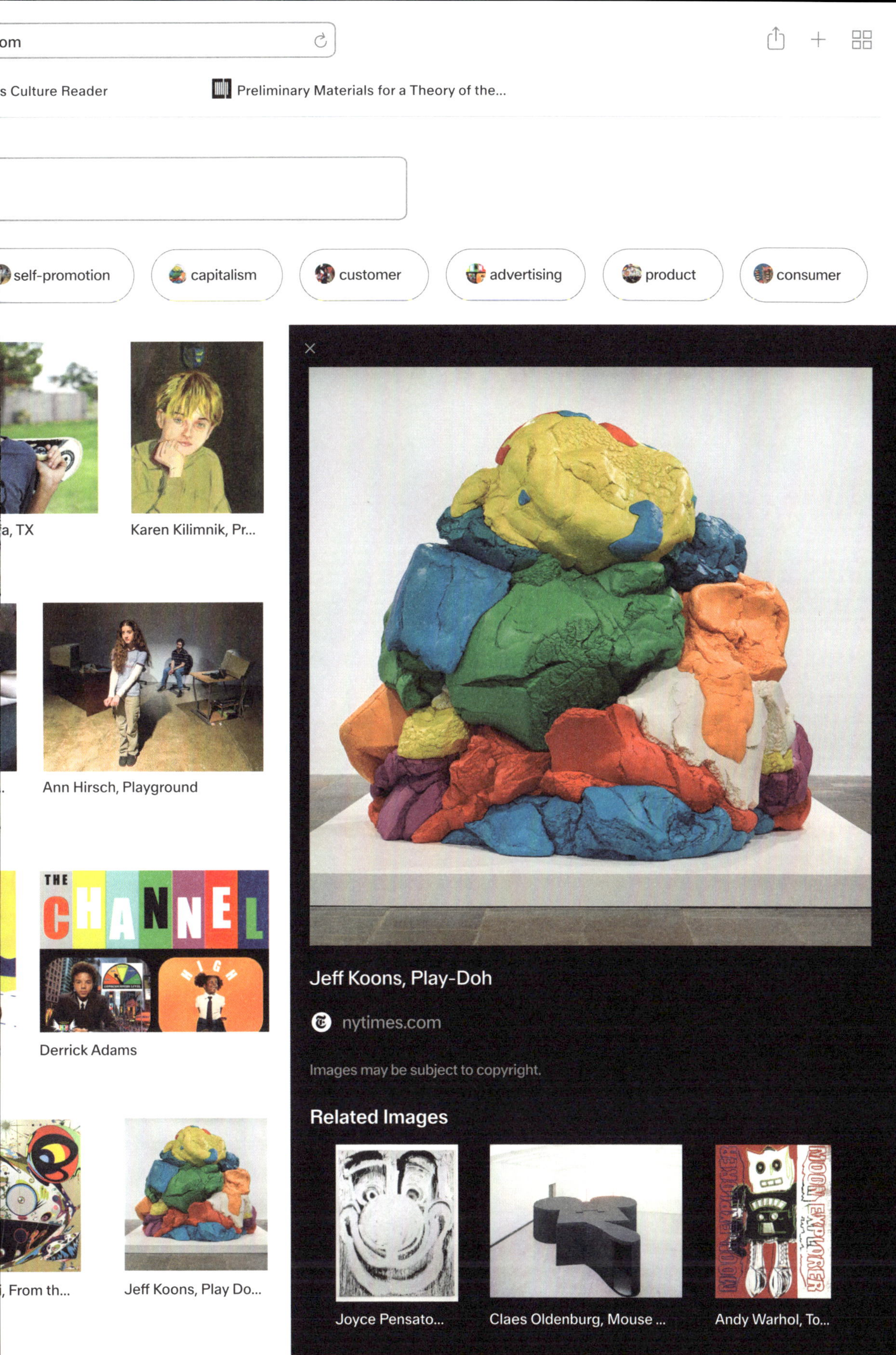
om
s Culture Reader
Preliminary Materials for a Theory of the...
self-promotion
capitalism
customer
advertising
product
consumer
fa, TX
Karen Kilimnik, Pr...
Ann Hirsch, Playground
THE CHANNEL
HIGH
Derrick Adams
, From th...
Jeff Koons, Play Do...
Jeff Koons, Play-Doh
nytimes.com
Images may be subject to copyright.
Related Images
Joyce Pensato...
Claes Oldenburg, Mouse ...
Andy Warhol, To...

Childishism

Nobody-Child

Nobody Child   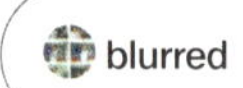 blurred   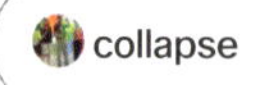 collapse   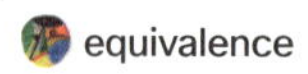 equivalence   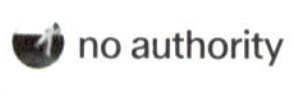 no authority

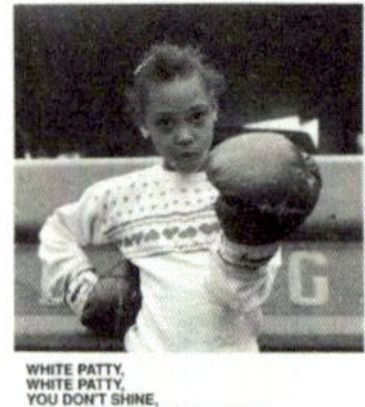

Carrie Mae Weem…

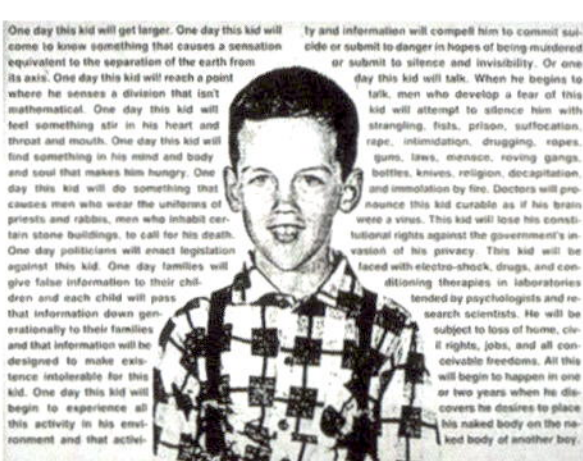

David Wojnarowicz, Untitled …

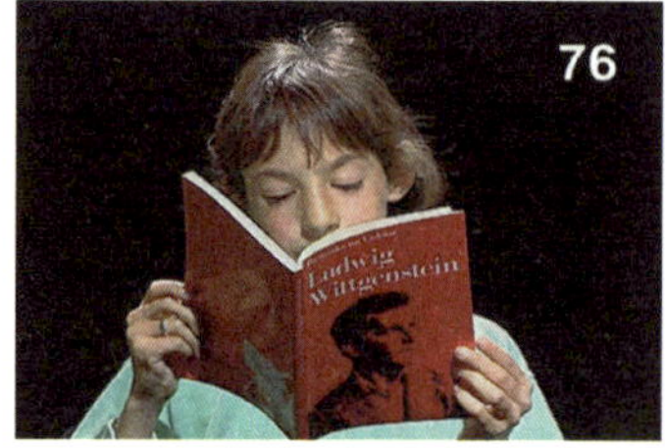

Gary Hill, Remarks on Color

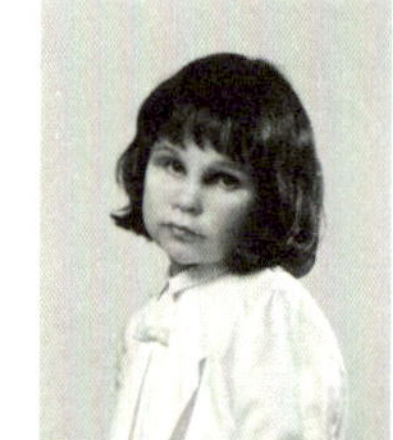

Gillian Wearing, S…

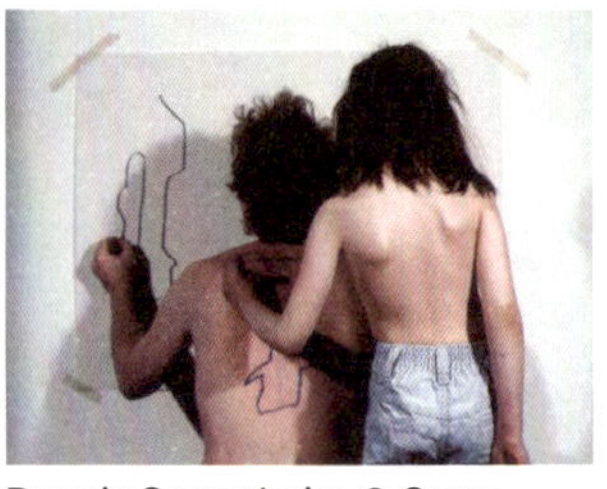

Dennis Oppenheim, 2-Stage…

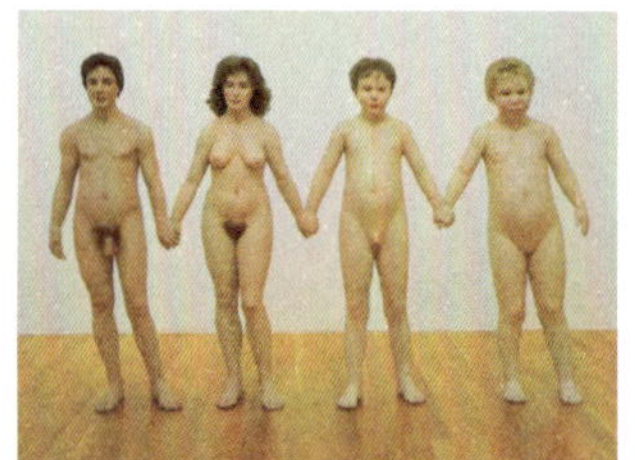

Charles Ray, Family Romance

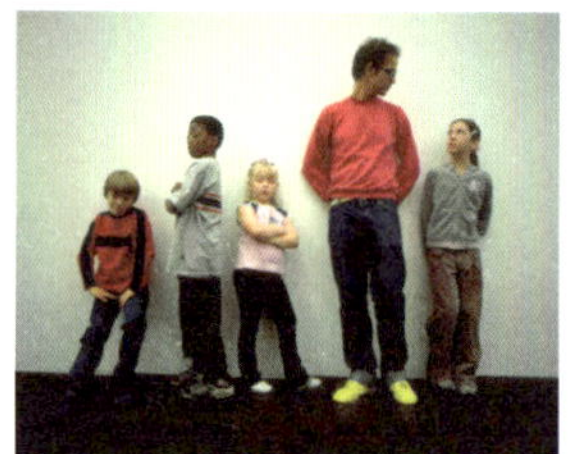

Tino Sehgal, Ann Lee

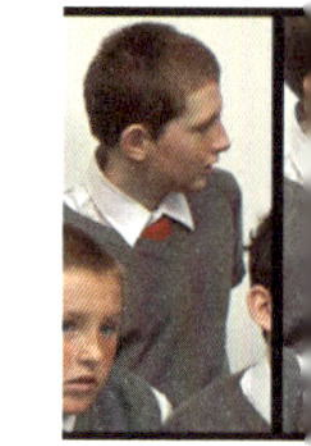

Rineke Dijkstr

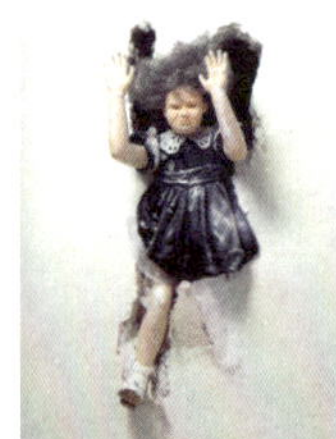

Kim Dingle, Fatt…

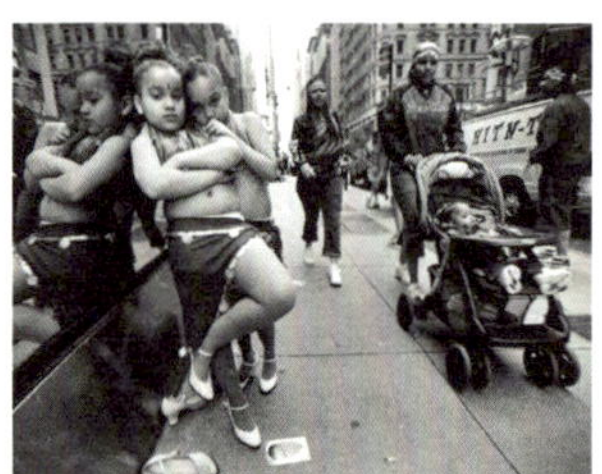

Mary Ellen Mark, Candice Loza…

Other Types

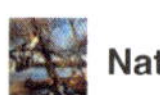 **Natural Child**

 **Primary Child**

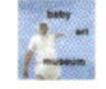 **Regressive Child**

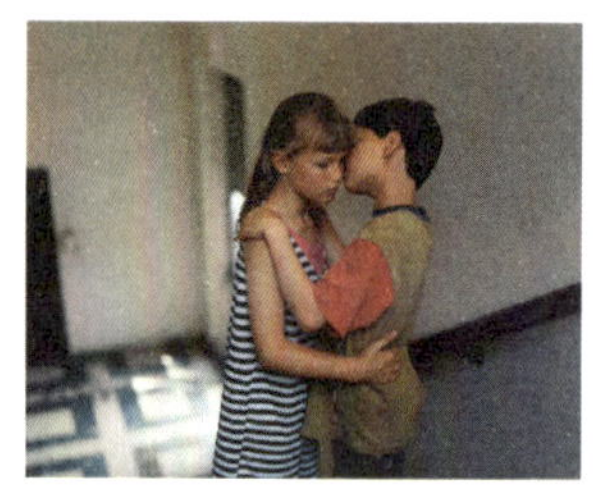

Sharon Lockhart, Audition Tw…

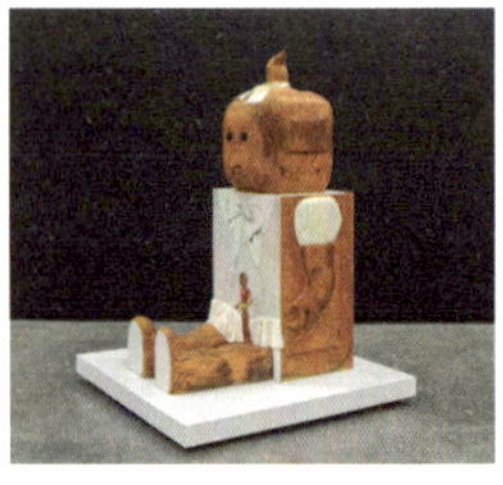

Marisol, Baby Girl

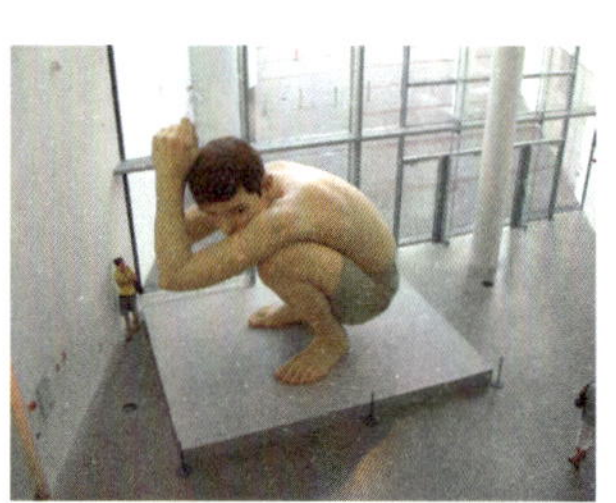

Ron Mueck, Boy

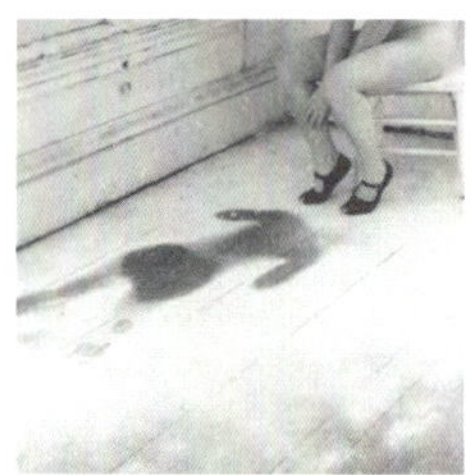

Francesca Woodman, …

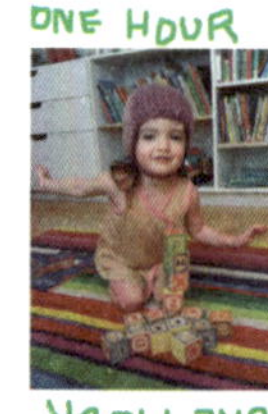

Harrell Fletc…

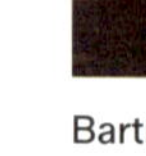

Bartl

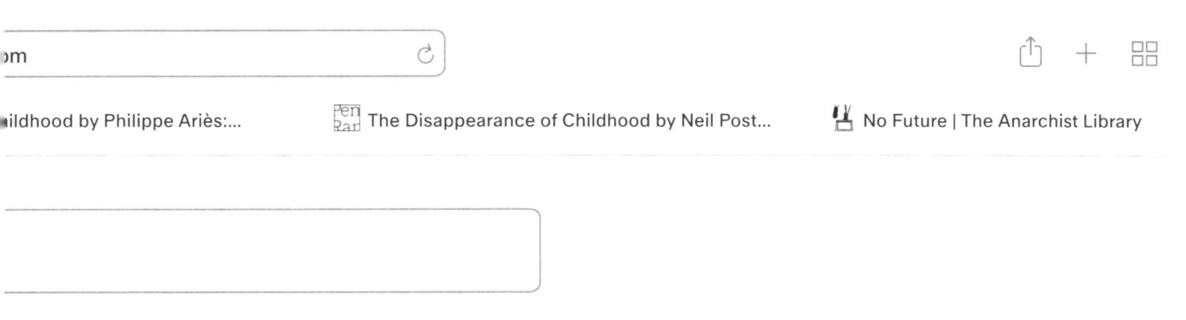
om
ildhood by Philippe Ariès:...
The Disappearance of Childhood by Neil Post...
No Future | The Anarchist Library
ensurate
fair
precocious
corresponding
limitless
ageless

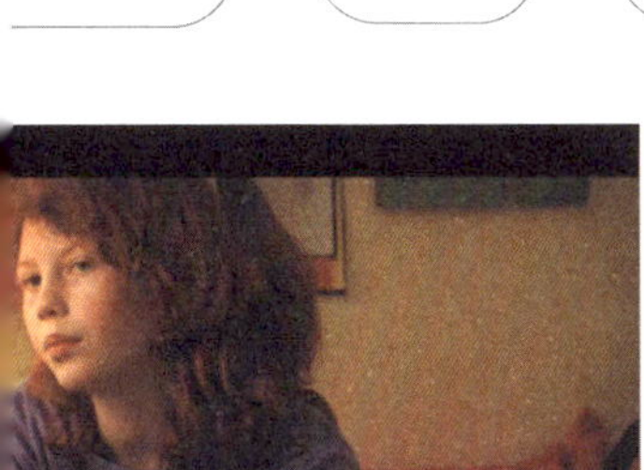
ere & Elsewhere

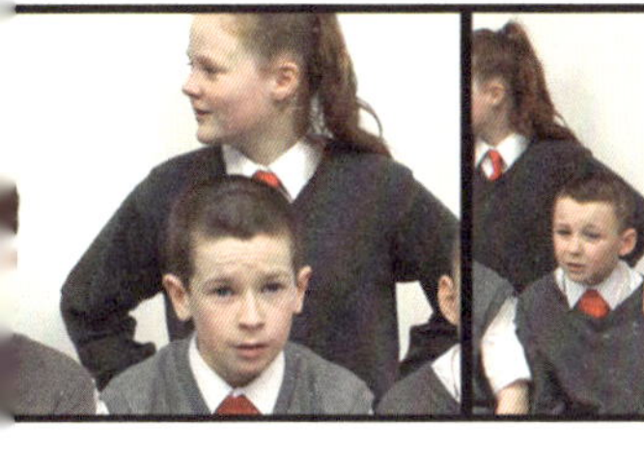
nan Crying

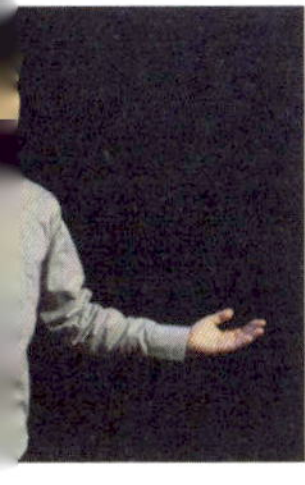
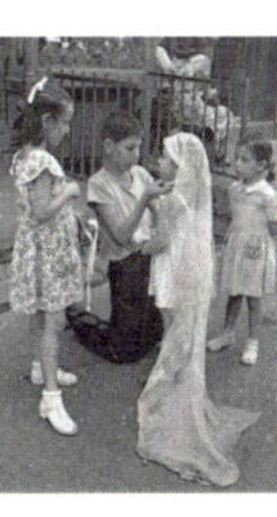
, The Thought...
Helen Levitt, N...

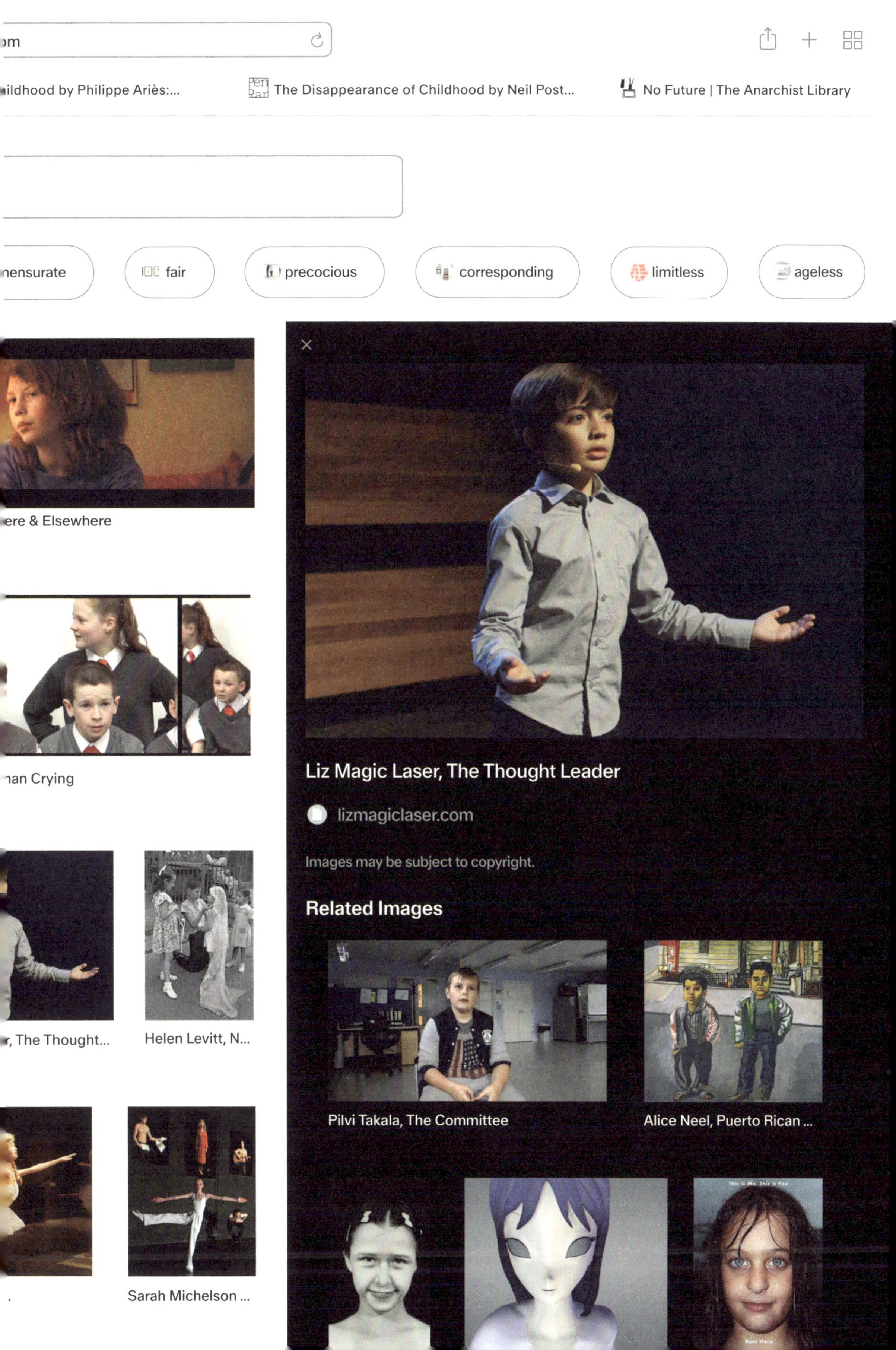

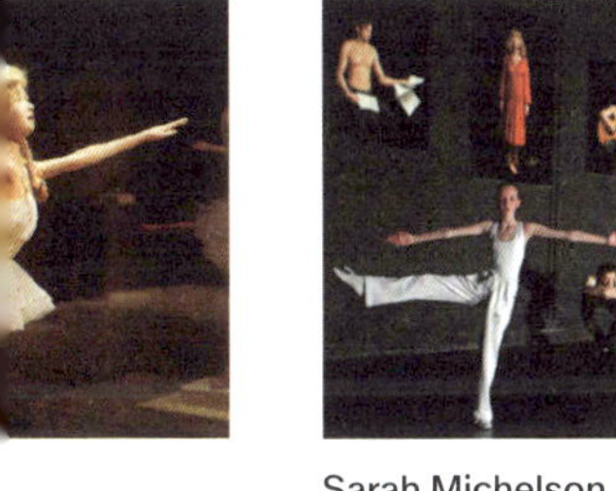
Sarah Michelson ...
Liz Magic Laser, The Thought Leader
lizmagiclaser.com
Images may be subject to copyright.
Related Images
Pilvi Takala, The Committee
Alice Neel, Puerto Rican ...

AM
Chil

ONG

dren

Duane Hanson
John Ahearn and Rigoberto Torres
Karon Davis
Berenice Olmedo
Tau Lewis
Charles Ray

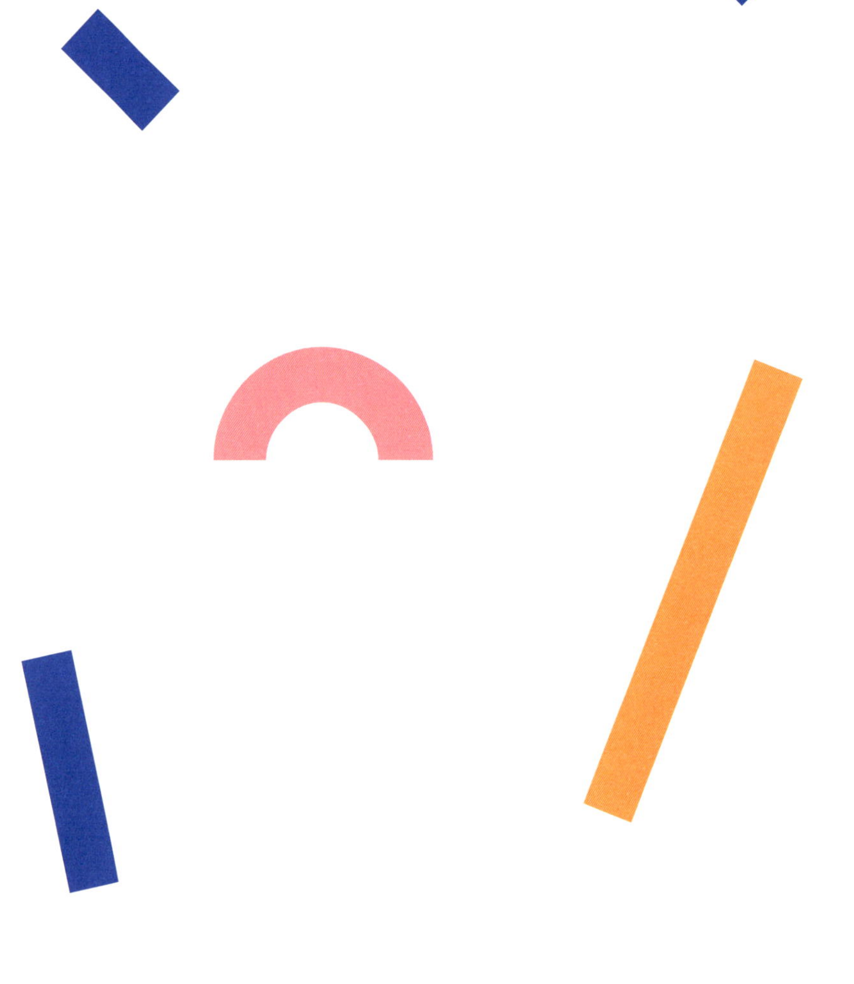

Sculptors today have employed the child figure to generate representations of childhood in rich and varied ways, registering experiences of joy, play, creativity, vulnerability, and resilience that reinvent centuries-old forms and motifs. A number of artists have worked directly with children as models. For his hyperrealistic sculptures, Duane Hanson modeled figures on his own young children—a decision that was as practical as it was conceptual—staging his daughter Maja in a couple of different works beginning in the 1970s. John Ahearn and Rigoberto Torres have been hosting plaster-casting sessions in their ground-floor studio in the Bronx since the 1980s, where being able to hold still for the painstaking process has become a badge of honor among young people in the neighborhood. Initially created as a public mural in the South Bronx, Ahearn and Torres's relief sculpture of four girls playing double Dutch captures the rhythmic coordination necessary for this iconic street game and monumentalizes the kids who call the place home. Karon Davis casts children from her neighborhood in Los Angeles to create dreamlike plaster sculptures with lifelike glass eyes that make her works feel inhabited. These seated girls appear frozen in the middle of a hand-clapping game, a pose as playful and simple as it is disarming and open-ended. Berenice Olmedo was volunteering at a facility in Mexico City that provides physical therapy to children when she came across a surplus of orthotic leg braces that children had outgrown; she began using them in her kinetic sculptures, which stage an unending cycle of falling and standing, expressing the hard work of recovery and survival. A hand-sewn soft sculpture by Tau Lewis approximates the artist as a young girl wearing patched-together fragments of her childhood clothes, a talismanic object that is the result of a reparative process of self-healing. Through scale and subject matter, Charles Ray's six-foot-tall, solid-stainless-steel sculpture of an adolescent boy dressed in a toga and holding a toy sword marks out the ever-changing borderline between childhood and what lies beyond, and reveals how children, like all people, learn how to "play the part." Conjuring the presence of children and their interior lives, these sculptures stage encounters in space between the viewer and the child figure. They negotiate the power of scale and perception, and they become containers for hopes, beliefs, fears, and ideas about humanity.

Duane Hanson
Child with Puzzle, 1978
Polyvinyl, polychromed in oil,
and mixed media with accessories
24 × 61 × 32 inches
(61 × 154.9 × 81.3 cm)

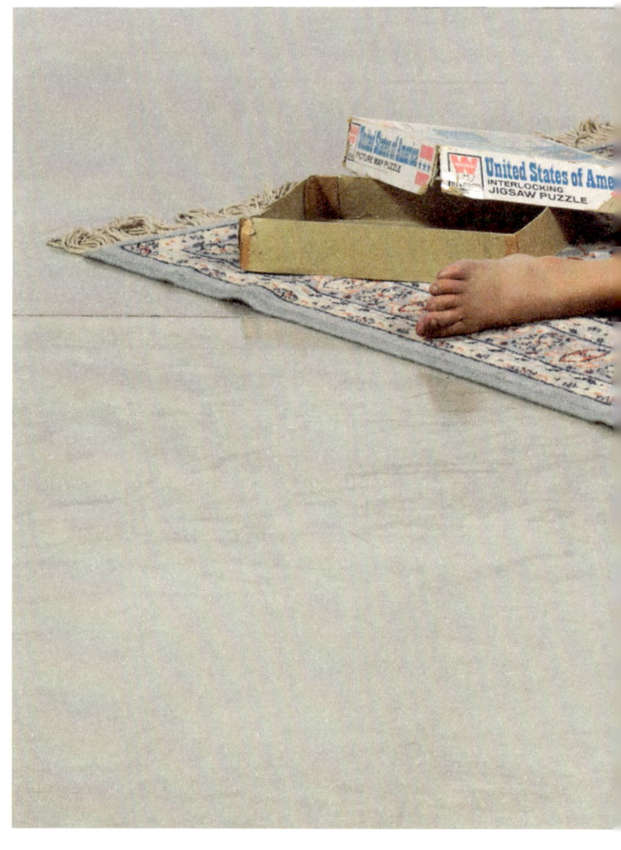

Among Children

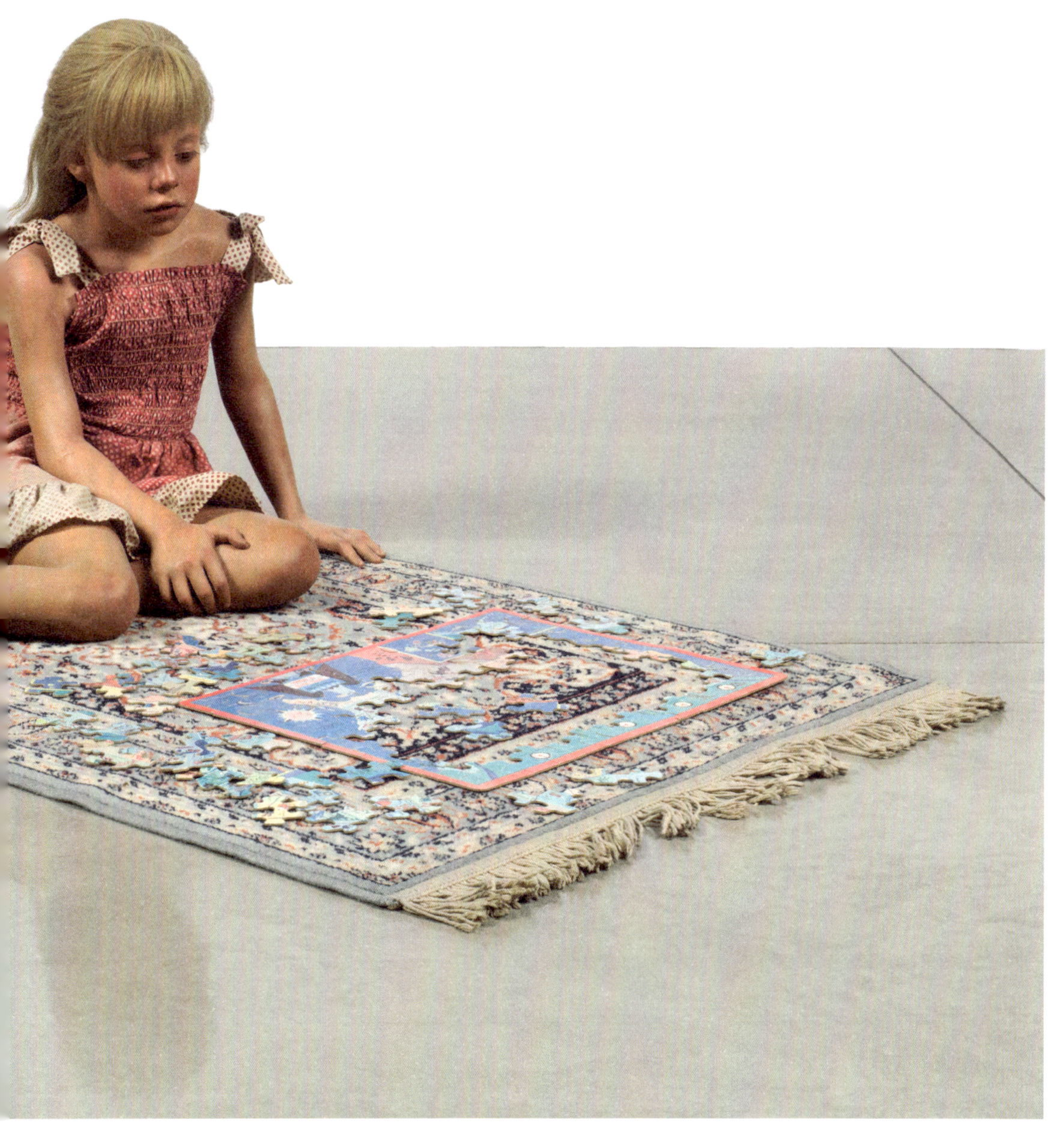

John Ahearn and Rigoberto Torres
Homage to the People of the Bronx: Double Dutch at
Kelly Street—La Freeda, Jevette, Towana, Staice, 1981–82
Oil on fiberglass
54 × 154 × 12 inches (137.2 × 391.2 × 30.5 cm)
(not pictured)

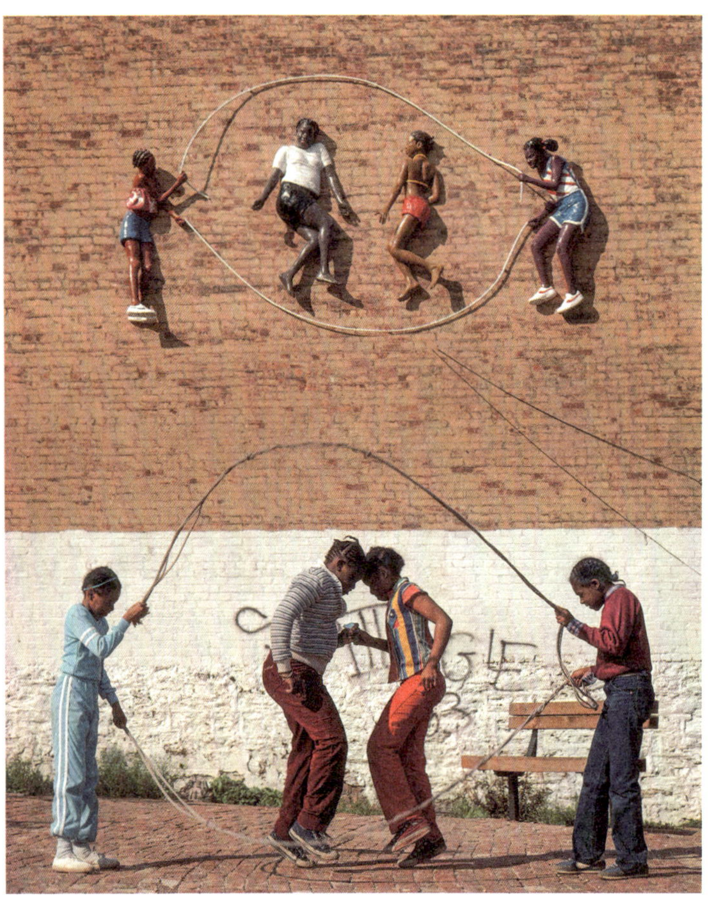

Martha Cooper, "*Banana Kelly Double Dutch*," *La Freeda, Jevette, Towana,*
Staice, The Bronx, NYC, 1982. 35mm Kodachrome slide. © Martha Cooper

                                                                 Among Children

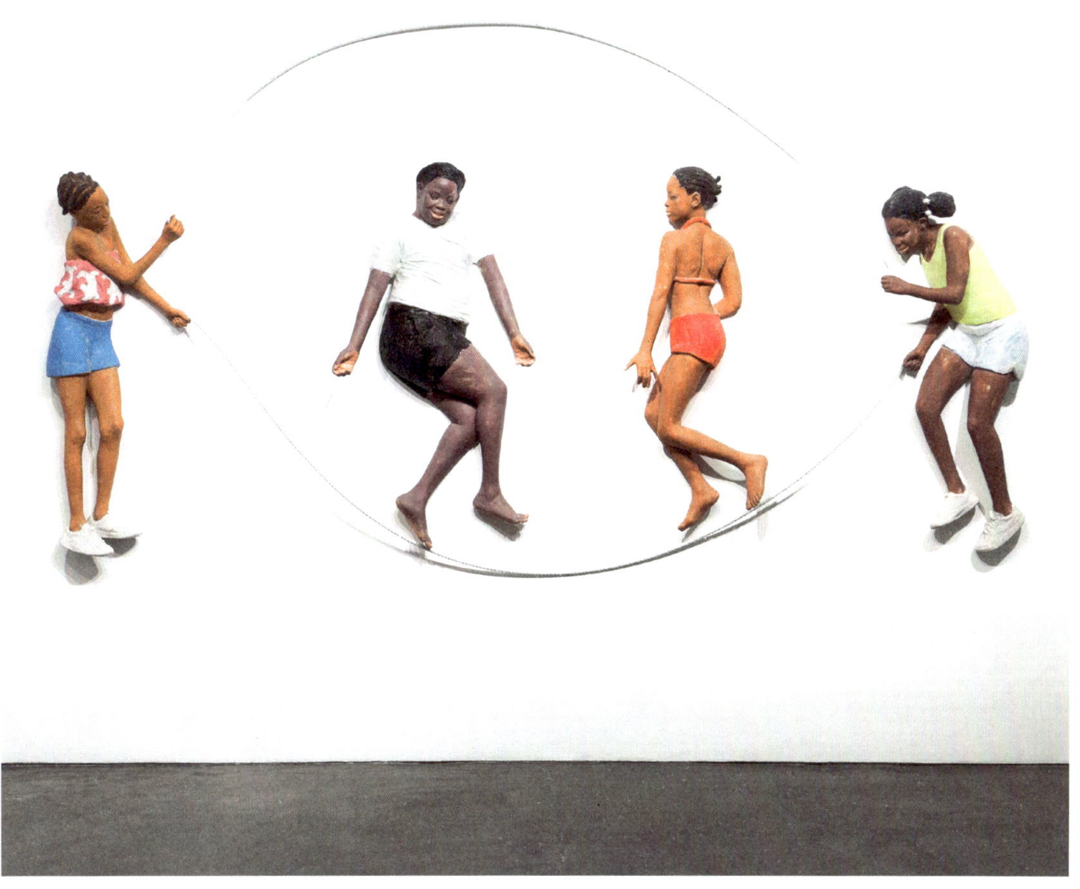

John Ahearn and Rigoberto Torres, *Double Dutch*, 1981/2010. Installation view, *John Ahearn: Works from Dawson Street and Walton Avenue*, Alexander and Bonin, New York, 2014

Karon Davis
Pattycakes, 2022
Plaster bandages, steel,
glass eyes, and chicken wire
31 × 56 ½ × 25 inches
(78.7 × 143.5 × 63.5 cm)

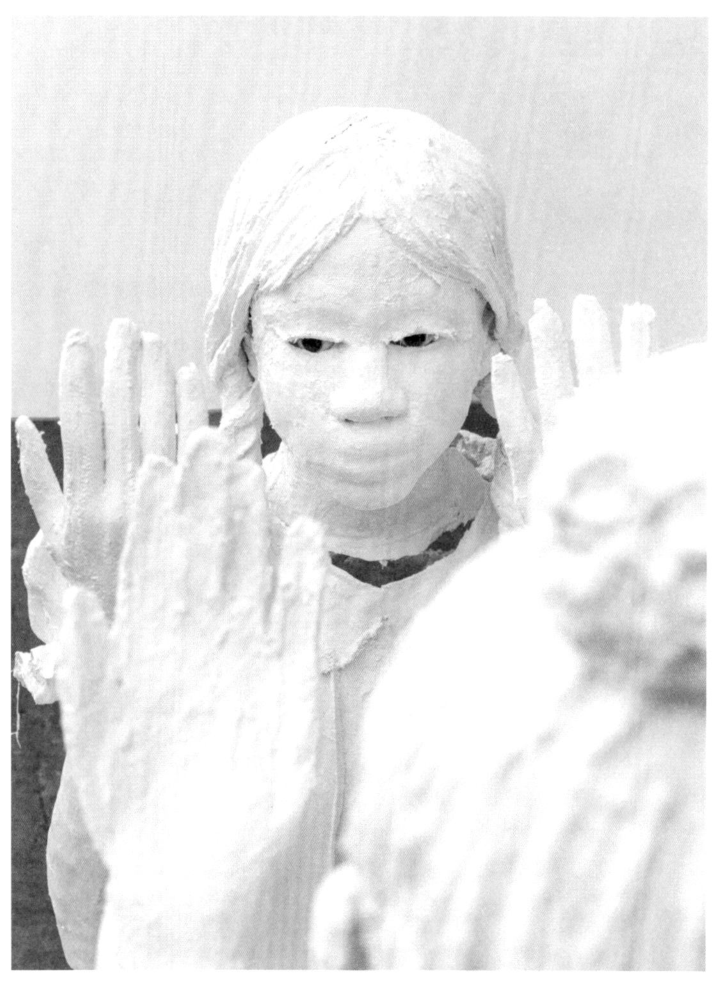

Among Children

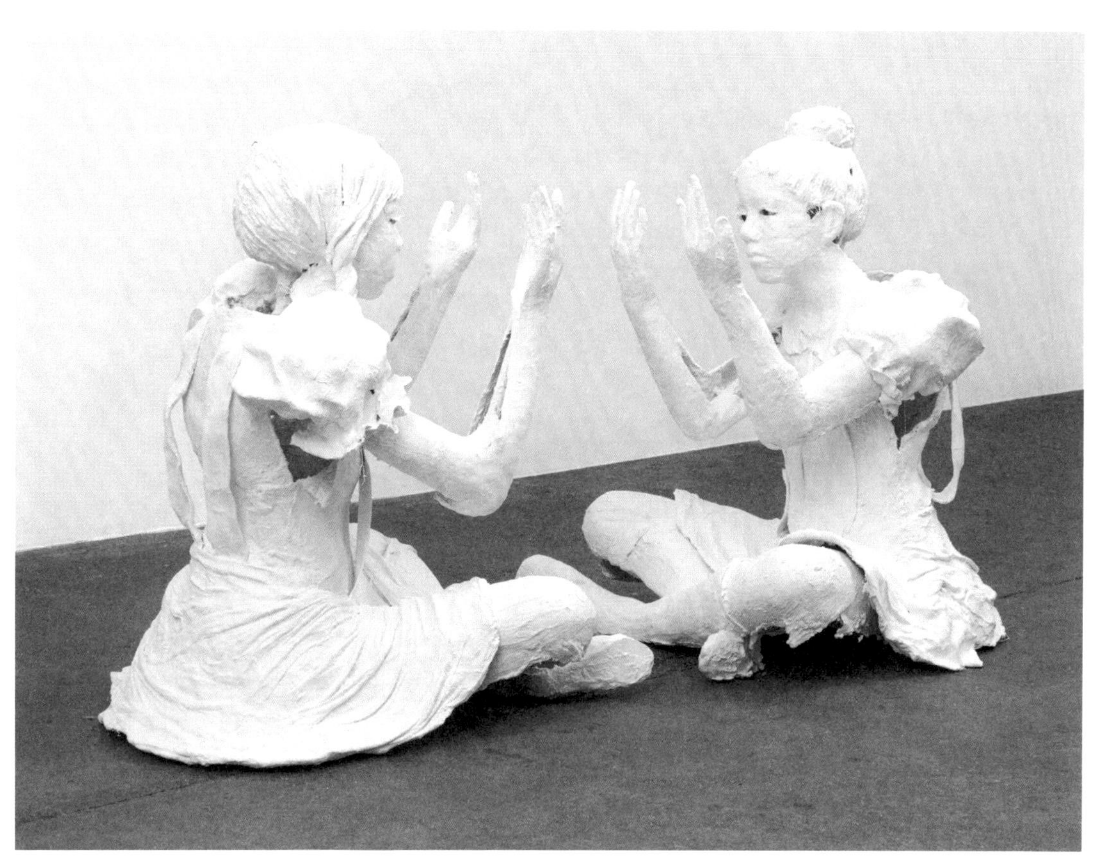

Berenice Olmedo
Olga, 2018
Hard plastic leg prostheses, steel rods
and joint screws, aluminum box, electrical
motor, and CPU-controlled hardware
29 ⅞ × 15 × 12 ⅝ inches (76 × 38 × 32 cm)

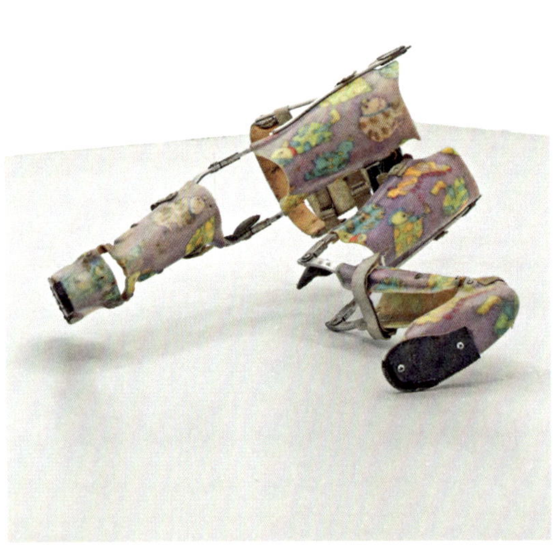 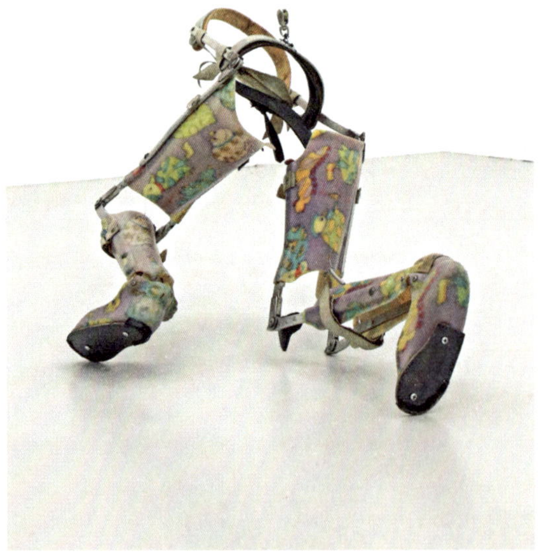

Among Children

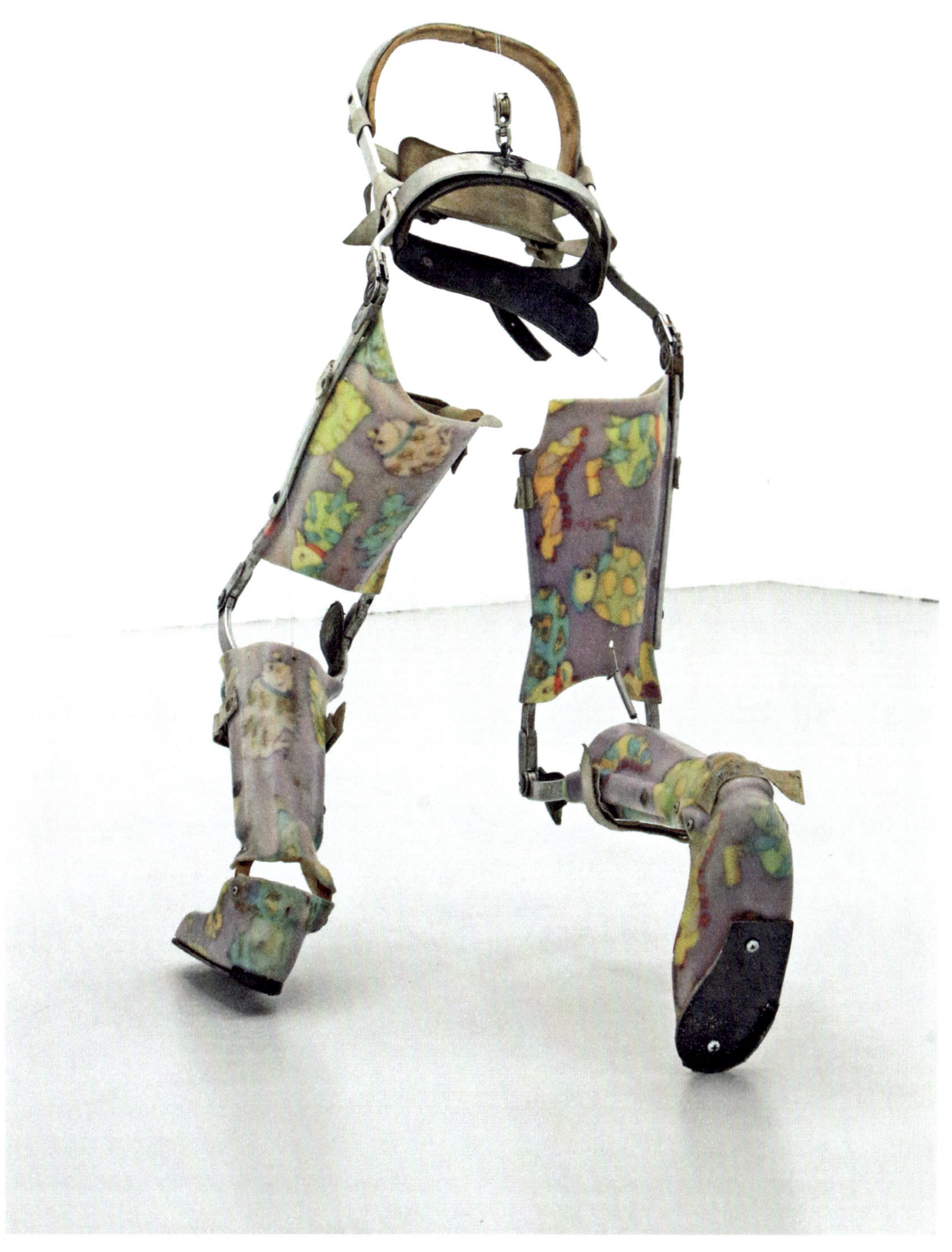

Tau Lewis
Untitled (play dumb to catch wise), 2017
Hand-sewn fabrics, wire, polyester stuffing,
plaster, acrylic paint, human hair, and stones
24 × 20 × 33 inches (61 × 50.8 × 83.8 cm)

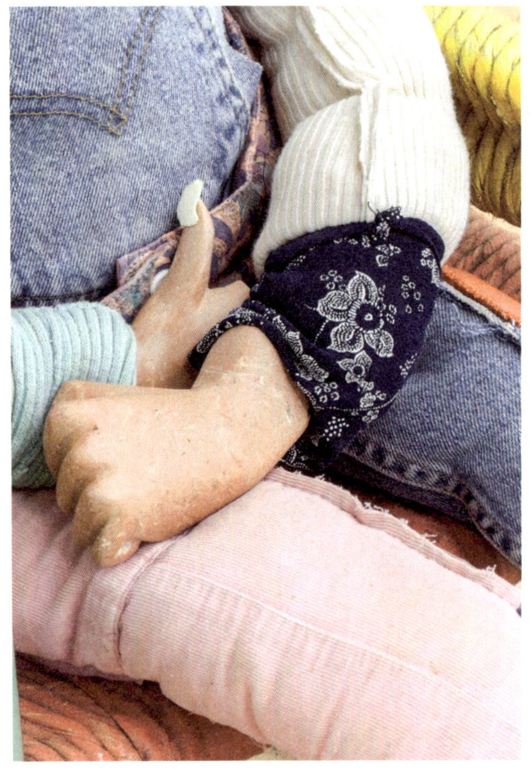

Among Children

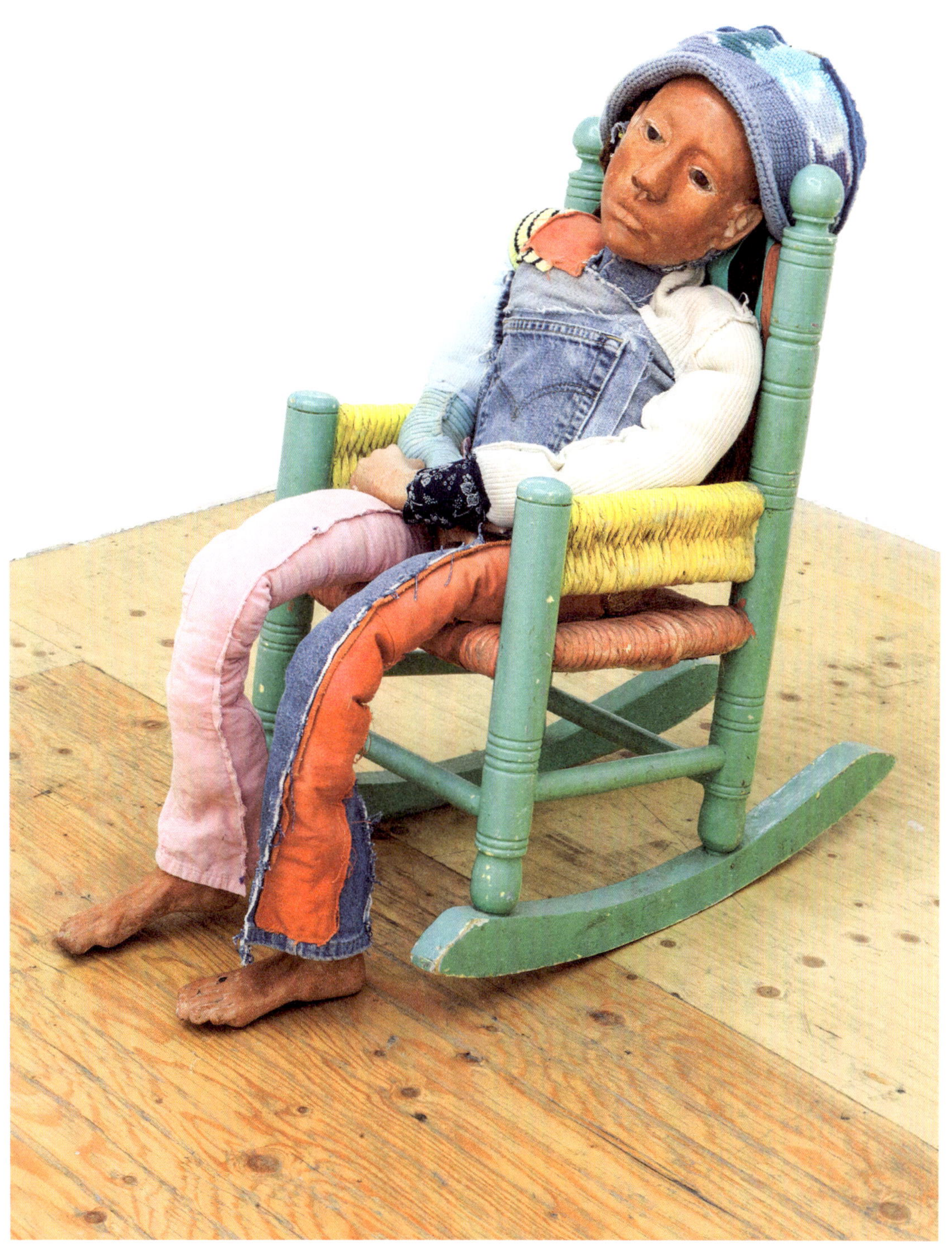

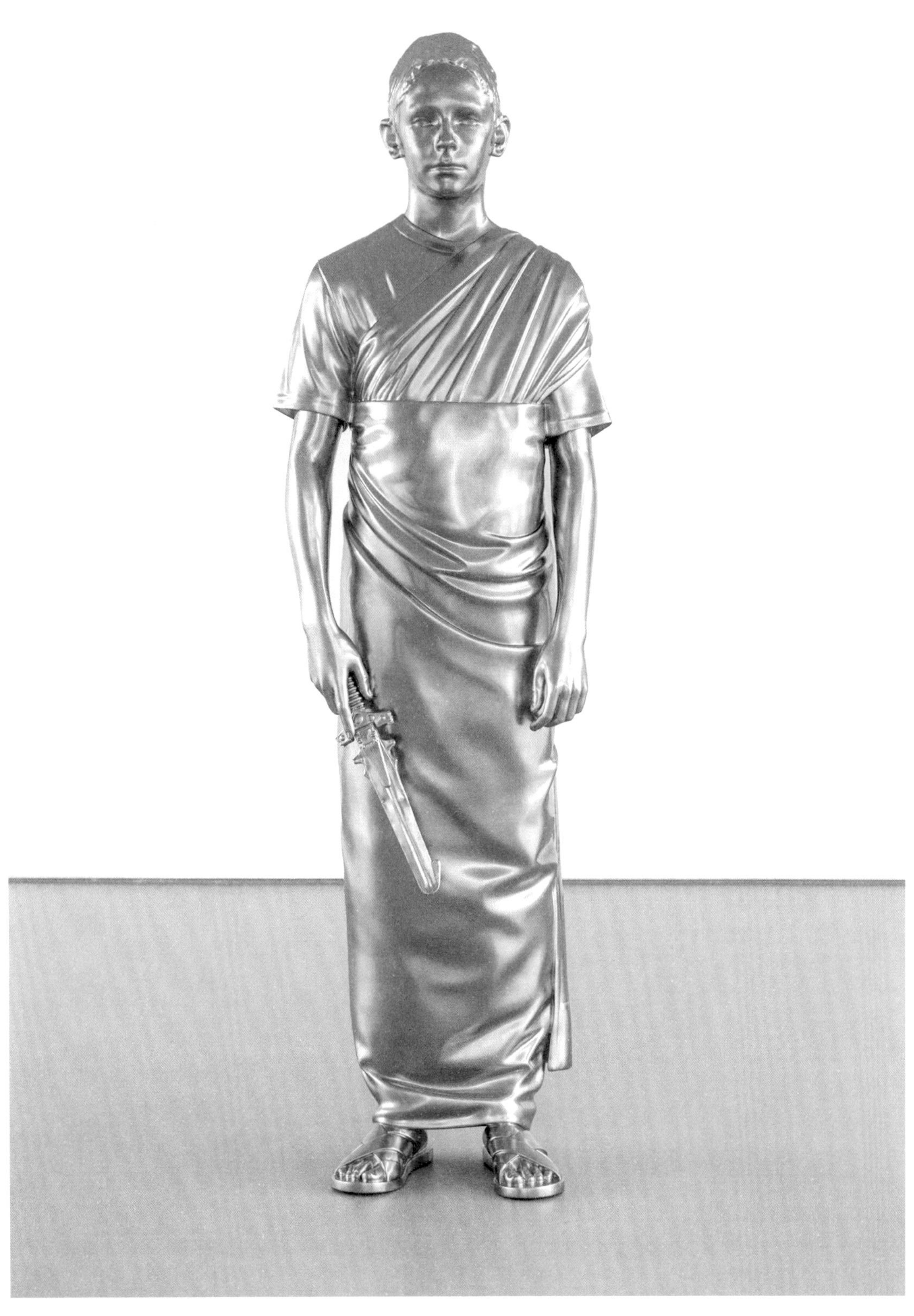

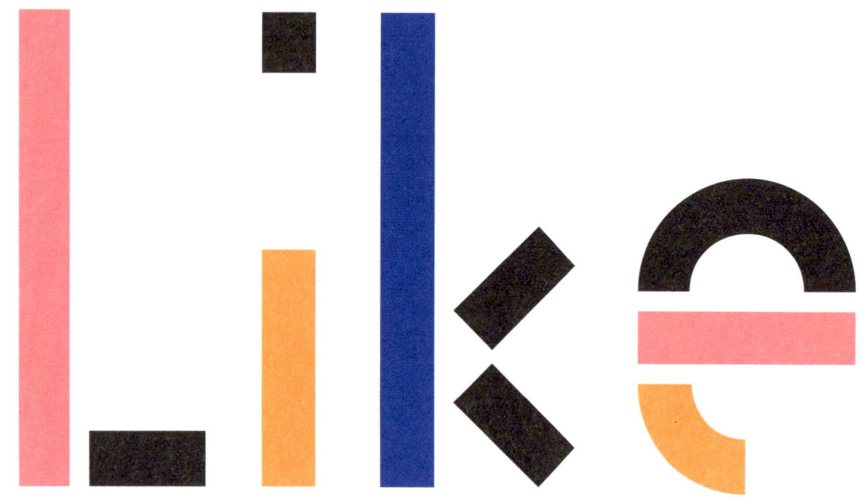
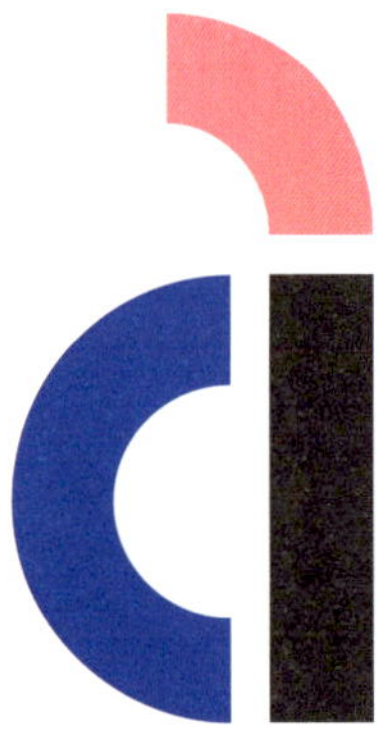

Draw

CHILD

Paul Klee
Allan Rohan Crite
Helen Levitt
Jean-Michel Basquiat
Mary Kelly
Glenn Ligon
Rivane Neuenschwander
Brian Belott

Artists have long sought to imitate, incorporate, or investigate "child-like" drawings in their own work. Paul Klee is emblematic of a number of vanguard twentieth-century European modernists for whom children's art played a critical role. In the United States, the vivid street scenes of mid-century artists such as Allan Rohan Crite and Helen Levitt depict the urban environment as a space of socialization and play for children, reflecting a widespread cultural interest in the lives of children at the time. Forty years later, emerging out of the graffiti community, Jean-Michel Basquiat integrated the city's visual languages into his paintings, including the street board game called "skully" drawn on concrete and played by children in Queens and the Bronx. Mary Kelly's infant son was the subject of and provided material for her important feminist artwork *Post-Partum Document* (1973–79), of which chapter three overlays her toddler son's scribbles in crayon with her own typewritten documentation of his speech and her reaction to these earliest attempts at communication. In his series of paintings called *Coloring*, Glenn Ligon derives imagery from coloring sessions he initiated at daycare centers in Minneapolis using 1970s coloring books featuring historical figures from African American history. The series addresses an emerging racial consciousness on the part of children and the role of media such as coloring books in constructing those identities. Rivane Neuenschwander, who has undertaken many collaborations with children through workshops, translated her nephew's drawings of his nightmares into a four-channel video work with a soundtrack by the experimental musician Arto Lindsay. Brian Belott builds his installation out of selections from the massive collection of children's art assembled by the early childhood educator and psychologist Rhoda Kellogg and his own "failed" copies of the children's art, staging a dialogue that invites closer reflection on the aesthetic and communicative qualities of children's drawings and modes of mark-making. Children's evolving ability to communicate is a fundamental aspect of their development, and within this uneven process, contemporary artists have discovered immense potential for invention and collaboration. These distinct artworks capture an enduring interest in the expressive and creative capacities of children.

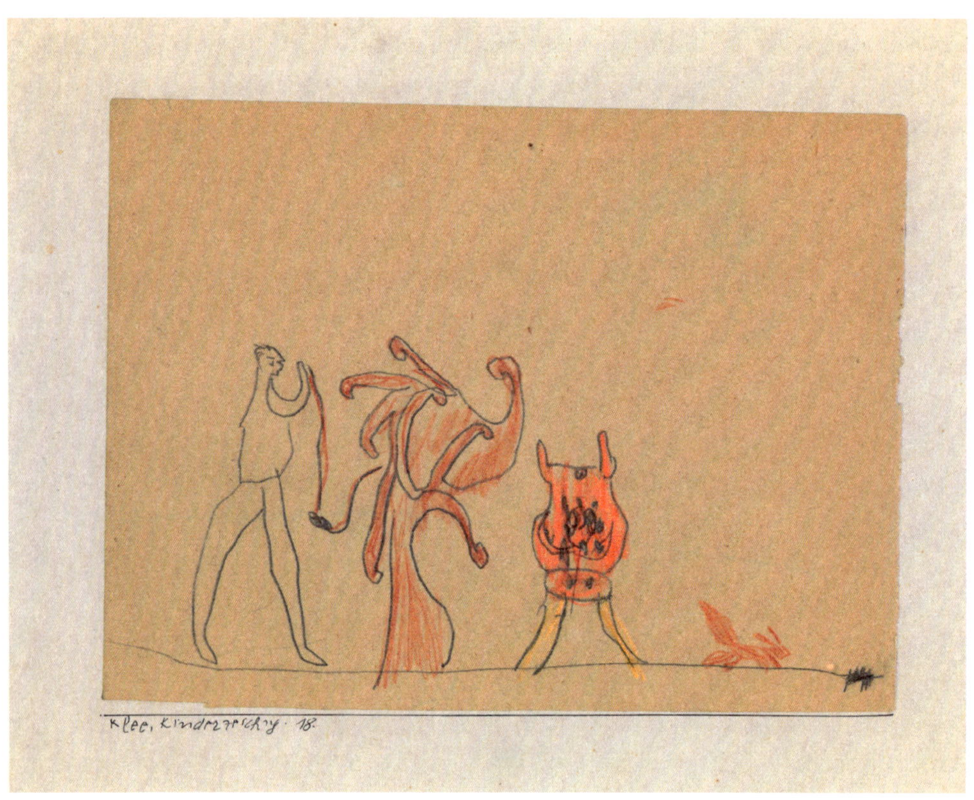

Draw Like a Child

Paul Klee
Hot Pursuit, 1939
Colored paste and oil on paper on jute
19 × 25 ½ inches (48.3 × 64.8 cm)

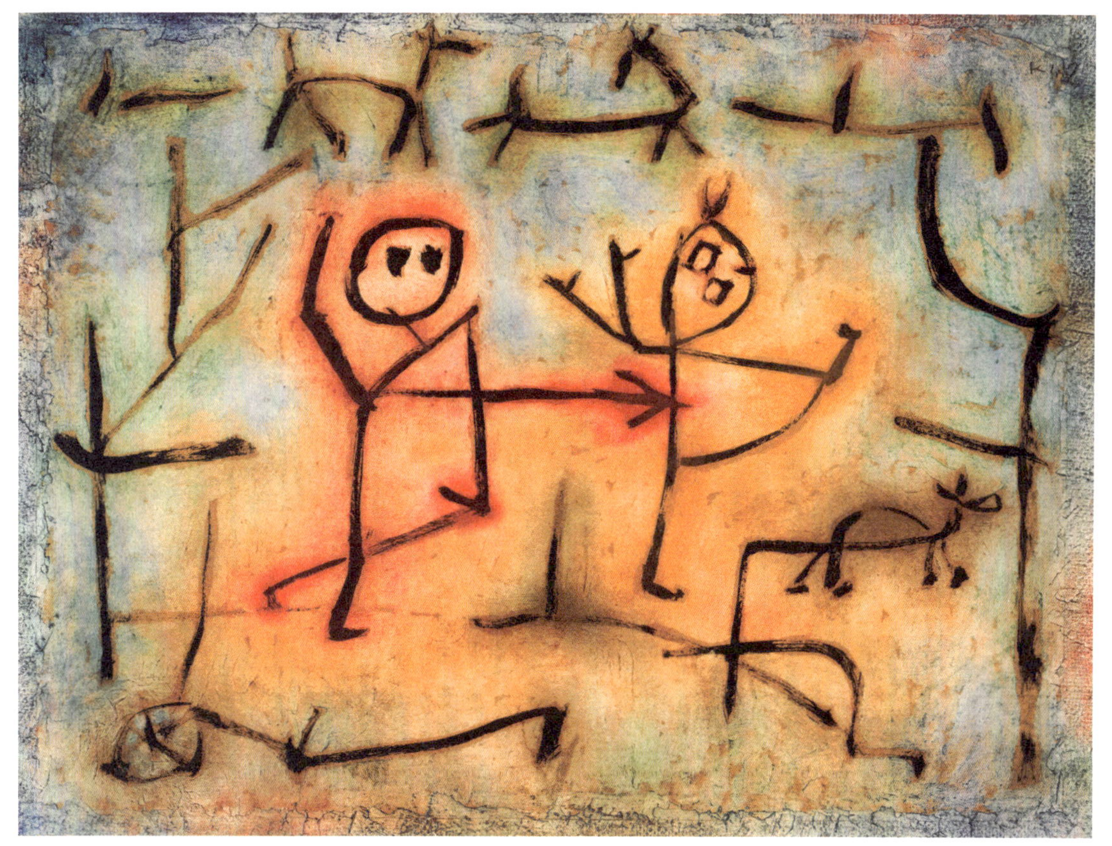

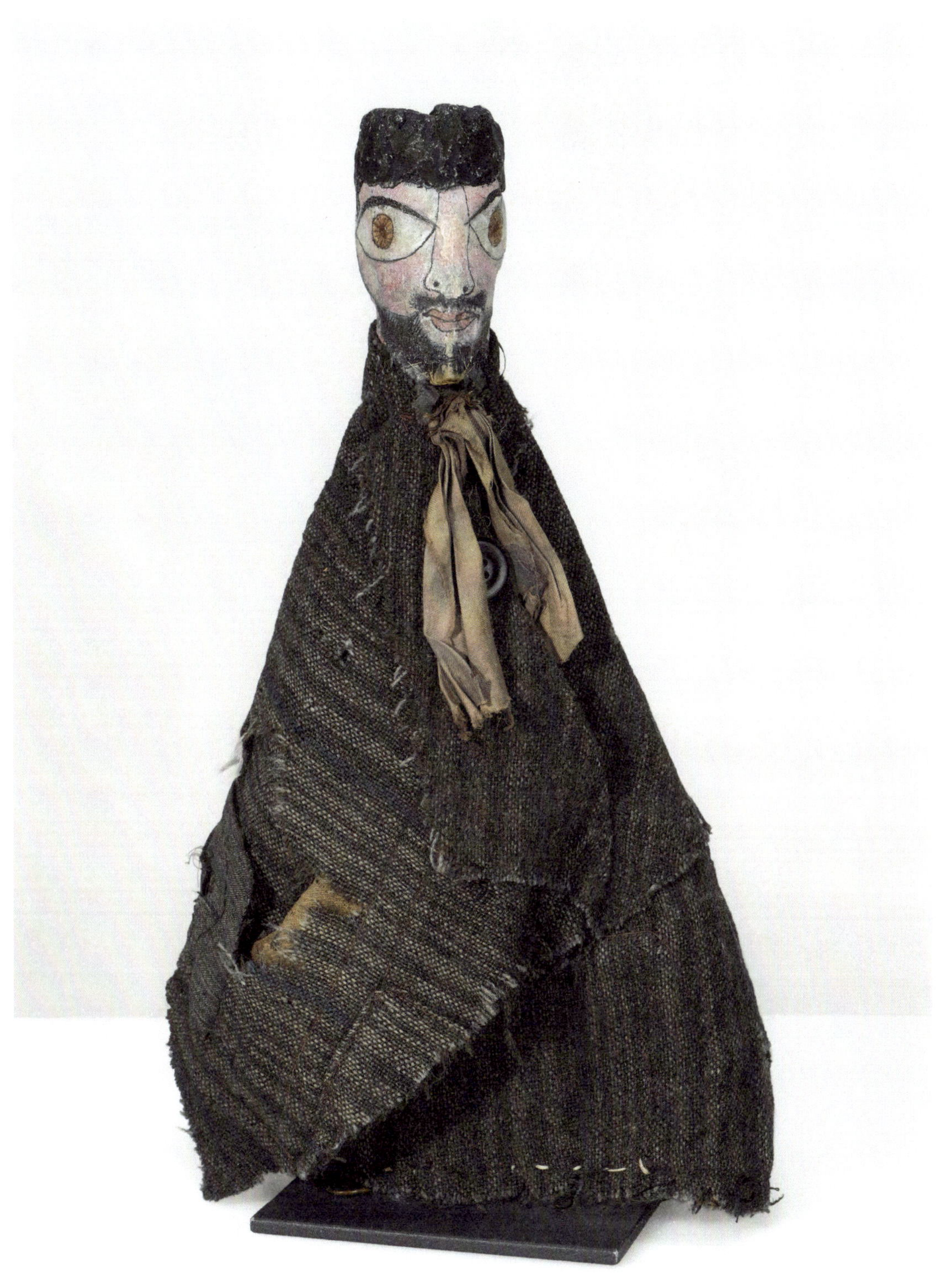

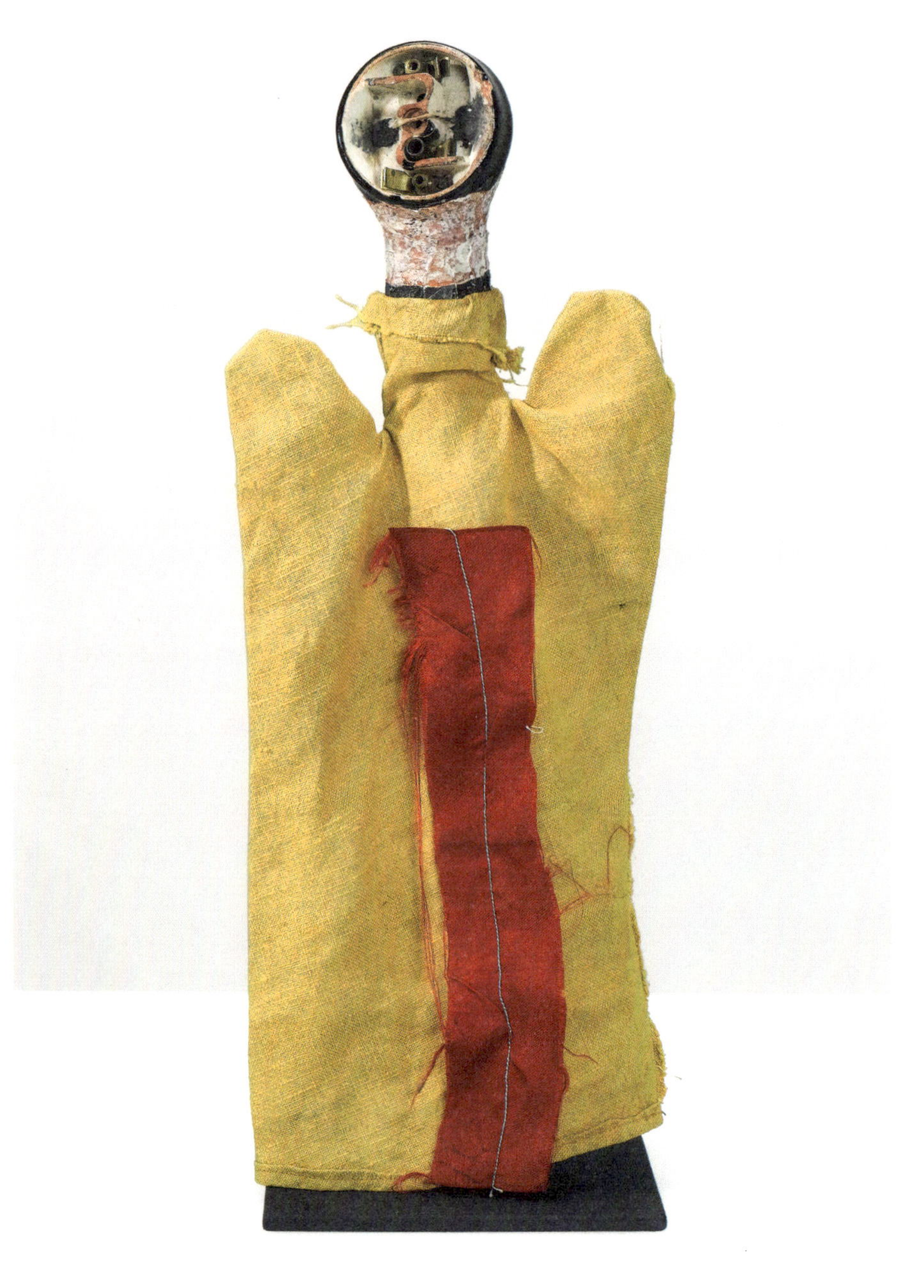

Paul Klee
Untitled (Electrical Spook), 1923
Hand puppet
14 ¼ × 6 × 3 ½ inches (36 × 15 × 9 cm)

Draw Like a Child

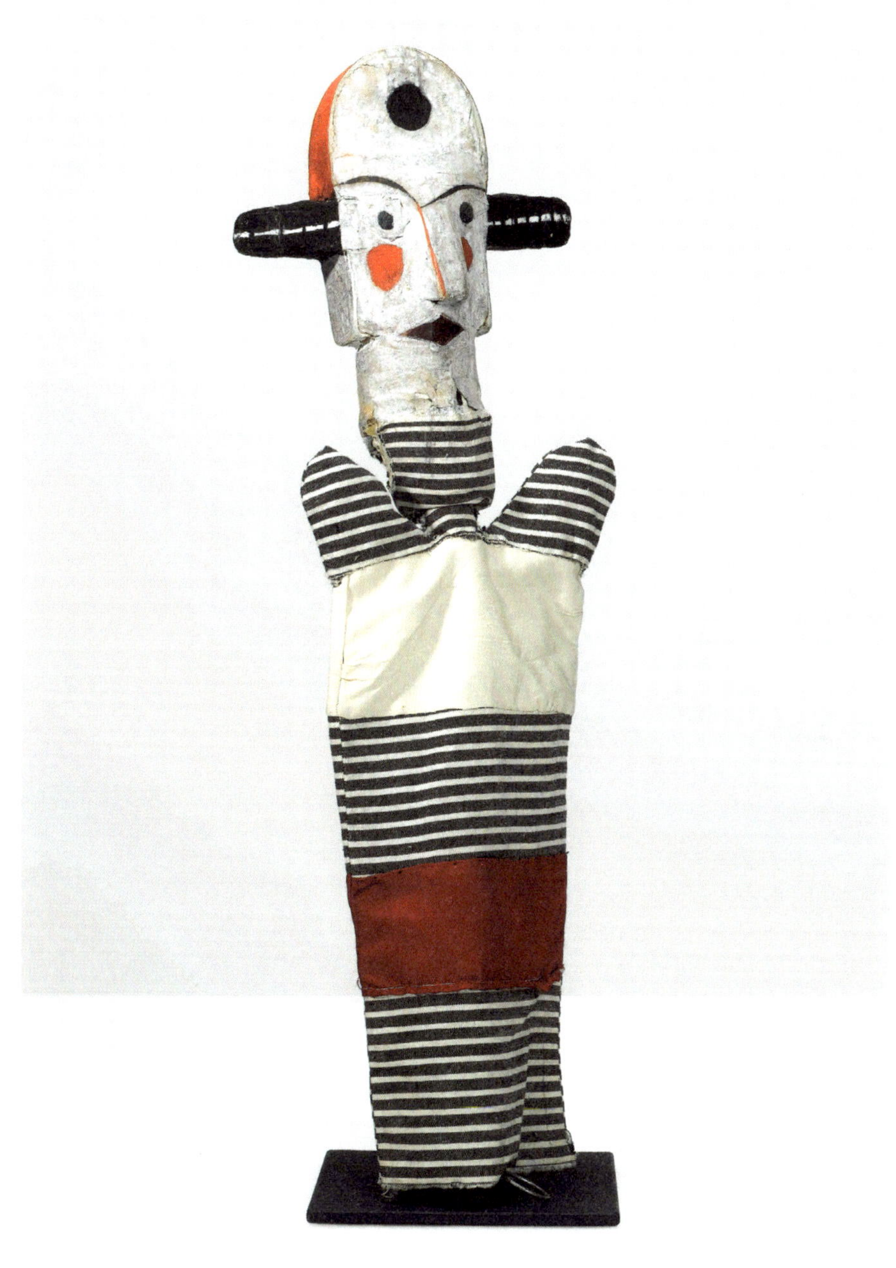

Paul Klee
Untitled (Big-Eared Clown), 1925
Hand puppet
19 ⅞ × 6 ¼ × 2 ¼ inches (48 × 16 × 7 cm)

Draw Like a Child

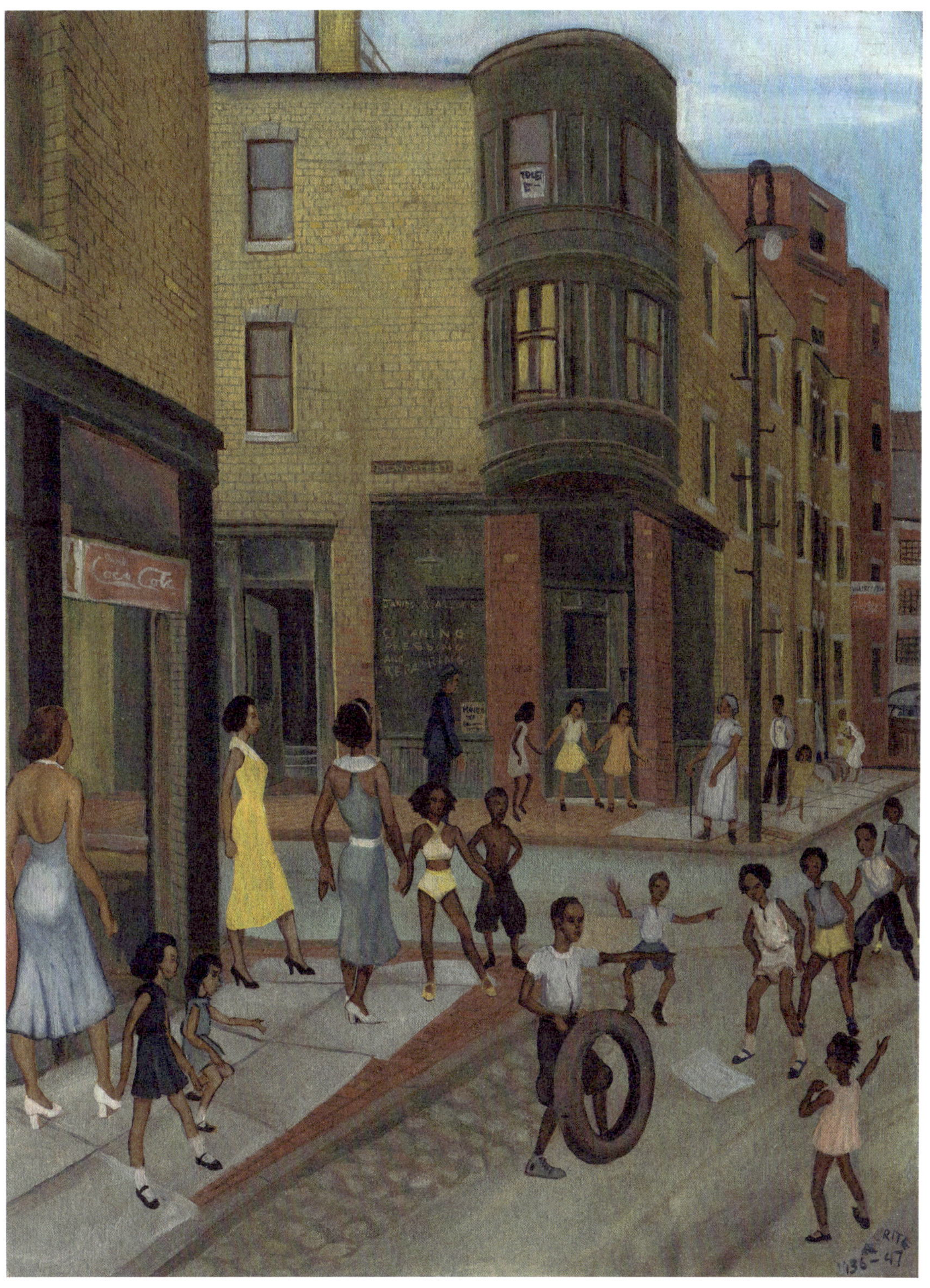

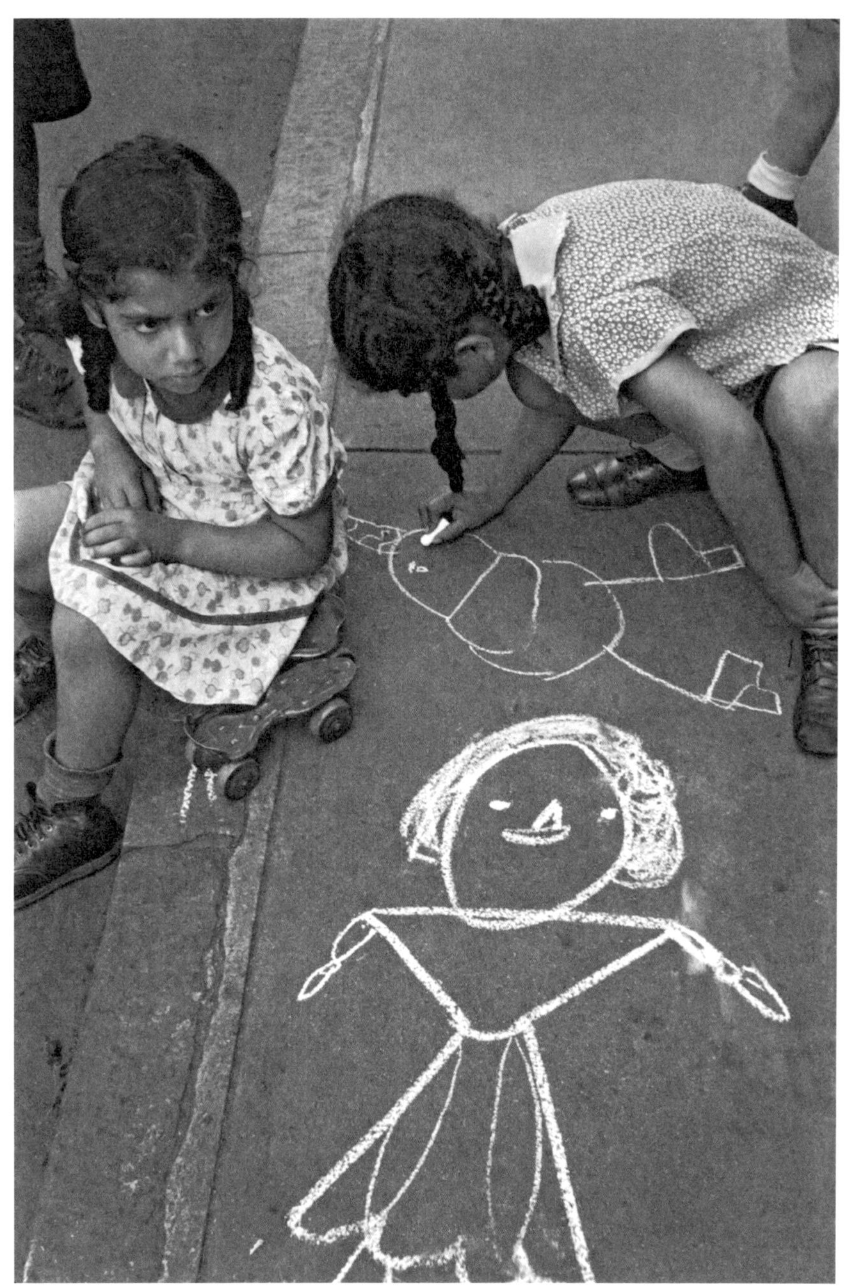

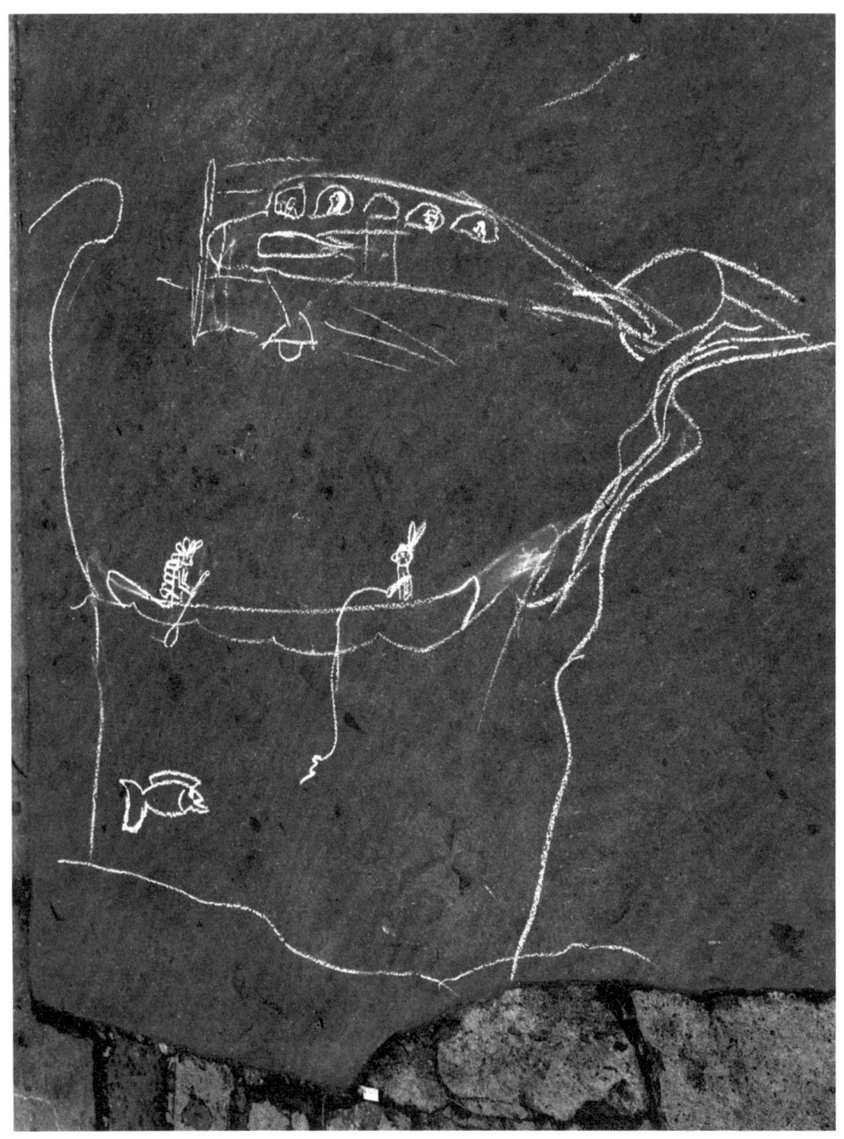

Helen Levitt
N.Y., ca. 1940
Gelatin silver print
10 ¼ × 8 ¼ inches (26.1 × 20.8 cm)

Draw Like a Child

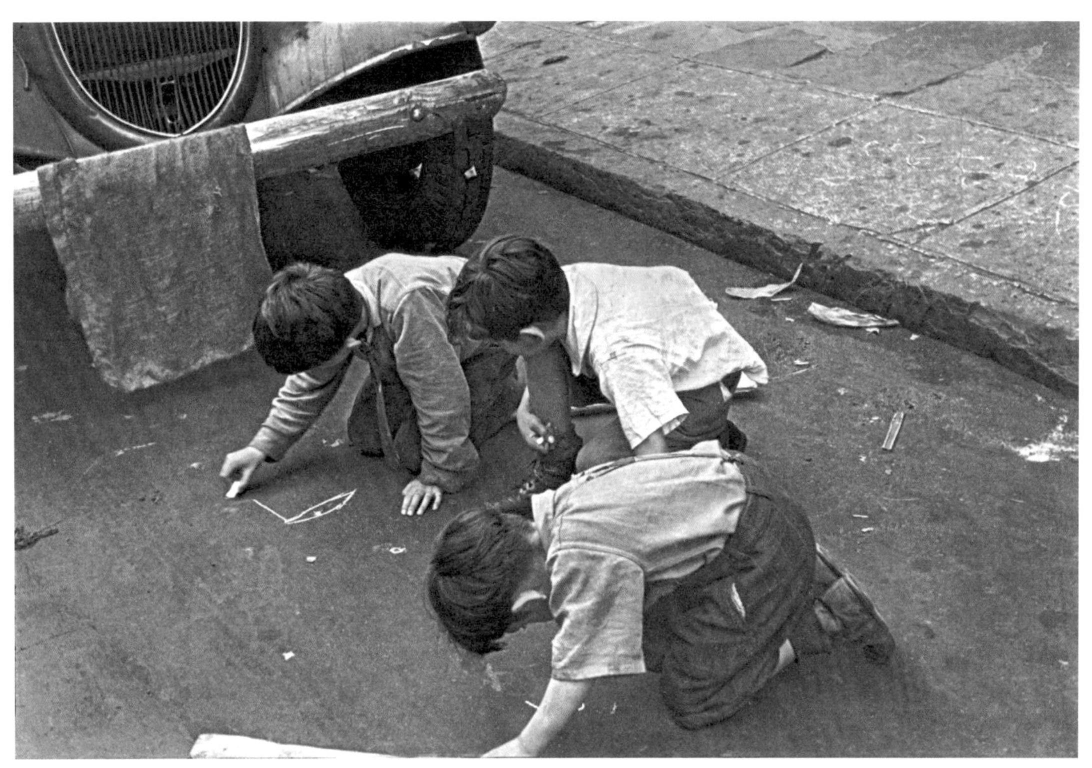

Helen Levitt
N.Y., ca. 1939
Gelatin silver print
8 ¼ × 10 ¼ inches (20.8 × 26.1 cm)

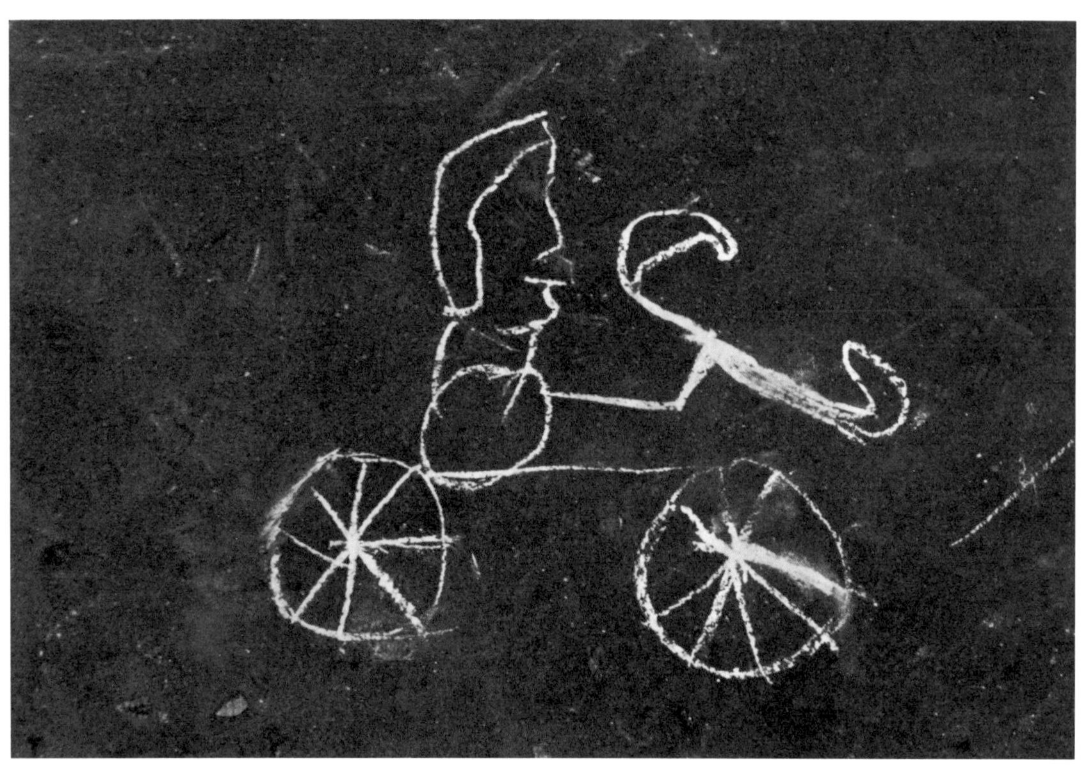

Helen Levitt
N.Y., ca. 1940
Gelatin silver print
8 × 10 ¾ inches (20.3 × 27.2 cm)

 Draw Like a Child

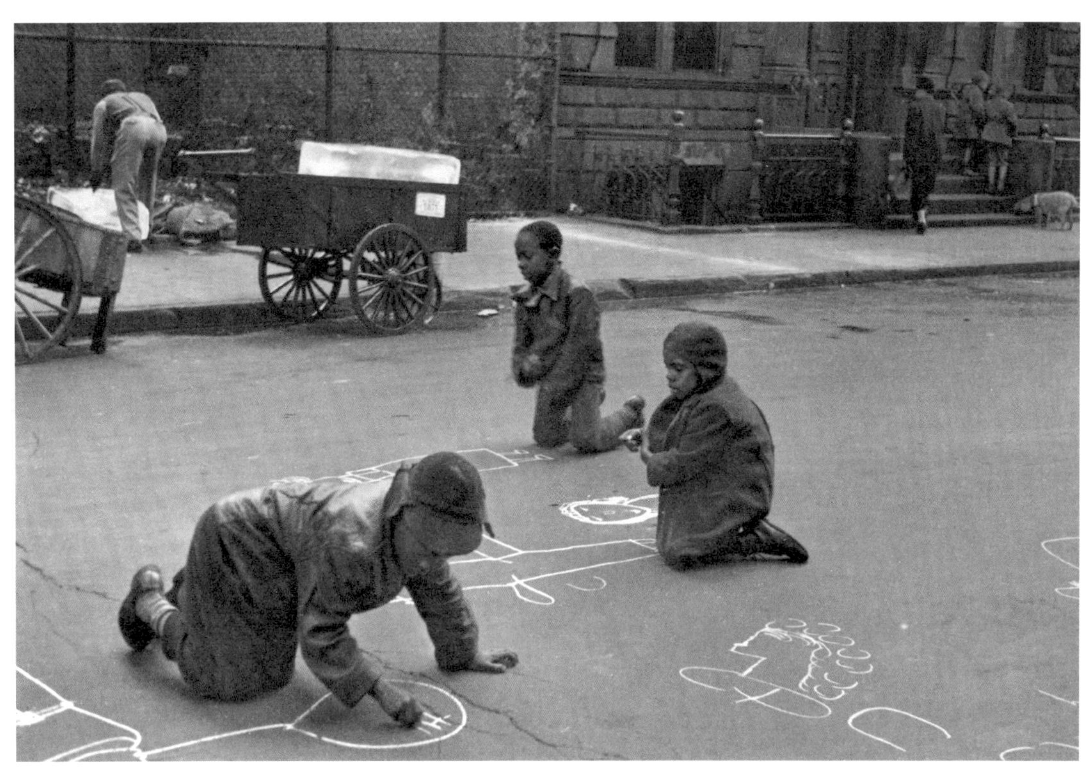

Helen Levitt
N.Y., ca. 1939
Gelatin silver print
7 × 10 inches (17.8 × 25.4 cm)

Jean-Michel Basquiat
Untitled, 1981
Acrylic and spray paint on canvas
80 × 80 inches (203 × 203 cm)

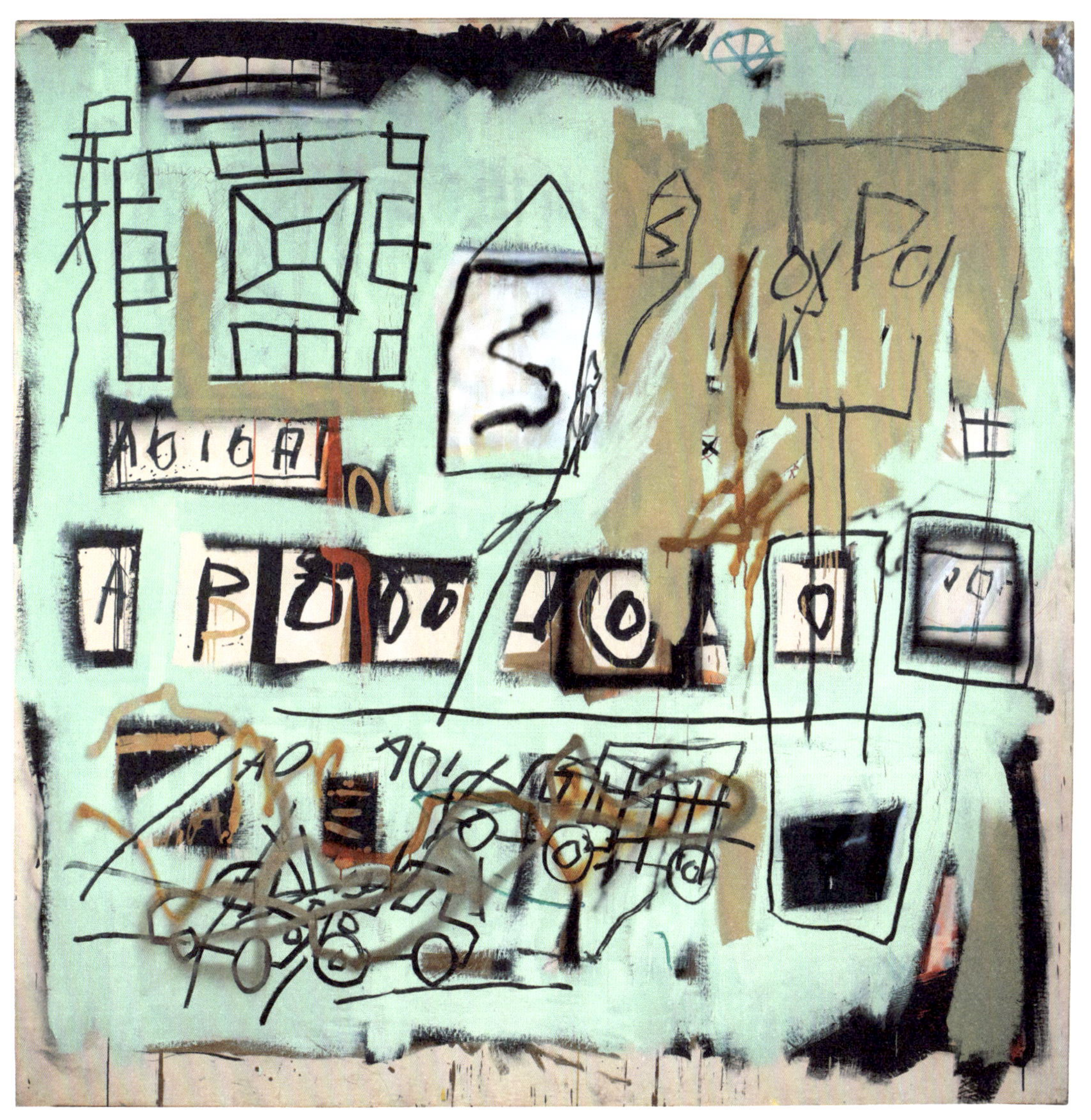

Mary Kelly
Post-Partum Document: Documentation III
Analysed Markings and Diary Perspective Schema, 1975
Works on paper, graphite, crayon, chalk, and
printed diagrams, mounted on paper
Thirteen parts, each 11 ¼ × 14 ¼ × 1 ⅜ inches
(28.6 × 36.1 × 3.5 cm)

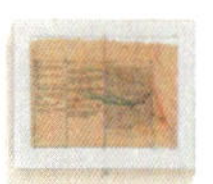

Draw Like a Child

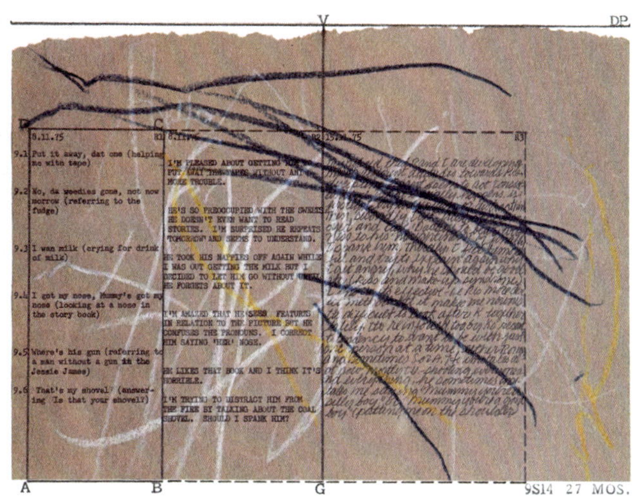

DP

8.11.75

9.1 Put it away, dat one (helping me with tape)

9.2 No, da weedies gone, not now morrow (referring to the fudge)

9.3 I wan milk (crying for drink of milk)

9.4 I got my nose, Mummy's got my nose (looking at a nose in the story book)

9.5 Where's his gun (referring to a man without a gun in the Jessie James)

9.6 That's my shovel? (answering 'Is that your shovel?')

I'M PLEASED ABOUT GETTING HIM TO PUT AWAY THE TAPES WITHOUT ANY MORE TROUBLE.

HE'S SO PREOCCUPIED WITH THE SWEETS HE DOESN'T EVEN WANT TO READ STORIES. I'M SURPRISED HE REPEATS 'TOMORROW' AND SEEMS TO UNDERSTAND.

HE TOOK HIS NAPPIES OFF AGAIN WHILE I WAS OUT GETTING THE MILK BUT I DECIDED TO LET HIM GO WITHOUT UNTIL HE FORGETS ABOUT IT.

I'M AMAZED THAT HE SEES FEATURES IN RELATION TO THE PICTURE BUT HE CONFUSES THE PRONOUNS. I CORRECT HIM SAYING 'HER' NOSE.

HE LIKES THAT BOOK AND I THINK IT'S HORRIBLE.

I'M TRYING TO DISTRACT HIM FROM THE FIRE BY TALKING ABOUT THE COAL SHOVEL. SHOULD I SPANK HIM?

A   B   G

9S14 27 MOS.

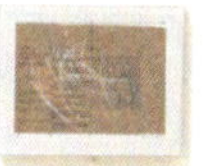
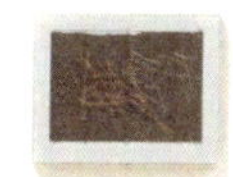
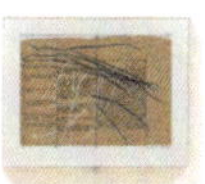
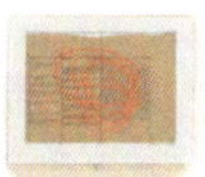
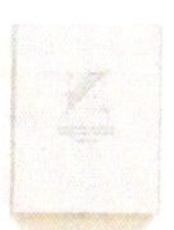
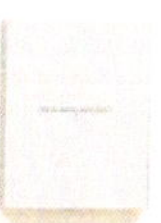

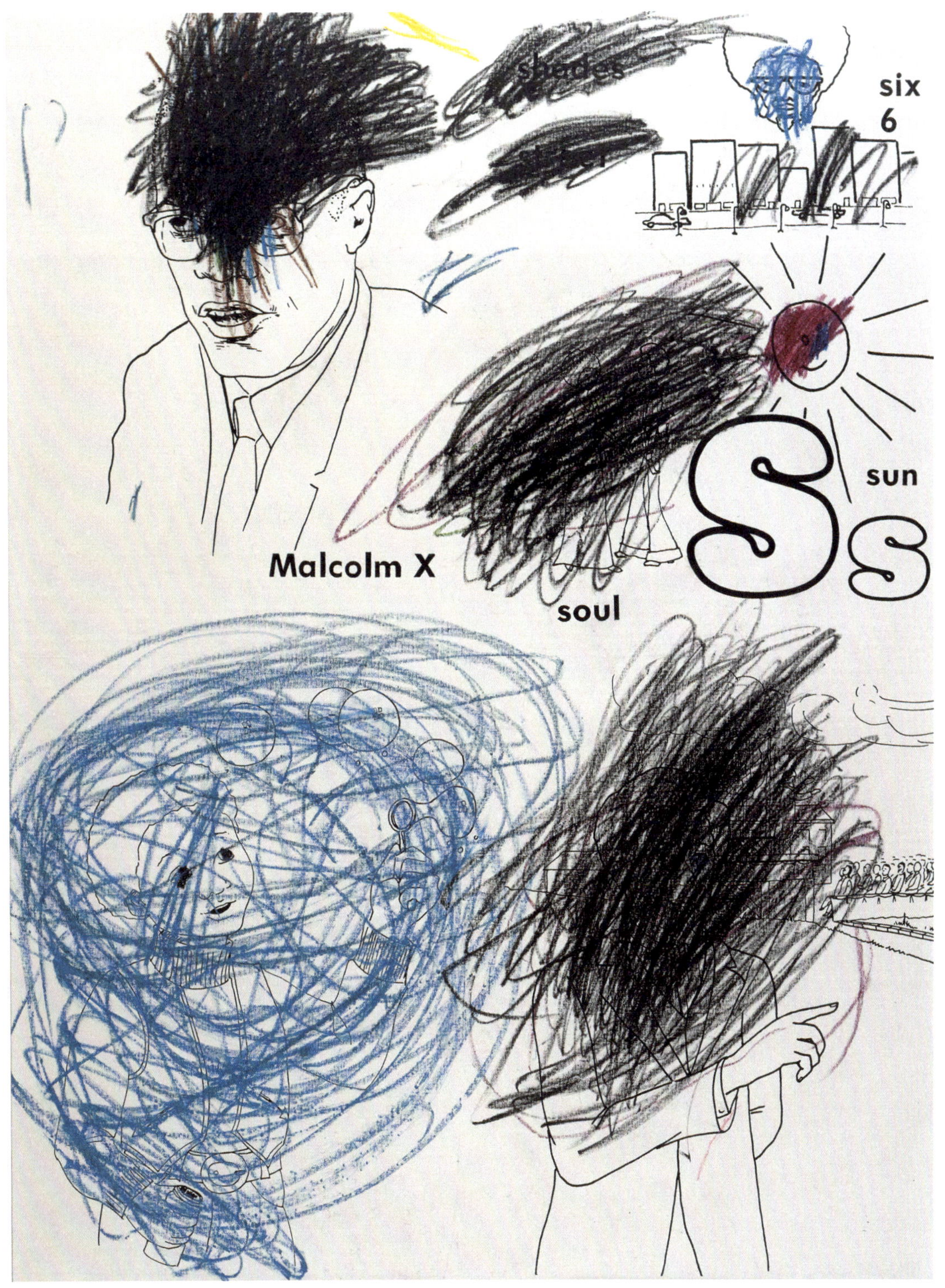

shades
six
6
sun
Ss
Malcolm X
soul

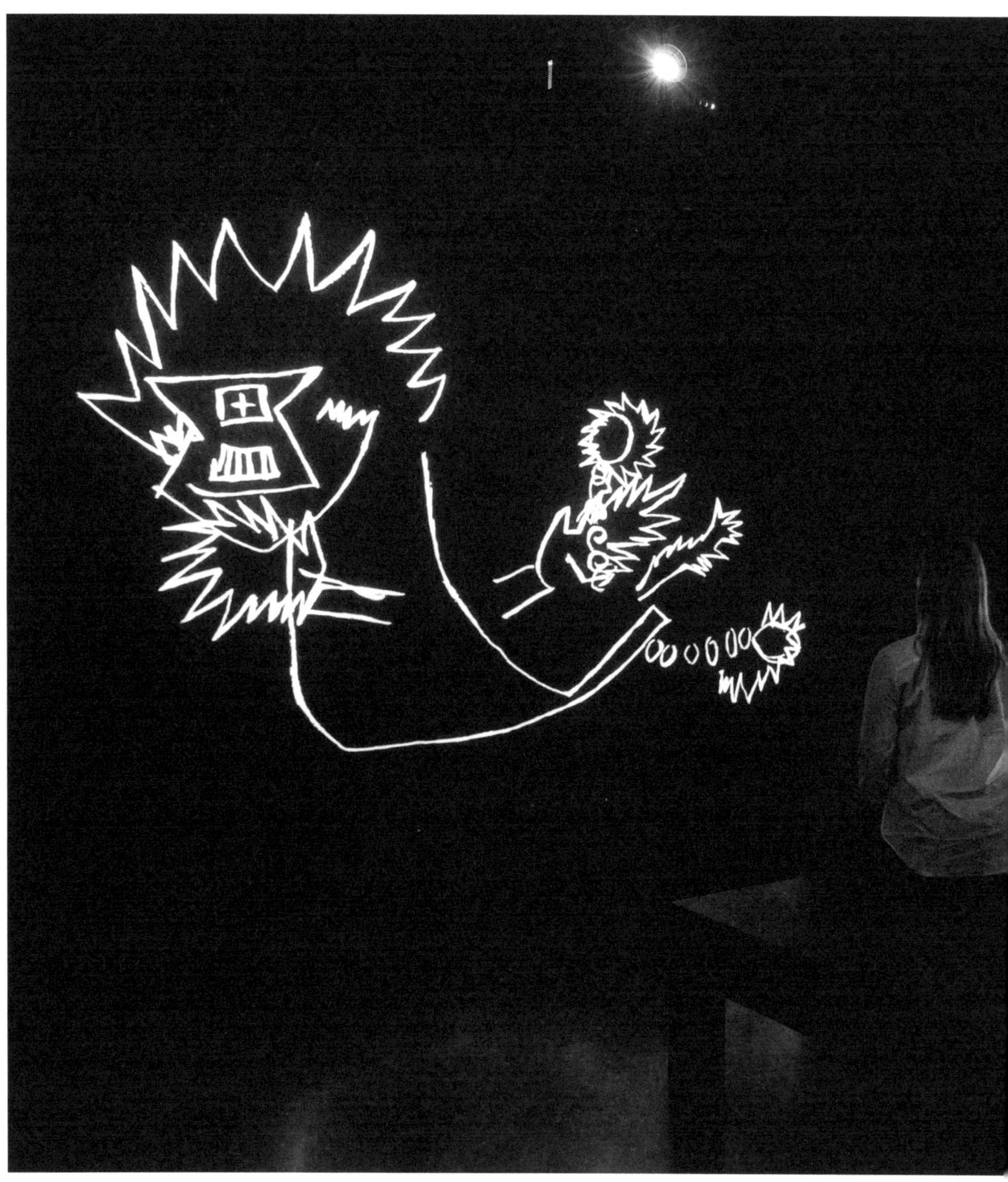

Draw Like a Child

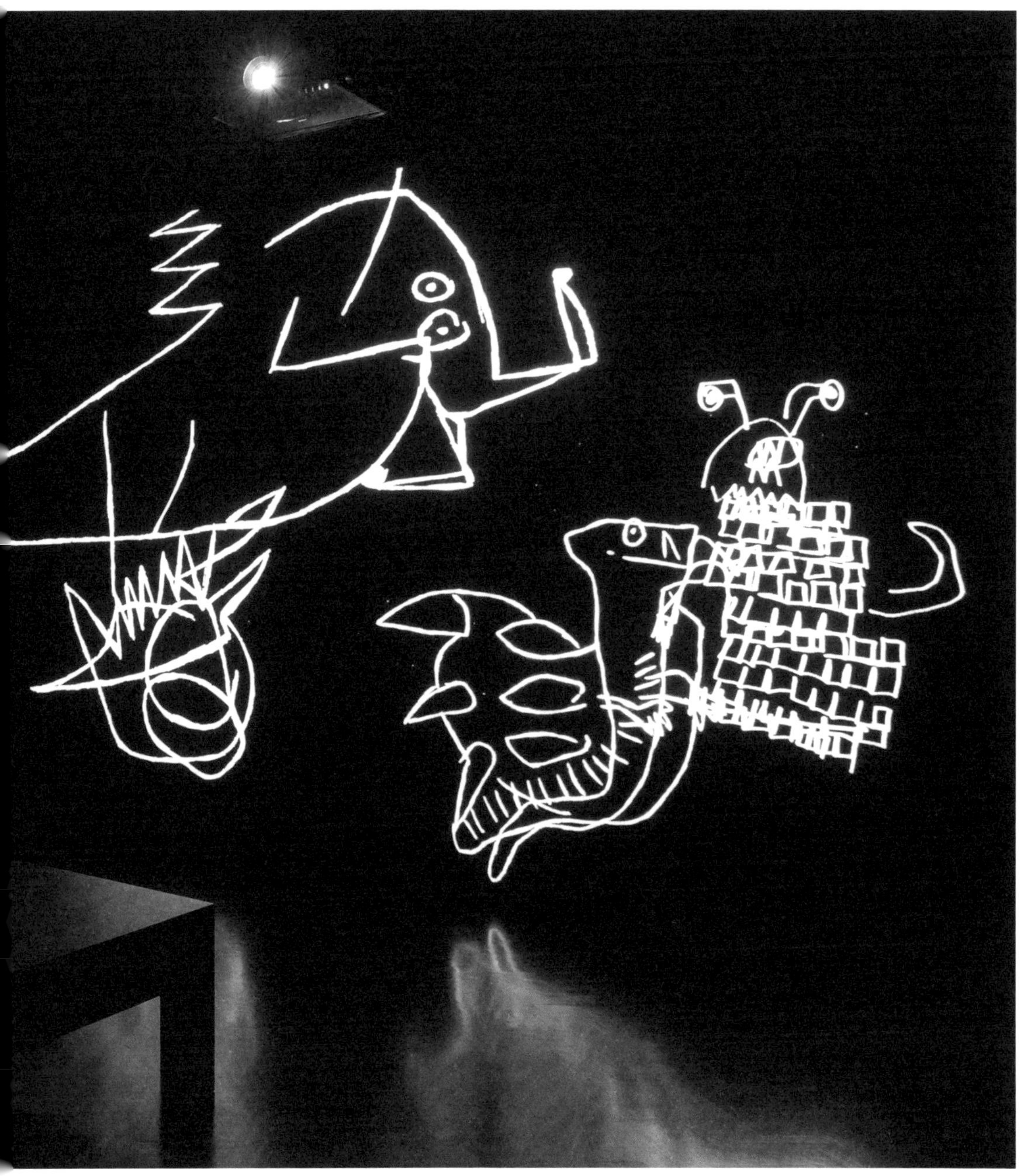

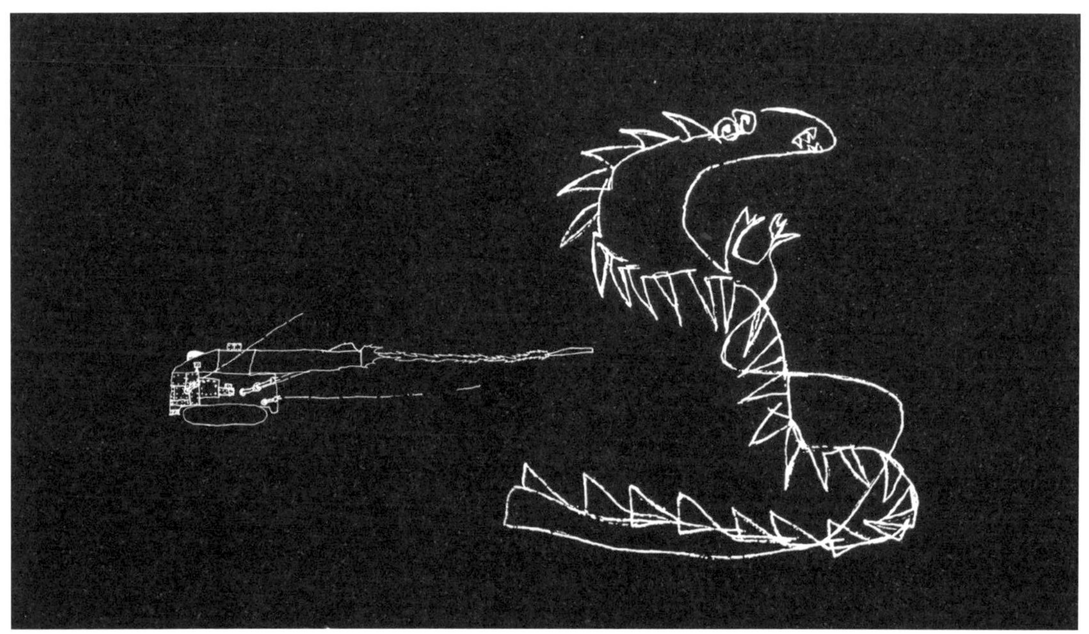

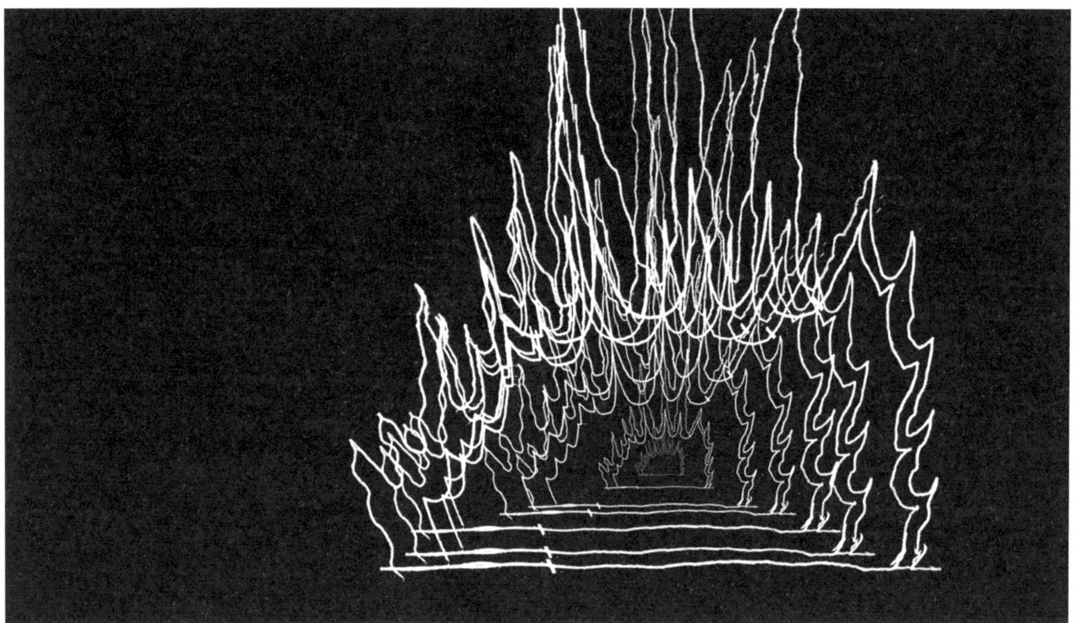

Rivane Neuenschwander
Cabra-Cega / Blind Man's Bluff (stills), 2016
Four-channel animated projection (black-and-white, sound; 2:31 minutes)
based on original drawings by Thomas N. Maciel Baron, sound by Arto Lindsay
Dimensions variable

                                    Draw Like a Child

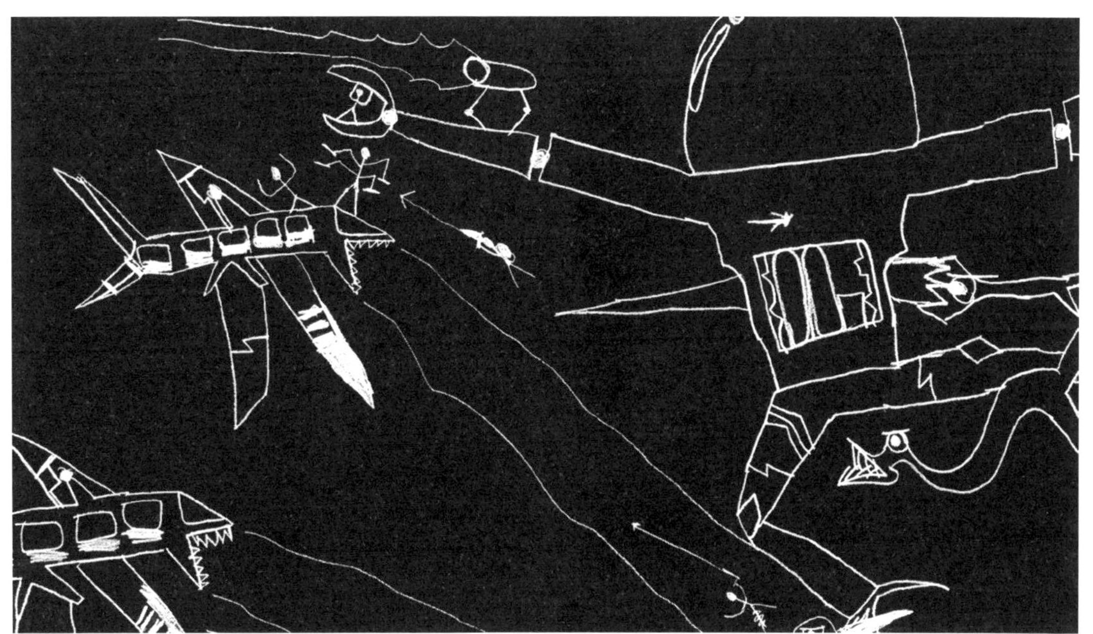

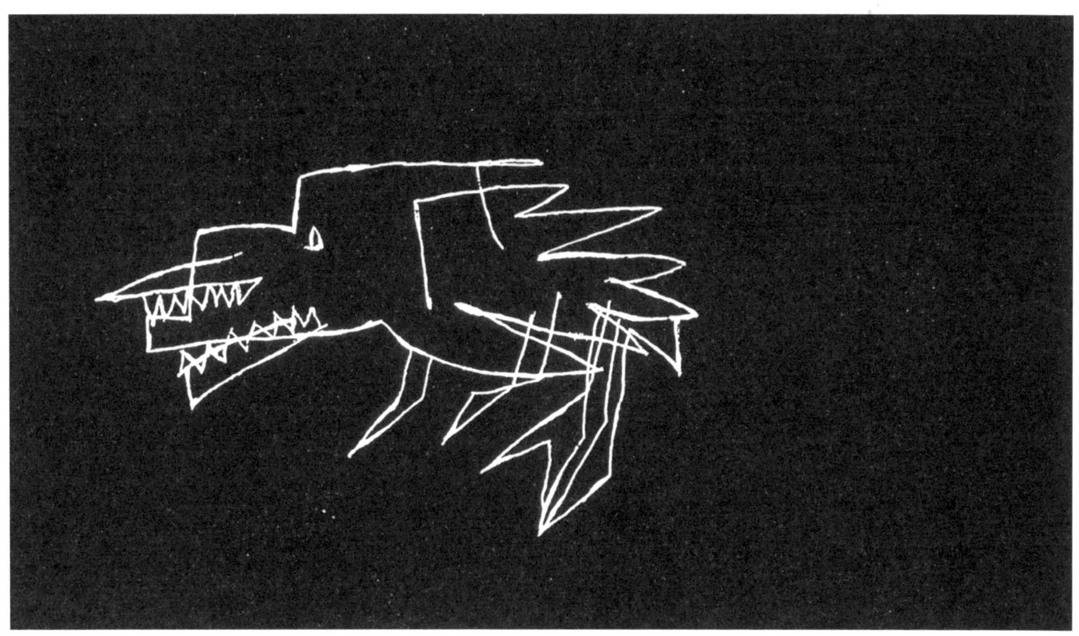

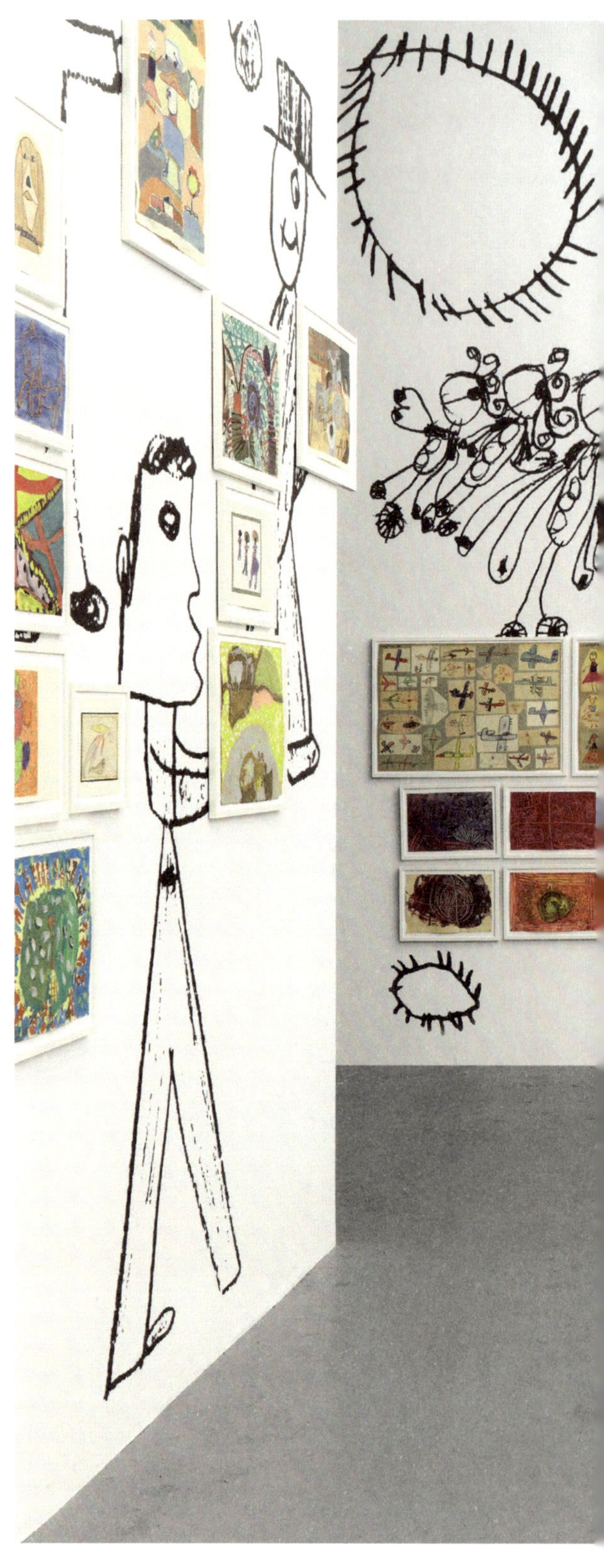

Draw Like a Child

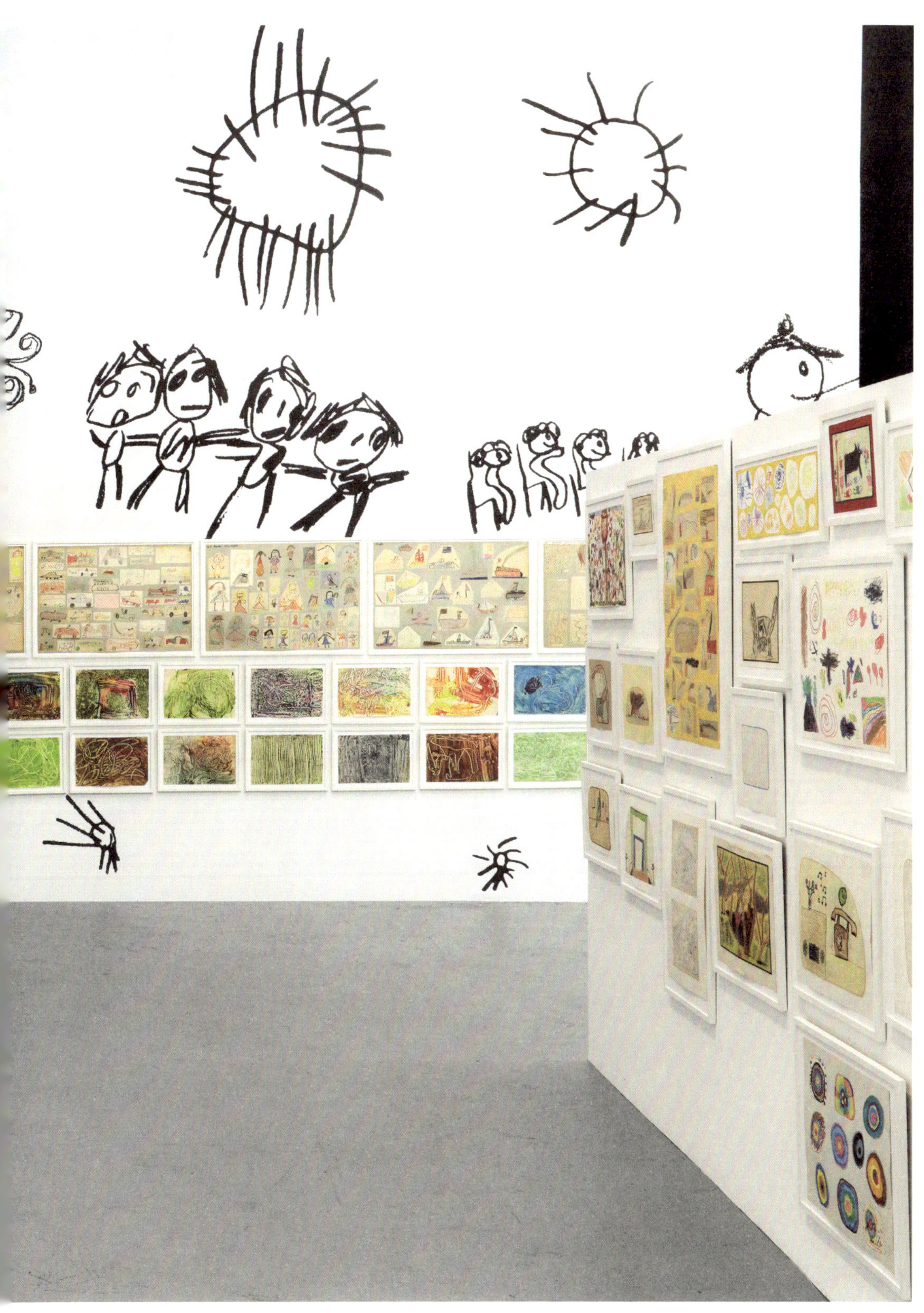

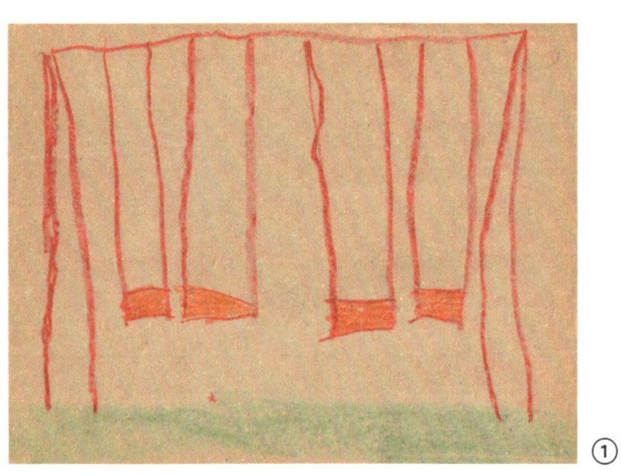

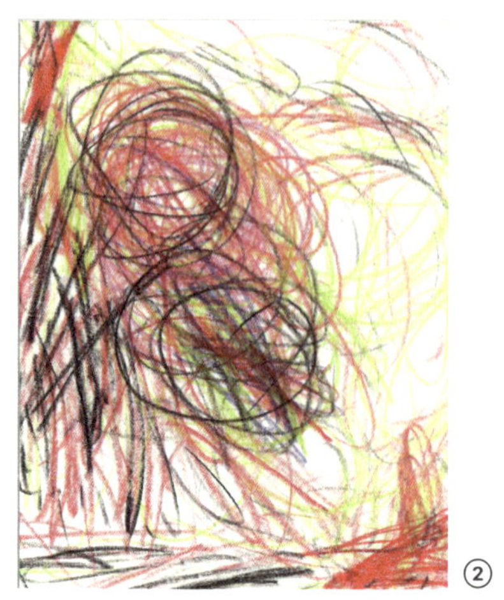

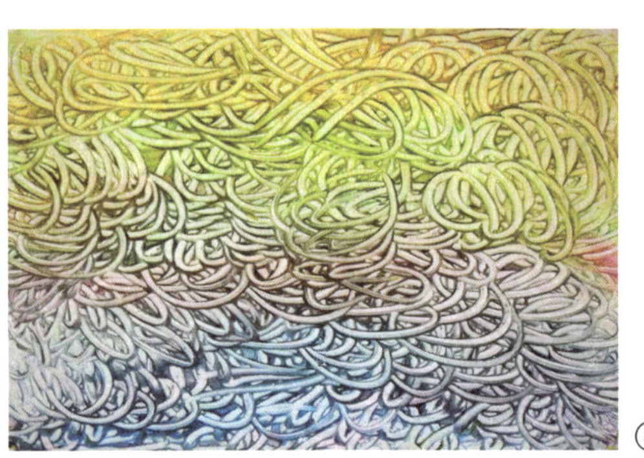

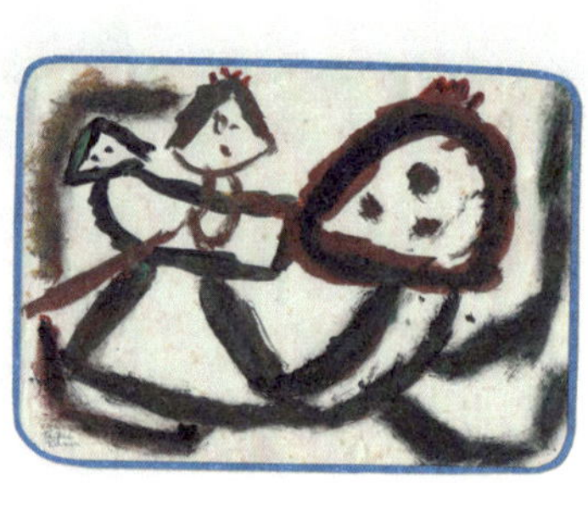

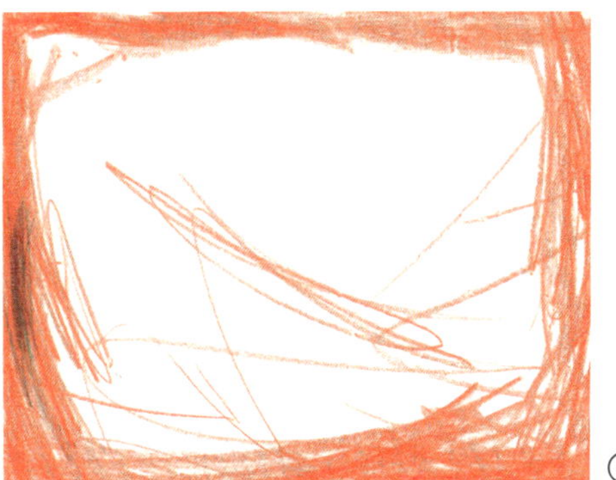

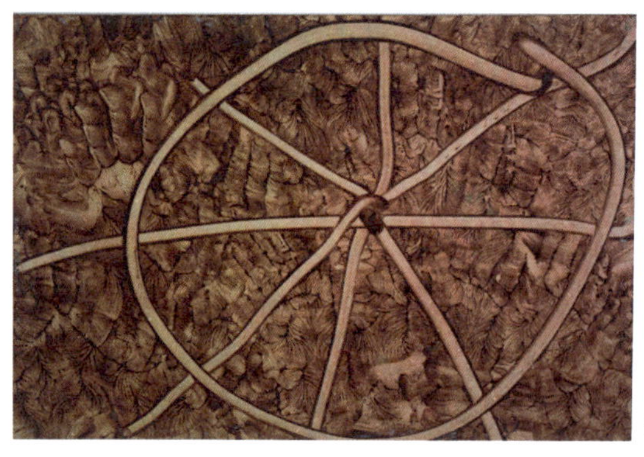

Draw Like a Child

1   Unknown, Apleane Swingset Red, n.d.
    Crayon on paper
    12 × 9 inches (30.5 × 22.9 cm)

2   Shana B., Page 516, n.d.
    Crayon on paper
    10 × 8 inches (25.4 × 20.3 cm)

3   Gina, Untitled, n.d.
    Acrylic on butcher paper
    18 × 12 inches (45.7 × 30.5 cm)

4   Unknown (Taipei, Taiwan), Untitled, n.d.
    Acrylic on paper mounted to board
    14 ½ × 12 inches (36.8 × 30.5 cm)

5   Alice L., Page 222, n.d.
    Crayon on paper
    8 × 10 inches (20.3 × 25.4 cm)

6   David W. (age 4–5), Untitled, 1954
    Acrylic on butcher paper.
    8 × 12 inches (45.7 × 30.5 cm)

7   Leslie S. (age 7 ½), Treed Mountain, n.d.
    Crayon on paper mounted to board
    13 ½ × 10 inches (34.3 × 25.4 cm)

8   David R. (age 7), 675 Edna Way, n.d.
    Graphite on paper mounted to board
    13 ½ × 11 ¼ inches (34.3 × 28.7 cm)

9   Sue (age 2), Untitled, n.d.
    Acrylic on butcher paper
    18 × 12 inches (45.7 × 30.5 cm)

10 Richard J. (age 8 ½), Cars on OP Road, n.d.
    Crayon on paper mounted to board
    13 ½ × 11 inches (34.3 × 27.9 cm)

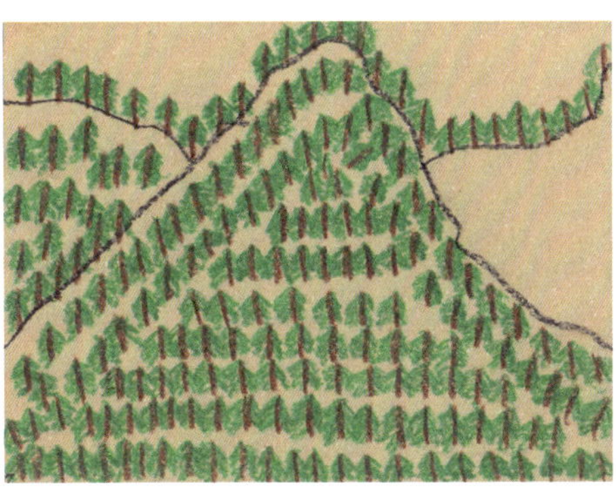

(7)

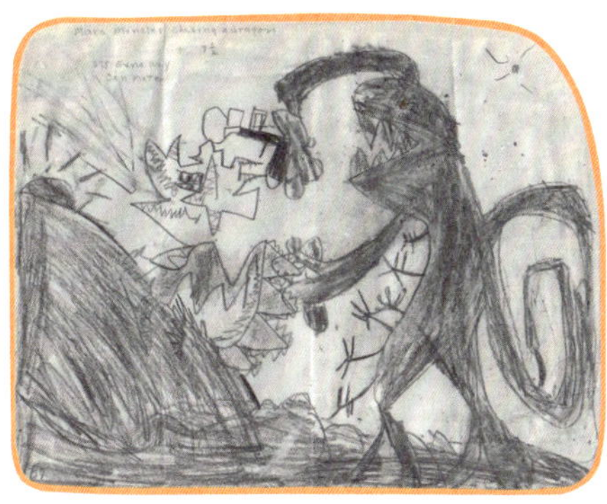

(8)

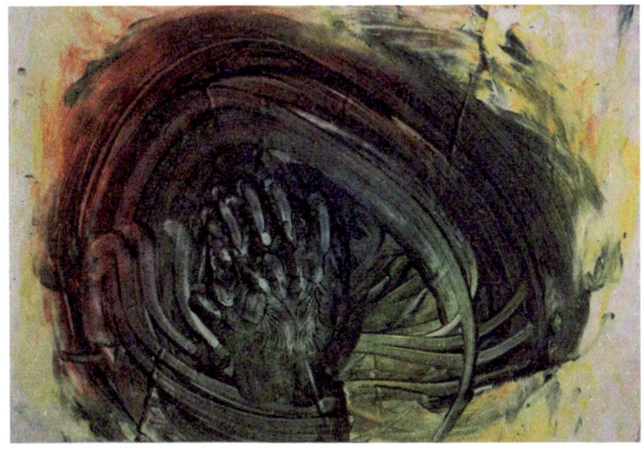

(9)

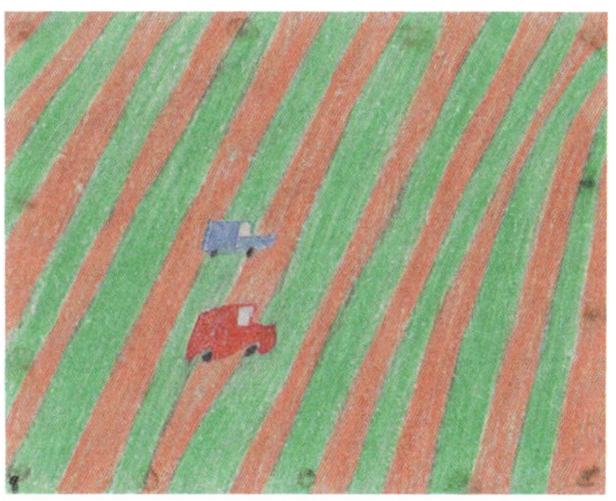

(10)

11 Unknown (girl, age 5), Untitled, n.d.
Crayon on paper mounted to board
14 ¼ × 11 ¼ inches (36.2 × 28.6 cm)

12 Shana B., Page 506, n.d.
Crayon on paper
10 × 8 inches (25.4 × 20.3 cm)

13 Cyn, Untitled, n.d.
Acrylic on butcher paper
18 × 12 inches (45.7 × 30.5 cm)

14 Unknown (Switzerland, boy, age 6),
Untitled, 1955
Colored pencil on paper mounted to board
12 × 7 ½ inches (30.5 × 19.1 cm)

15 Unknown (Egypt, boy, age 10), Untitled, n.d.
Watercolor on paper ,mounted to board
15 ½ × 10 inches (39.4 × 25.4 cm)

16 Adrian P. (age 8), Untitled, n.d.
Crayon on paper mounted to board
14 × 11 inches (35.6 × 27.9 cm)

17 Unknown (Vietnam, age 8), Exercise, n.d.
Graphite and crayon on paper mounted to board
14 ¼ × 10 ¼ inches (36.3 × 26.2 cm)

18 Unknown (Israel, girl, age 8), Untitled, n.d.
Mixed media on paper mounted to board
8 ½ × 13 inches (21.6 × 33 cm)

19 Margaret G. (age 9), Untitled, 1960
Graphite and crayon on paper mounted to board
11 ¾ × 9 inches (30 × 22.9 cm)

20 Unknown, Yellow Circle Scribble, n.d.
Crayon on paper
17 × 11 inches (43.2 × 27.9 cm)

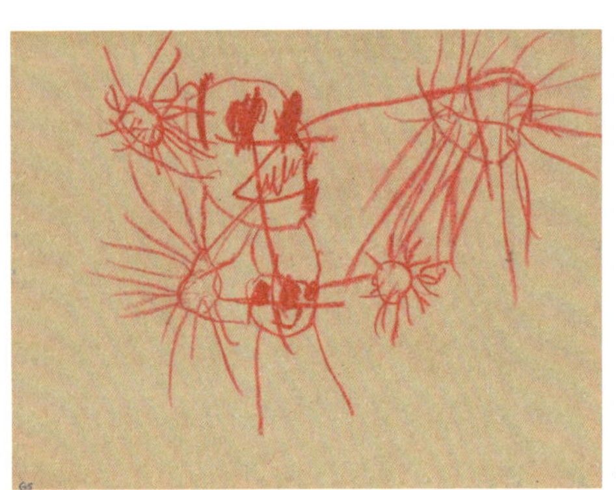

(11)

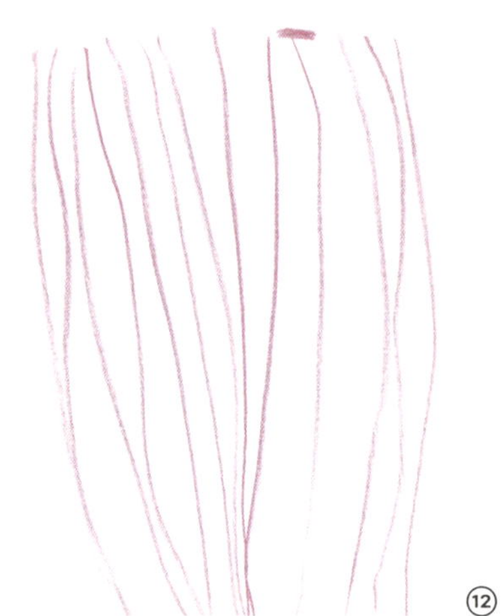

(12)

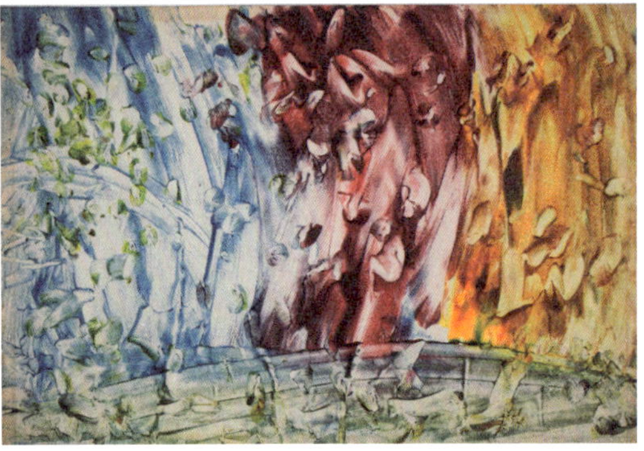

(13)

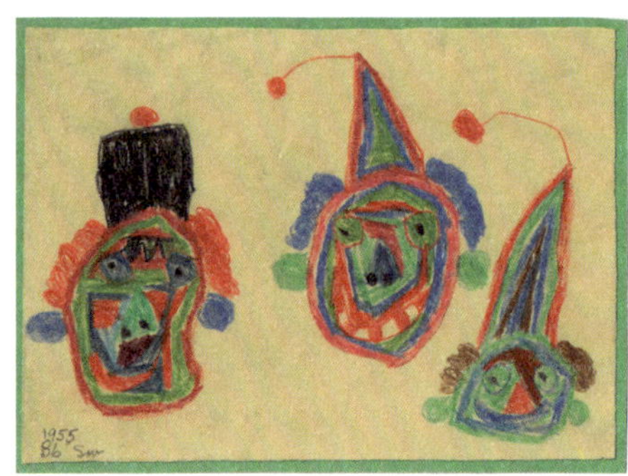

(14)

Draw Like a Child

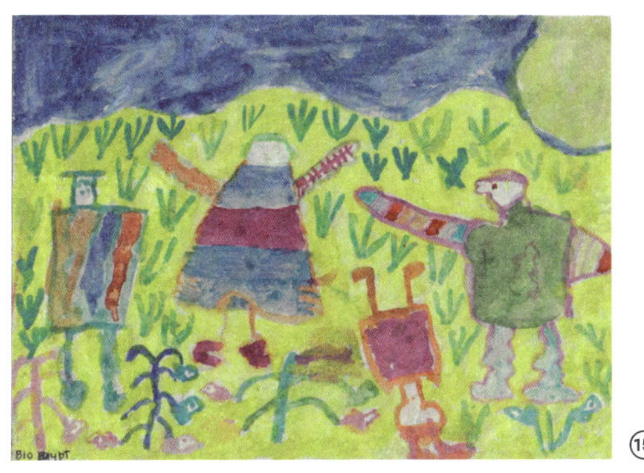

15

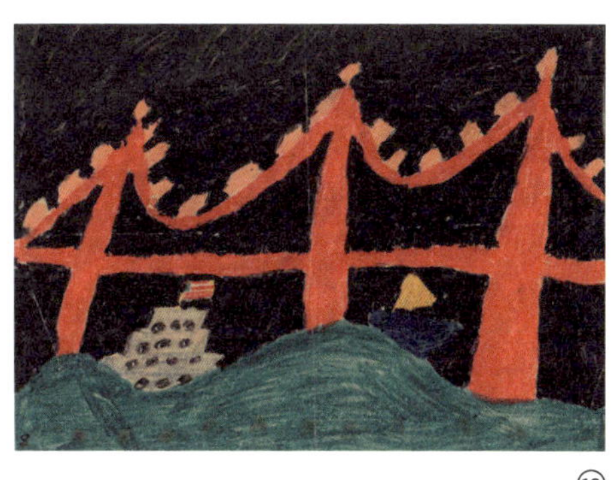

16

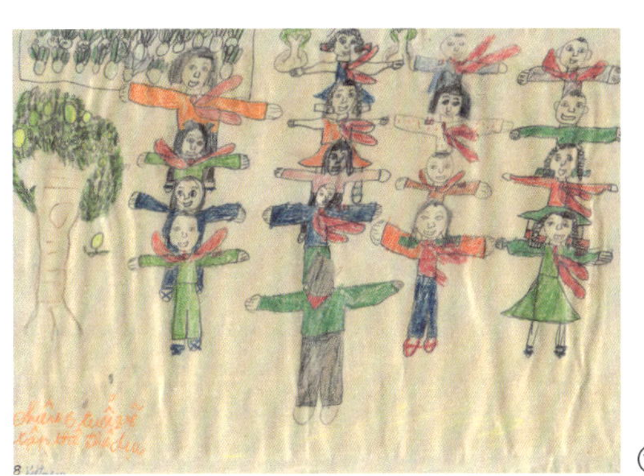

17

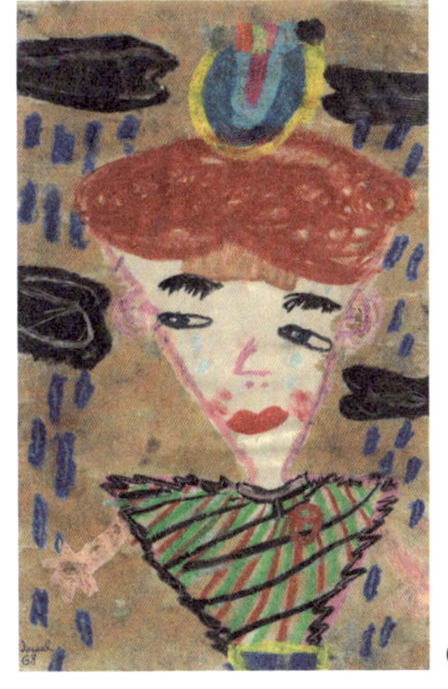

18

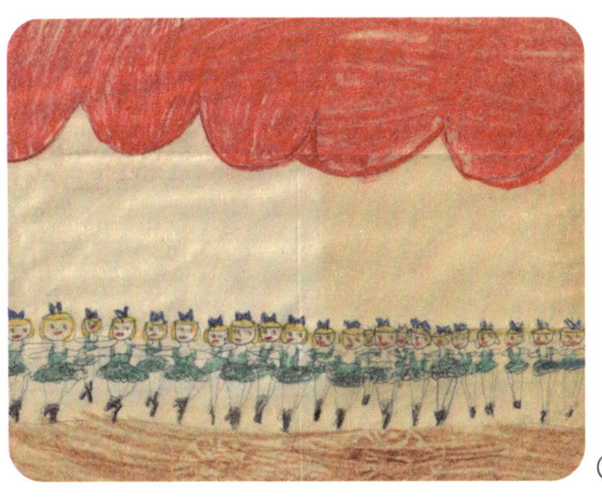

19

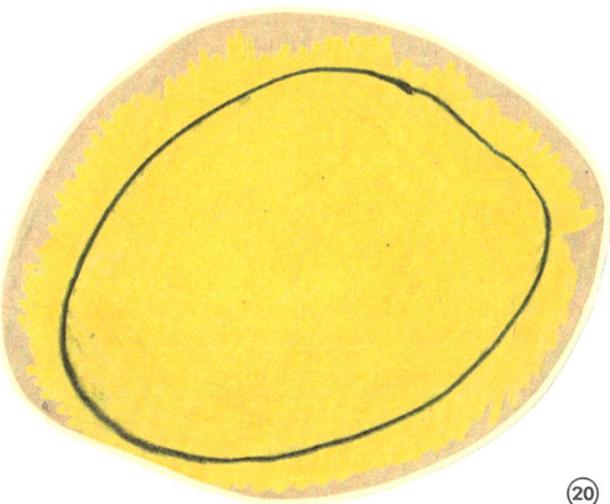

20

The Is a V

PAGE

WORLD

Henry Darger
Trenton Doyle Hancock
Rachel Rose
Faith Ringgold
Ekua Holmes
Becky Suss

Just as books shape the lives of children, the vast world of children's literature has also affected artists. Since the twentieth century, illustrated books intended for young people have offered platforms to innovatively explore relationships between word and image, and provided source material for artists to articulate their own novel visions and worlds. In his mid-twentieth-century epic tale of the Vivian Girls, Henry Darger modeled his imaginary protagonists on popular images drawn from magazines, consumer catalogues, and even the yellow-haired girl from the Morton salt label, each beautifully traced or redrawn in graphite and watercolor. Half a century later and inspired by Darger's world building, Trenton Doyle Hancock draws upon a superhero he invented as a ten-year-old to account for the dearth of Black figures in the children's literature and popular culture of his youth, signaling the importance of comics, graphic novels, and other forms of popular media in a child's self-imagination. Rachel Rose scanned hundreds of children's books from the eighteenth and nineteenth centuries, incrementally building the cells of her 2016 animated single-channel video *Lake Valley* from the forms and patterns found within those pages. Faith Ringgold and Ekua Holmes have each created works of art grounded in their illustrations for children's books and their shared commitment to depicting the love and strength of Black families. Ringgold's story quilt based on her Caldecott award–winning children's book *Tar Beach* (1991) envisions female liberation through the book's spirited eight-year-old narrator, and Holmes's depictions of the life of Kahlil Gibran are intended for young audiences. Children's books have been a consistent source of inspiration for Becky Suss, who recently created a series of paintings of her own childhood bedroom aimed at capturing the spaces of imagination that open like portals in a child's bedroom. The page has offered artists and children a tremendously rich space for reflecting the world and imagining it anew.

6 Episode 3 Place Not Mentioned. Escape during violent storm,
still fighting though persed for long distance (recto), mid-20th century
Double-sided watercolor, pencil, and carbon tracing on pieced paper
24 × 74 ¾ inches (61 × 189.9 cm)

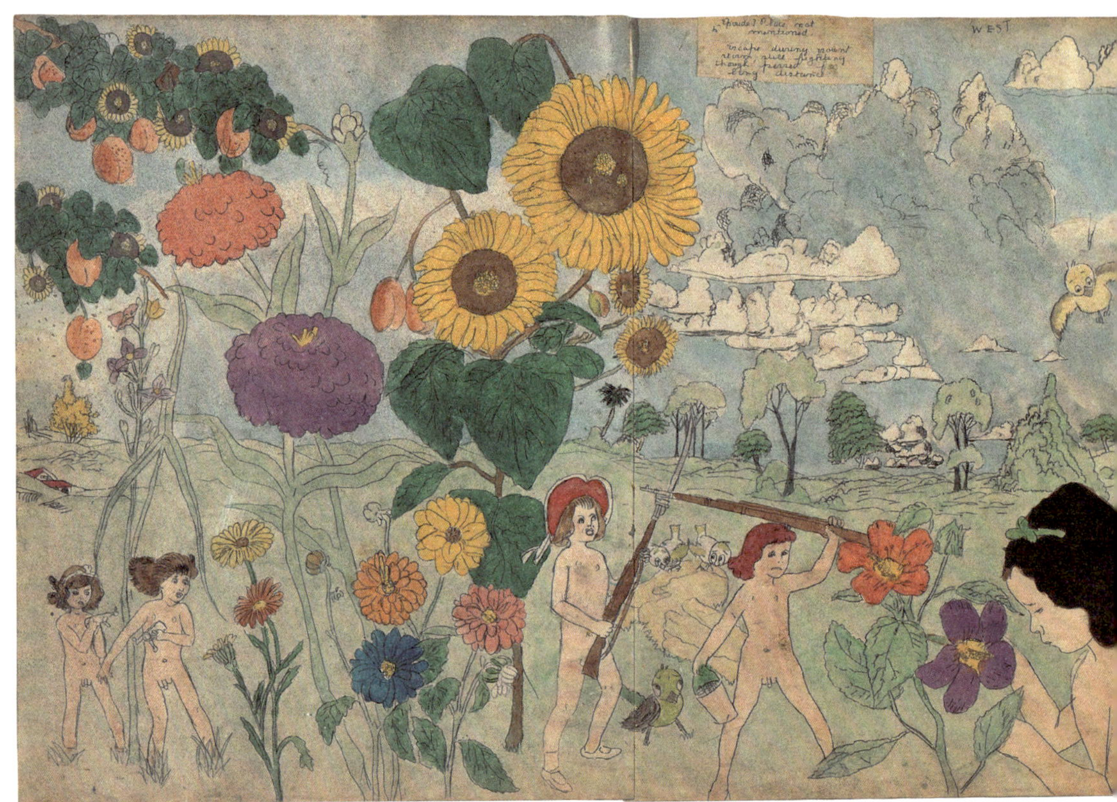

The Page Is a World

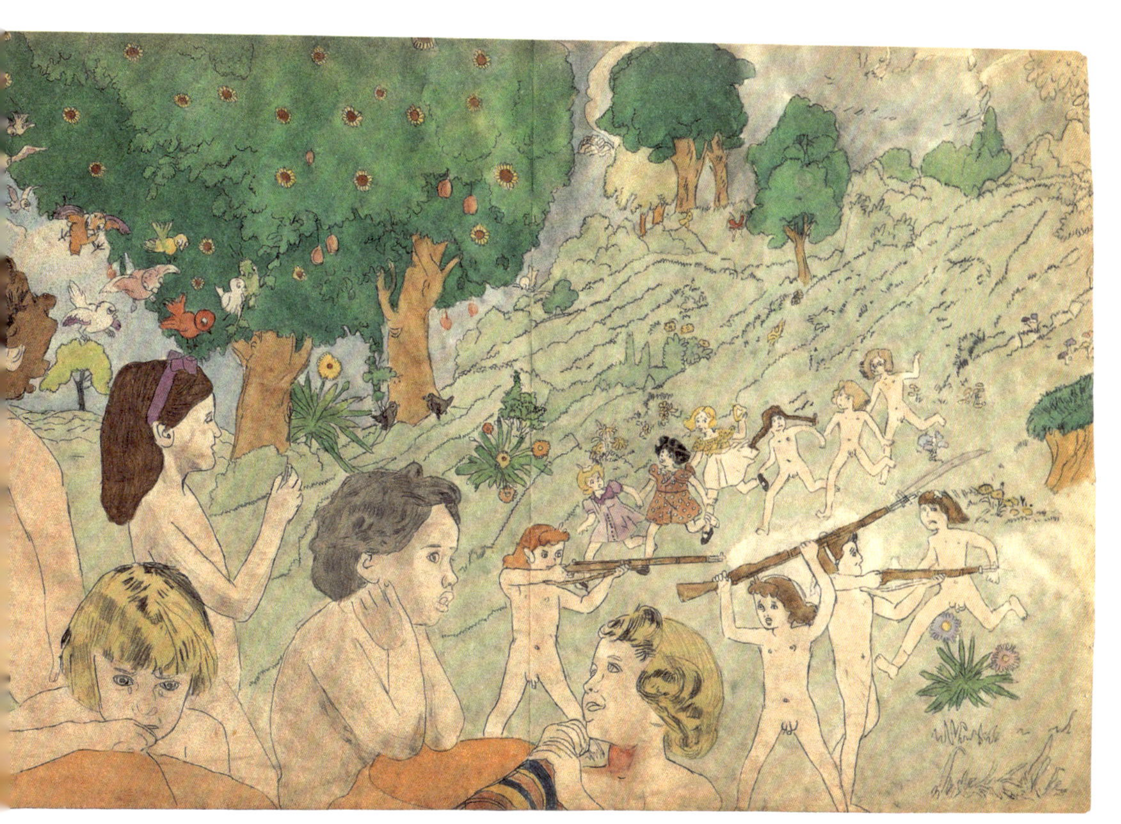

Henry Darger
6 Episode 3 Place Not Mentioned. Escape during violent storm,
still fighting though persed for long distance (verso), mid-20th century
Double-sided watercolor, pencil, and carbon tracing on pieced paper
24 × 74 ¾ inches (61 × 189.9 cm)

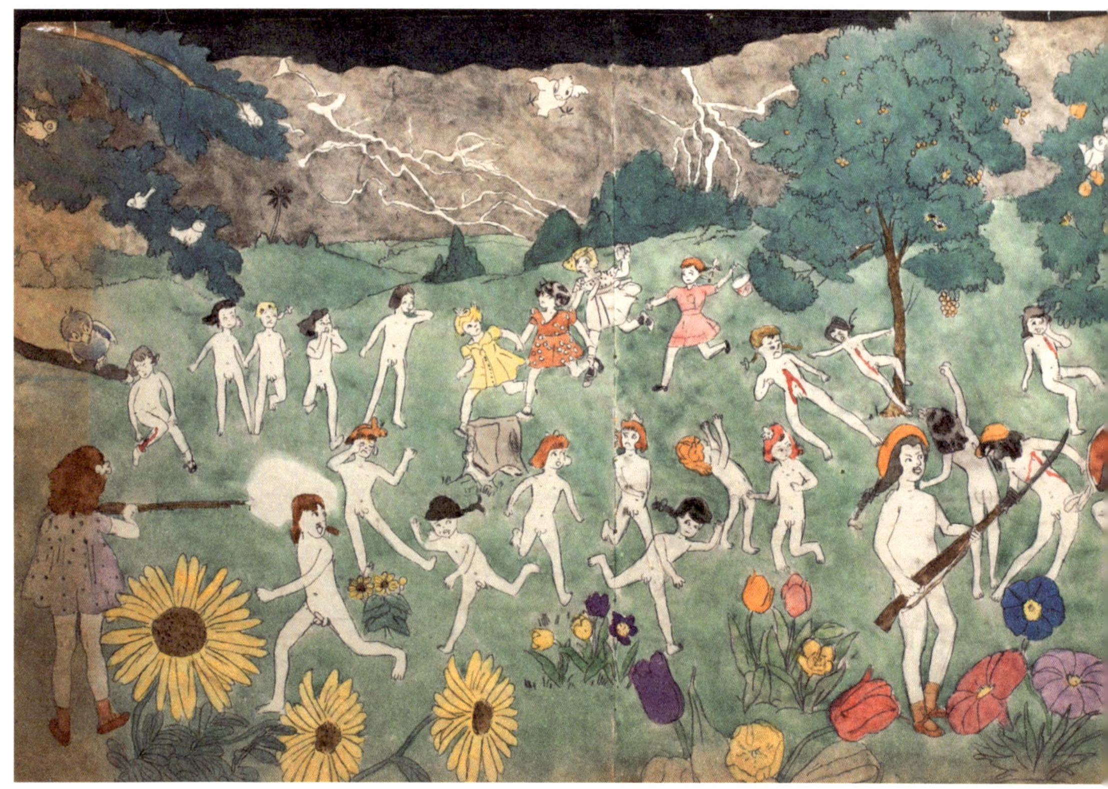

The Page Is a World

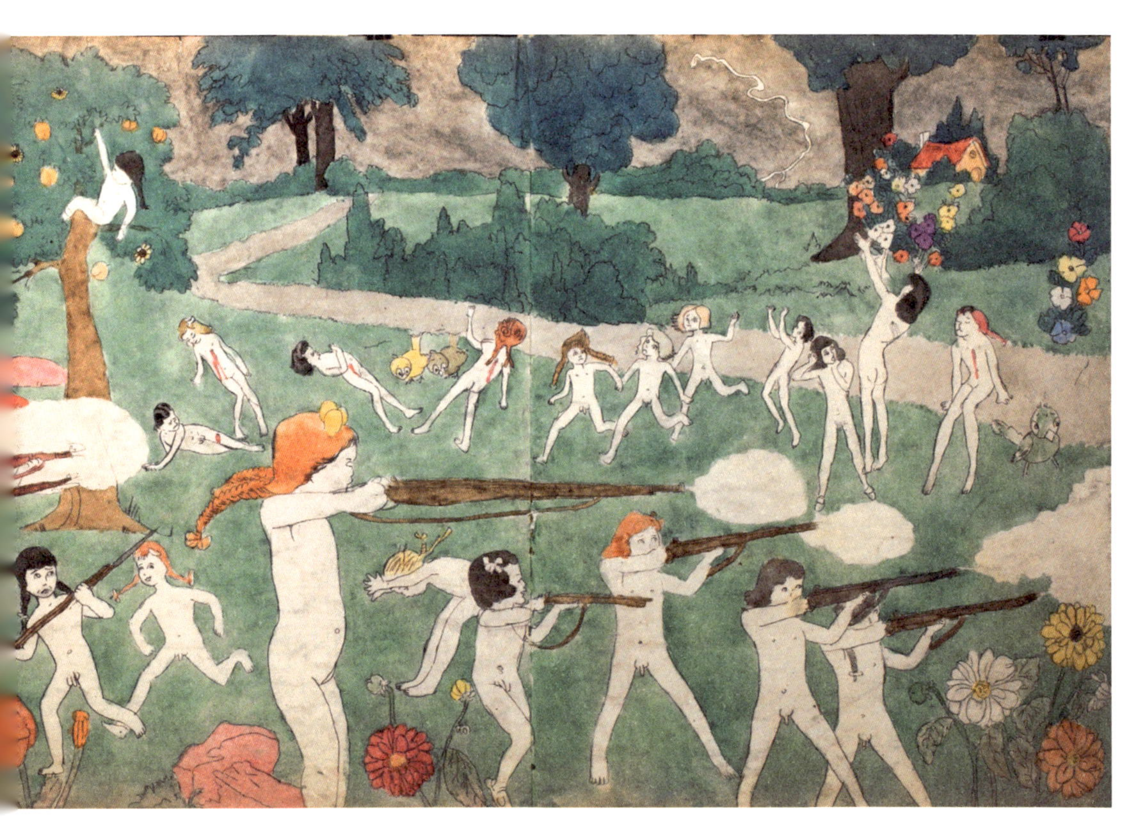

Torpedoboy Fights a Bear, 1984
Graphite on notebook paper
7 ¾ × 10 ½ inches (19.7 × 26.7 cm)

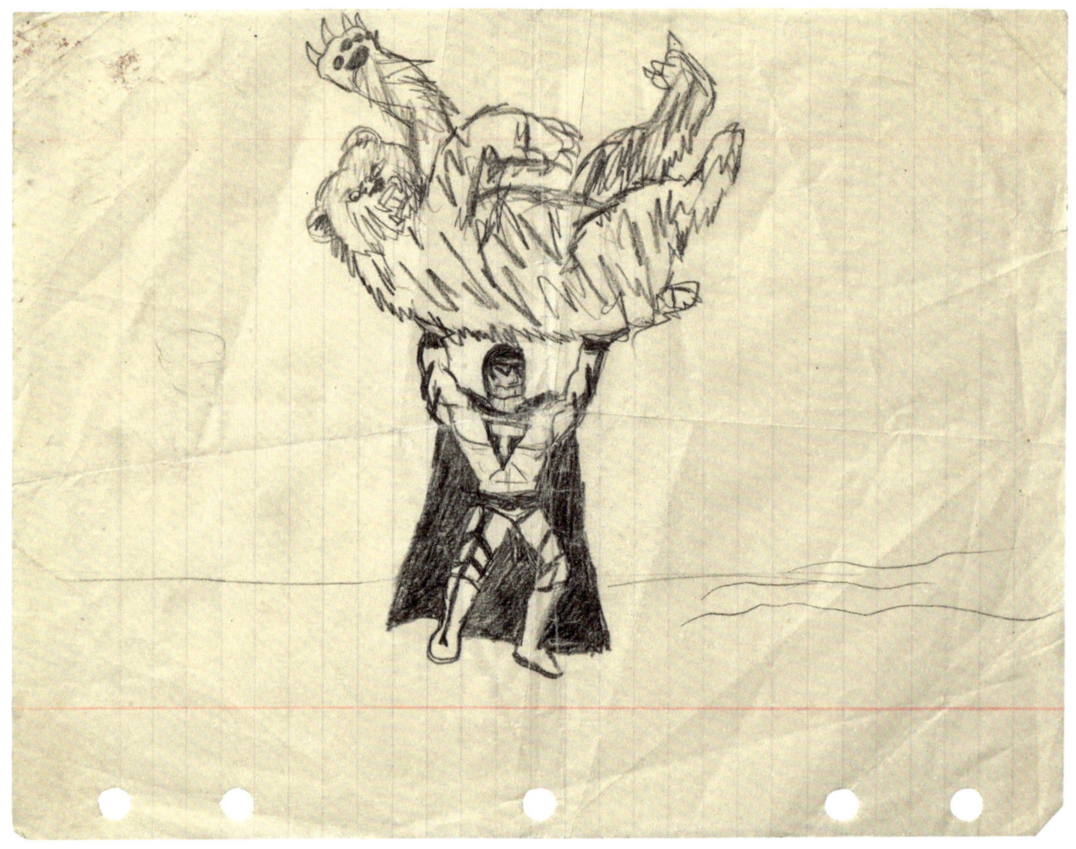

Trenton Doyle Hancock
Torpedoboy Fights Aliens, 1984
Graphite on notebook paper
7 ¾ × 10 ½ inches (19.7 × 26.7 cm)

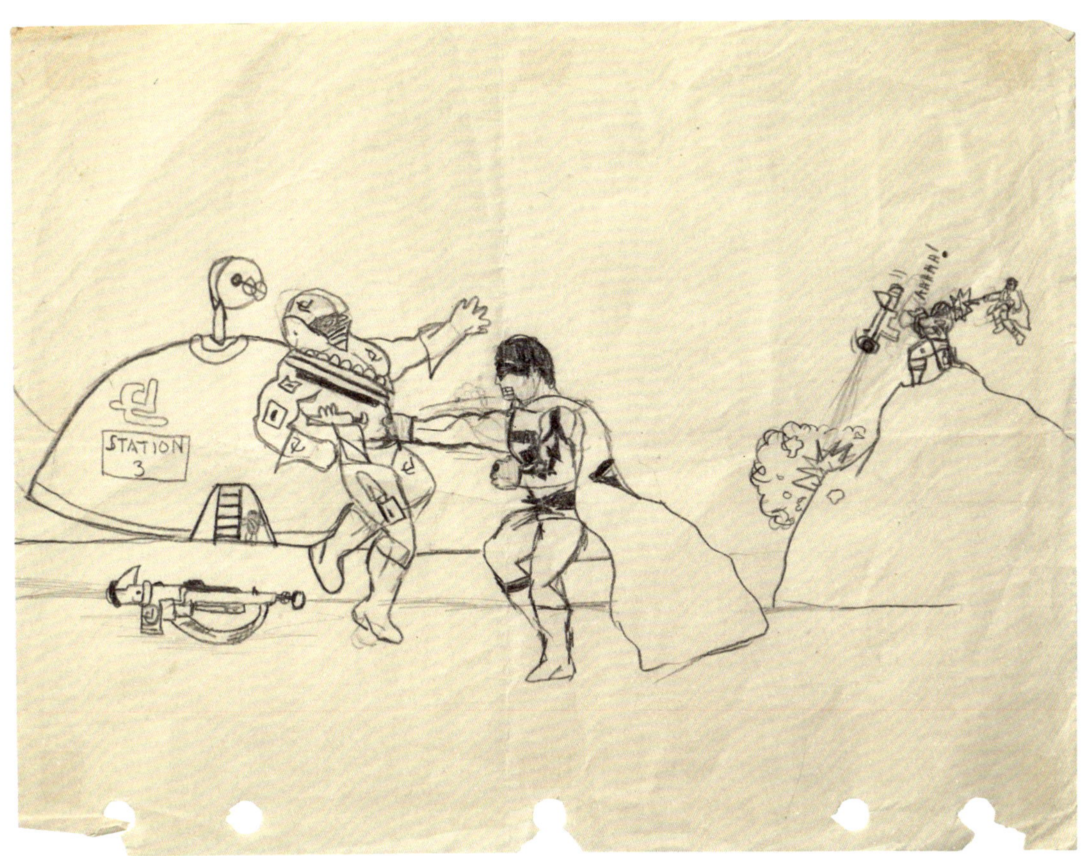

Trenton Doyle Hancock
Torpedoboy Flying, 1984
Graphite on notebook paper
7 ¾ × 10 ½ inches (19.7 × 26.7 cm)

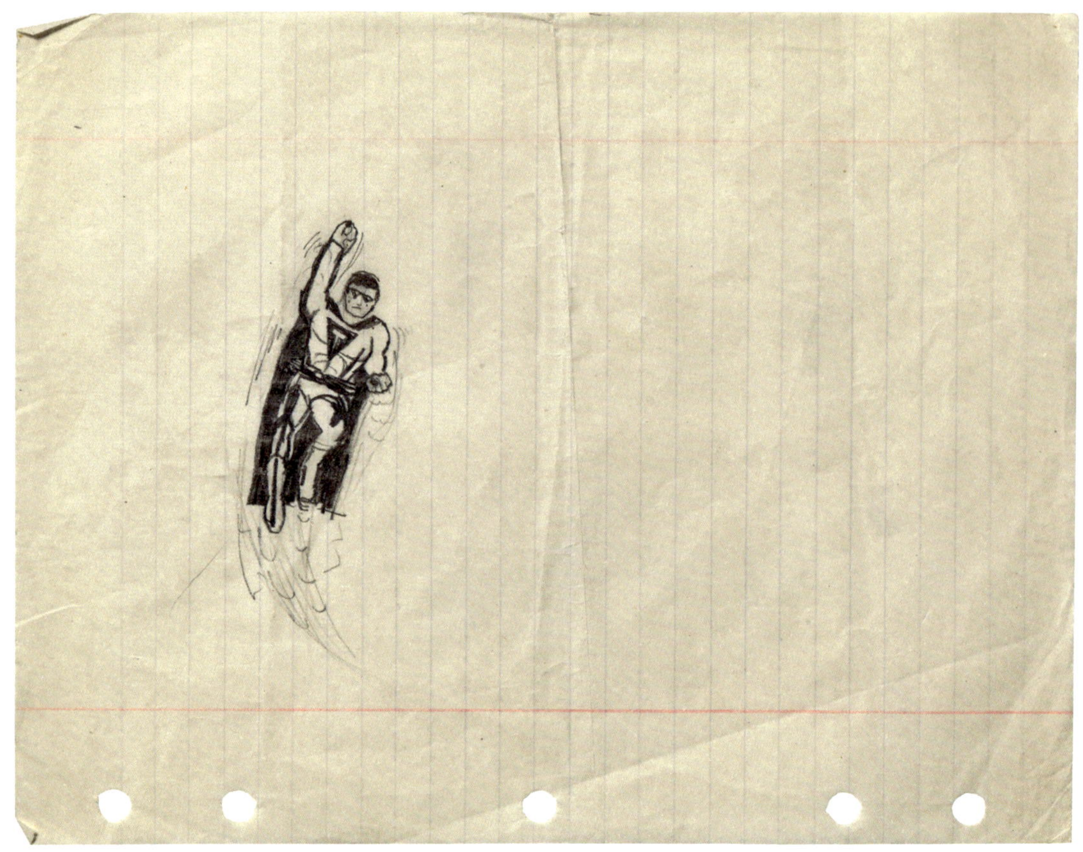

The Page Is a World

Trenton Doyle Hancock
Torpedoboy vs. A Giant, 1984
Graphite on notebook paper
7 ¾ × 10 ½ inches (19.7 × 26.7 cm)

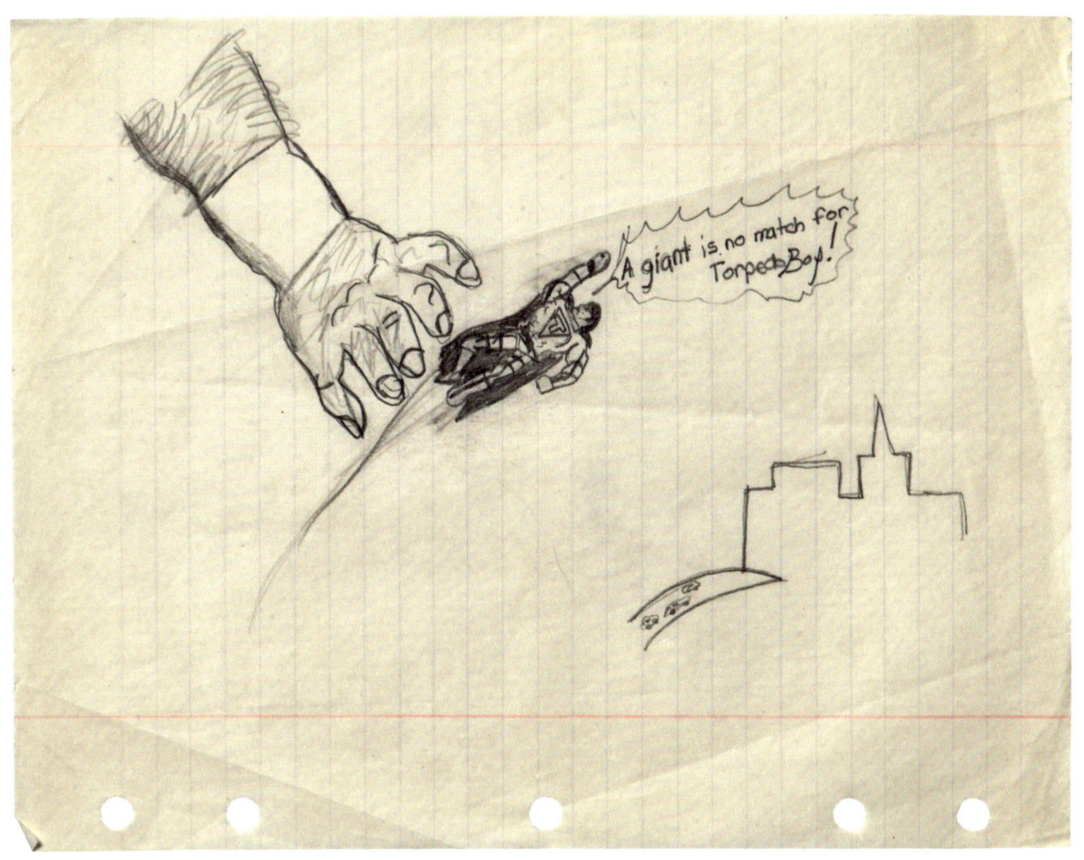

Trenton Doyle Hancock
8 Back Icon Series: Torpedoboy—
Protector of the Mounds, No. 5185, 2016
Acrylic and mixed media on canvas
66 × 38 inches (167.6 × 96.5 cm)

The Page Is a World

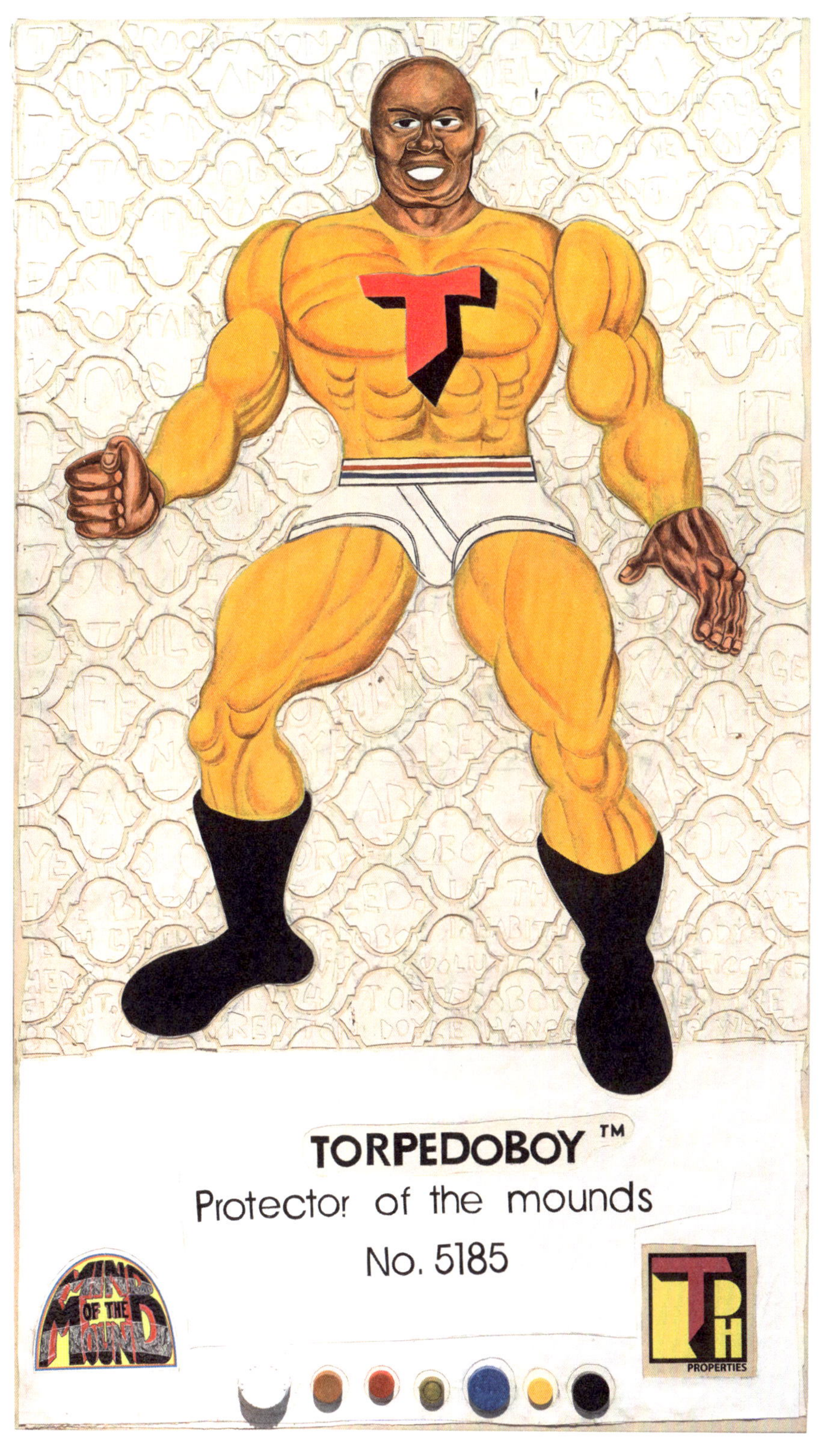

TORPEDOBOY ™
Protector of the mounds
No. 5185
PROPERTIES

Trenton Doyle Hancock
Torpedoboy, Moundverse Infants Doll, 2018
Vinyl, factory-applied paint, artist-designed
packaging, and Risograph booklet
16 × 7 ½ × 5 ½ inches (40.6 × 19.1 × 14 cm)

The Page Is a World

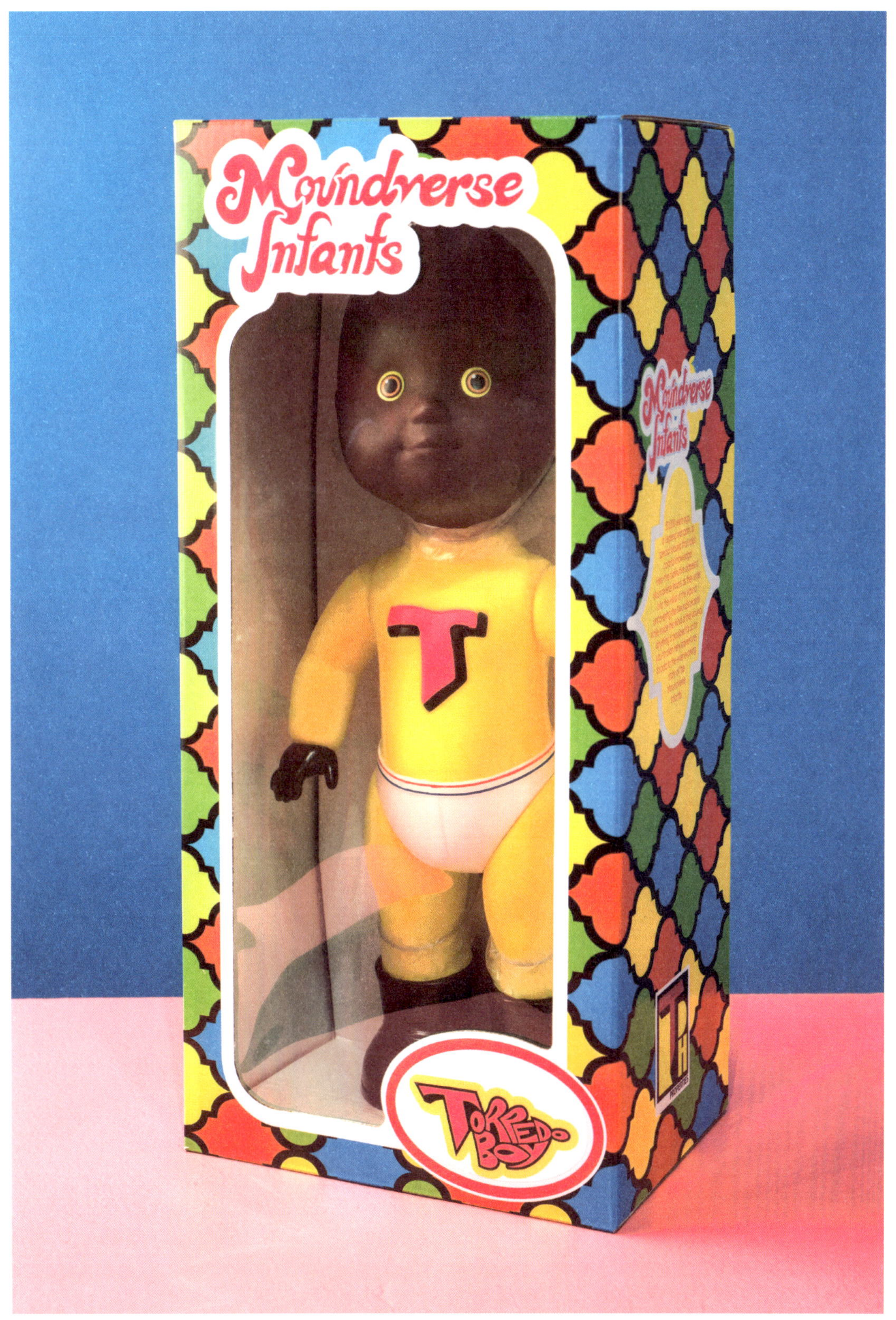
Moundverse
Infants
T
Moundverse
Infants
TORPEDO
BOY

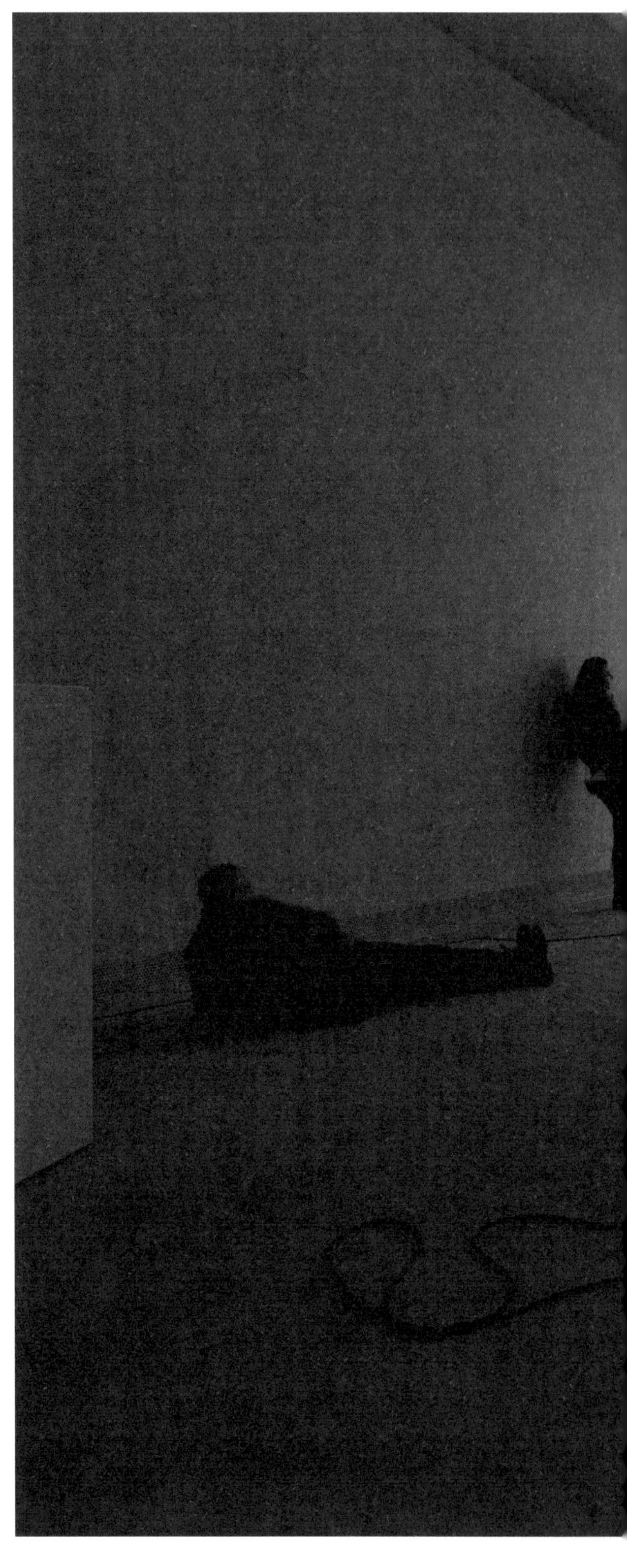

The Page Is a World

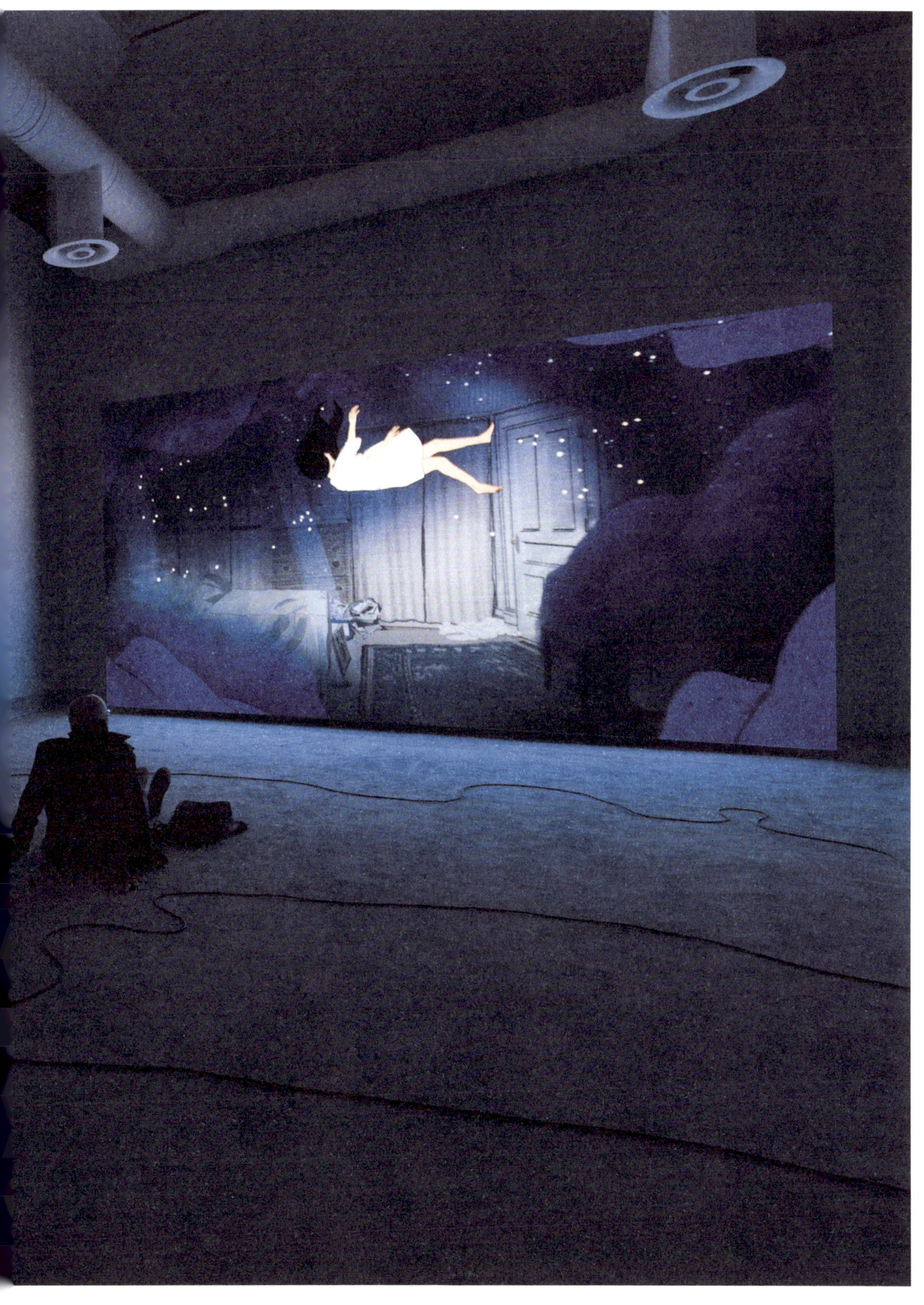

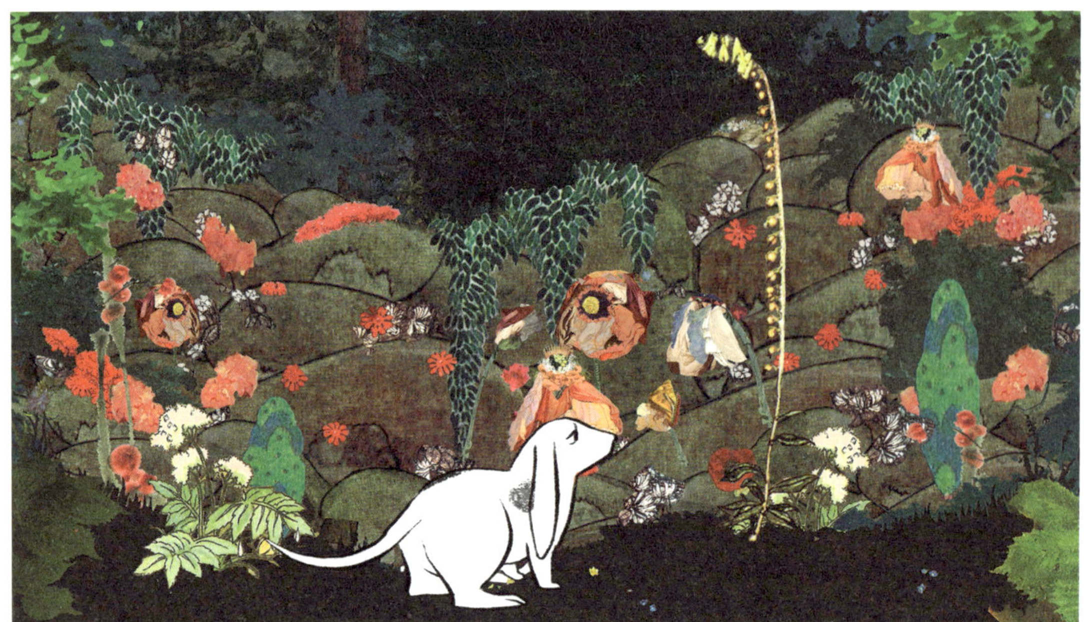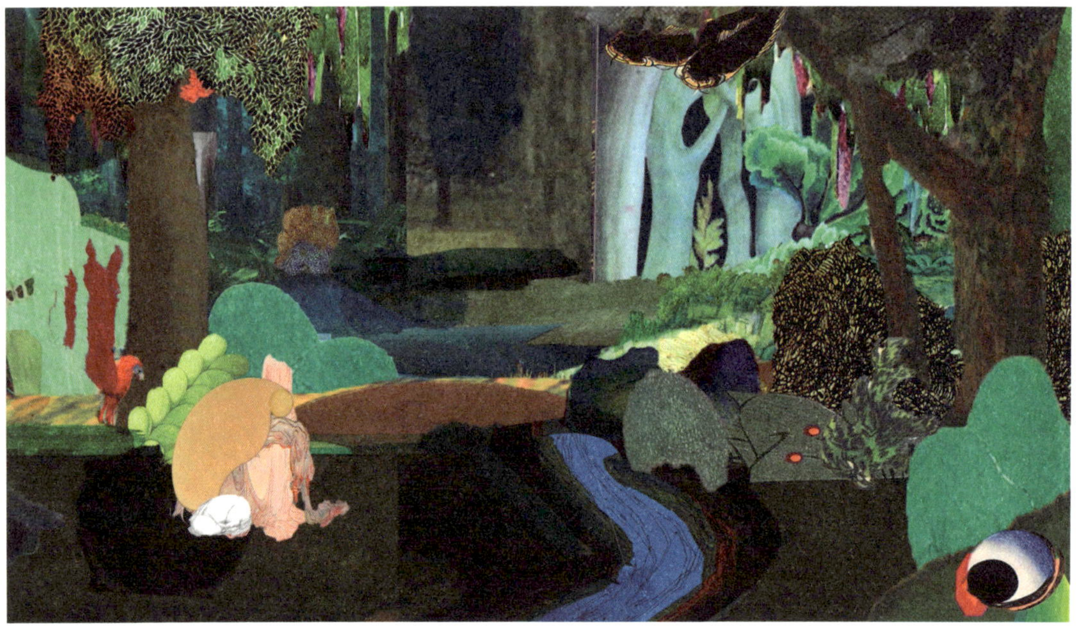

The Page Is a World

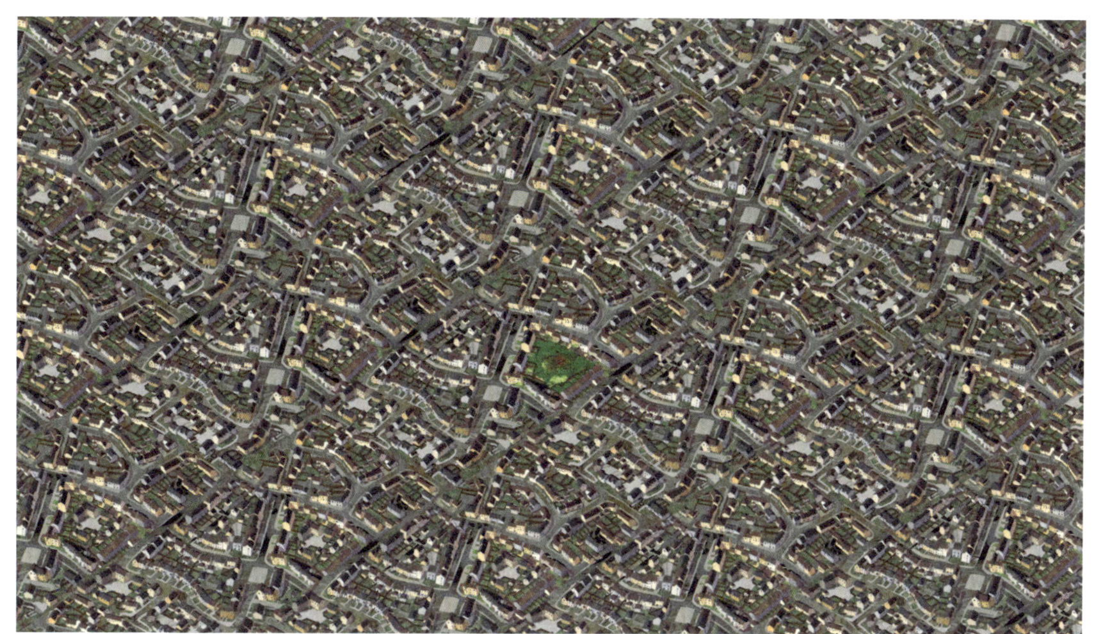

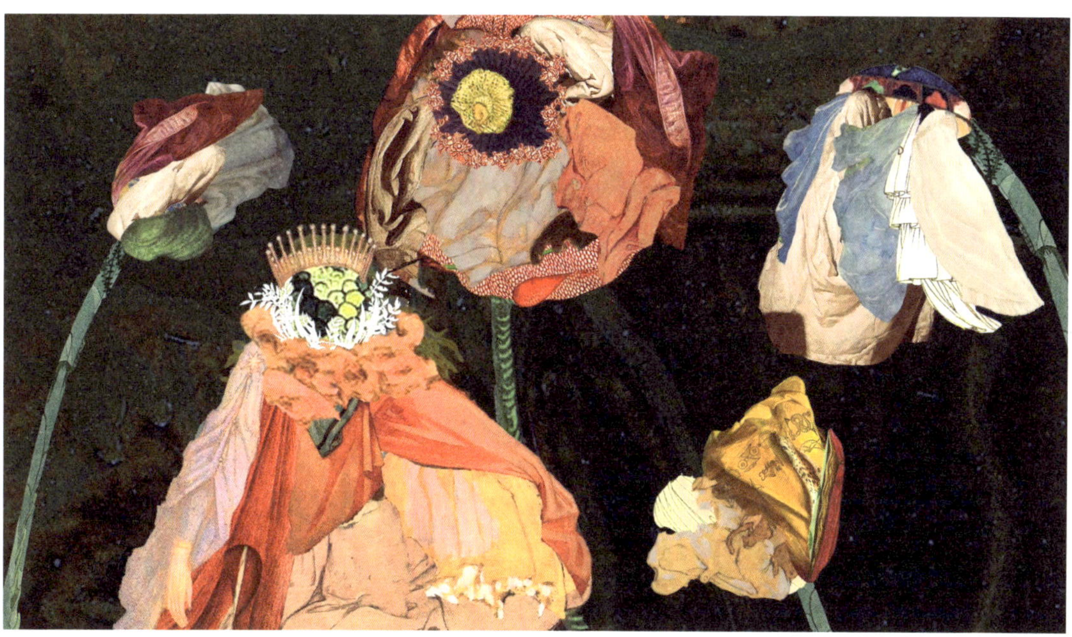

Rachel Rose
Lake Valley (stills), 2016
Single-channel video
(color, sound; 8:25 minutes)

Faith Ringgold
Tar Beach #2, 1990–92
Silkscreen on silk
60 × 59 inches (152.4 × 149.9 cm)

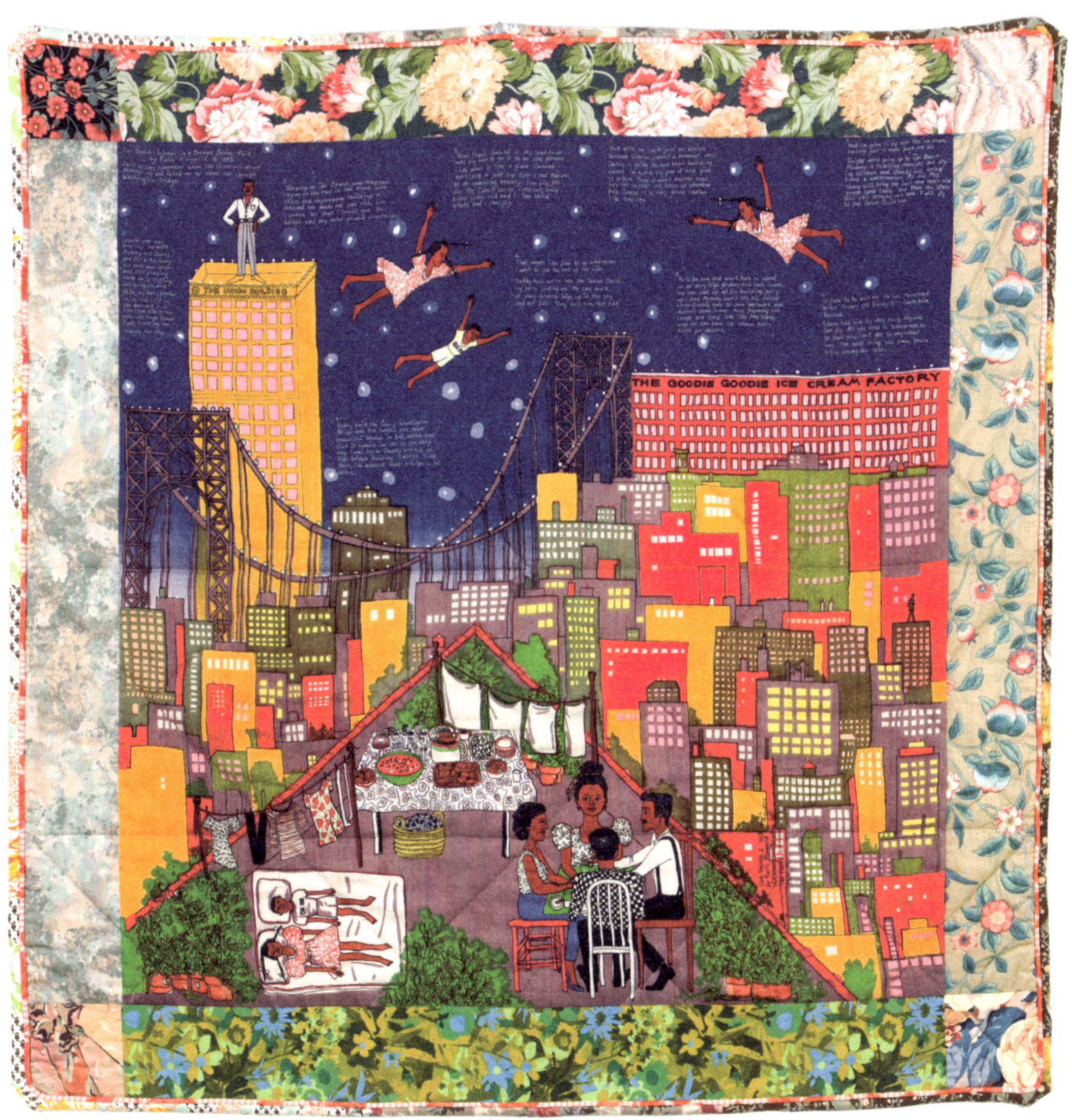

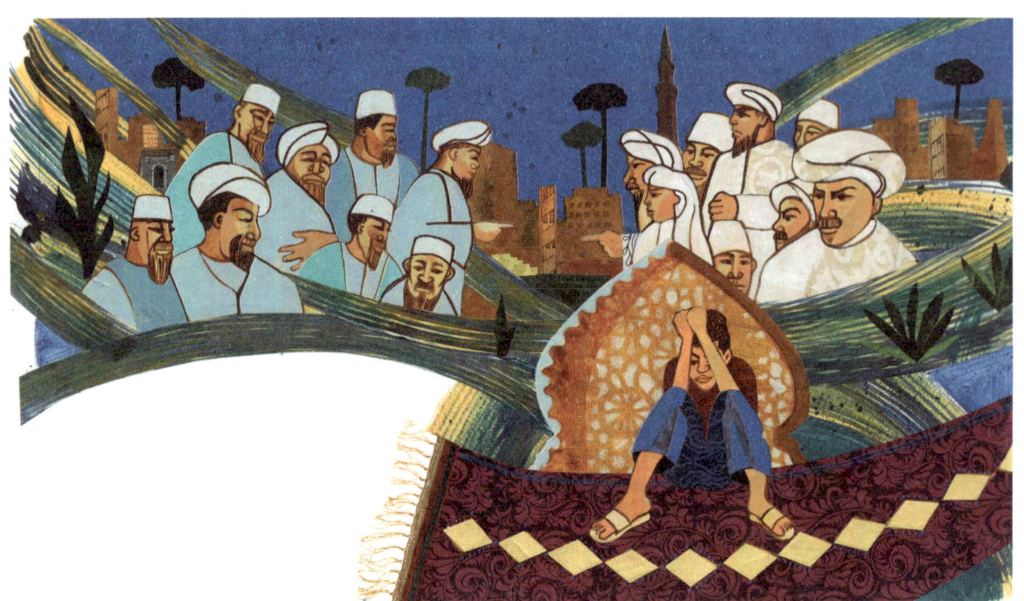

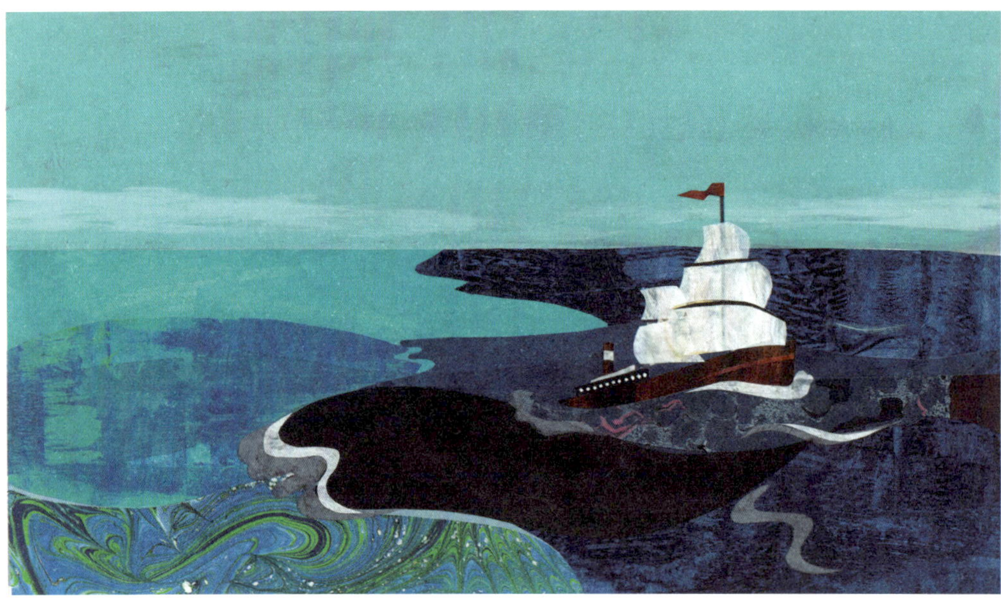

Ekua Holmes
Crashing Winds, 2021
From *Hope Is an Arrow*, 2022
Paper and acrylic on paper
12 × 20 inches (30.5 × 50.8 cm)

Ekua Holmes
Oceanality, 2021
From *Hope Is an Arrow*, 2022
Paper and acrylic on paper
12 × 20 inches (30.5 × 50.8 cm)

The Page Is a World

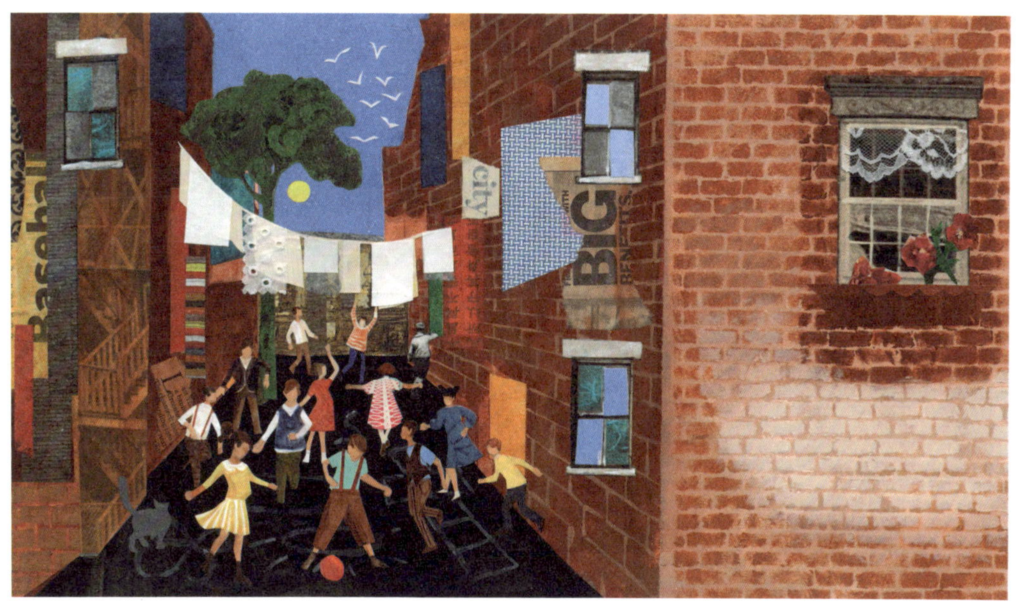

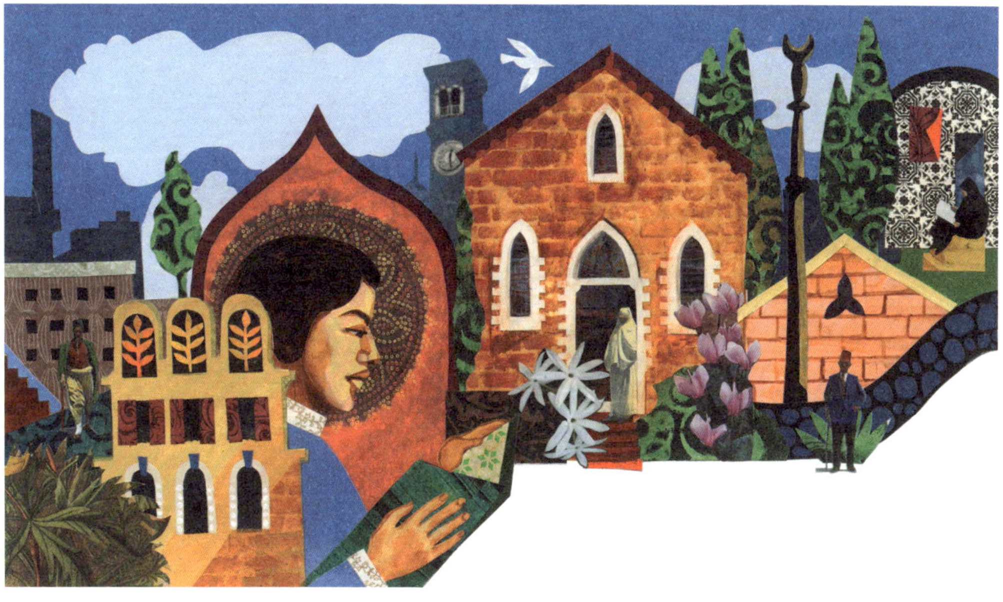

Ekua Holmes
Boston, 2021
From *Hope Is an Arrow*, 2022
Paper, fabric, and acrylic on paper
12 × 20 inches (30.5 × 50.8 cm)

Ekua Holmes
Bold Beirut, 2021
From *Hope Is an Arrow*, 2022
Paper and acrylic on paper
12 × 20 inches (30.5 × 50.8 cm)

Ekua Holmes
Precarious, 2017
Collage on board
24 ½ × 18 inches (62.2 × 45.7 cm)

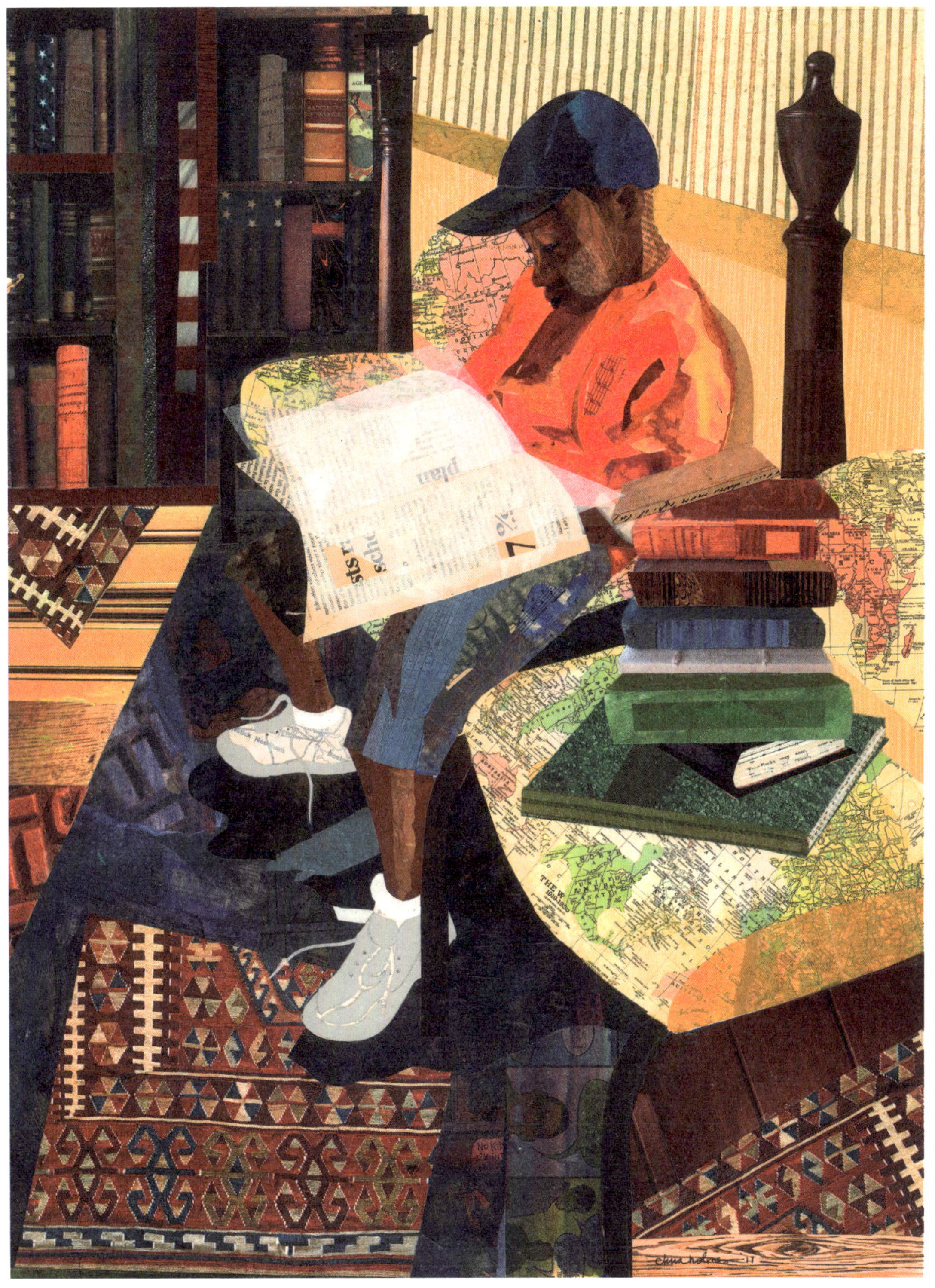

Becky Suss
8 Greenwood Place (1985–88), 2021
Oil on canvas
84 × 60 × 1 ½ inches (213.4 × 152.4 × 3.8 cm)

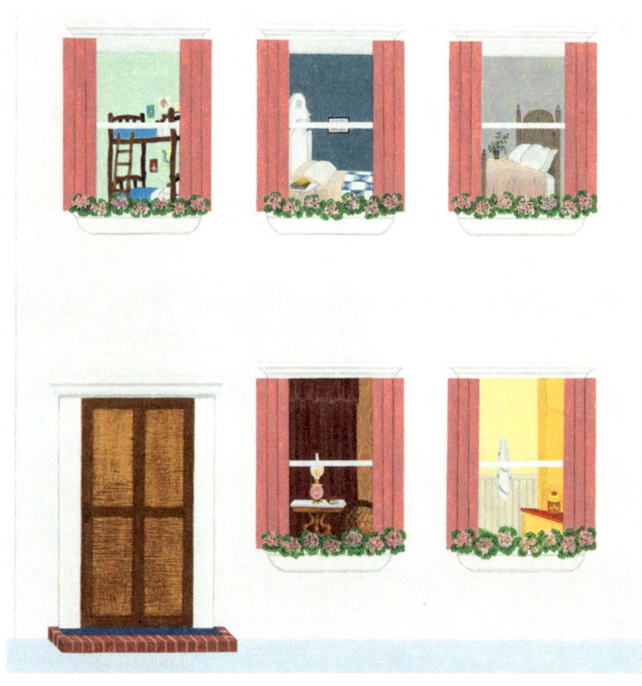

The Page Is a World

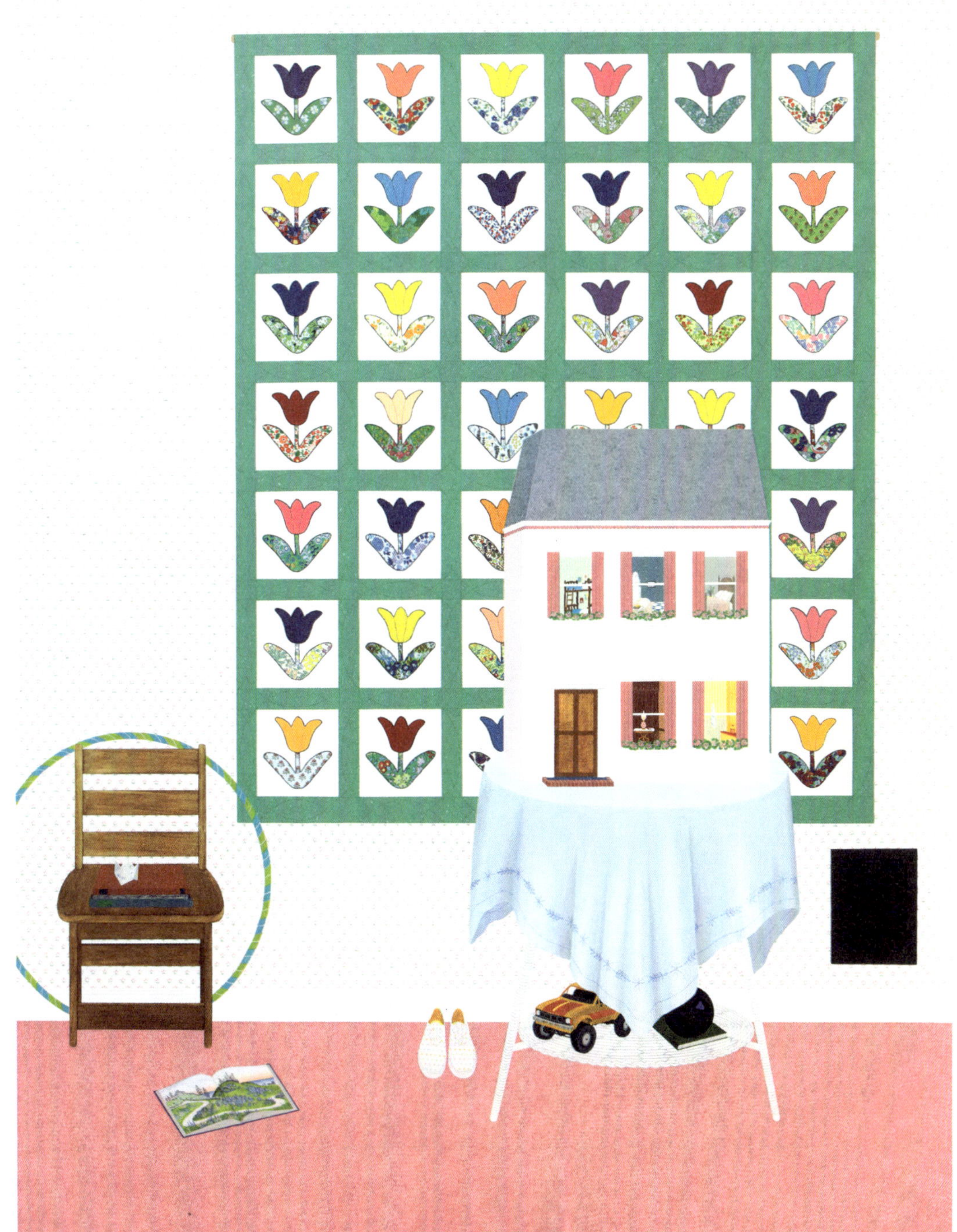

INTO

BORN

BEING

Heji Shin
Sharon Hayes
Robert Gober
Mona Hatoum
Sable Elyse Smith
Deborah Roberts
Njideka Akunyili Crosby

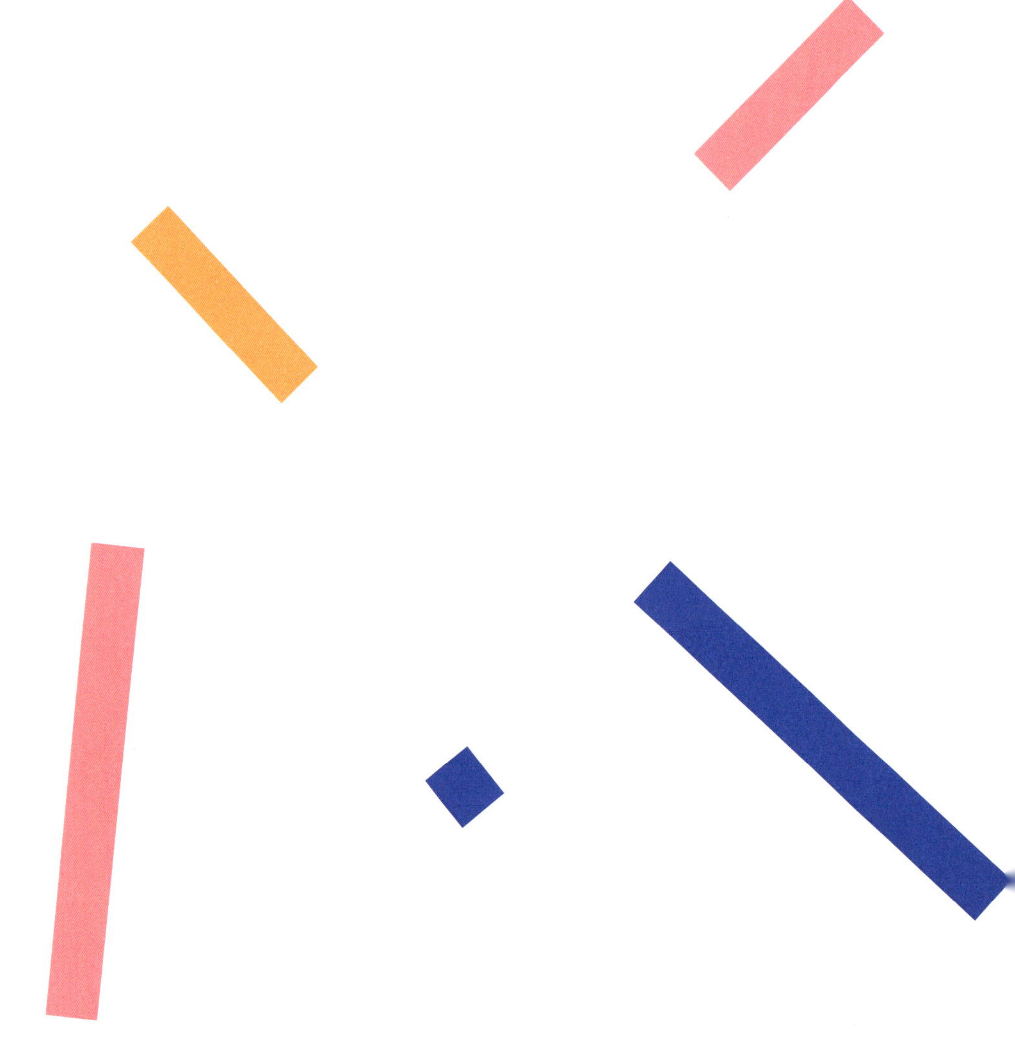

Dynamics of power—and attendant issues of disenfranchisement and agency—shape the experiences of children from the moment of their birth. Those dynamics are sometimes visible and can be named or even inscribed by the rule of law, but at other times and in other places, they are invisible and unconscious yet inform conceptions of childhood. Heji Shin captures the moment of an infant's head emerging from a vagina, a powerful document of how so many come into this world and yet signaling the immediately distinct ways that we will come to live in this world. Sharon Hayes, in creating her video work that explores expansive ideas about nonnormative family structures, invites children of LGBTQ+ families to respond to questions about birth, reproduction, and challenges they face. Sculptors Robert Gober and Mona Hatoum both use the form of the playpen or crib in their unique works to probe diverse sentiments of estrangement, violence, and fear, which too often characterize the lives of children, especially when facts of biology or economics come into play. The tile floor of Gober's sculpture and the glass-beaded web of Hatoum's invoke the inhospitality of places intended for comfort and security. Sable Elyse Smith bases her paintings on a coloring book intended for children in the waiting rooms of courts and prisons. Her interventions in these found pages signal the presence of—and resistance to—the carceral system in the lives of some children. Deborah Roberts contends with dominant portrayals and narratives of Black youth, narratives that she teases out, challenges, and subverts through her use of found media and collage. Her distinctive, bold works reflect a spectrum of Black childhood experience, from the increased rates of incarceration to bountiful joy and deeply held bonds. Njideka Akunyili Crosby's portraits of Nigerian youth, built from a layered ground of historical, popular, and personal photographs transferred to canvas, stage the interactions between sociohistorical conditions and the individual that are at the heart of human development. These artists give form to the complex processes of becoming, attending to the structures that empower and marginalize young people.

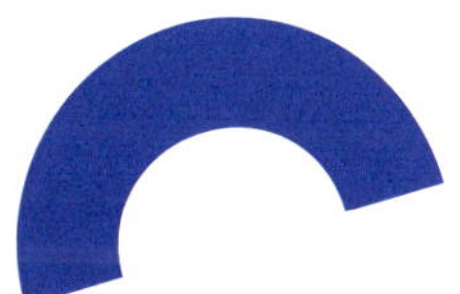

Heji Shin
Baby 6, 2016
Inkjet print
31 ¼ × 23 ¼ inches (79.5 × 59 cm)

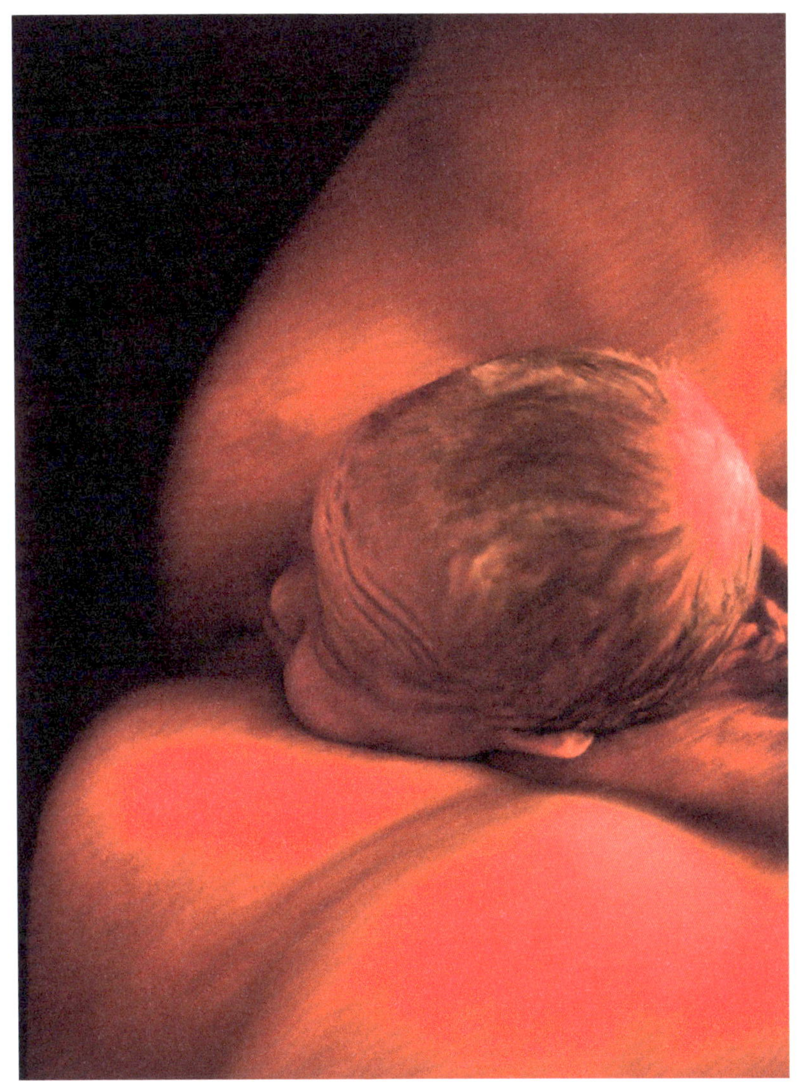

Heji Shin
Baby 10, 2017
Inkjet print
23 ¼ × 31 ¼ inches (59 × 79.5 cm)

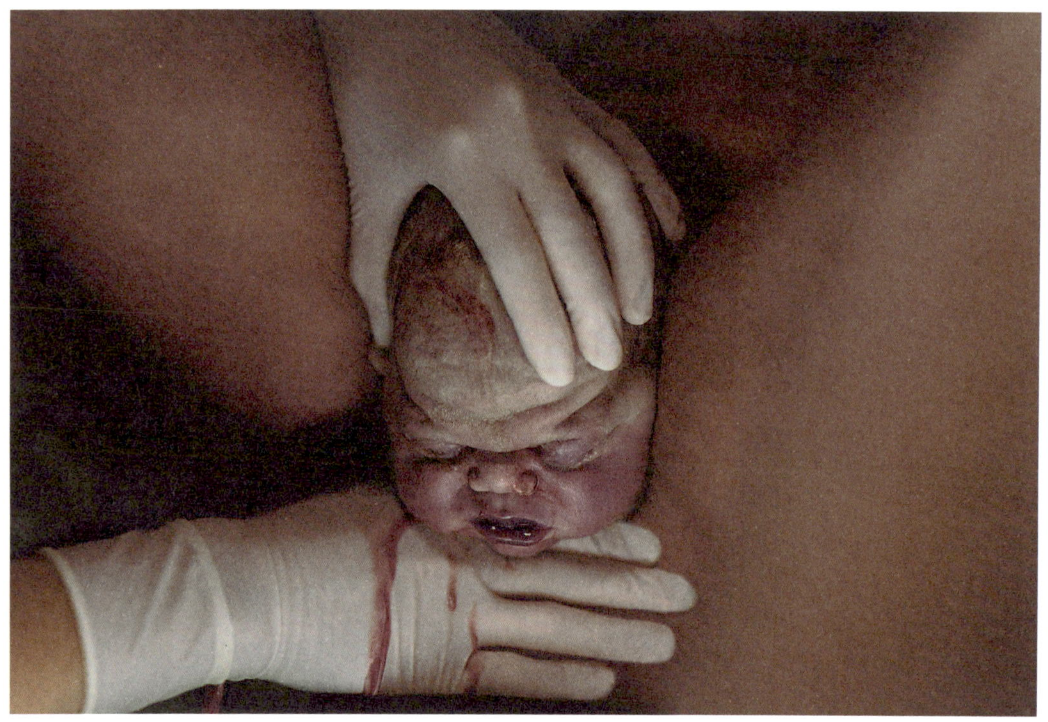

Born into Being

Heji Shin
Baby 7, 2016
Inkjet print
31 ¼ × 23 ¼ inches (79.5 × 59 cm)

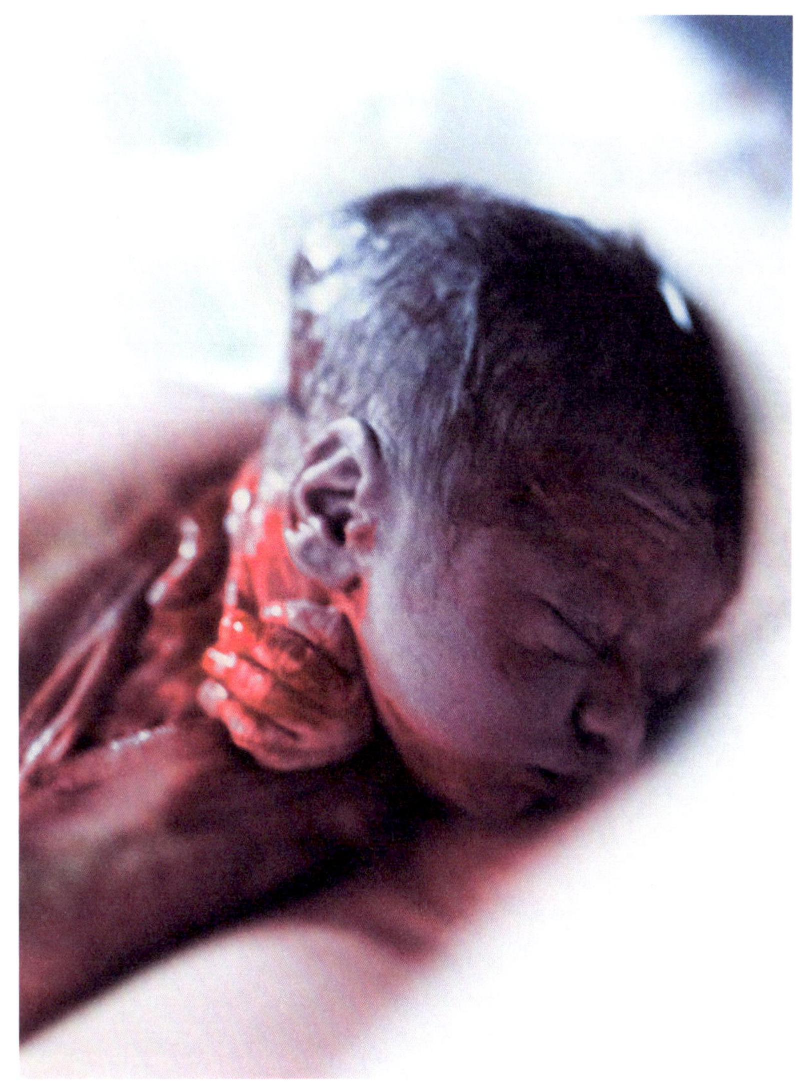

Sharon Hayes
Ricerche: one (stills), 2019
Two-channel HD video
(color, sound; 28:00 minutes)

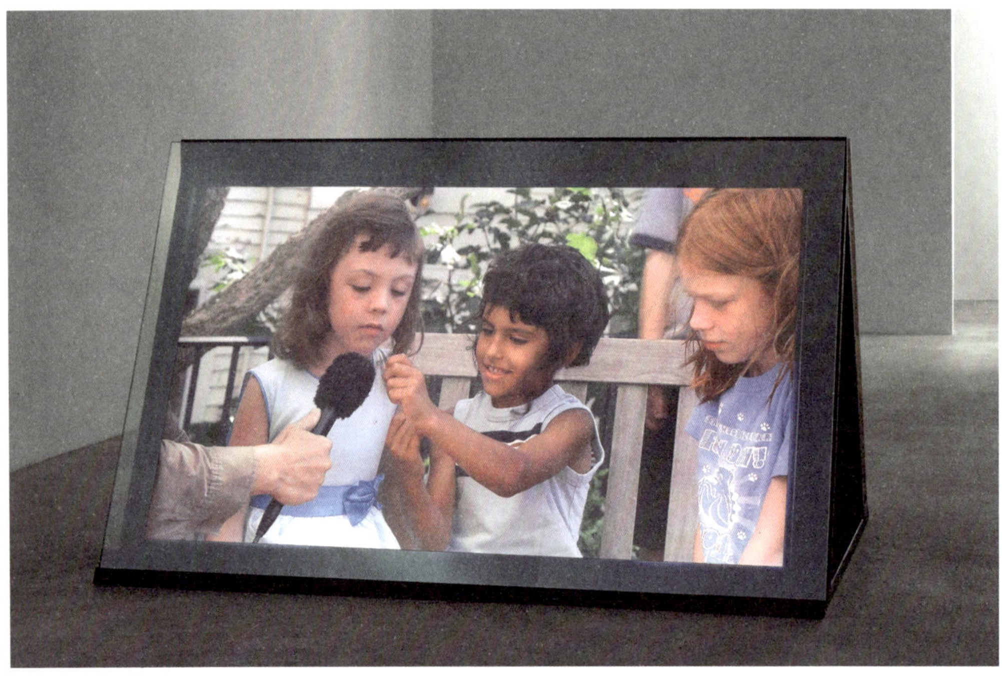

Installation view: *Sharon Hayes: Nel Mezzo*, Tanya Leighton Gallery, Berlin, 2019

Born into Being

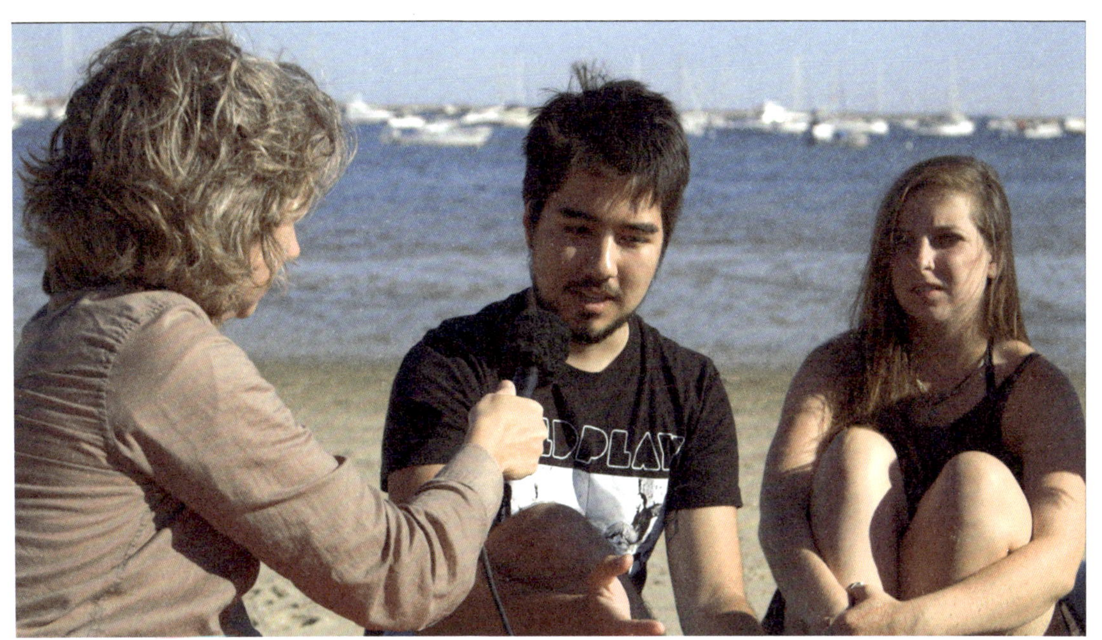

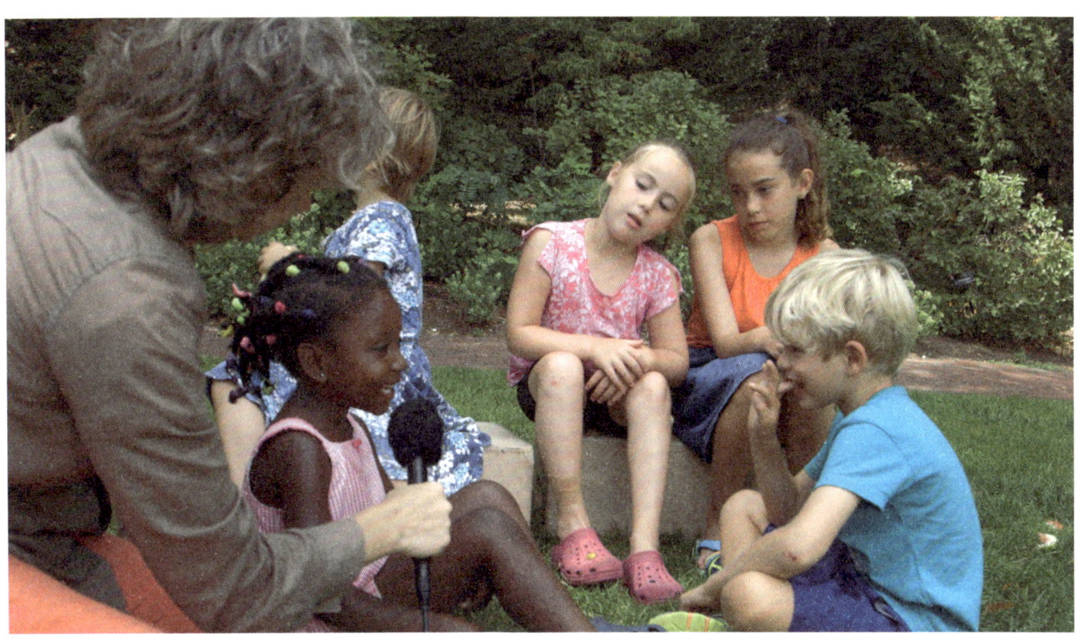

Robert Gober
Untitled, 2006–7
Wood and enamel paint
27 × 39 ⅛ × 39 ⅛ inches (69 × 99 × 99 cm)

Born into Being

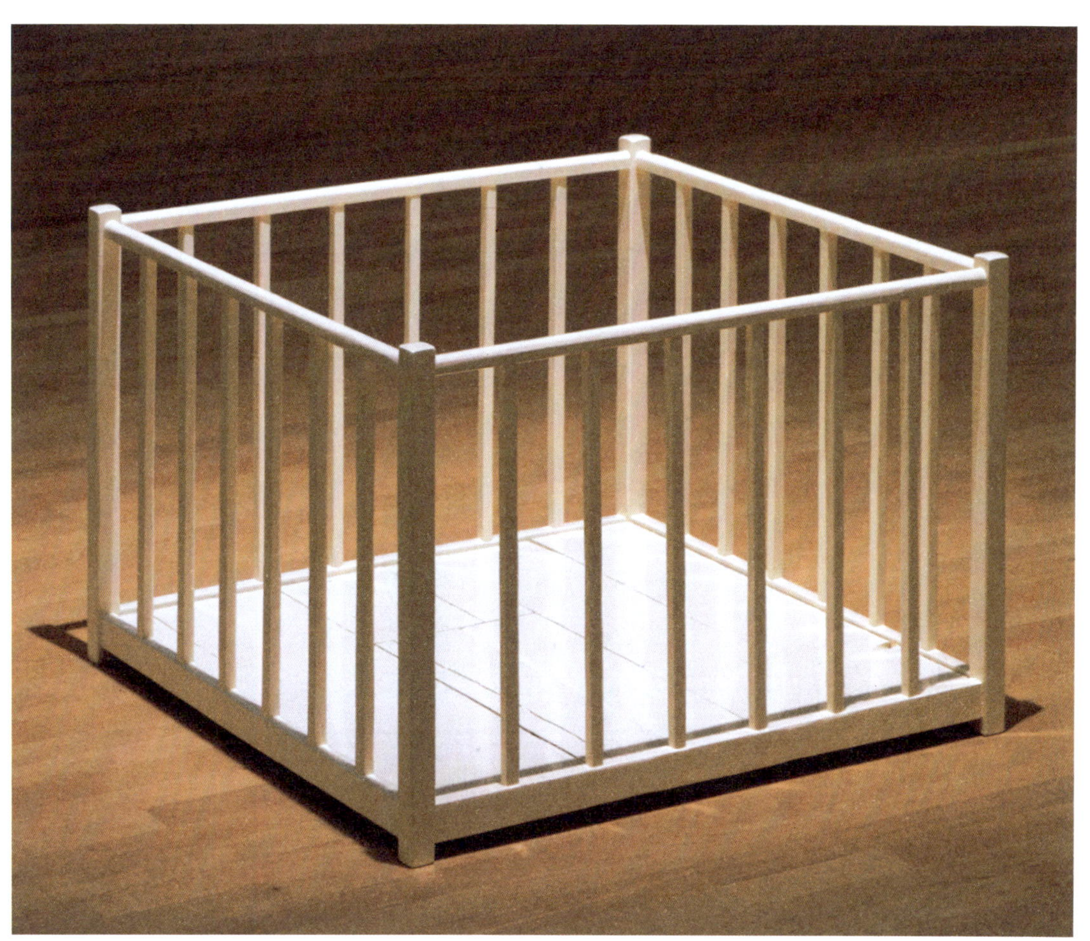

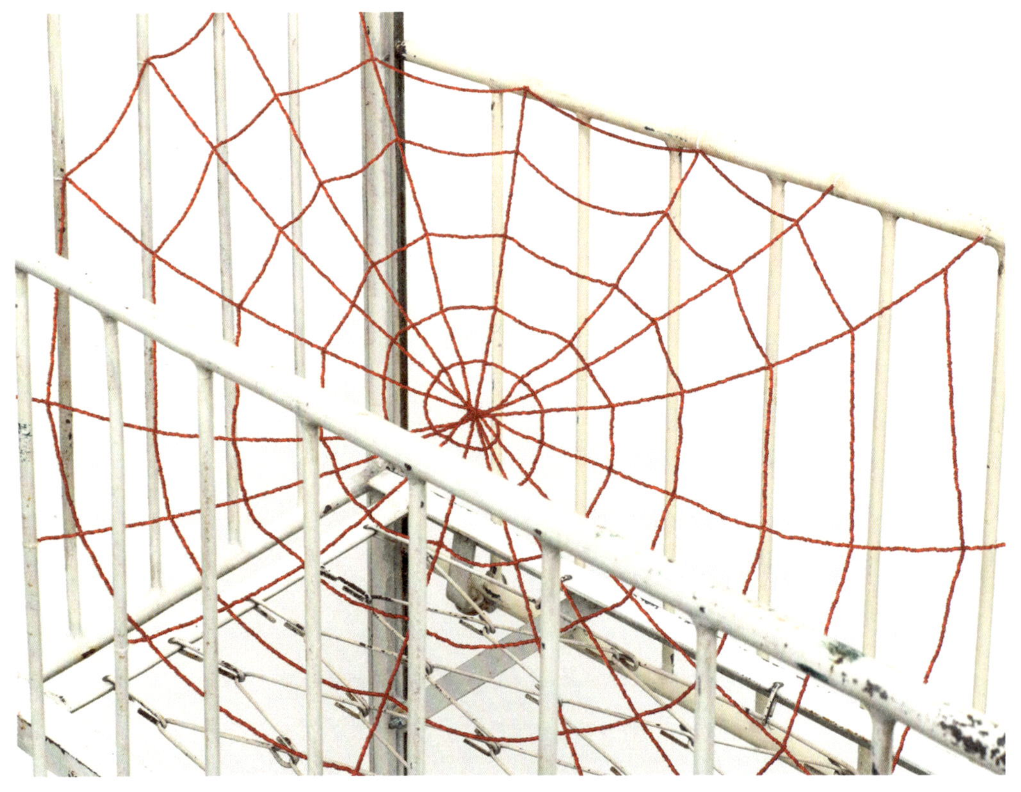

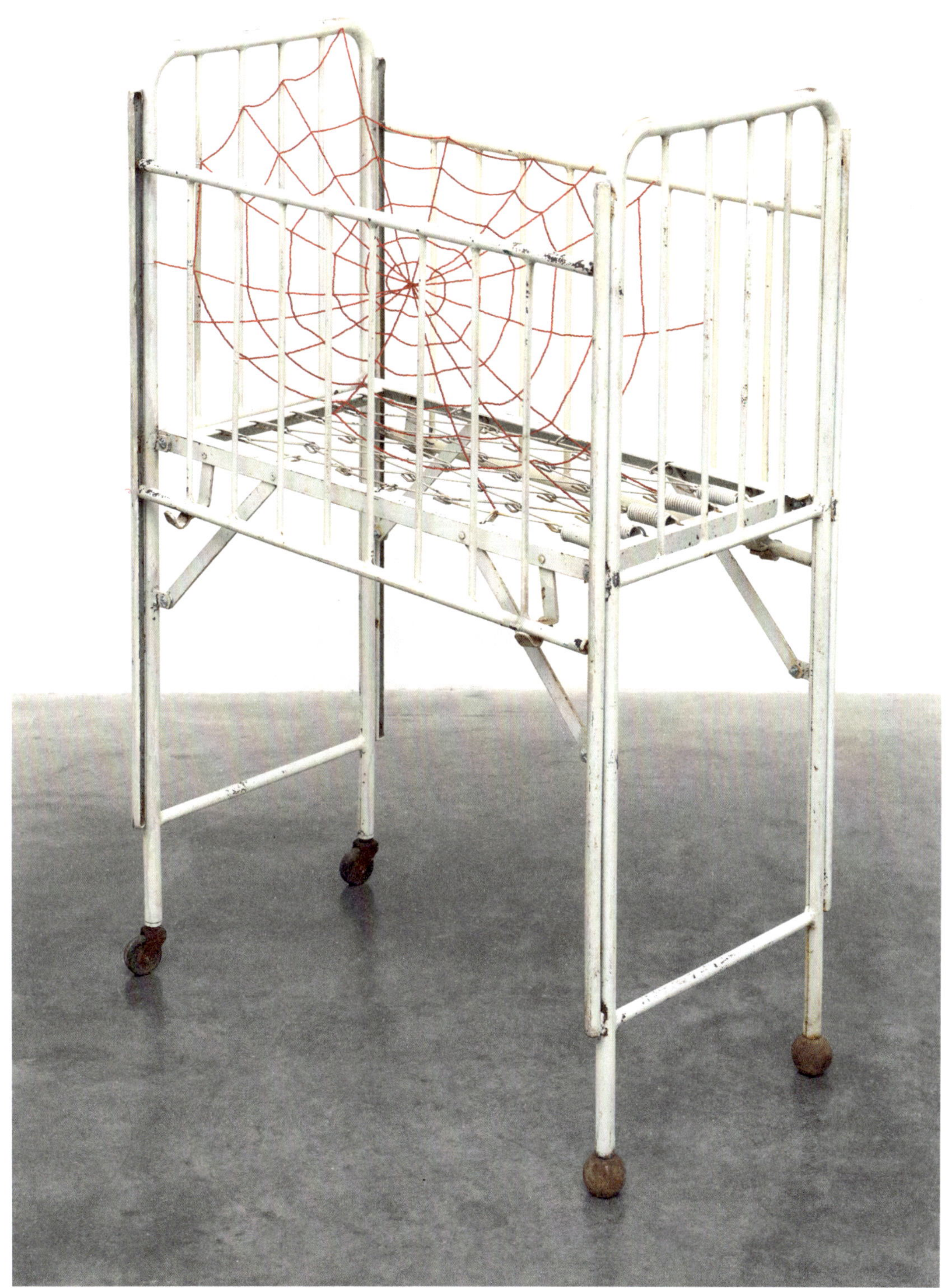

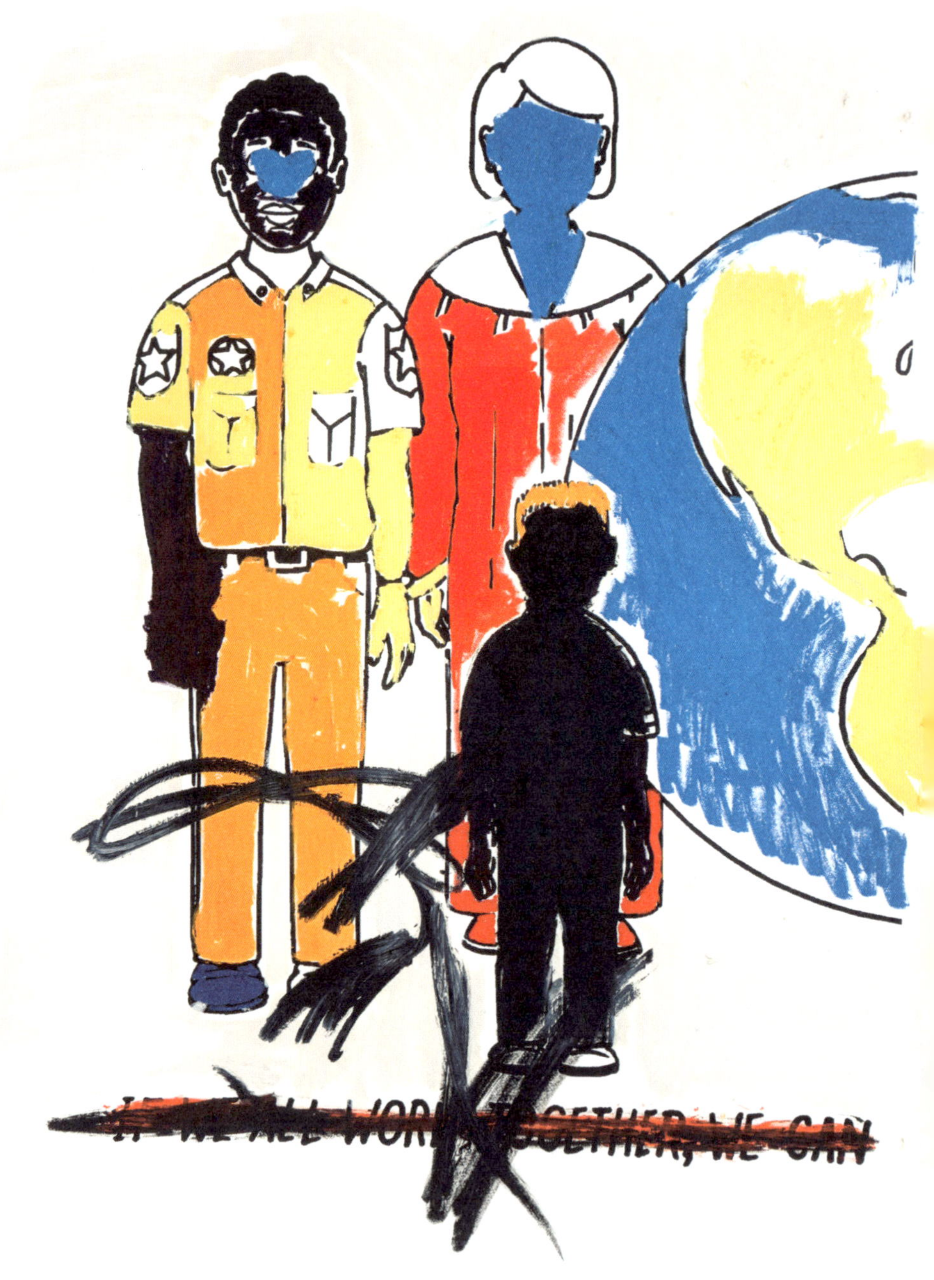

Born into Being

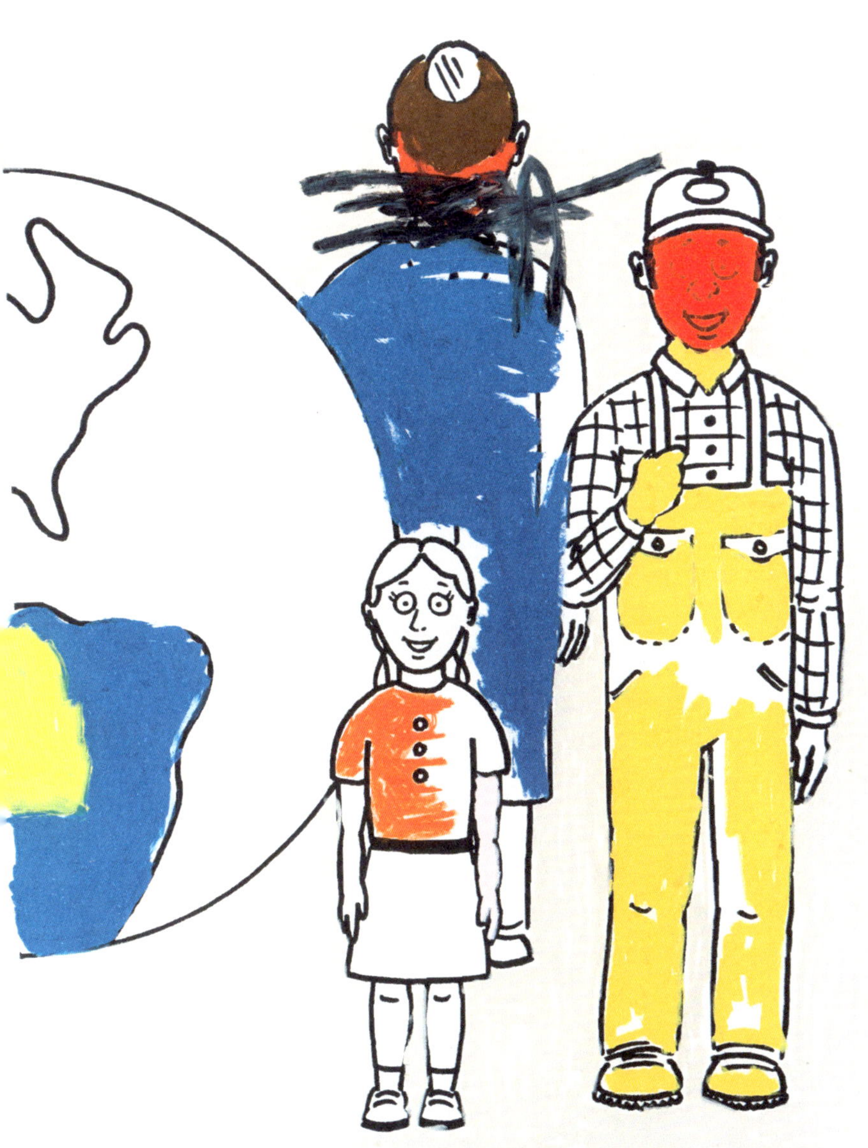

MAKE THE ~~WORLD~~ A BETTER PLACE.

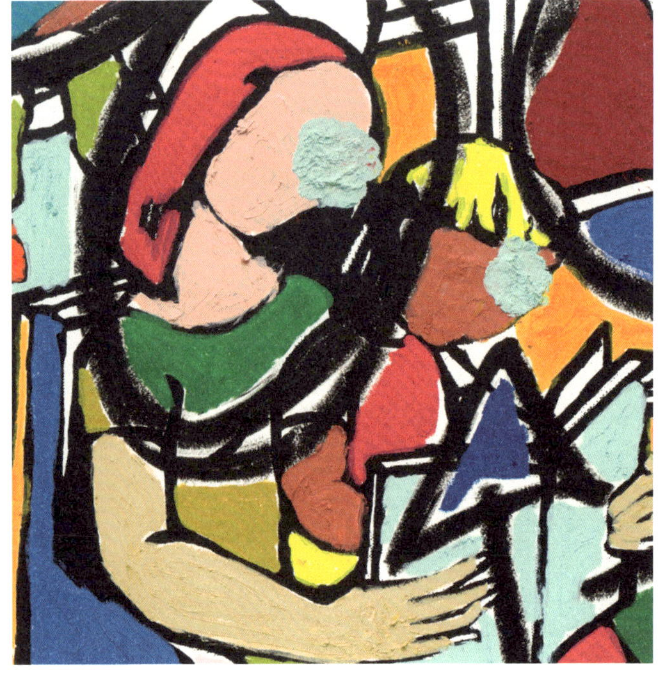

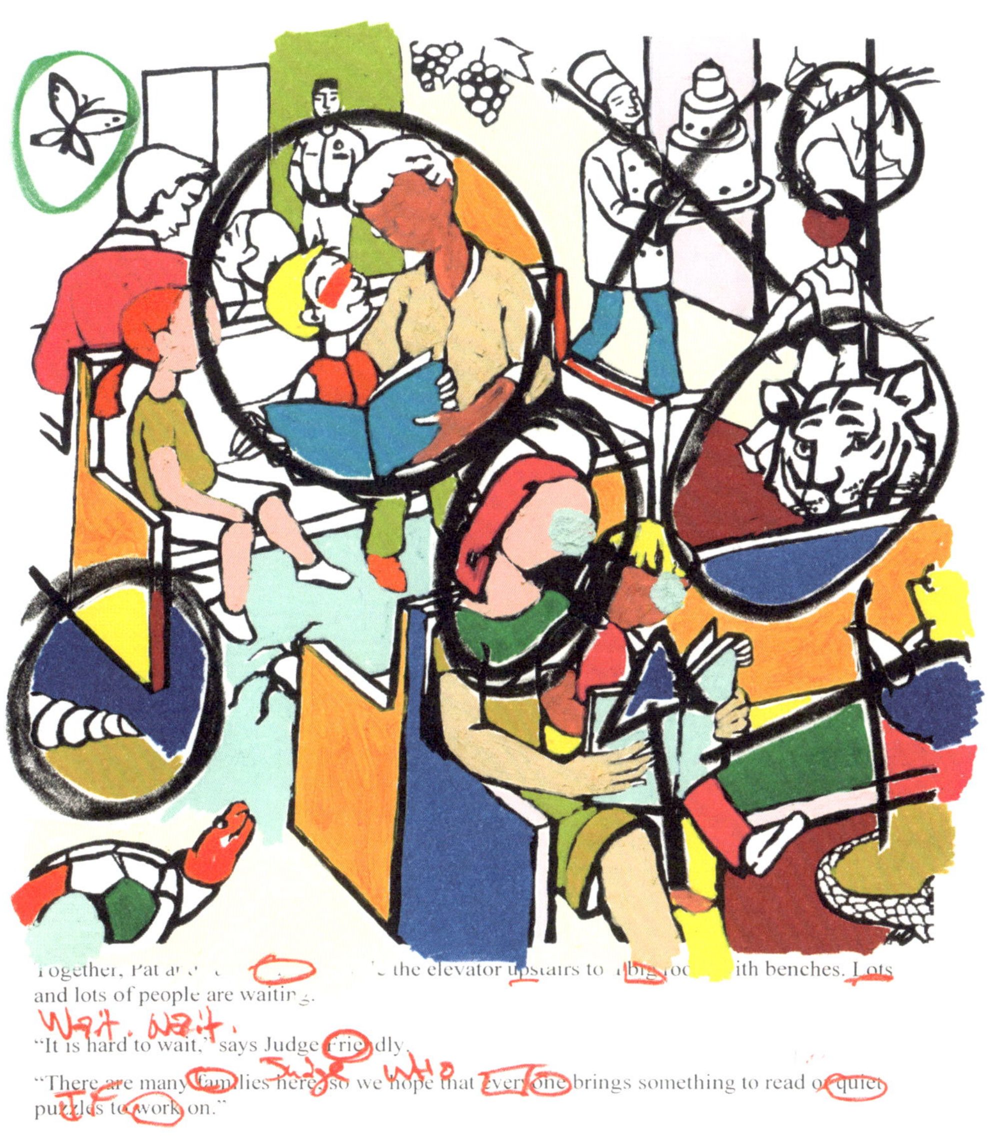

Together, Pat and Jo take the elevator upstairs to a big room with benches. Lots and lots of people are waiting.

"It is hard to wait," says Judge friendly.

"There are many families here, so we hope that everyone brings something to read or quiet puzzles to work on."

What 10 things don't belong in this picture?

Deborah Roberts
Ulysses, 2019
Mixed media and collage on linen
65 × 45 inches (165 × 114.3 cm)

Born into Being

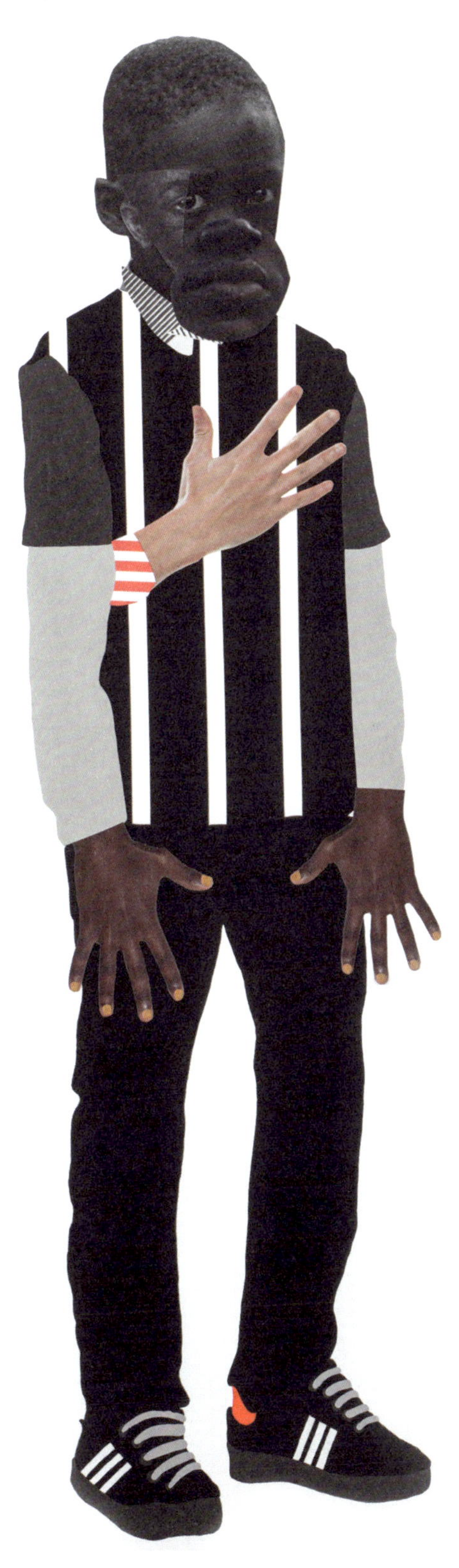

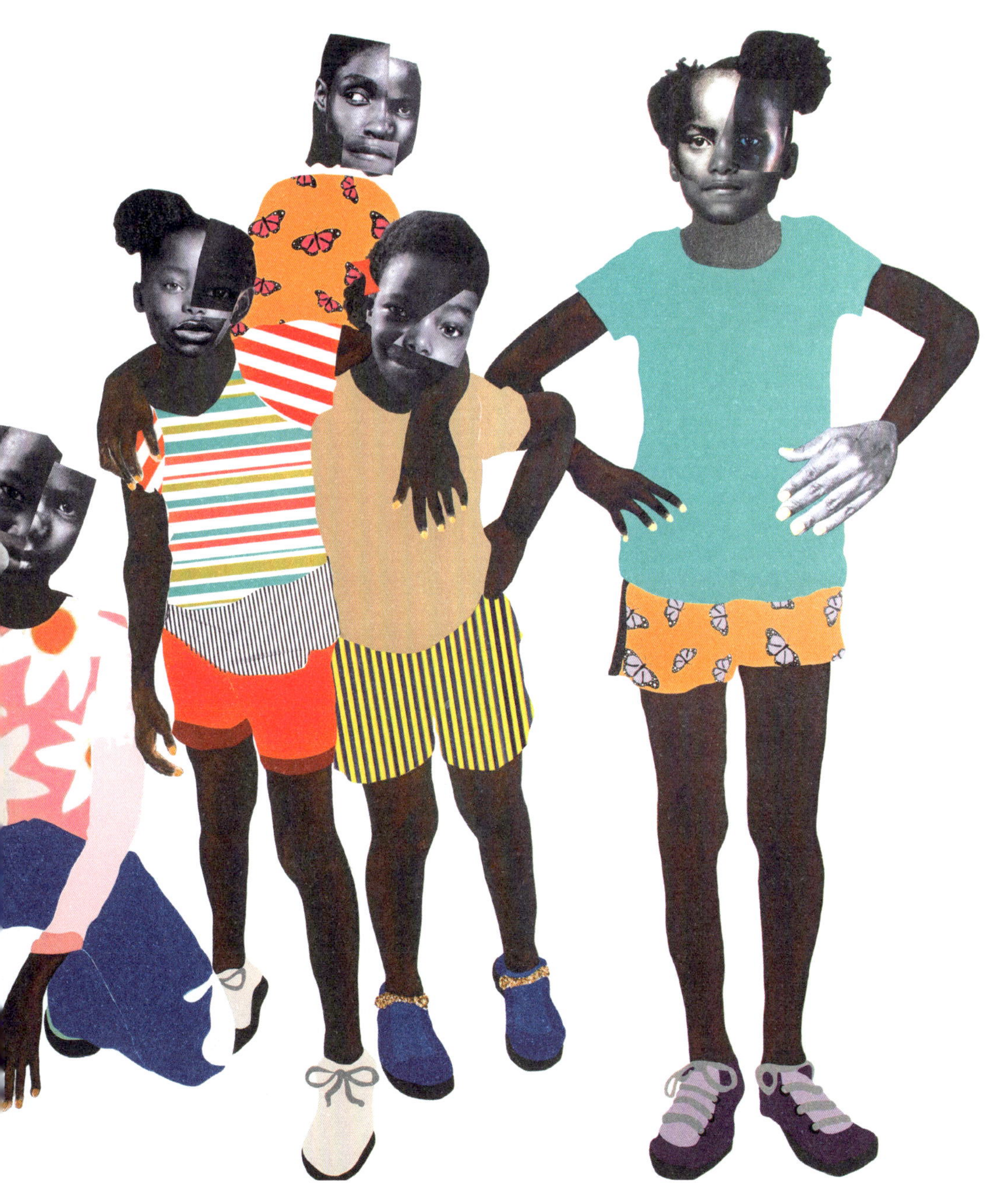

Njideka Akunyili Crosby
"The Beautyful Ones" Series #7, 2018
Acrylic, colored pencil, and transfers on paper
59 ⅞ × 42 ½ inches (152.1 × 108 cm)

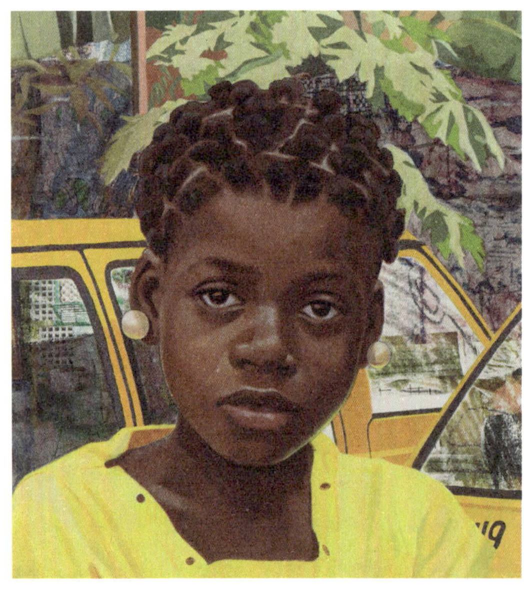

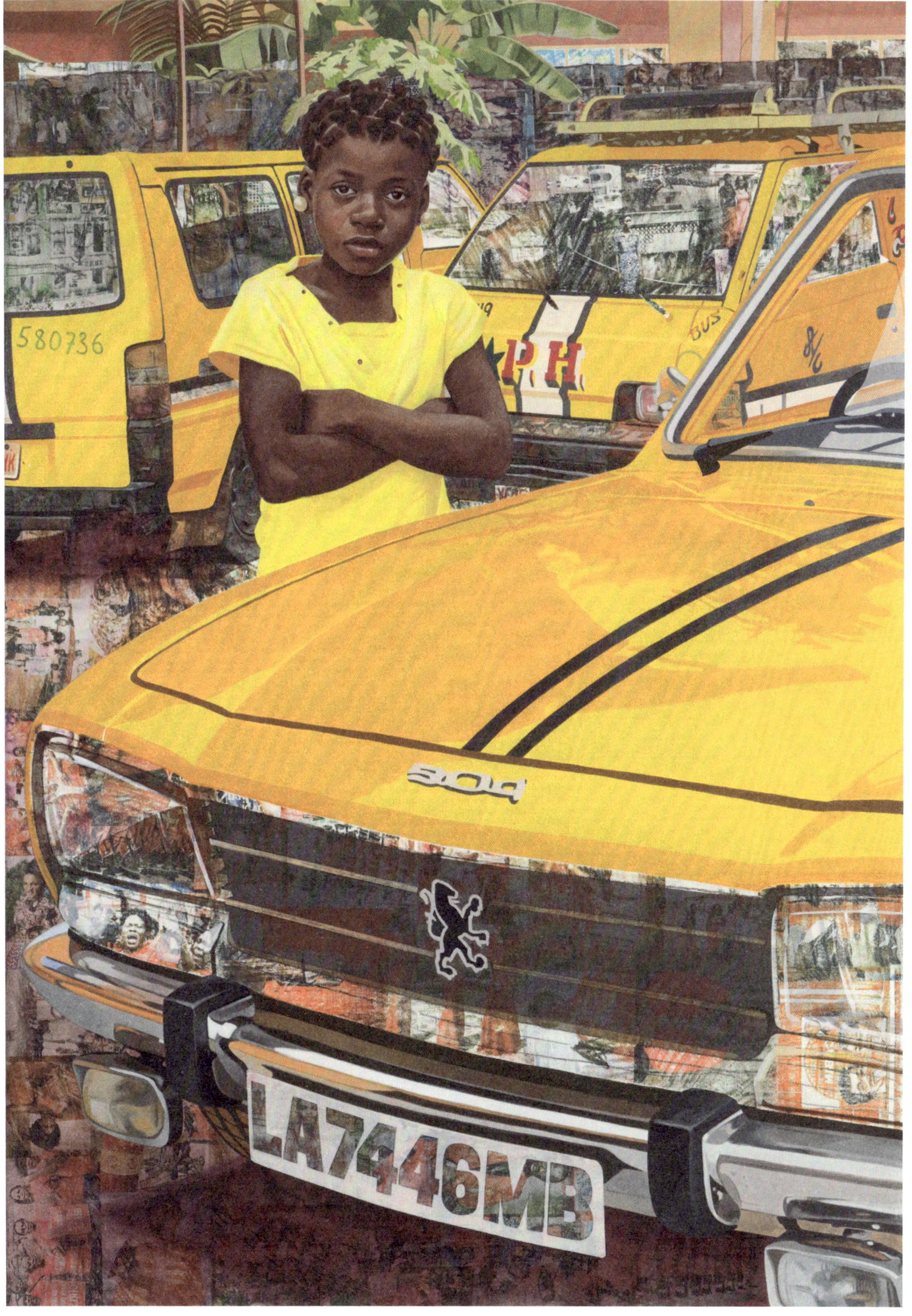

580736
PH
BUS
504
LA7446MB

Njideka Akunyili Crosby
"The Beautyful Ones" Series #1b, 2014
Acrylic, colored pencil, and transfers on paper
60 × 52 inches (152.4 × 132.1 cm)

Born into Being

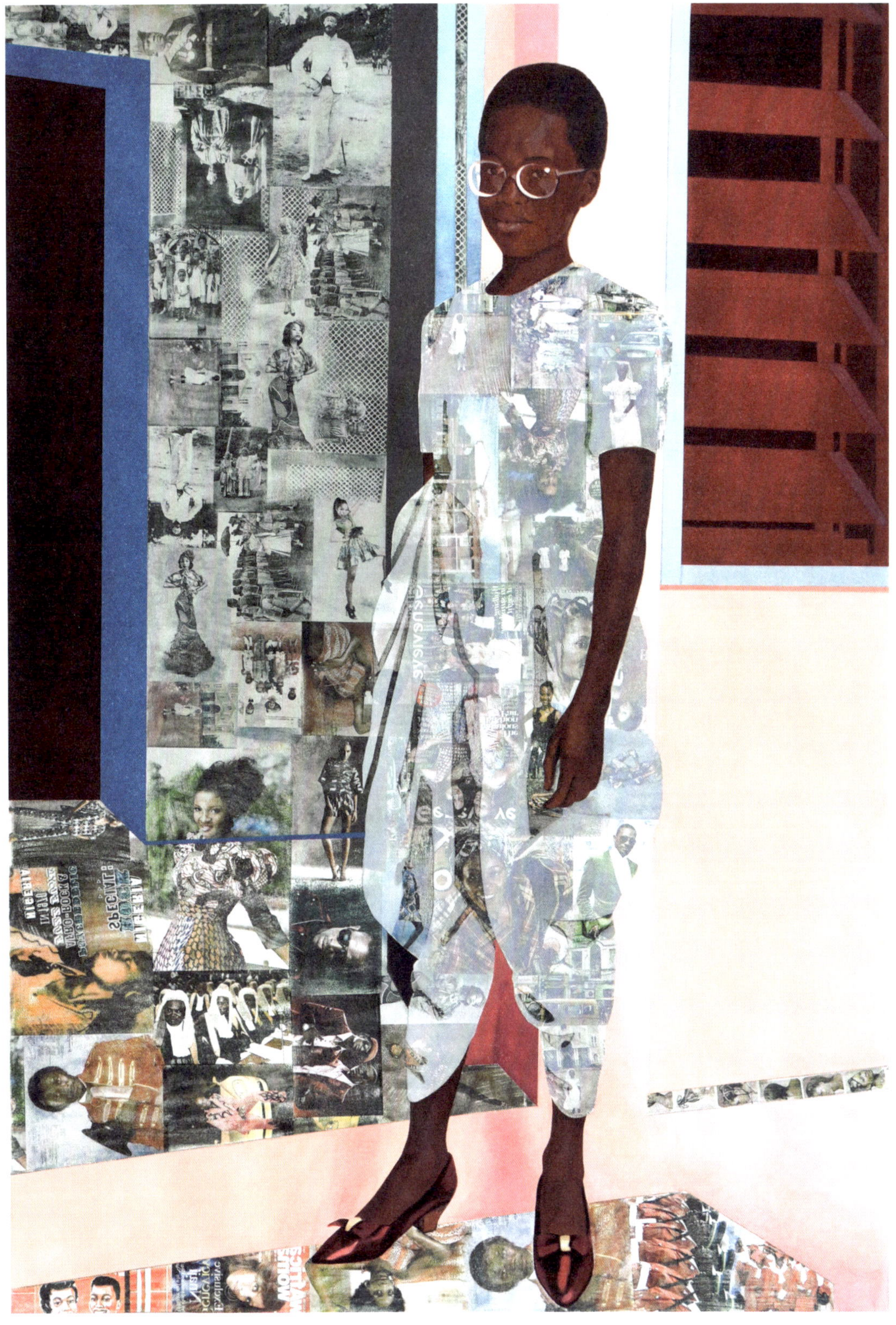

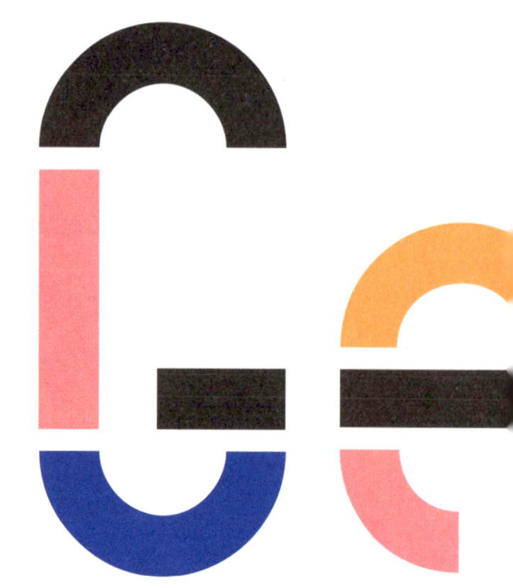
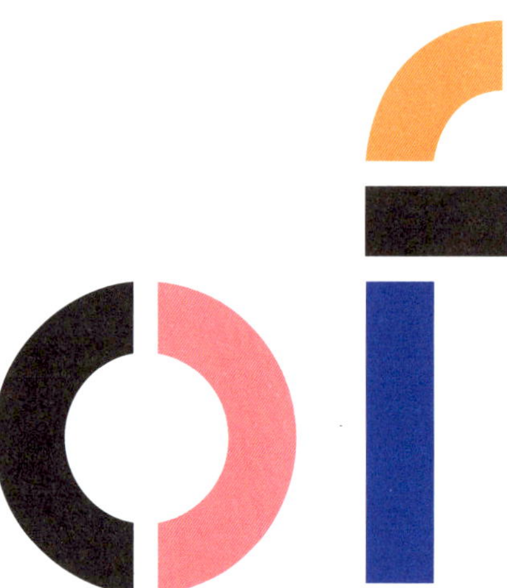

stures

CARE

Ann Agee
Mierle Laderman Ukeles
Lenka Clayton
Cathy Wilkes
Jay Lynn Gomez
Jordan Casteel
Justine Kurland

Numerous artists reflect on the practical and intangible needs of children and the many individuals who meet those needs, often with an extended hand or a warm embrace. Ann Agee reimagines the iconography of the Madonna and Child in inventive clay and porcelain sculptures that suggest the centrality of the mother-and-child bond both in the history of art and in historical consciousness writ large; she renovates this prototype by inserting a girl child and depicting a wide array of physical engagements, from nursing and biting to playing and pushing away. Historically overlooked labors of the mother are a subject for the pioneering feminist artist Mierle Laderman Ukeles, who in a series of photographs from the 1970s documents the acts of dressing and undressing her two children to go outside, part of her lifelong effort to raise awareness of invisible forms of labor. Her inclusion of a cotton rag to the right of the framed piece connects the acts of the mother figure with those of museum staff whose cleaning of artworks and spaces likewise goes largely unseen. Lenka Clayton's videos draw attention to the little acts of love, assistance, and control that structure the everyday care of her toddler son during her "Artist Residency in Motherhood." In her poetic and charged sculptural tableau, Cathy Wilkes shows a family performing the roles of reproductive labor, of fulfilling needs, and of play, despite impoverished circumstances. Jay Lynn Gomez (formerly Ramiro Gomez), who has painted the largely immigrant workforce that keeps many houses, yards, and families functioning, portrays a nanny and toddler holding hands as the latter learns to walk in tentative steps that the nanny will witness in all their minute development. Jordan Casteel's striking paintings capture passing subway scenes that speak to myriad forms of care: two twins topple onto each other in sleep, and a toddler clings to a man's jeans at a subway door. Justine Kurland's staged photographs from her Girl Pictures series imagine a troop of runaways who craft homes in suburban brush and next to underpasses, and fulfill the roles of family and care no longer available to them from those associated through biology. These works invite us to reconsider caretaking as an act shared in communion rather than the labor of an individual.

Ann Agee
Green Pleated Shift Madonna, 2021
Glazed earthenware with slip
30 × 15 × 14 inches (76.2 × 38.1 × 35.6 cm)

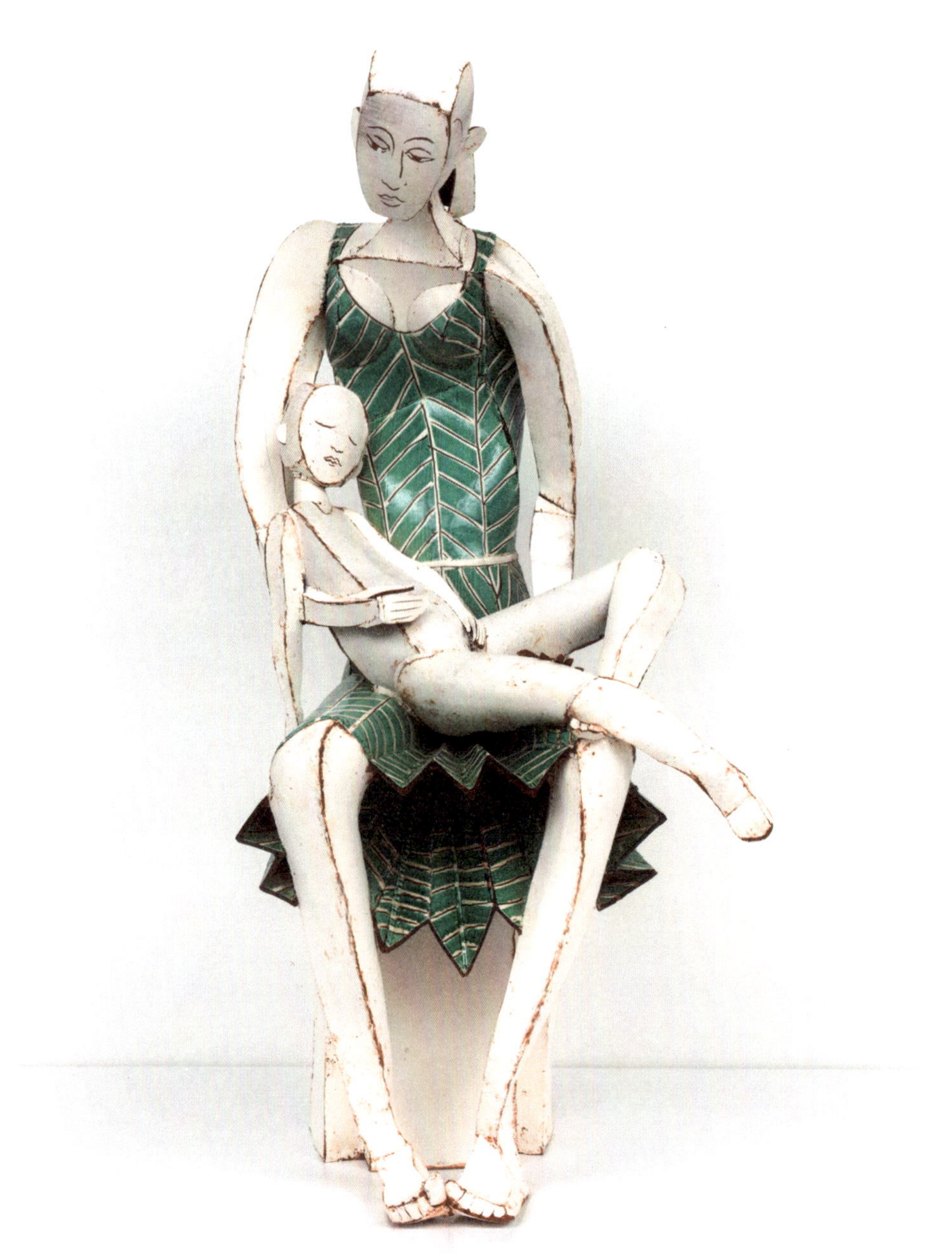

Ann Agee
Spandex Madonna with a Ball, 2021
Earthenware with colored slips
35 ½ × 13 × 12 inches (90.2 × 33 × 30.5 cm)

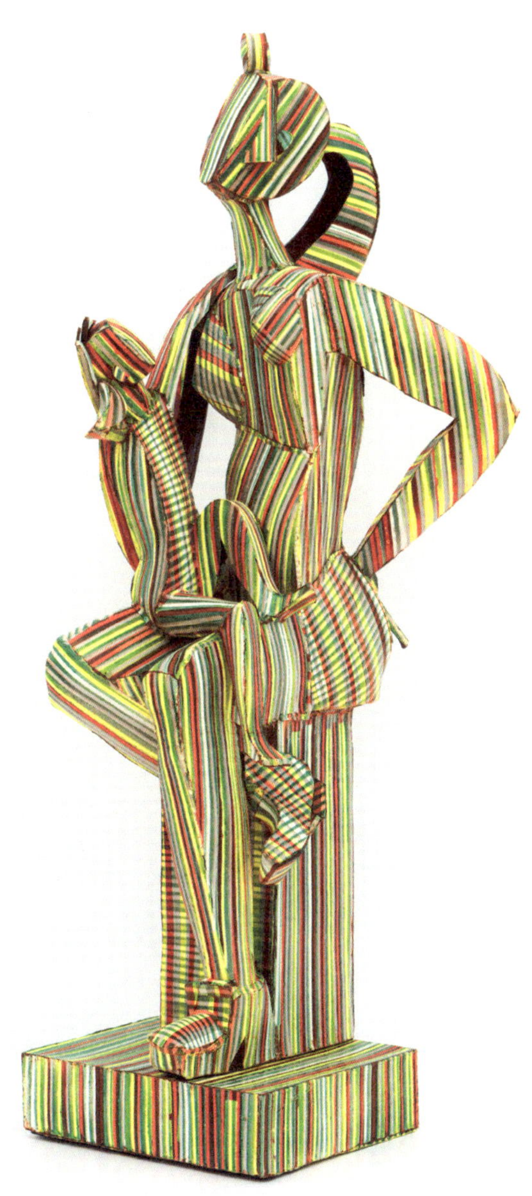

Ann Agee
Nursing Bra Madonna, 2019
Glazed porcelain with red overglaze enamel
17 ¼ × 4 × 5 ¾ inches (43.8 × 10.2 × 14.6 cm)

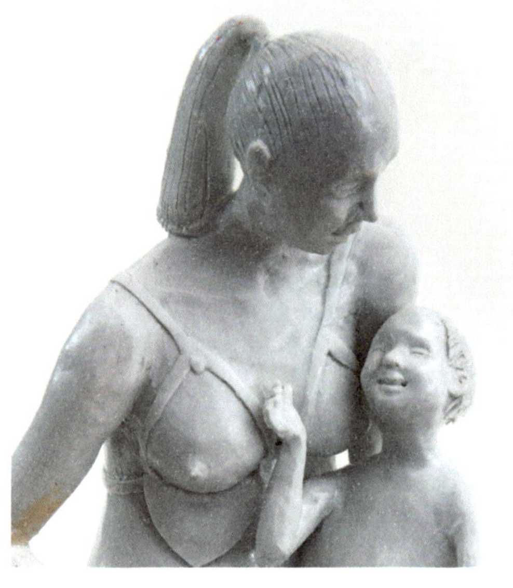

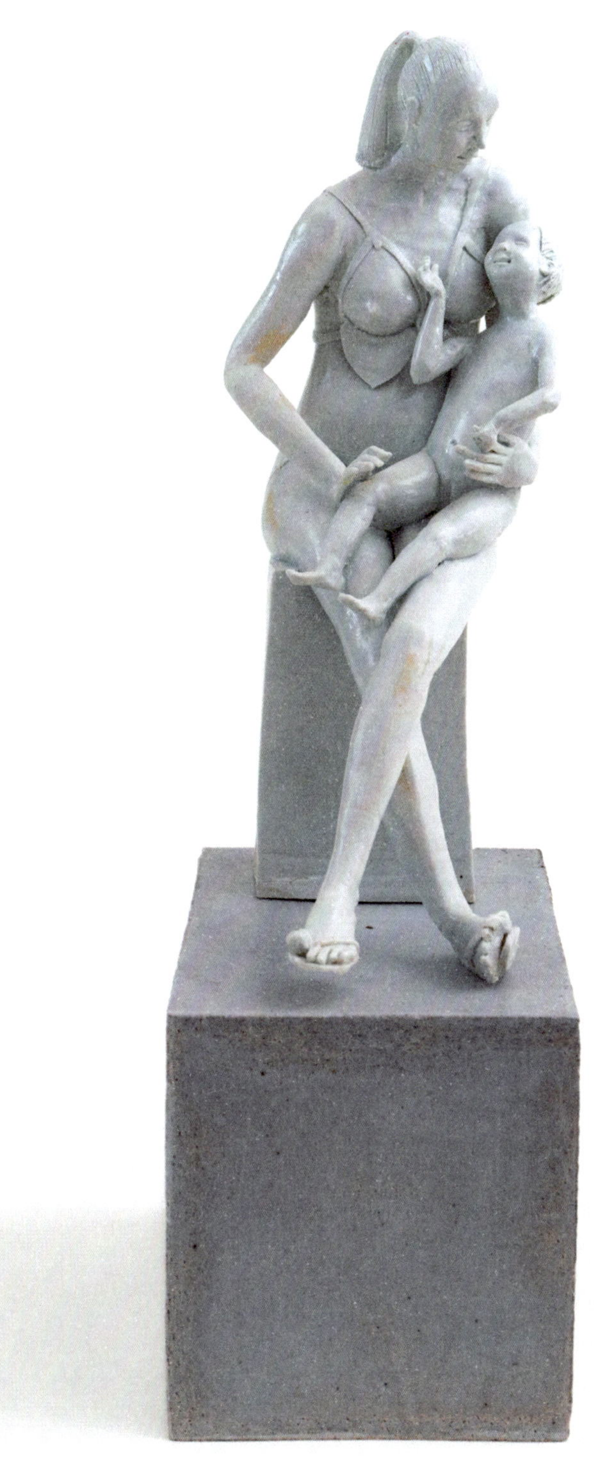

Ann Agee
Sideways Plaid Madonna with Drawer, 2021
Earthenware with glaze and underglaze
26 ½ × 14 ⅞ × 6 ⅞ inches (67.3 × 37.8 × 17.5 cm)

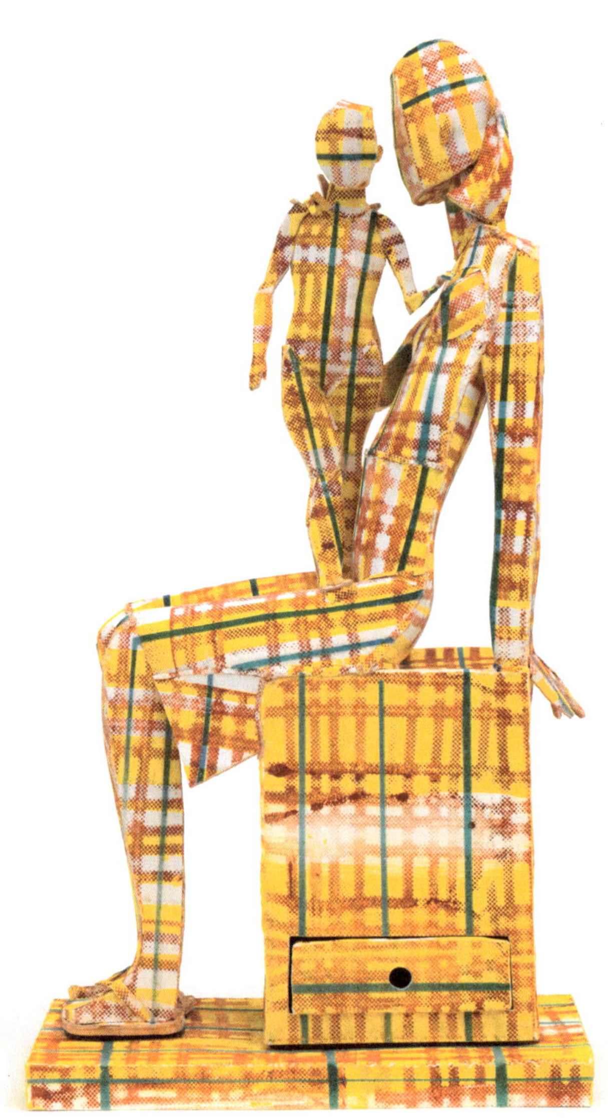

Ann Agee
Raised Curtain Madonna, 2020
Glazed porcelain with matte blue glaze
14 ¾ × 10 ¼ × 8 ½ inches (37.5 × 26 × 21.6 cm)

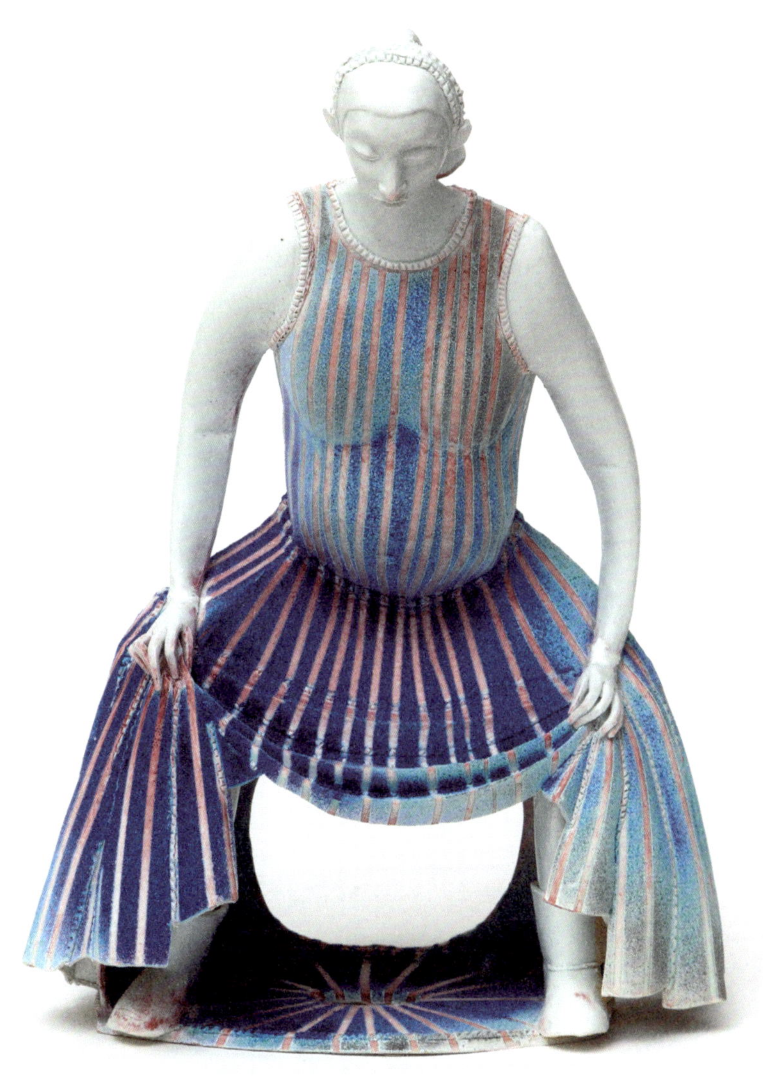

Mierle Laderman Ukeles
Dressing to Go Out / Undressing to Go In, 1973
Gelatin silver prints mounted on
foamcore with chain and dust rag
57 ¼ × 44 ⅜ × ¾ inches (145.6 × 112.9 × 2.1 cm)

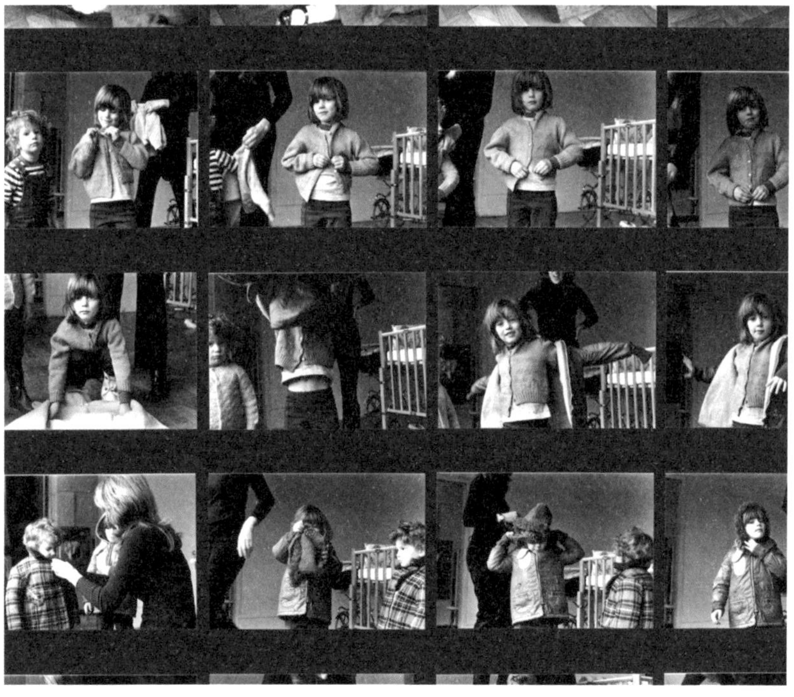

Gestures of Care

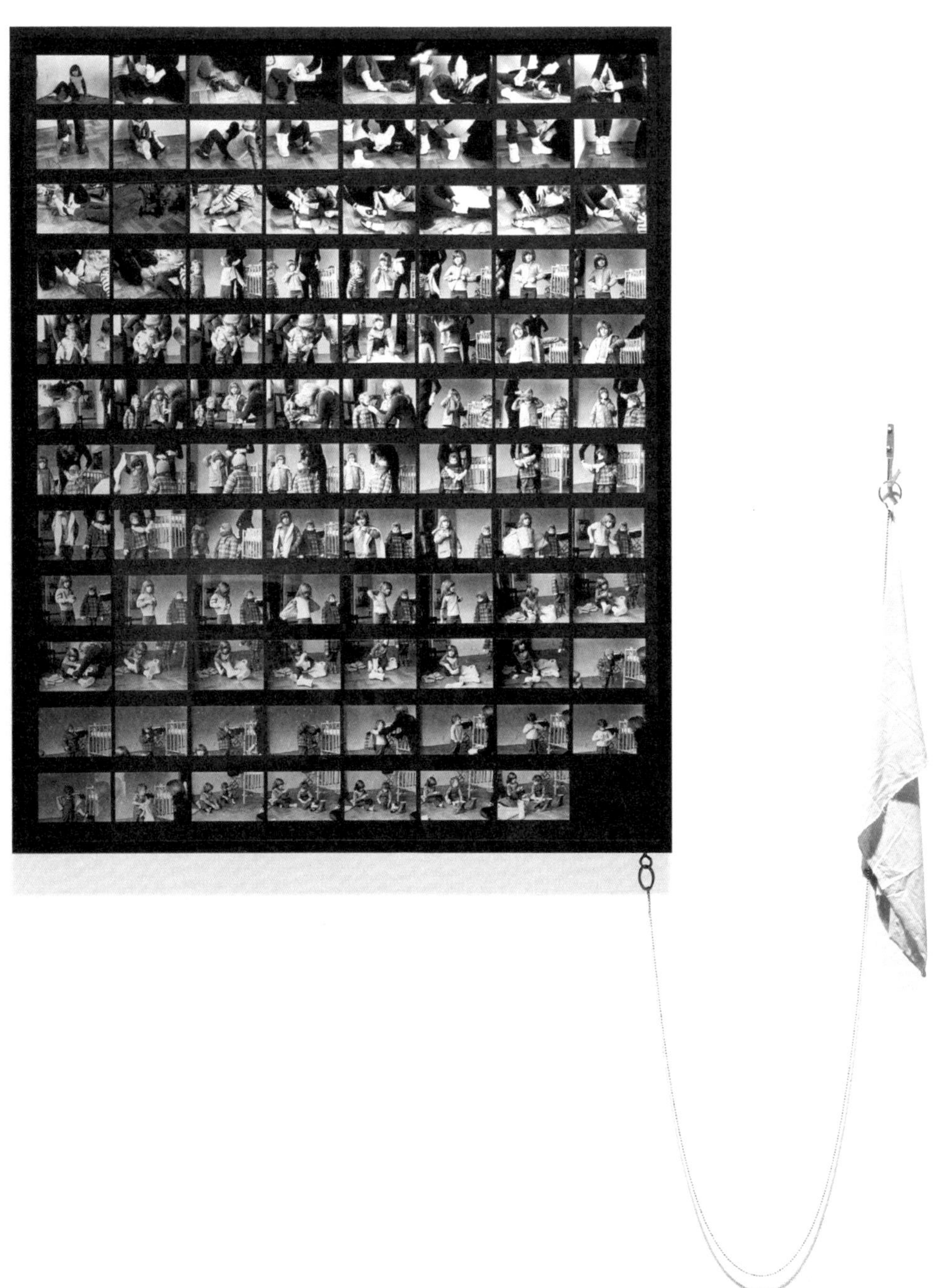

Lenka Clayton
An Artist Residency in Motherhood, 2012
Typewriter ink on paper
11 × 8 ½ inches (27.9 × 21.6 cm)

<u>Artist's Statement</u>

<u>An Artist Residency in Motherhood</u>

In common with all new parents, the birth of my first child in
April 2011 changed many things in my life. One of those changes
has been the way I and others think about my career as an artist.
I find now that many aspects of the professional art world are
closed to artists with families. Most prestigious artist reside-
-ncies for example specifically exclude families from attending.
Despite a legacy of public artist-parents it still seems to be a
commonly held belief that being an engaged mother and serious
artist are mutually exclusive endeavors. I don't believe or
want to perpetrate this. I like to imagine the two roles not as
competing directions but to view them, force them gently if
necessary, to inform one another.

I will undergo this self-imposed artist residency in order to
fully experience and explore the fragmented focus, nap-length
studio time, limited movement and resources and general upheaval
that parenthood brings and allow it to shape the direction of
my work, rather than try to work "despite it".

Lenka Clayton September 2012

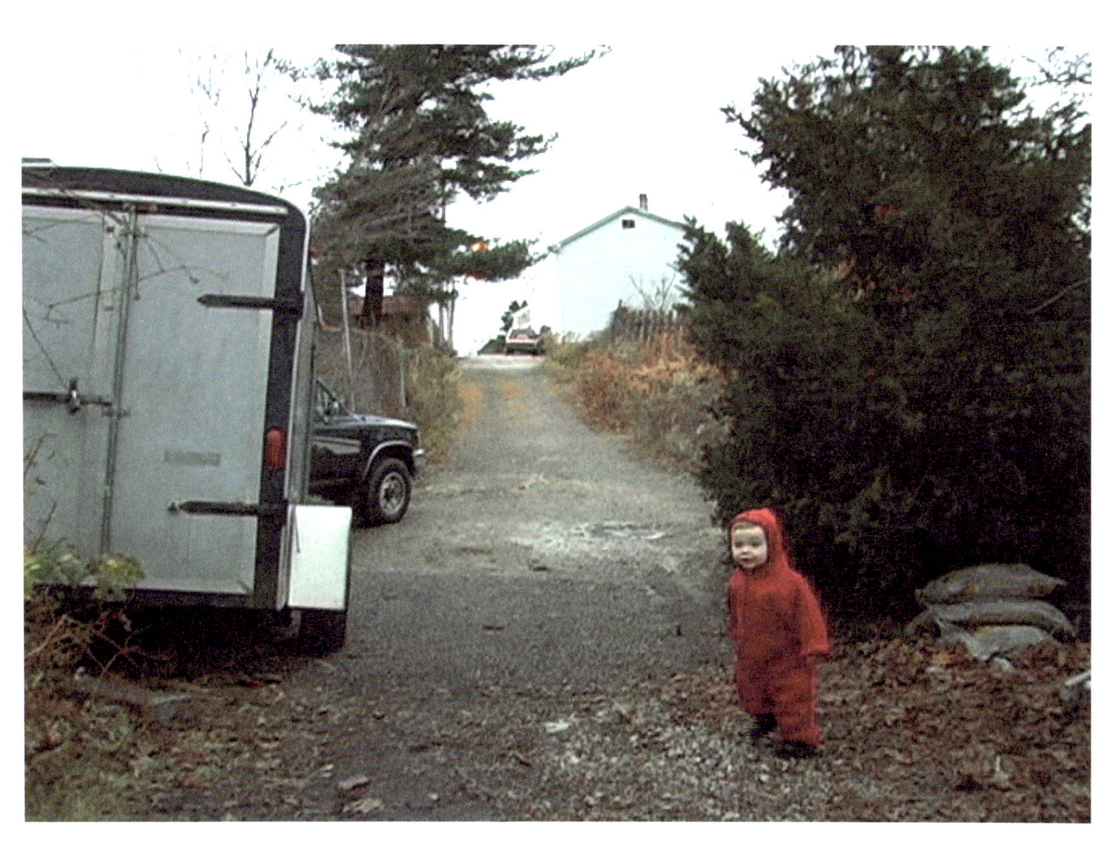

Lenka Clayton
The Distance I Can Be from My Son (Back Alley) (still), 2013
Video (color, sound; 1:53 minutes)

Lenka Clayton
The Distance I Can Be from My Son (Supermarket) (still), 2013
Video (color, sound; 00:52 minutes)

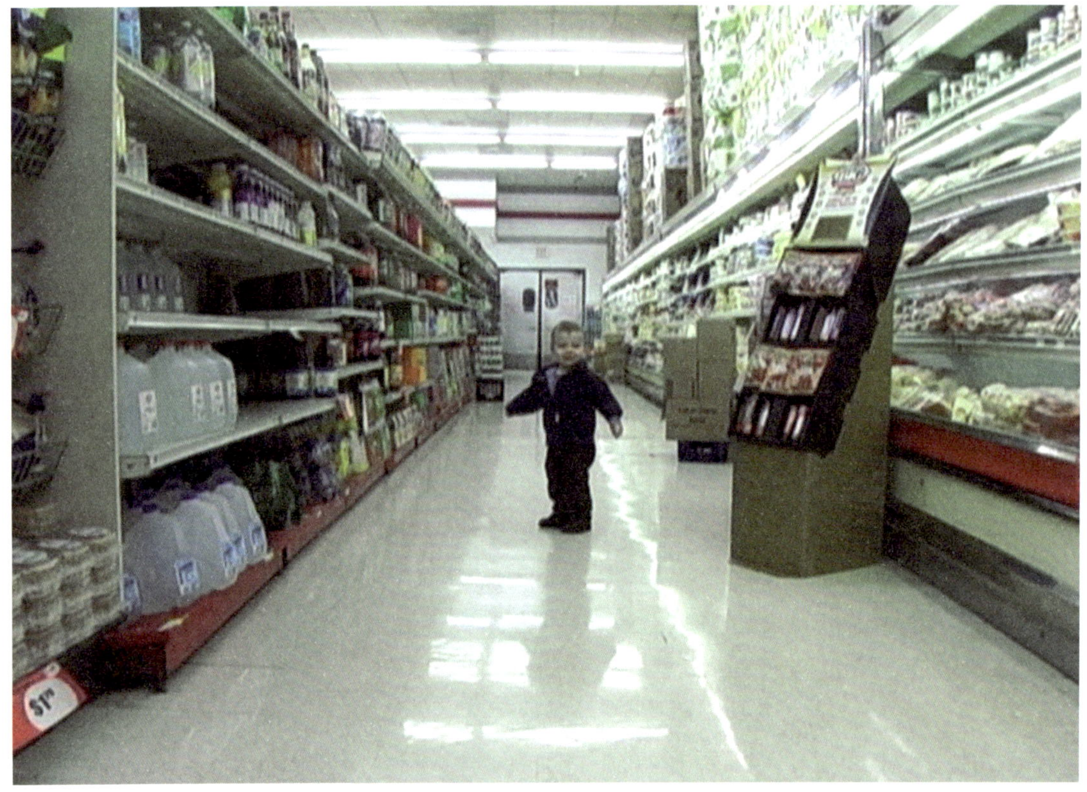

Lenka Clayton
The Distance I Can Be from My Son (Park) (still), 2013
Video (color, sound; 1:43 minutes)

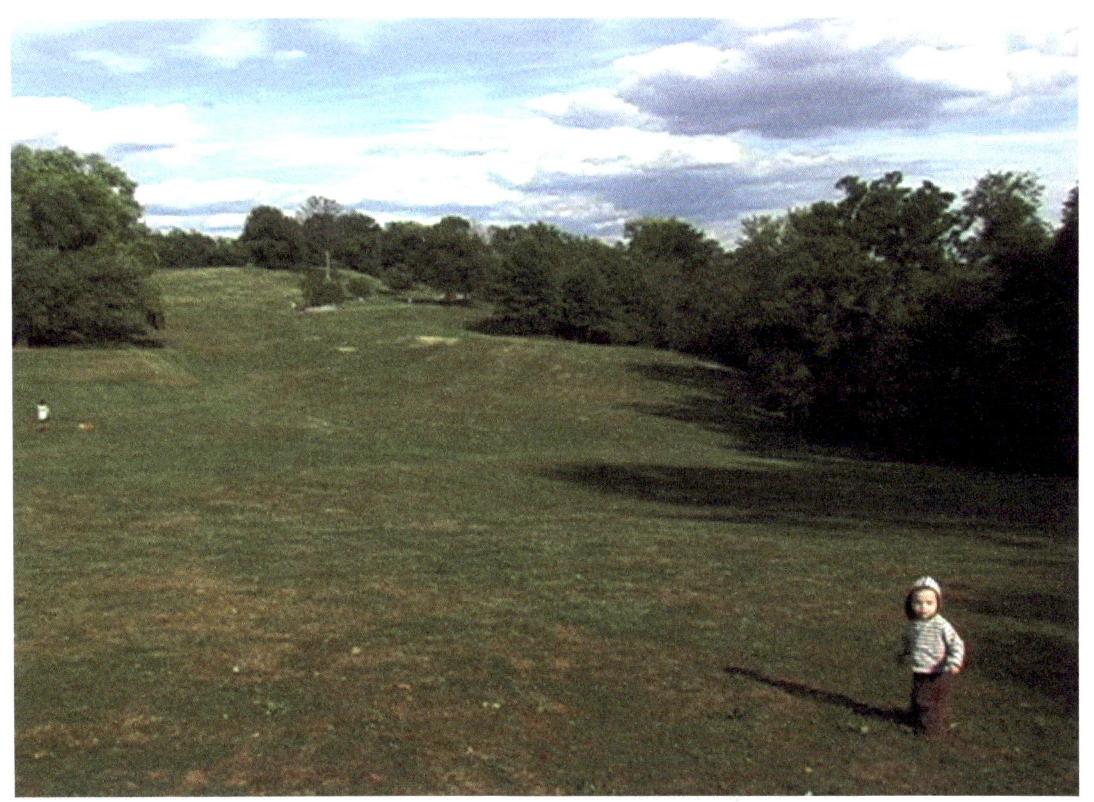

Cathy Wilkes
Untitled, 2012
Mixed media
Overall dimensions variable

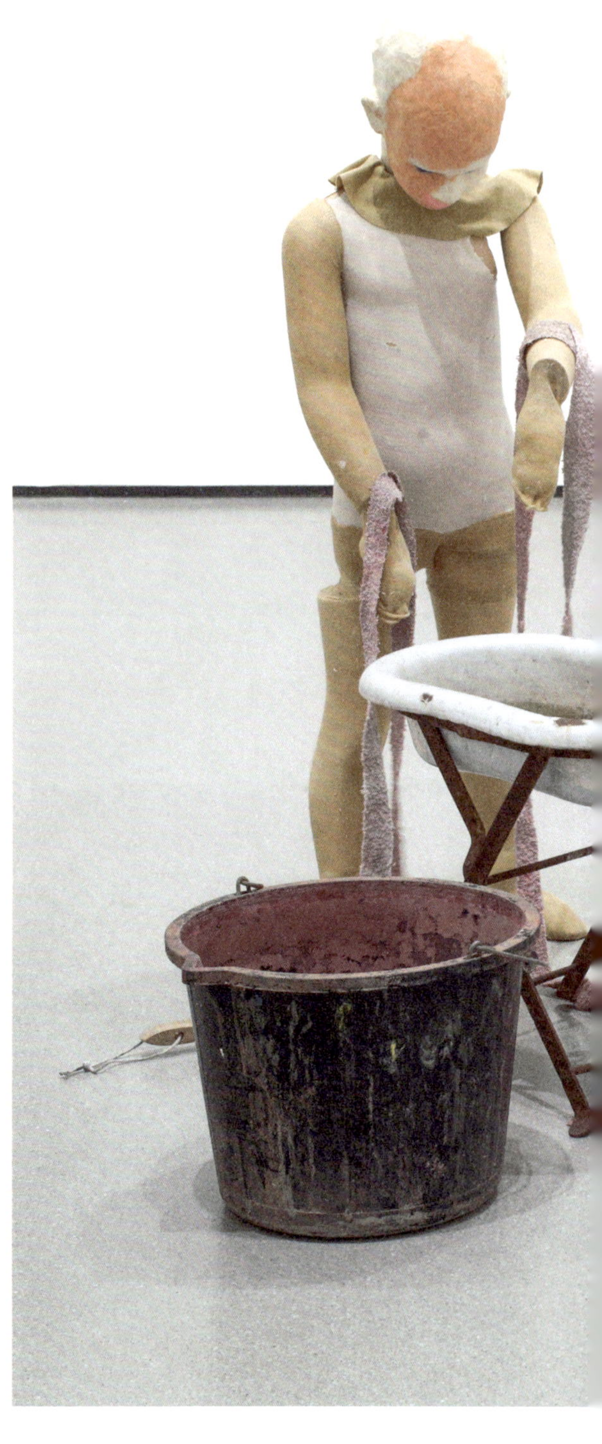

Gestures of Care

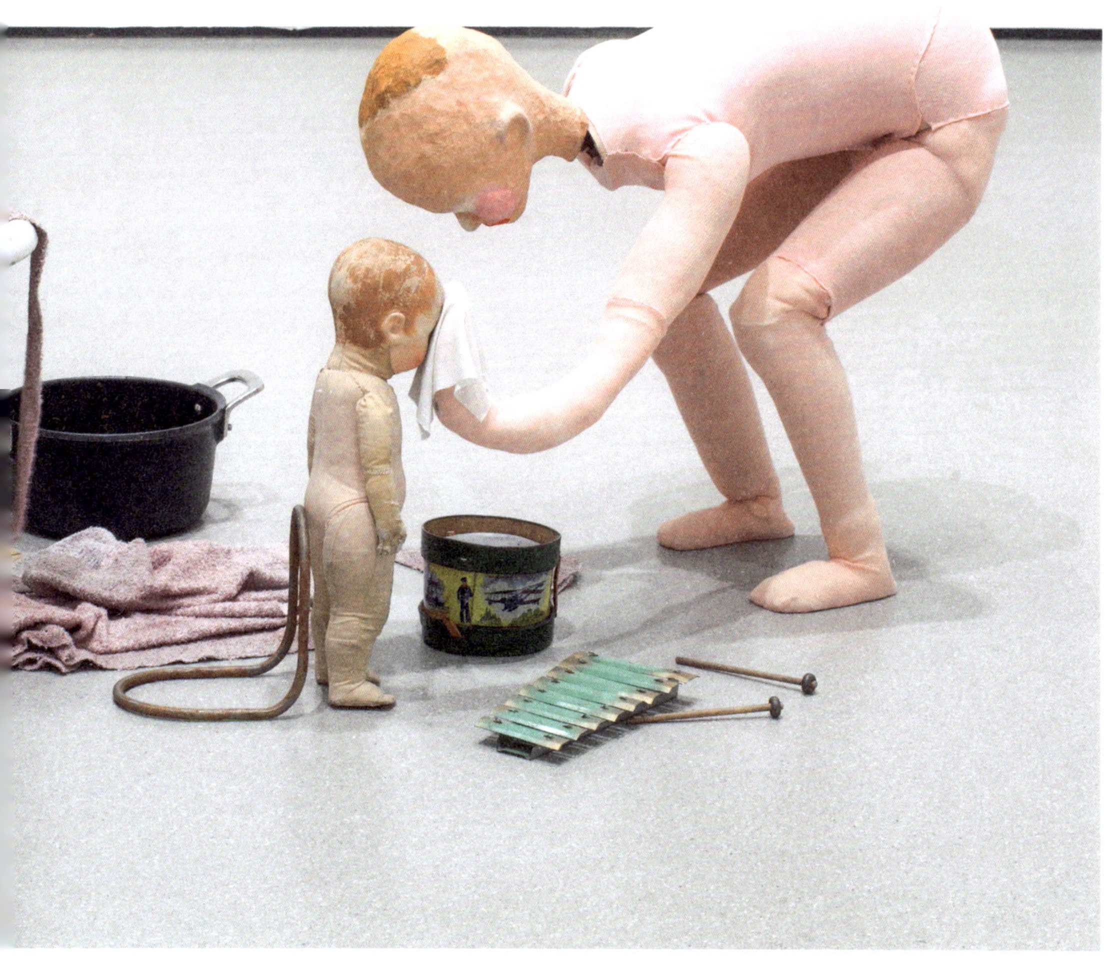

Ramiro Gomez
(now Jay Lynn Gomez)
Nanny and Child (Madison Square Park), 2018
Mixed media on canvas
72 × 72 inches (182.9 × 182.9 cm)

Gestures of Care

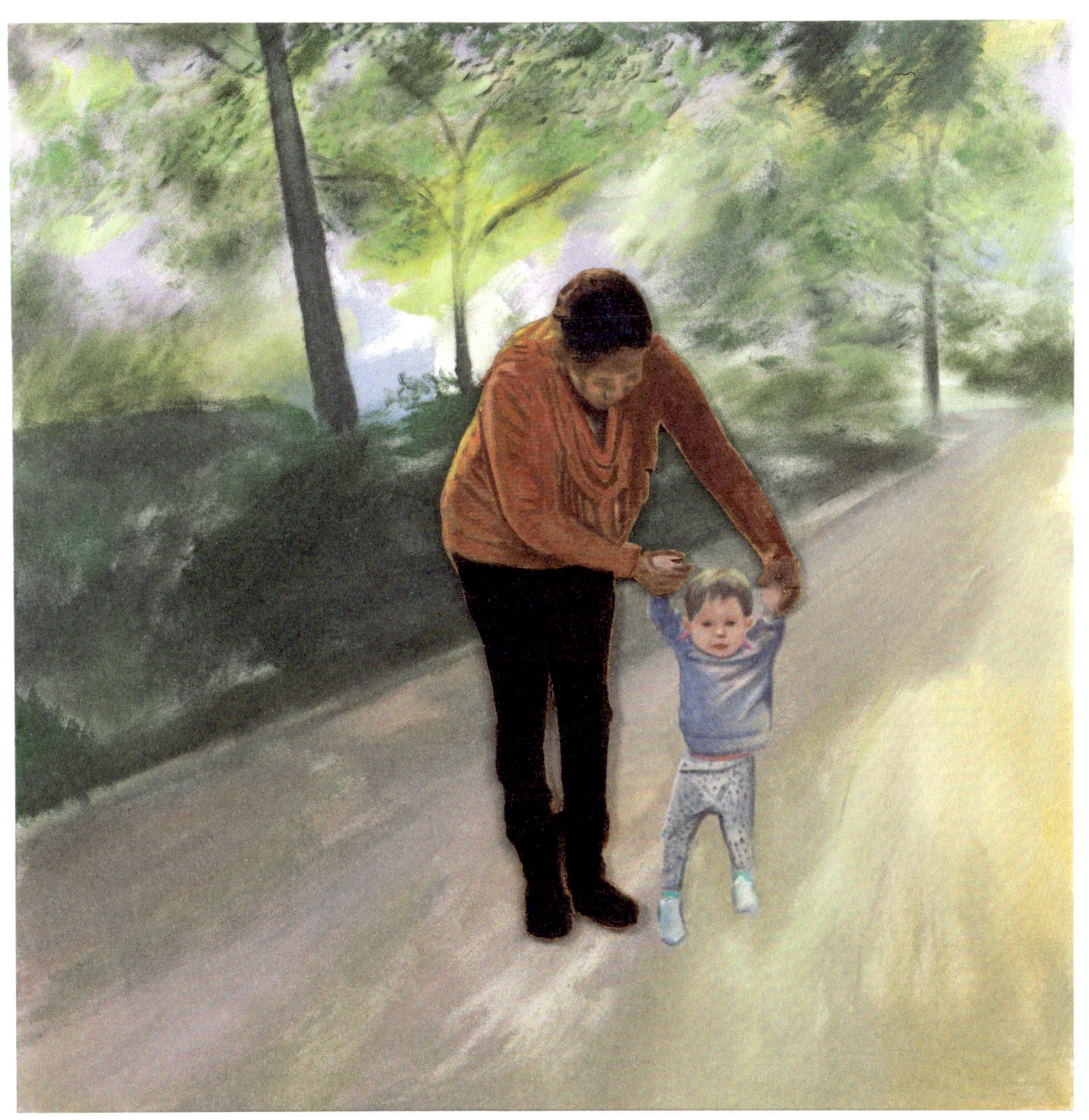

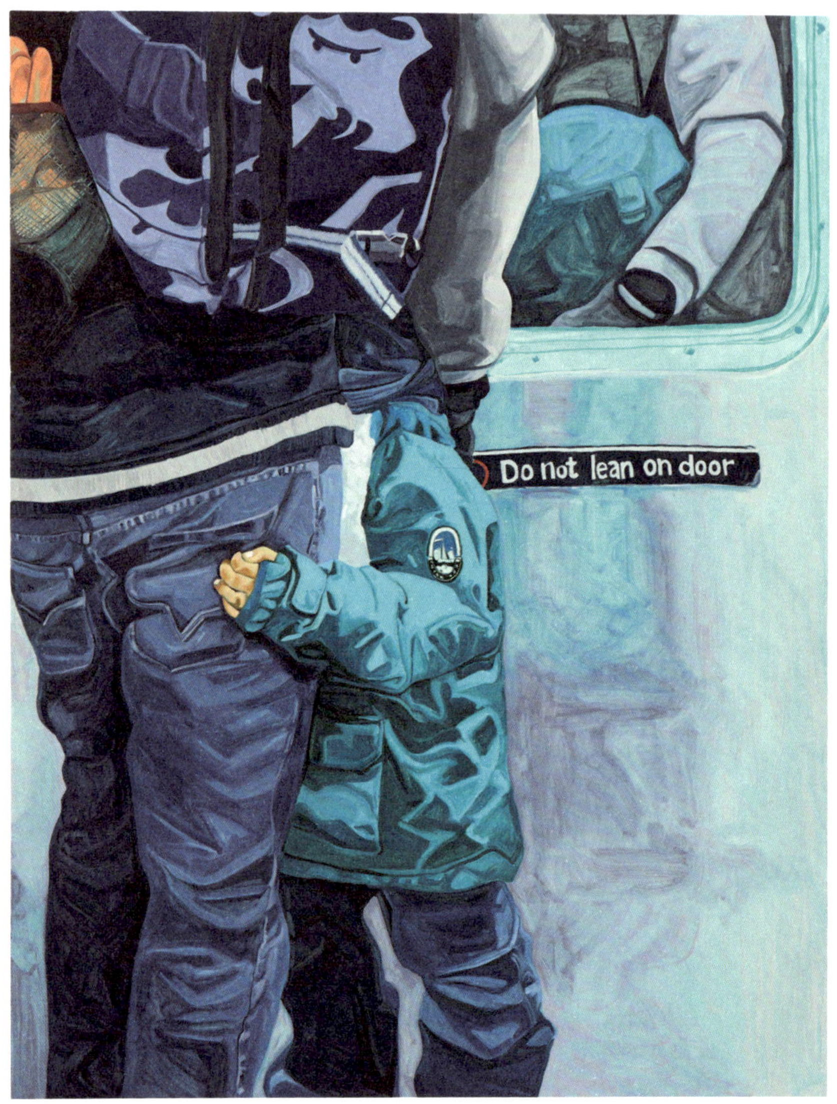
Do not lean on door

Jordan Casteel
Twins (Subway), 2018
Oil on canvas
56 × 72 inches (142.2 × 182.9 cm)

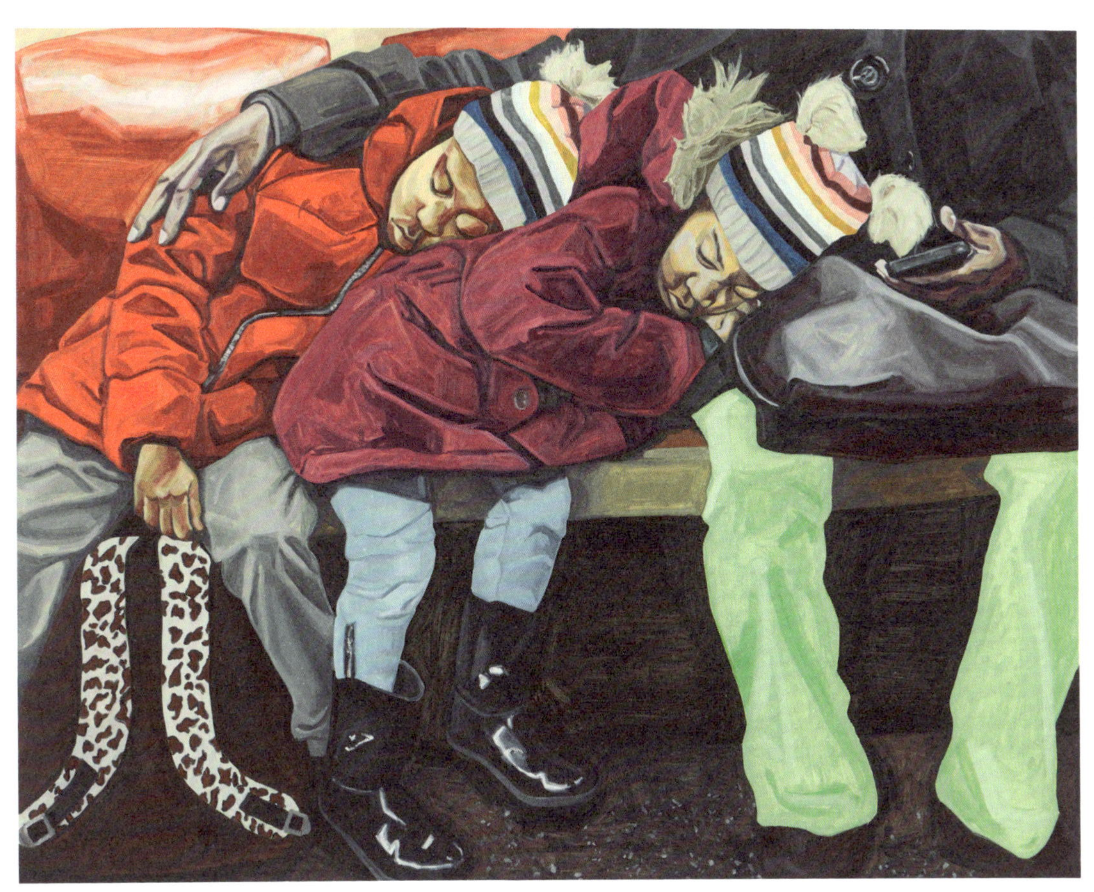

Justine Kurland
Girls Curled Up, 1997
Chromogenic color print
24 × 36 inches (61 × 91.4 cm)

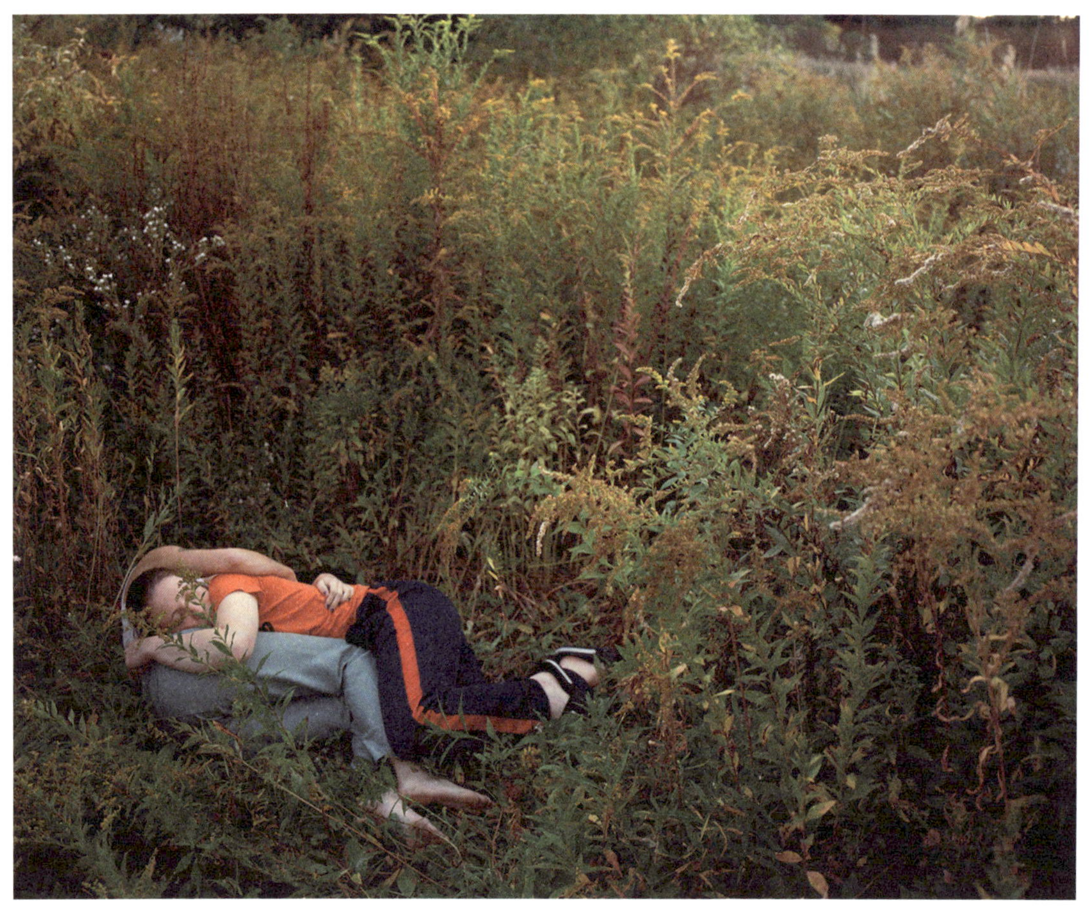

Justine Kurland
Feminine Hygiene, 2000
Chromogenic color print
24 × 30 inches (61 × 76.2 cm)

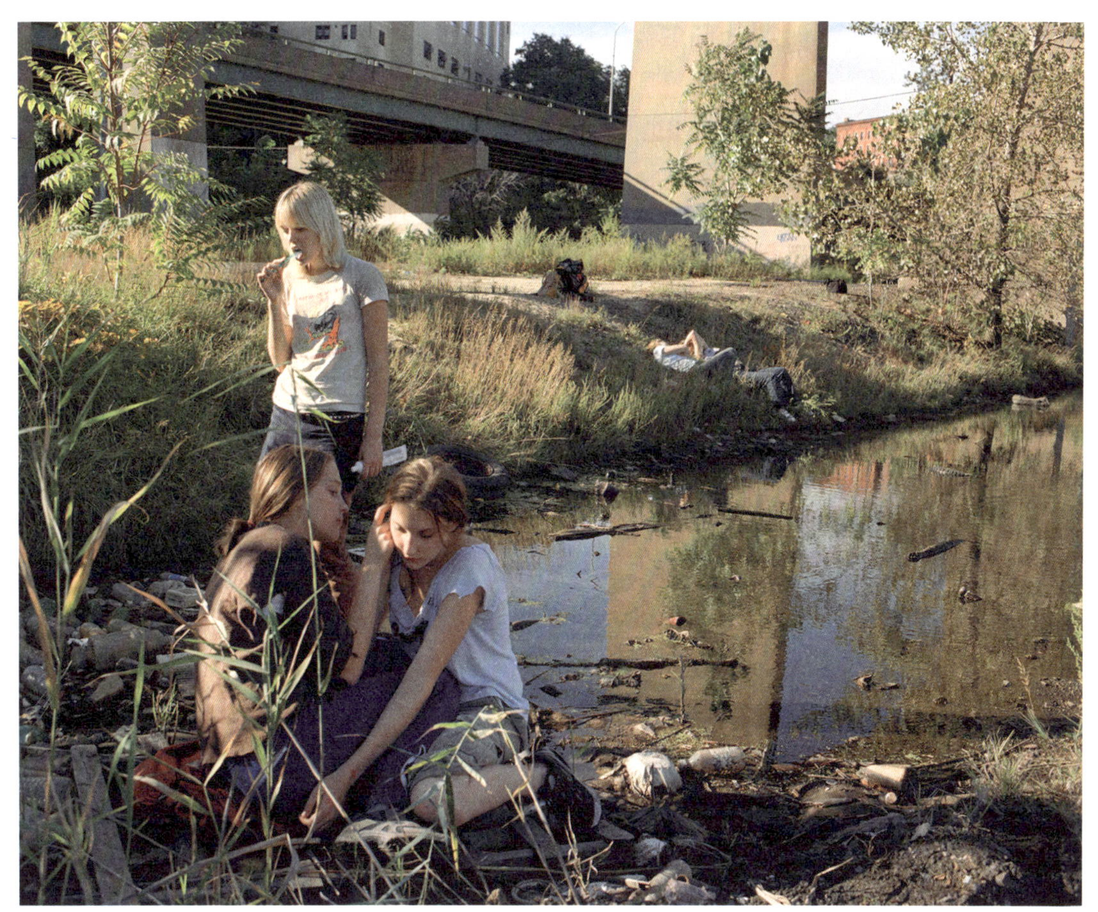

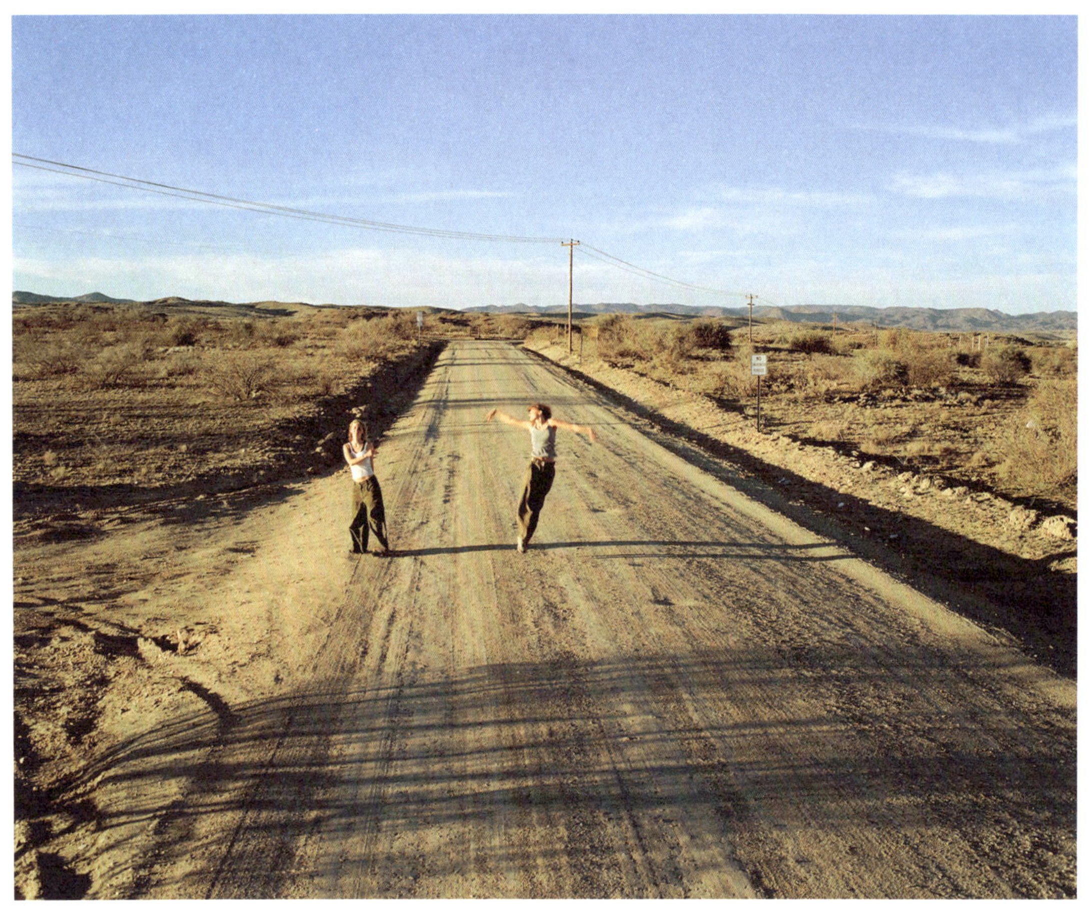

Gestures of Care

Justine Kurland
Blood Sisters, 2000
Chromogenic color print
24 × 30 inches (61 × 76.2 cm)

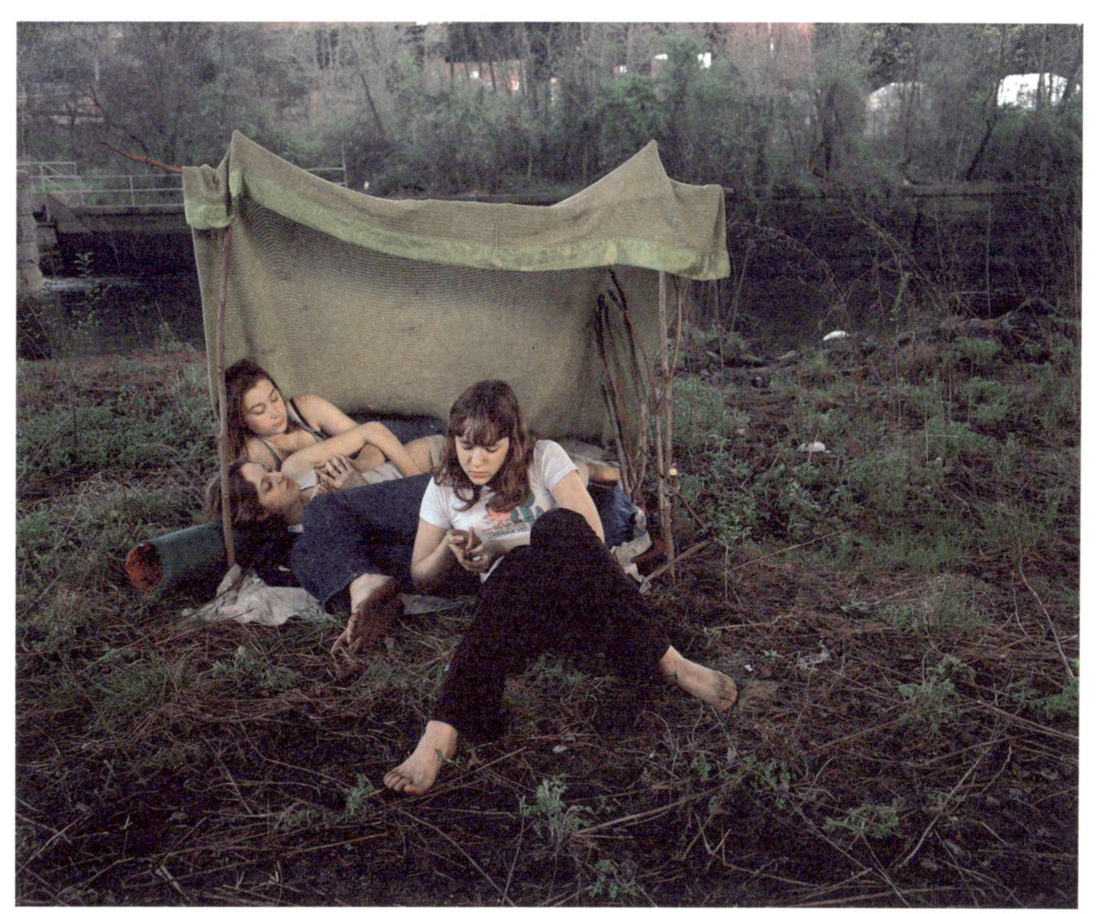

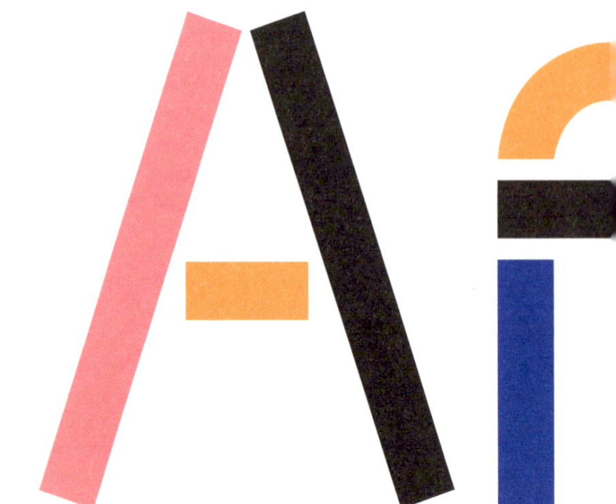

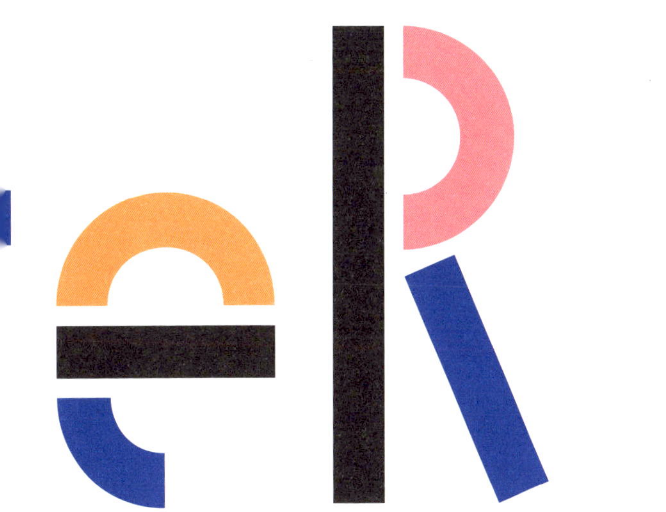
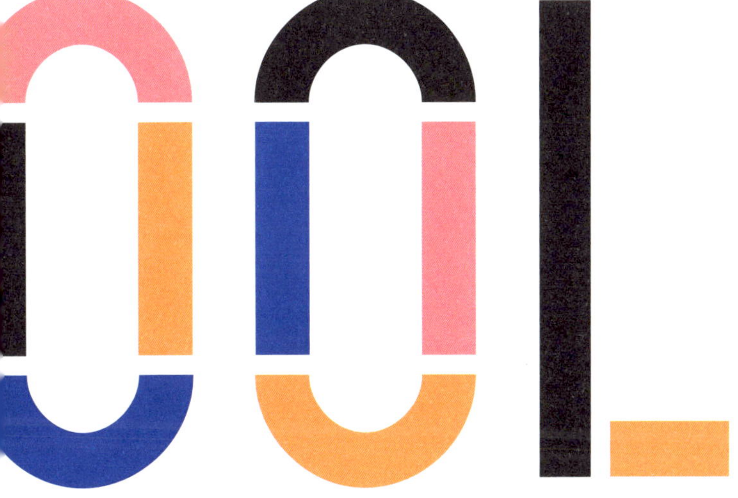

Tim Rollins and K.O.S.
Carmen Winant
Oscar Murillo
Francis Alÿs

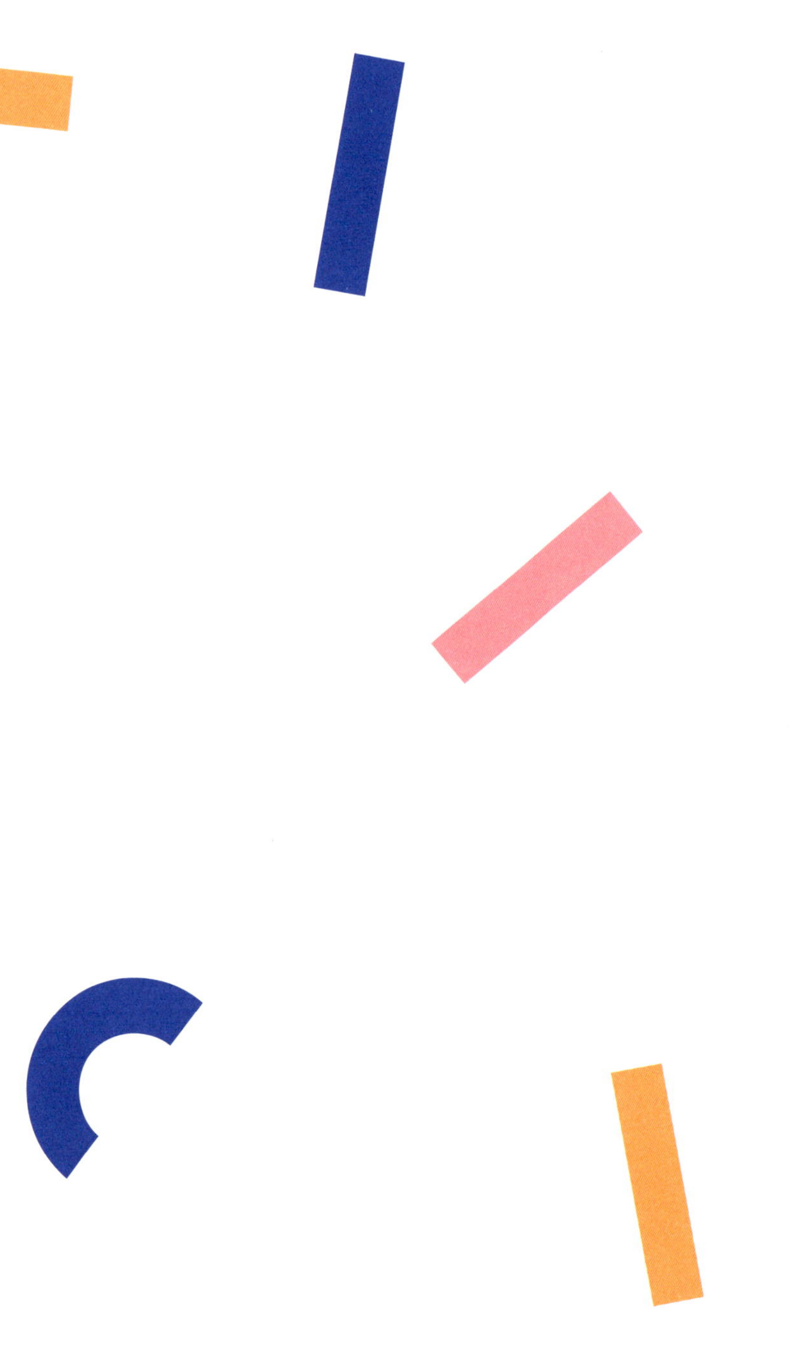

Models of learning sometimes appear at the margins of institutions and sanctioned structures, and often involve the imagination of artists and children collaborating. Tim Rollins's influential work with a group of teenagers in the Bronx (who became known as K.O.S., Kids of Survival) beginning in the early 1980s led to the creation of the Art & Knowledge Workshop, a collaborative approach to reading and writing that Rollins and K.O.S. brought across the country, including to the Institute of Contemporary Art/Boston in 1988. The 1987–88 painting *The Interior of the Heart* layers a series of red A's painted by Rollins and his young collaborators over a grid of pages from Nathaniel Hawthorne's 1850 book *The Scarlet Letter*. Carmen Winant's large-scale installation assembles more than three hundred instructional books intended for young people on subjects ranging from geography and ceramics to familial relationship-building. Her project traces the capacity of books and their images to travel, to teach outside of language, and to have unintended lives. Oscar Murillo's *Frequencies* project (2013–ongoing) totals some forty thousand canvases, each made by installing a blank canvas on a classroom desk and leaving it in place for a few months. Described by Murillo and his collaborators as inserting a free space into the school, the installations have taken place in more than thirty countries throughout the world, generating a vast collection that registers the presence and creative self-expression of students. Francis Alÿs's short videos *Children's Games* (begun 1999) depict children playing games across the world, including on a street in Mexico City, in the Sharya Refugee Camp in Iraq, and on a beach in Belgium. The videos record the valuable roles of such play as children learn to negotiate with one another and with larger societal structures; they also highlight the unique rituals and customs of each location, while representing the universal fact that children will find ways to play. These distinct projects illuminate unexpected paths of learning and the unique competencies of children and artists in navigating them. They also reveal the breadth of expression, play, and knowledge generated by and for children, reminding us that there is no single childhood but rather as many childhoods as there are children.

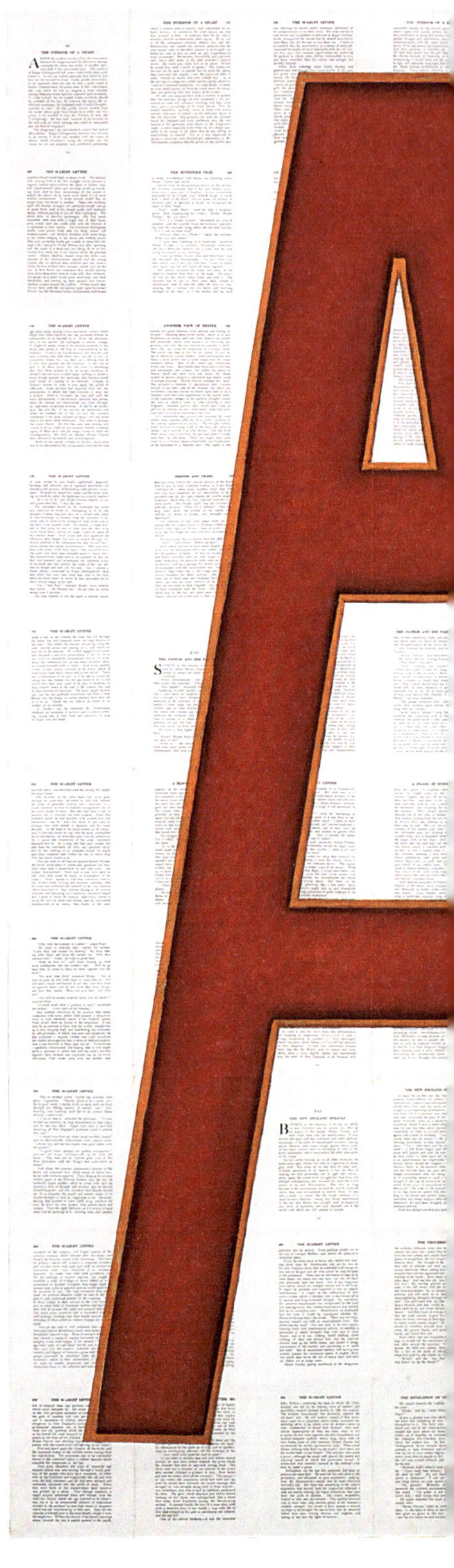

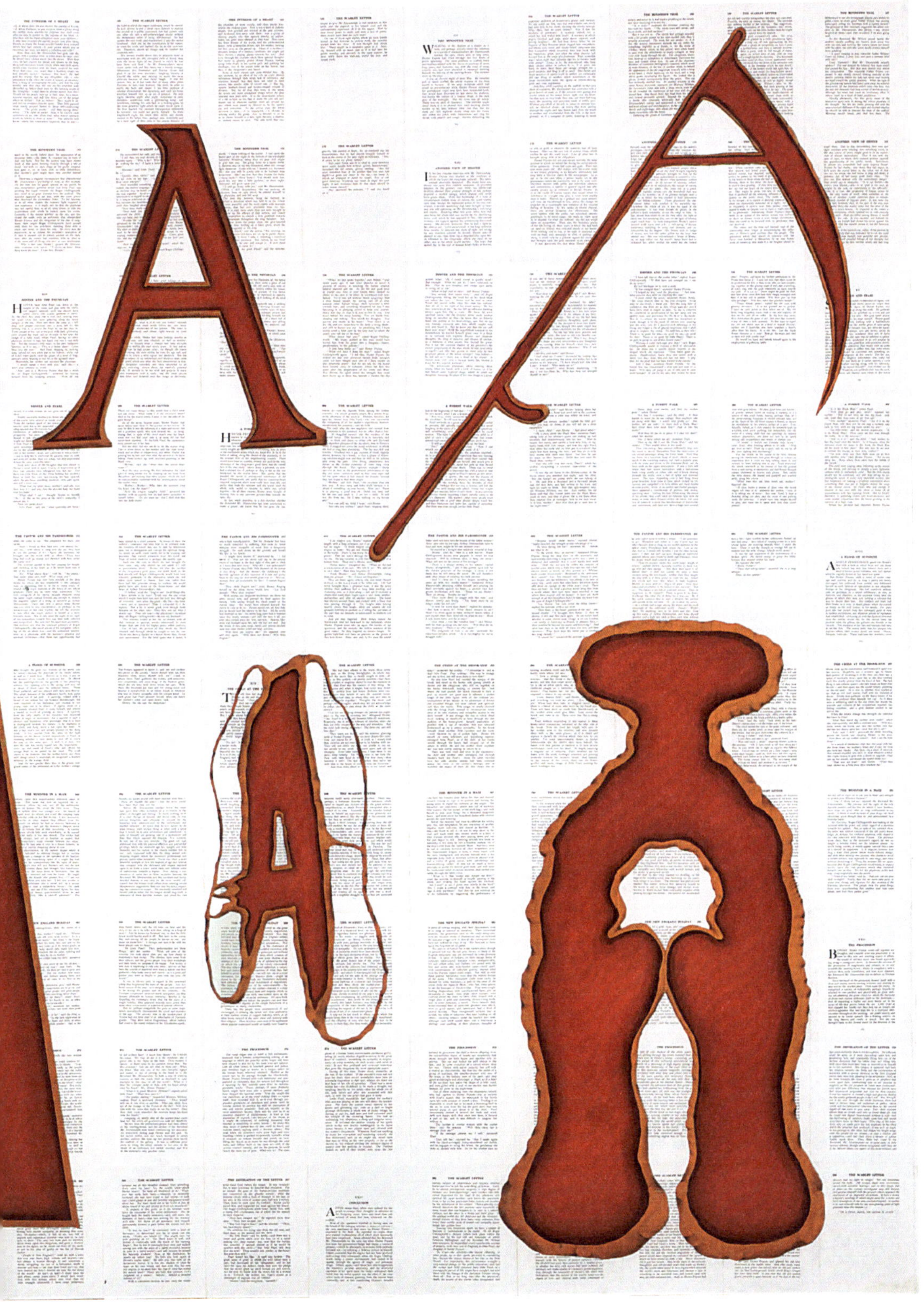

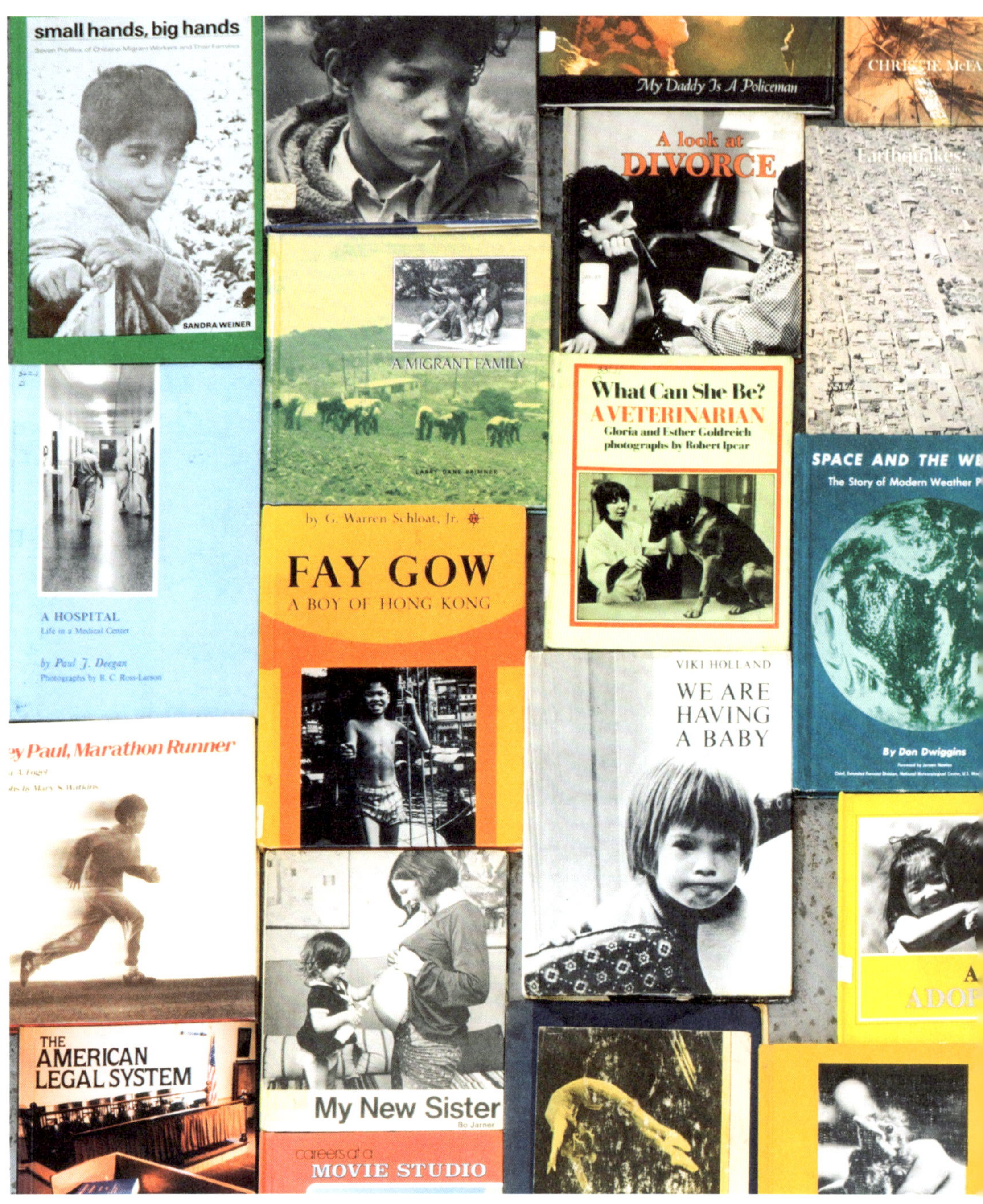
small hands, big hands
SANDRA WEINER
A MIGRANT FAMILY
My Daddy Is A Policeman
A look at DIVORCE
CHRISTIE McFA
Earthquakes:
A HOSPITAL
Life in a Medical Center
by Paul J. Deegan
Photographs by B. C. Ross-Larson
by G. Warren Schloat, Jr.
FAY GOW
A BOY OF HONG KONG
What Can She Be?
A VETERINARIAN
Gloria and Esther Goldreich
photographs by Robert Ipcar
SPACE AND THE WE
The Story of Modern Weather P
By Don Dwiggins
y Paul, Marathon Runner
VIKI HOLLAND
WE ARE
HAVING
A BABY
A
ADOP
THE AMERICAN LEGAL SYSTEM
My New Sister
Bo Jarner
careers at a
MOVIE STUDIO

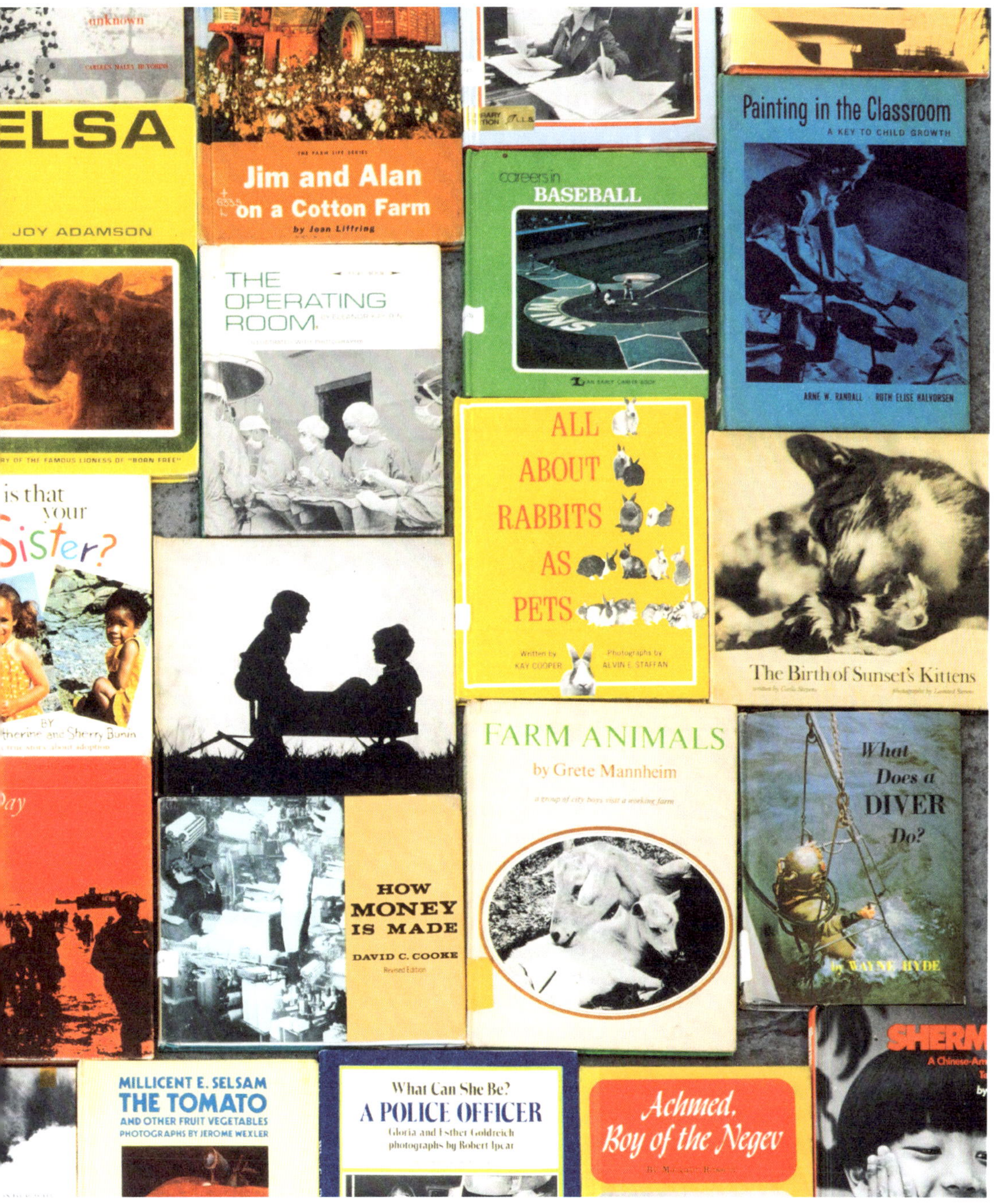

Carmen Winant
What it is like to be (details), 2022
Found books
Dimensions variable

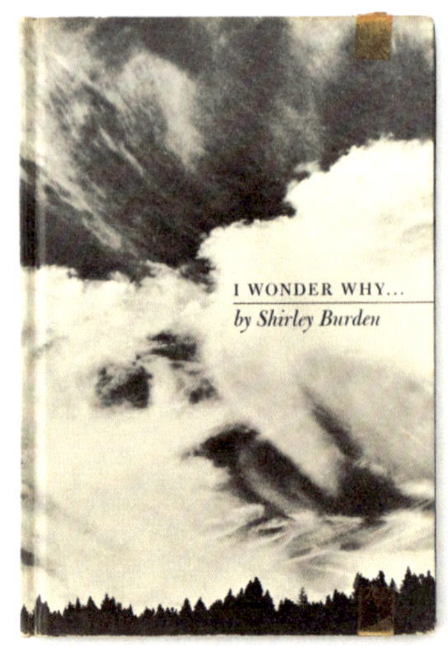

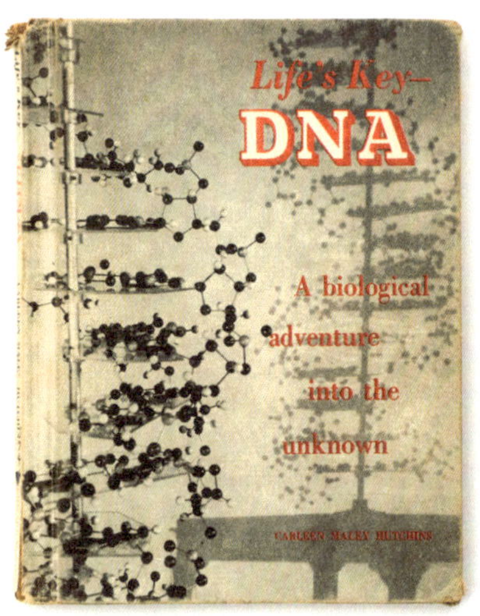

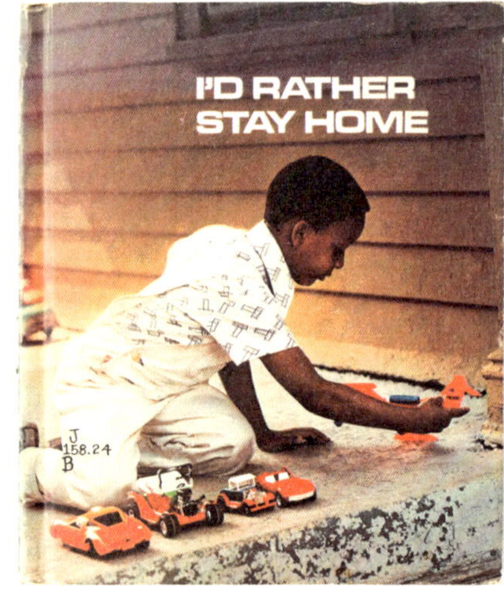

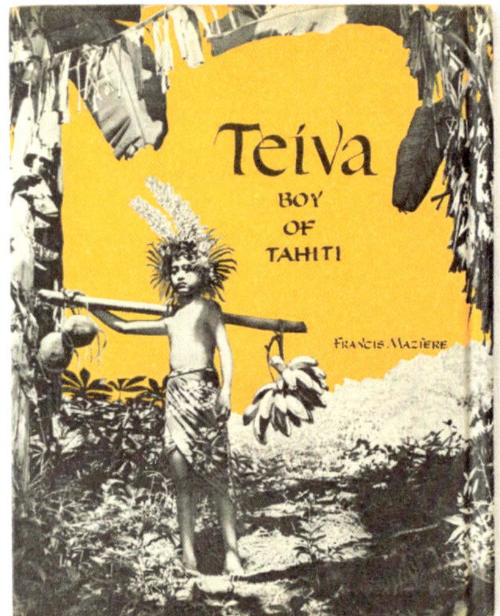

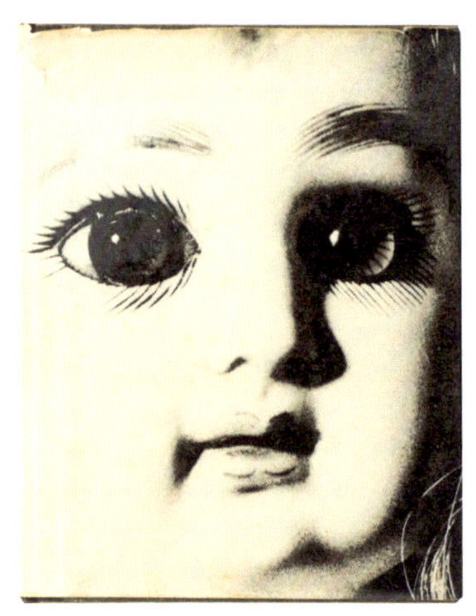

After School

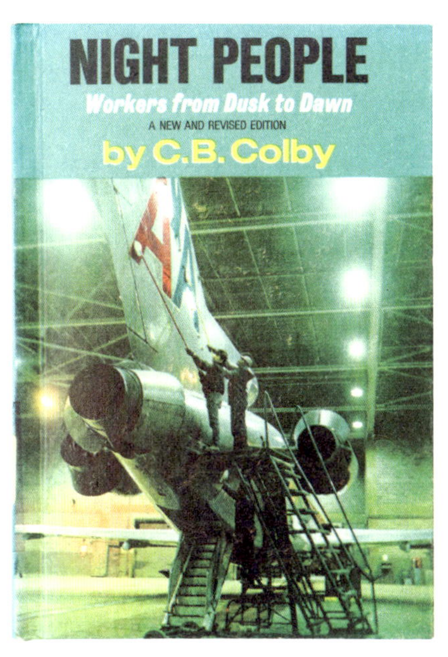
NIGHT PEOPLE
Workers from Dusk to Dawn
A NEW AND REVISED EDITION
by C.B. Colby

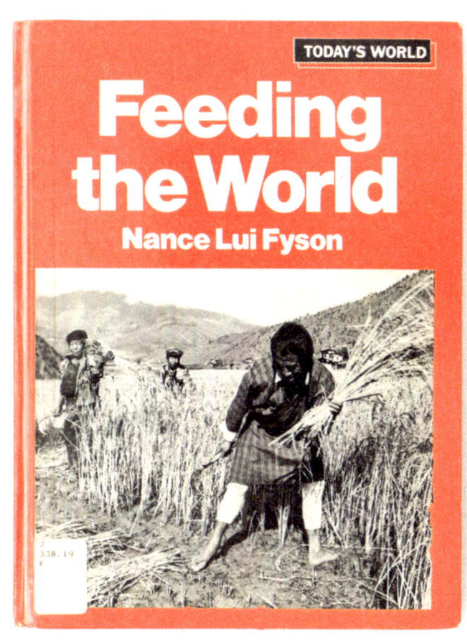
TODAY'S WORLD
Feeding the World
Nance Lui Fyson

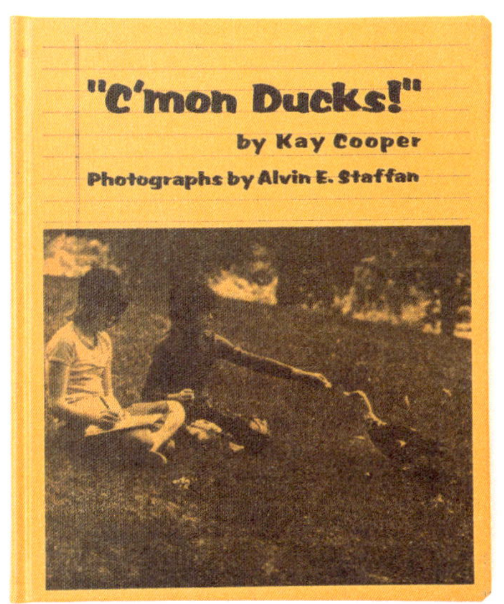
"C'mon Ducks!"
by Kay Cooper
Photographs by Alvin E. Staffan

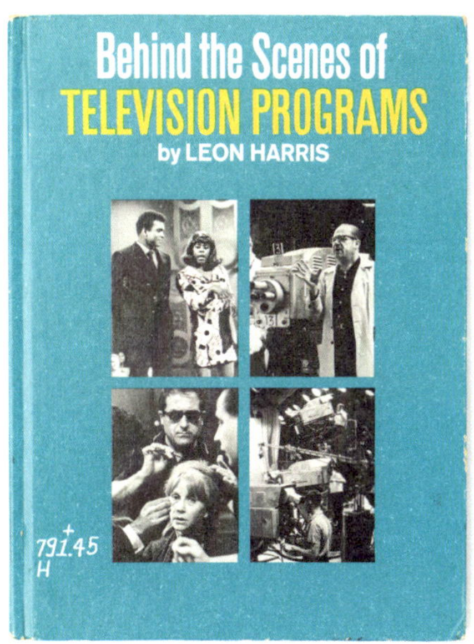
Behind the Scenes of
TELEVISION PROGRAMS
by LEON HARRIS
791.45
H

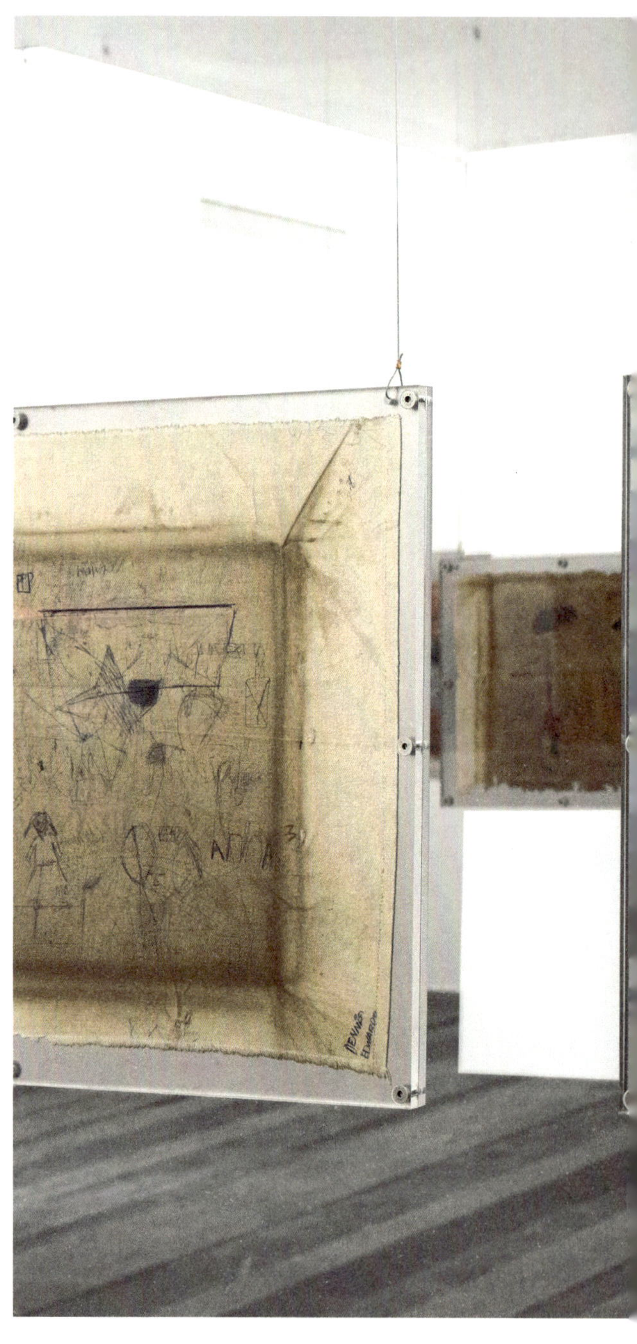

166   **After School**

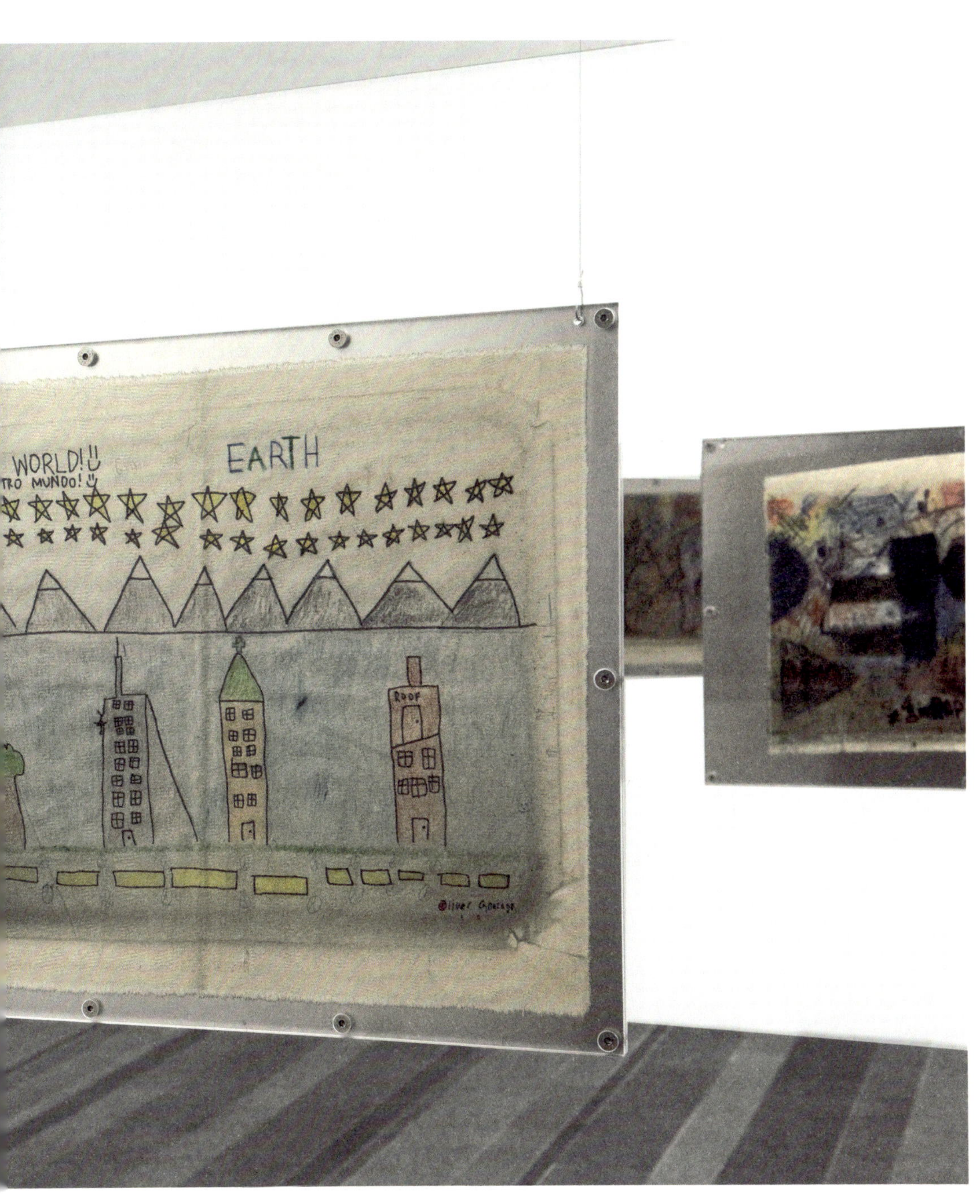
WORLD!!
TRO MUNDO!
EARTH
ROOF
Oliver Gonzaga

Oscar Murillo
Frequencies, 2013–ongoing (Yiyang, China, 2016)
Ballpoint pen, fountain pen, graphite, felt tip pen, highlighter pen,
permanent marker, paint, crayon, staples, natural pigments, debris,
and other mixed media on canvas
19 ¾ × 26 inches (50 × 66 cm)

Oscar Murillo
Frequencies, 2013–ongoing (Toyohashi, Japan, 2016)
Ballpoint pen, fountain pen, graphite, felt tip pen, highlighter pen,
permanent marker, paint, crayon, staples, natural pigments, debris,
and other mixed media on canvas
21 ¼ × 30 ¾ inches (54 × 78 cm)

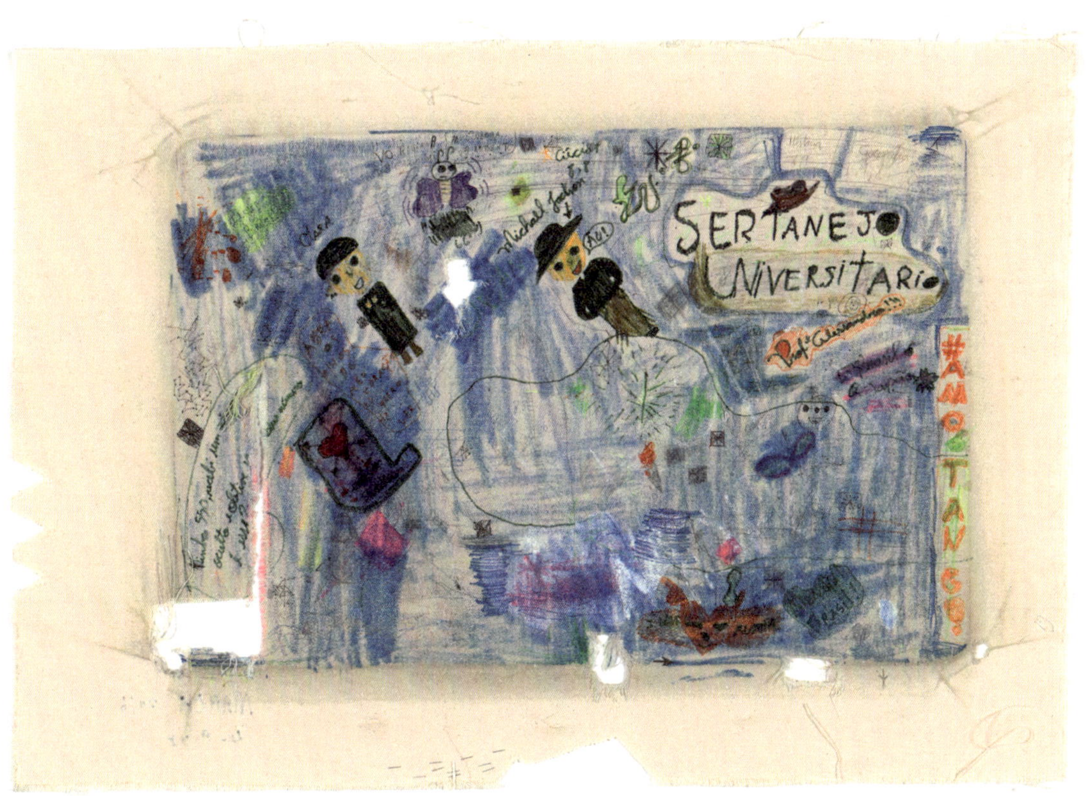

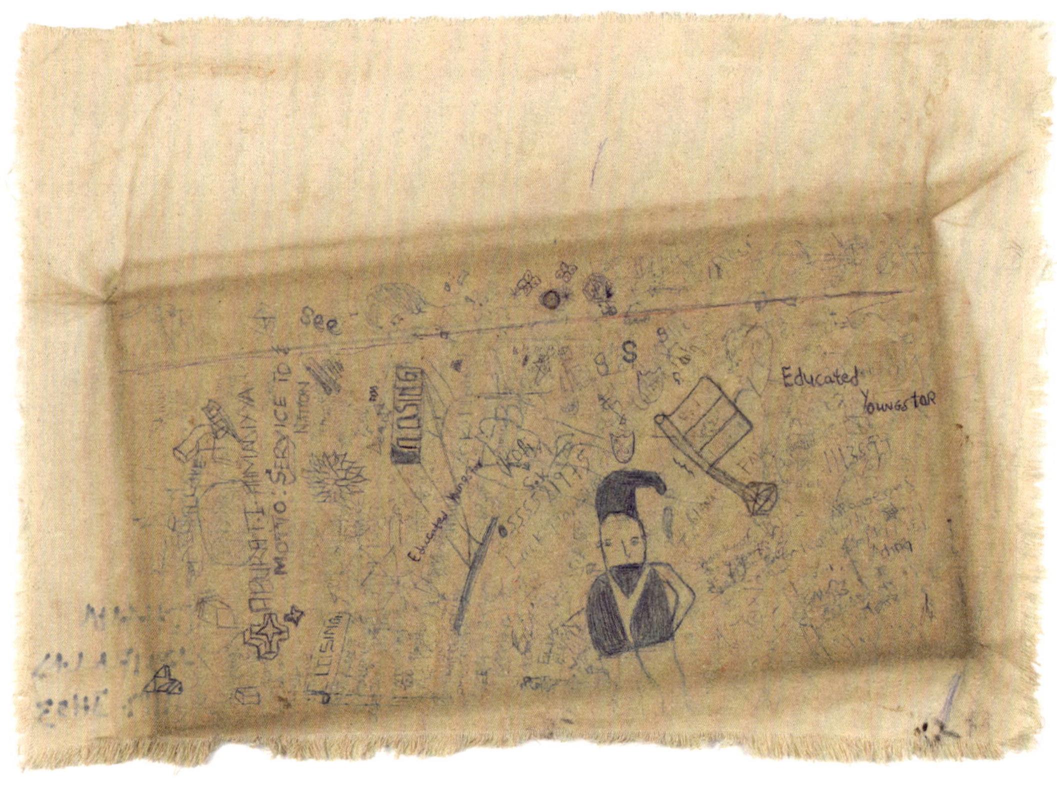

After School

Oscar Murillo
Frequencies, 2013–ongoing (Manila, Philippines, 2016)
Ballpoint pen, fountain pen, graphite, felt tip pen, highlighter pen,
permanent marker, paint, crayon, staples, natural pigments, debris,
and other mixed media on canvas
28 × 13 inches (71 × 33 cm)

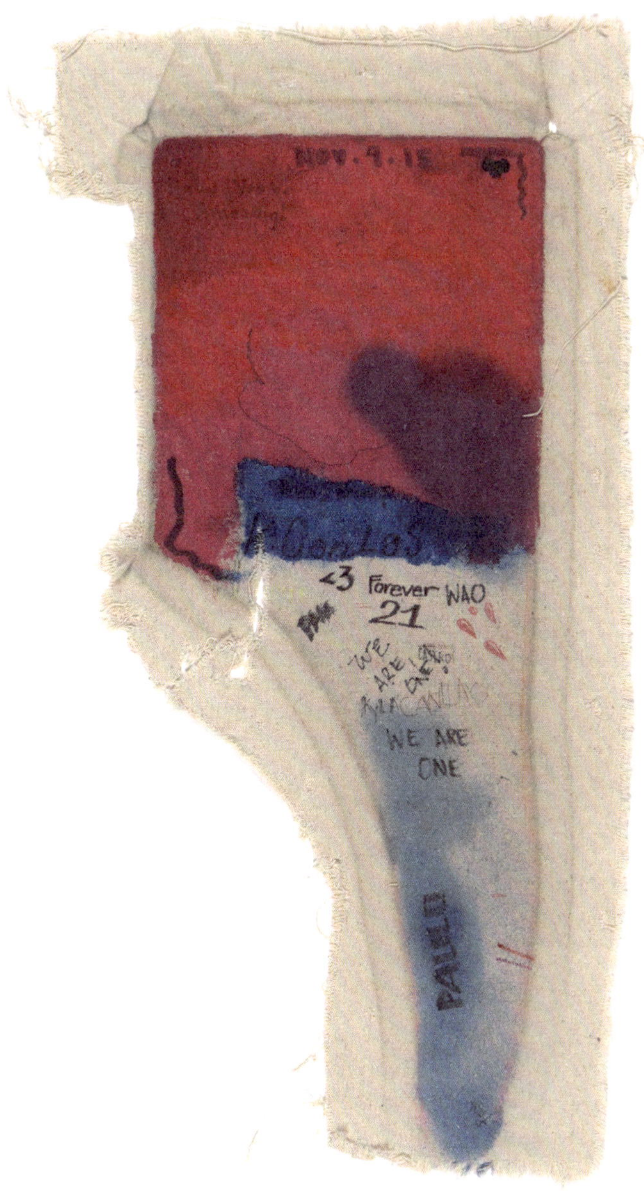

Francis Alÿs
Children's Game #1: Caracoles (Mexico City, Mexico) (still), 1999
Video (color, sound; 4:34 minutes)
In collaboration with Julien Devaux

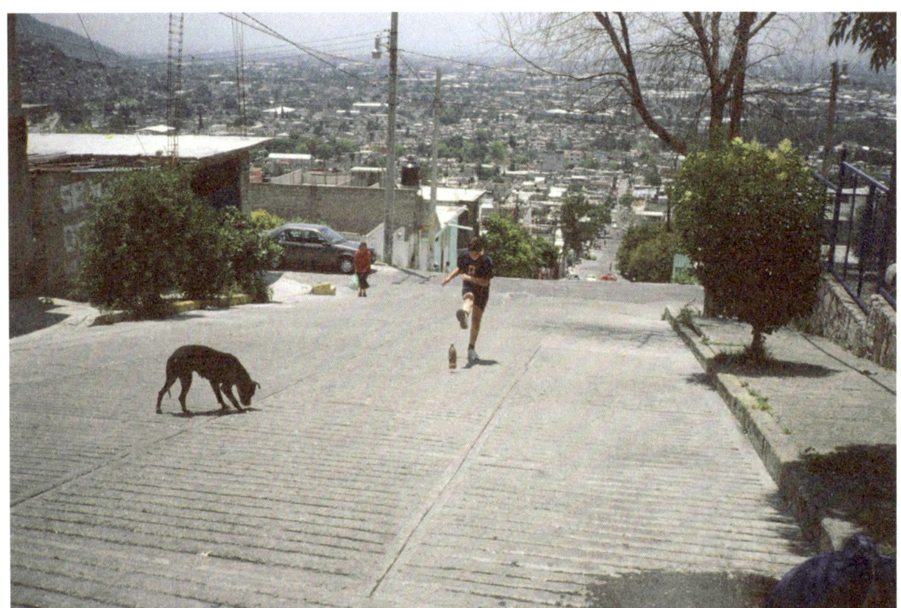

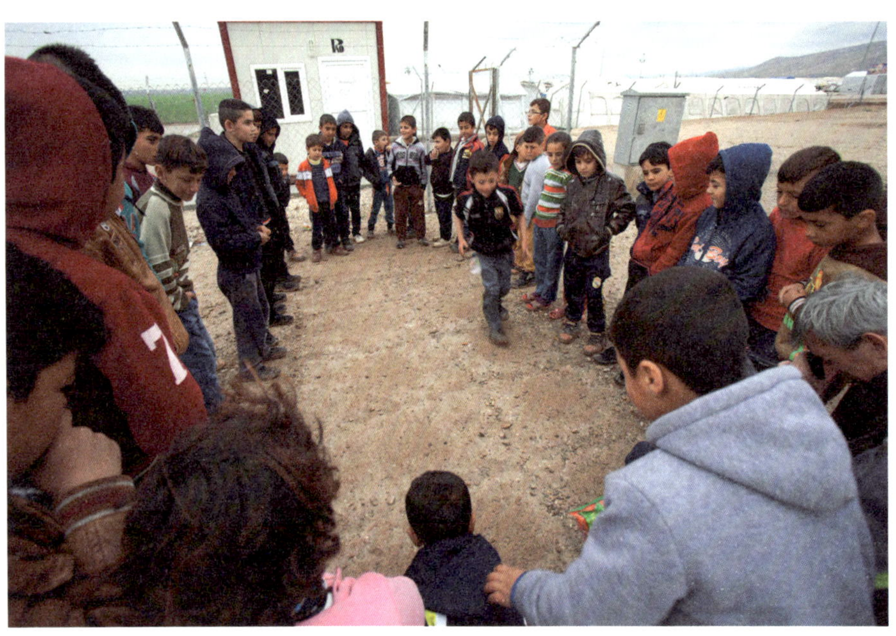

After School

Francis Alÿs
Children's Game #6: Sandcastles (Knokke-Le-Zoute, Belgium) (still), 2009
Video (color, sound; 6:04 minutes)
In collaboration with Julien Devaux, Cristian Manzutto, and Félix Blume

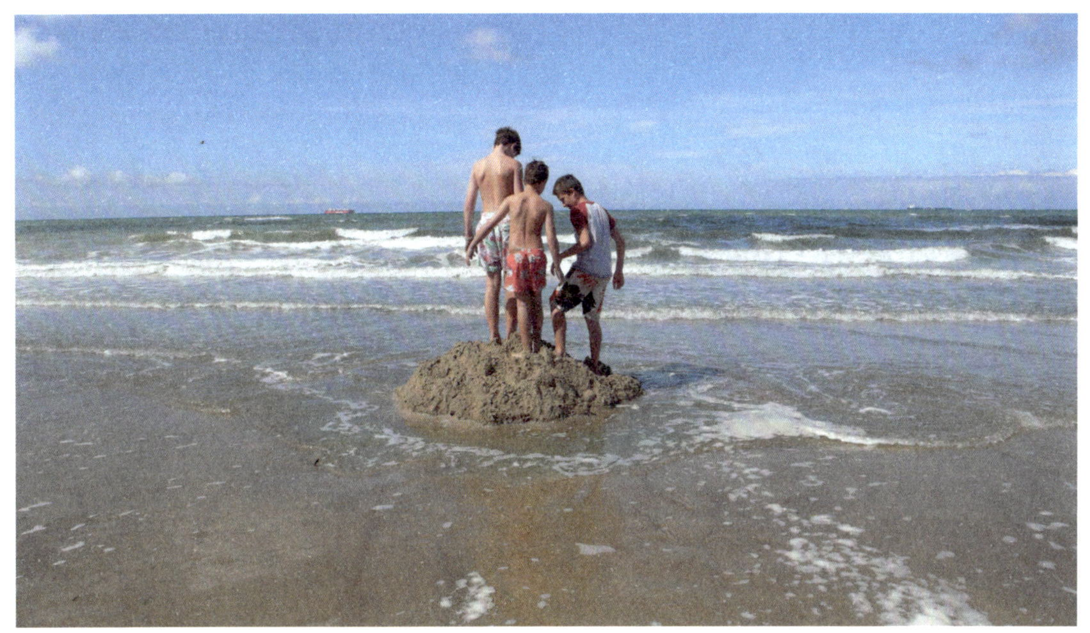

bottom left: **Francis Alÿs**
Children's Game #16: Hopscotch (Sharya Refugee Camp, Iraq) (still), 2016
Video (color, sound; 4:02 minutes)
In collaboration with Julien Devaux and Félix Blume

Francis Alÿs
Photograph taken during the filming of *Children's Game #16: Hopscotch
(Sharya Refugee Camp, Iraq)*, 2016
Video (color, sound; 4:02 minutes)
In collaboration with Julien Devaux and Félix Blume

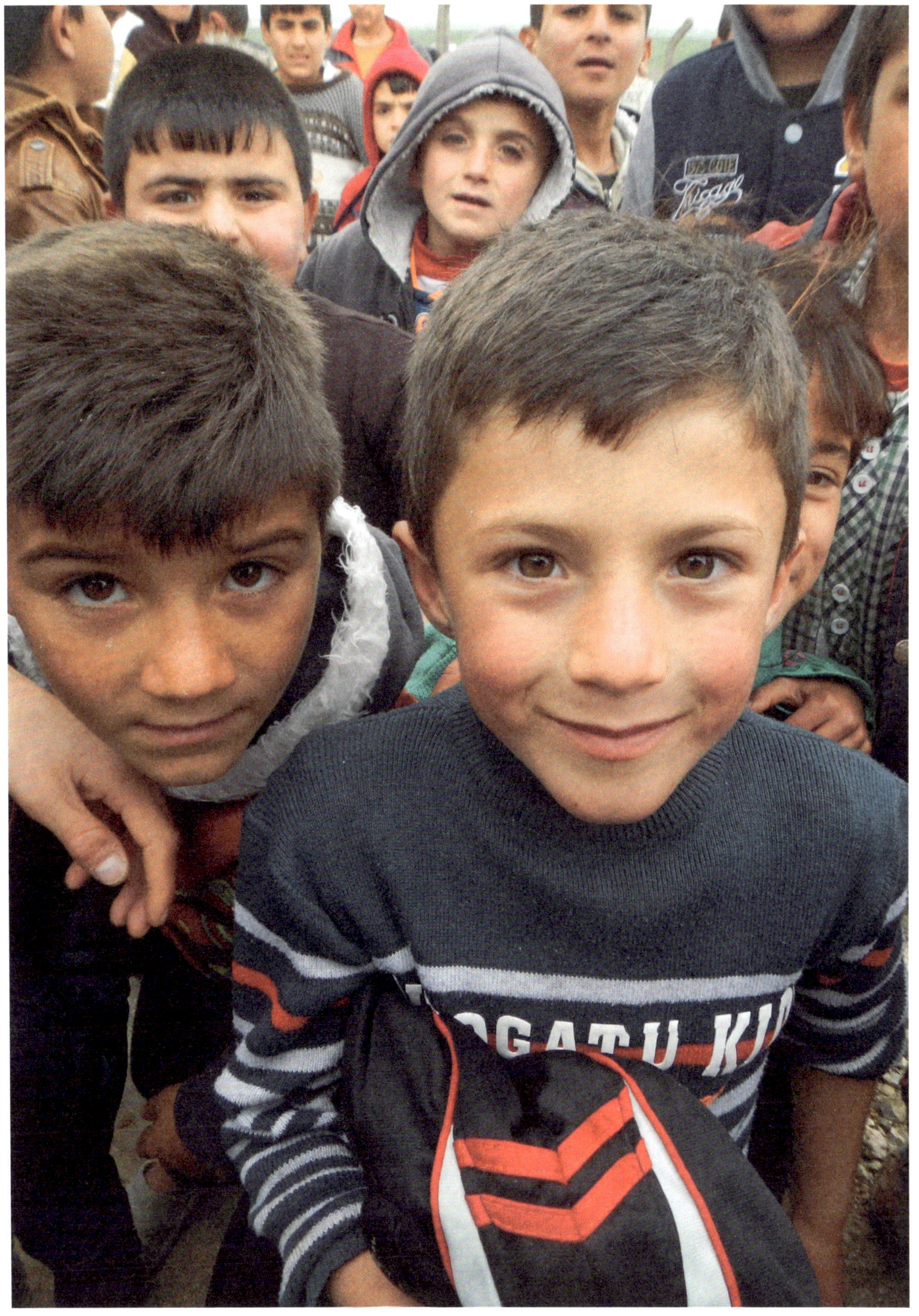

BeGin

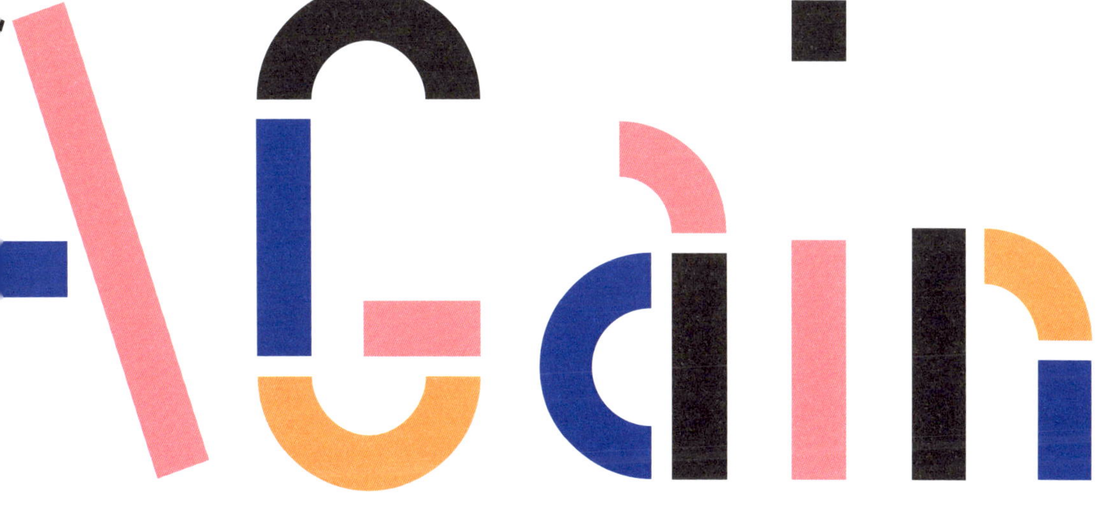
To
Again

Slightly Closer to the Heart of Creation than Usual, but Still Not Close Enough

Jeffrey De Blois

Paul Klee and Children's Art in European Modernism

In October of 1902, at the tender age of twenty-two and having recently completed training at the Academy of Fine Arts in Munich, Paul Klee returned to his parents' house in Bern, Switzerland, where he found a cache of his childhood drawings that had been saved and stored in the shed. The rediscovery of his childhood drawings was revelatory for the fledgling artist, who had been disappointed and uninspired by his traditional academic training. Writing to his fiancée, Lily Stumpf, Klee described these drawings as "among the most significant" of his to date.[1] Indeed, he later formalized this significance by entering eighteen drawings he made between the ages of three and ten into his handwritten "oeuvre catalogue," a methodical accounting of his artworks following an exacting process in which he signed, dated, titled, numbered, and mounted each of them to board. Like many artists, Klee consciously constructed a genealogy for his artistic development in the oeuvre catalogue, retroactively locating a meaningful point of origin for his vocation in his rediscovered childhood drawings.[2] A few months before he came across the drawings, almost as if to foretell things to come, Klee wrote in his diary: "I want to be as though newborn, to know nothing of Europe, nothing at all. Ignorant of poetry, wholly uninspired; to be almost primitive."[3]

Klee's artworks, writings, and lectures all evince a complicated relationship to the multivalent influence of children's art on his creative output, which changed for him over the course of his career. Throughout, however, his work repeatedly displayed an inventory of stylistic features often attributed to the drawings of children, such as scribbles and seemingly rudimentary mark-making; simplified forms, shapes, and compositions; and figures rendered geometrically or even reduced to stick forms. Klee's turn toward imitating the stylistic characteristics of children's art was part of a larger, decisive turn away from traditional training and academicism in art by vanguard modernists, for whom children's art exemplified romantic notions of innocence, immediacy, unencumbered vision, raw expressiveness, and unschooled authenticity. These artists pushed back against certain cultural values and dogmatic approaches to art-making that were long held to be incontrovertible but now, according to the artist Jean Dubuffet, began "to appear doubtful, and even quite false."[4] For the art historian Jonathan Fineberg, "the vanguard of the new century sought to peel back the layers of an overcultivated, fin-de-siècle Europe and discover what lay buried beneath that skillfully rendered facade."[5]

In 1911, the same year Klee entered his childhood drawings into his oeuvre catalogue, he famously wrote, in a review of the first exhibition by the group of German artists called Der Blaue Reiter (The Blue Rider), that "the primitive beginnings in art" can be found "in ethnographic collections or at home in one's nursery."[6] The following year, Klee was included in the second Blaue Reiter exhibition, and one of his works was reproduced in the group's almanac, alongside illustrations of thirteen children's drawings, Russian folk paintings, Egyptian puppets, Chinese paintings, Native American, African, and Oceanic artifacts, and more. It was not until 1923 that Klee first exhibited one of his own childhood drawings—*Man, ?, Chair, Hare* (1884; page 46), made at the age of five, which he presented alongside his current works.[7] A year later, in 1924, perhaps tiring of the extent to which the reception of his work was so often compared to children's art, Klee publicly addressed the issue in a lecture delivered in Jena, Germany: "The legend about the childishness of my drawing must have started with those of my linear compositions in which I tried to combine a concrete representation, let us say a man, with a pure use of the linear element."[8] Though he appears to have wanted to curtail the association of his art with that of children, such connections are evident right up until his death in 1940. Klee's epitaph, placed on his tombstone by his son Felix, is telling in this context; its final line

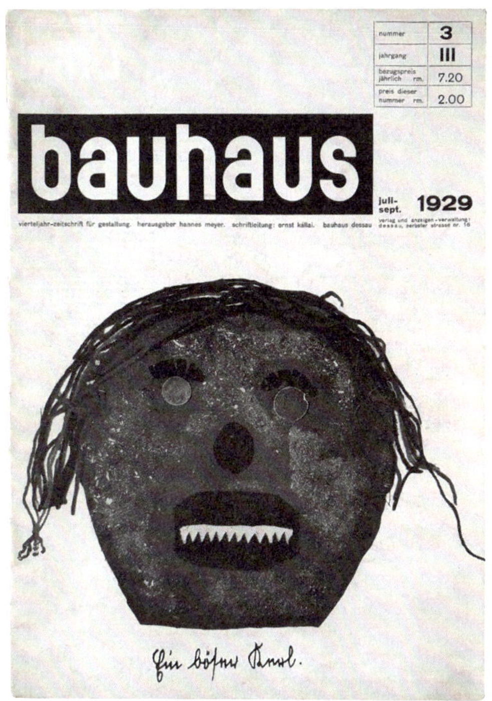

Fig. 1. Child's collage. *Bauhaus* 3, no. 3 (July–September 1929), cover

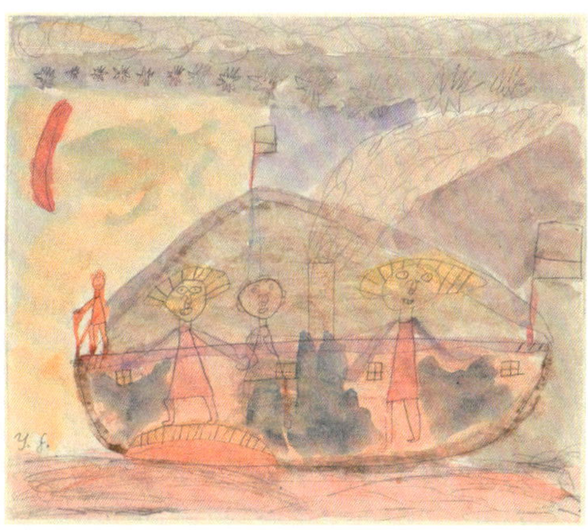

Fig. 2. Child from the class of Hans-Friedrich Geist, *Ohne Titel (Schiff mit drei Figuren und Steuermann* (Untitled [ship with three figures and helmsman]), ca. 1930. Pencil and watercolor on paper. 13 ⅜ × 15 ¾ inches (34 × 40 cm)

reads: "Slightly closer to the heart of creation than usual, but still not close enough."

Klee's sustained fascination with children's art and the search for "the heart of creation" are emblematic of broader, commonly held artistic concerns of early twentieth-century European modernism.[9] In addition to his affiliation with Der Blaue Reiter, he worked in close proximity to several defining movements in modern art, including Dada, cubism, and surrealism, each of which privileged some aspect of an idealized notion of childhood. Klee taught at the Bauhaus in Germany for ten years, from 1921 to 1931, during which time an exhibition of children's art was reportedly organized at the school by one of his former students, Lene Schmidt-Nonne. In the summer 1929 issue of *Bauhaus* magazine (fig. 1), which contains several articles on children's art, Schmidt-Nonne credits Klee with having influenced her interest in the subject.[10] Another contributor to that issue of the journal, the educational psychologist Hans-Friedrich Geist, later gifted a collection of children's watercolors to Klee for his fiftieth birthday (fig. 2).

Klee is but one of a number of predominantly male, white European modernists—including Jean (Hans) Arp, Jean Dubuffet, Joan Miró, Pablo Picasso, and many more—for whom children's art offered a unique direction in the search for the "primitive beginnings of art." Children's art, in this context, might be understood as one of what the art historian Hal Foster refers to as a "trio of exotics," alongside the problematic Western construct of "primitive" art and the art of individuals with psychiatric disorders, though adding "folk" art would form a more broadly representative quartet.[11] Each of these categories represents an "other" integral to the self-construction of several dominant, and still influential, strains of European modernism that depends, if not insists, on the passivity and lack of agency for a marginalized, de-subjectified subject.[12] Foster succinctly outlines the interrelated impulse to articulate a counterposition to now suspect European cultural formations as "modernist fantasies either of a pure origin of art or an absolute alterity to culture."[13]

In a similar vein, the art historian Rosalind E. Krauss elucidates this troublingly pervasive and culturally symptomatic equivalency at work in the 1926 book *Primitive Negro Sculpture* written by the Parisian art collector Paul Guillaume, who in 1914 was one of the first to display African sculpture as art in Europe. "What is insisted upon throughout the text," Krauss writes, "is the continuous presence of a will to art, an aesthetic drive that is understood to be originary, or primal. Preceding all ideas, religious or otherwise, this instinct is the joint possession of children of all races as well as those 'children' of the human race: primitive men and women."[14] Likewise, in his 1930 comparative study of children's drawings and "primitive" art, the philosopher and Freemason Georges-Henri Luquet concluded that "these artistic works, whose common characteristic is their opposition to the works of civilized adults, can legitimately be united into a single genre, suited by the name of primitive art."[15] Against the backdrop of such charged equivalencies—which in the case at least of Luquet lay claim to a sense of legitimacy afforded by rigorous analysis—the modernist fascination with the "other" in which children's art figured prominently comes into focus. These fantasies about children's art must therefore be understood in part as interwoven with the broader context of a prevailing racist and colonialist European worldview.

The ability to fantasize (a privilege long enjoyed by male artists) and the perceived necessity of othering to establish a way out of dubious cultural formations are also part of what was a protracted crisis in the symbolic order of European culture. According to the art historian Joyce S. Cheng, primitivism is a "critical machine . . . arguably at its most powerful in the period between the two world wars, when its primary target—the life forms and values of the secular, industrial-capitalist societies of western Europe—faced the possibility of total collapse."[16] At a historical moment defined in many ways by this crisis in the symbolic order, an idealized notion of childhood and children's art functioned for artists like Klee as an aesthetic model and a stylistic device that offered a way out, but one that was still fraught with and overburdened by a colonialist and racist paradigm. As such, the legacy of the function of childhood and children's art in European modernism is one that is still largely unresolved, a fact with which artists working today have to contend.

Children's Art in an Expanded Field

Today, approaches to children's art take diverse forms, and artists are often keenly aware of the complex dynamics inherited from modernism that surface in their work sometimes obliquely. Like Klee, Trenton Doyle Hancock returned home from college in his early twenties to discover a cache of hundreds of childhood drawings he saved for himself in the attic of his parents' house. What he found provided the jumping-off point for the complex mythology and world-building at the center of his practice. In 1984, at the age of ten, thanks mostly to his Auntie Fan Fan, who taught him to draw at the age of three, Hancock imagined himself as a superhero named Torpedoboy. In pencil drawings on notebook paper, a young Hancock turns into Torpedoboy, flies, and fights a bear, aliens, killer plants, and a giant (pages 84–87). On seeing these early drawings, Hancock felt compelled to reconsider the characters he had imagined as a child, the profound possibilities of which he is still exploring today. These are now enshrined in the myth around Torpedoboy, who in Hancock's narrative has been around for seven hundred years: "Around the year 1973, Torpedoboy's body dissipated and his consciousness was transferred to the unborn child of an Oklahoma City schoolteacher, Carolyn Joyce Hancock. The child, Trenton Doyle Hancock, was born and, when he came of age, resumed the role of Torpedoboy."[17]

Around the time he rediscovered his childhood drawings, Hancock came in contact with back issues of *Raw* magazine, where he was exposed to the work of Henry Darger and Chéri Samba, and other artists from graphic culture such as Gary Panter, who attended the same college as Hancock. Hancock was particularly influenced by Darger's fifteen-thousand-page *The Story of the Vivian Girls, in What Is Known as the Realms of the Unreal, of the Glandeco-Angelinnian War Storm, Caused by the Child Slave Rebellion* (pages 80–83), illustrated in several hundred scroll-like watercolors and collage paintings with figures repurposed from children's books, magazines, or comics. This use of materials and visual information, and especially Darger's elaborate creation of an alternate world, were empowering of Hancock's own proclivities for narrative and mythmaking.[18]

For Hancock, Torpedoboy addresses a specific exclusion in broader American culture: that Black kids like himself were largely missing from children's literature. And not just books; they were also missing in other popular forms such as lines of toys and comic books. Hancock felt as if he had been "brainwashed into thinking Black characters were tertiary. On a deep level [Torpedoboy] was about seeing something I didn't see before."[19] In that sense, Torpedoboy is an assertion of presence, and this presence can evoke a living complexity: despite his superhero strength, his "near genius intellect" is "dampened by his inflated ego and lack of common sense."[20] Across a staggering array of media—drawings, paintings (page 89), sculptures, installations, tableaux, dolls (page 91), toys, trading cards, comics, graphic novels, and more—Hancock follows the blueprint he established as a child, and honored as a young adult, to breathe life into an alternate universe capacious enough for him to explore timeless questions. The seeds were planted by his childhood imagination, and he continues to tend to them as an adult who pays homage to and values his younger self.

Brian Belott is also the son of a schoolteacher, and he has described how even as a young person he would go to his mother's classroom at the end of the school year to rescue children's art from its "inevitable trajectory" into the trash can.[21] Belott's deep and manifold engagement with children's art is inspired by a prevailing interest in ideas of amateurism, which found new expression when he came into contact with the work of Rhoda Kellogg (fig. 3). Kellogg was a suffragette, an educator, an early childhood scholar, and perhaps the world's leading collector of children's art. The Rhoda Kellogg International Child Art Collection, with artworks numbering in the hundreds of thousands if not millions, is an extensive collection amassed from

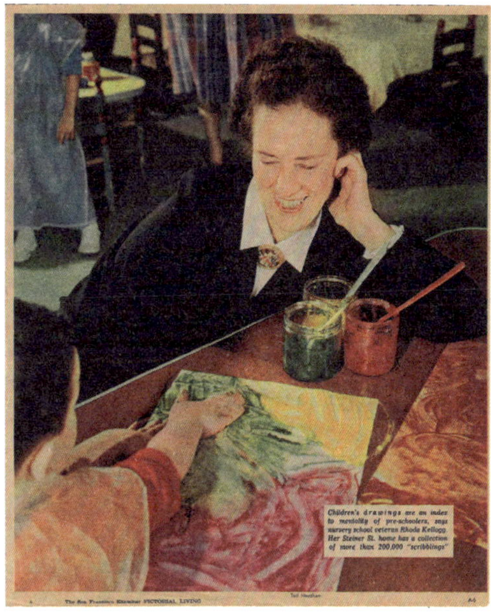

Fig. 3. Rhoda Kellogg pictured in the *San Francisco Examiner*, ca. mid-to-late 1960s

Kellogg's travel to more than thirty countries and through her work at the Phoebe A. Hearst Preschool Learning Center in San Francisco, which she designed and founded in 1966.[22] Kellogg's rigorous study of children's art convinced her that "children in all cultures follow the same graphic evolution in their drawing, from scribbles through certain basic forms, and that children's art can be a key to understanding the mental growth and educational needs of children."[23] Kellogg fleshed these theories out in a series of books, including *What Children Scribble and Why* (1955)—which Belott describes as Kellogg's first attempt "to put the science on this storm of the scribble"[24]—and later *The Psychology of Children's Art* (1967, with Scott O'Dell) and *Analyzing Children's Art* (1969), a compendium of her ideas about children's art. Kellogg's overriding concern throughout her work was the health and development of the child, not some notion of the "will to art."

Belott is now co-custodian of the Child Art Collection with Jennifer DiGioia, an early childhood educator who took up the mantle of advocate at Kellogg's Phoebe A. Hearst Preschool Learning Center. Belott also works with the collection as an archivist, advocate, curator, artist, and interloper who frequently makes forgeries of the children's

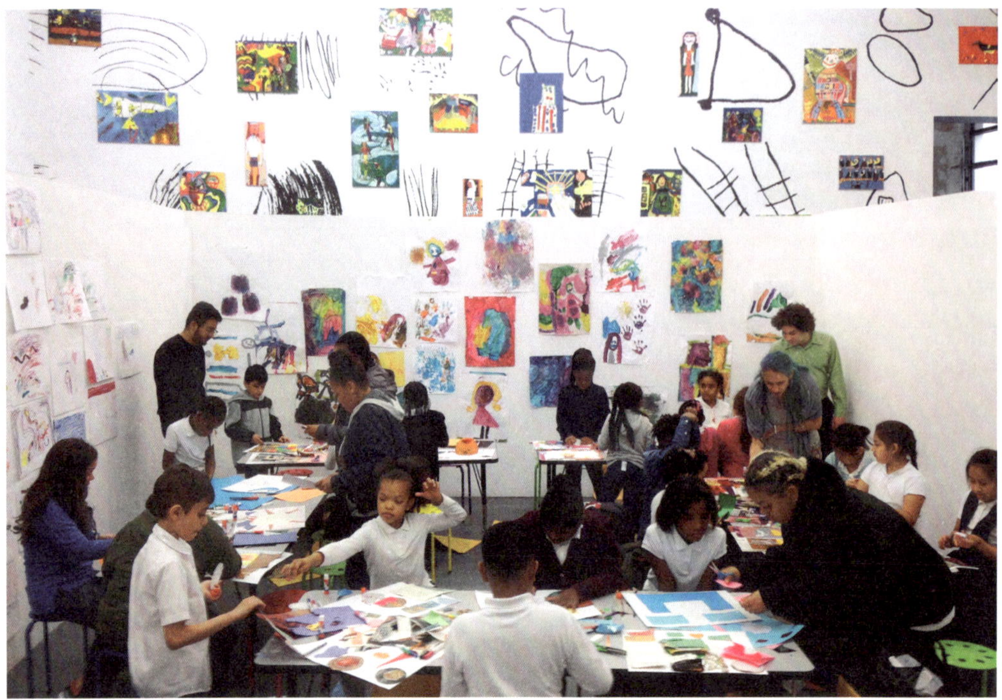

Fig. 4. Installation view, *Brian Belott: Dr. Kid President Jr. 2*, Gavin Brown's enterprise, New York, 2017

art that he lovingly refers to as "failures." Copying the children's art was part of Kellogg's almost ethnographic approach to her collection, and she would trace works over and over in an attempt to apprehend their pictorial development. Kellogg's own artworks, which she developed later in life, stemmed from the innumerable copies she made as part of her obsessive drive to understand child development through comparison of one child's work to another, or that of a single child over a long period of time.

Belott's installations visualize a sometimes bizarre and layered triangulation between children's art from the collection, Kellogg's tracings, and his own failed attempts to imitate the "whimsical, slapdash, hit and run" works of children.[25] The installations insist at once on letting children's art stand on its own, on the driving necessity and historical importance of Kellogg's life's work, and on the impossibility that the trained adult artist can capture the vitality of children's art. Belott staged this triangulation in his 2017 exhibition *Dr. Kid President Jr. 2* at Gavin Brown's enterprise in Harlem, the first time a large selection from Kellogg's collection was exhibited; he furthermore included, in the heart

                                                                 De Blois

of the exhibition, a classroom for open-ended, walk-in art-making sessions for New York City children, whose works were hung on the walls and accumulated throughout the run of the show (fig. 4). Channeling the pedagogical spirit of Kellogg, who asserted that "our aesthetic sense is biological" and that adults should take a hands-off approach toward children's art-making,[26] *Dr. Kid President Jr. 2* modeled a dynamic understanding of children's art in the present, one that simply yet radically values it on its own terms for its aesthetic possibilities, regardless of adult proclivities. The child is allowed a sense of agency and autonomy that was often denied in early modernist appropriations of children's art.

In 2013 Oscar Murillo returned to the school he had attended as a child in La Paila, Colombia, where he was inspired by the densely graffitied wooden desks he found there. This motivated the artist to initiate what would quickly become a globally scaled project called *Frequencies*. Murillo, in close collaboration with his family and studio team, set about wrapping school desks in classrooms around the world with a blank canvas, inviting students to freely draw, write, or otherwise leave their mark, or not, over a period of several months. An artist whose painterly work has often been associated with childlike mark-making, Murillo imagines *Frequencies* as a collaborative project rooted in the poetics of relation articulated by the Martinican writer, poet, and philosopher Édouard Glissant. In the context of *Frequencies*, Murillo is drawn particularly to Glissant's idea of horizontality, which offers a model for thinking about mutually held values across categorizations that does not privilege any position above another. Murillo's collaborative project therefore extends beyond the artist himself and any individual student to include all students who sit at a given desk, or even to the natural environment of some schools, where exposure to the elements causes the canvases to gather a patina.

Like Kellogg's collection of child art, Murillo's collection is extensive: before its first phase was brought to a close during the global COVID-19 pandemic, *Frequencies* was taken to 350 schools in more than thirty countries and grew to encompass some forty thousand individual canvases (pages 166–71). When the archive is activated through its exhibition, it functions like a kind of map of global childhoods whose borders and characteristics are imagined anew each time canvases from the collection are differently installed. At times Murillo selects which canvases are to be shown; at other times the canvases are displayed as a living archive in stacks or on tables for visitors to leaf through, encouraging them to draw their own connections through intimate encounters. Many presentations also include what Murillo refers to as an agora—a place of community, of events and educational workshops—where the interpretation of the archive is collectively performed in real time, often by young people themselves. Recently, Murillo has engaged groups of young people to periodically reinstall new selections of canvases during the run of a show; he considers this a means for "agitating the archive through the physical gesture of selection."[27] Murillo himself began intervening in the collection by sewing together select canvases to create supports for large-scale paintings in his signature expressionistic style, enacting a kind of violence he sees as always latent in the act of choosing works from the archive for exhibition.

Frequencies Foundation (now Frequencies Institute) was founded by Murillo at the outset of the project, as a space where all the school relationships and social interactions could be held. The Institute now functions as a home for the archive, for research and reflection on the project, and for the development of new strategies for dissemination of the archive. In the same way that Kellogg's collection has been opened up by Belott's relentless curiosity and depth of engagement, scholars studying the *Frequencies* trove will enrich our understandings of children's art and its significance, speaking in different voices and from a range of perspectives, to move, as Murillo says, "from volume to meaning."[28]

Even as modernism's often essentializing approach to children's art casts a long shadow on artists working today, their envisioning of new modes of critical engagement and expansive possibilities for children's art moves it into an expanded field. No longer searching with reckless abandon for the "heart of creation," artists such as Hancock, Belott, Murillo, and many others are consciously aware of the fraught politics at work in the historical idealizations of children's art widespread in the early twentieth century. Instead, these contemporary artists open up new pathways that bring us still closer to understanding the cultural value of children's art by meeting it on its own terms.

My sincere thanks to Samuel Adams, Fabienne Eggelhöfer, Anni Pullagura, and Rachel Tang for their support on aspects of this essay.

1

Paul Klee to Lily Stumpf, October 3, 1902, in *Paul Klee: Briefe an die Familie, 1893–1940*, ed. Felix Klee, 2 vols. (Cologne, 1979), 1:273, quoted in Marcel Franciscono, "Paul Klee and Children's Art," in *Discovering Child Art: Essays on Childhood, Primitivism, and Modernism*, ed. Jonathan Fineberg (Princeton, NJ: Princeton University Press, 1998), 96.

2

Klee further narrativized his artistic development by crediting his grandmother, Frau Frick, with teaching him "very early to draw with crayons." Paul Klee, "Memories of Childhood," in *The Diaries of Paul Klee, 1898–1918*, ed. Felix Klee (Berkeley: University of California Press, 1964), 4. It is noteworthy that women have been foundational to the early artistic development of many artists, including Klee, Trenton Doyle Hancock, Brian Belott, and others outside of those discussed here.

3

Paul Klee, Tagebücher 1898–1918, text-kritische Neuedition, ed. Wolfgang Kersten (Stuttgart: Paul-Klee-Stiftung, Kunstmuseum Bern, 1988), 153. This English translation is quoted from *Paul Klee: I Want to Know Nothing* (Bern: Zentrum Paul Klee, 2021), 3.

4

Jean Dubuffet, "Anticultural Positions," in *Dubuffet and the Anticulture* (New York: Richard L. Feigen & Co., 1969), insert, 1; the text was originally delivered as a lecture in English at the Arts Club of Chicago, December 20, 1951.

5

Jonathan Fineberg, "Reawakening the Beginnings: The Art of Paul Klee," in *The Innocent Eye: Children's Art and the Modern Artist* (Princeton, NJ: Princeton University Press, 1997), 82.

6

Klee, *Diaries of Paul Klee*, 266.

7

Paul Klee: I Want to Know Nothing, 11.

8

Paul Klee, "Survey and Orientation in Regard to Pictorial Elements and Their Spatial Arrangement," in *Paul Klee Notebooks, Volume 1: The Thinking Eye*, ed. Jürg Spiller (London: Lund Humphries, 1961), 95.

9

While the focus here is on European modernism, following the works included in the exhibition, children's art was also significant in the development of strands of American modernism. For example, between 1912 and 1916, Alfred Stieglitz's "291" gallery hosted four exhibitions of children's art, perhaps influenced by the *Blaue Reiter Almanac*, which was known in his circle at that time. Stieglitz's influential journal *Camera Work* planned an issue dedicated to "Children's Work, in pictures and in words," that was never published. See Debra Bricker Balken, *Debating American Modernism: Stieglitz, Duchamp, and the New York Avant-Garde* (New York: American Federation of Arts; Distributed Art Publishers, 2003), 56, and Sarah Archino, "The Critical Deployment of Amateurism in 1910s New York," in *Panorama: Journal of the Association of Historians of American Art 5*, no. 1 (Spring 2019), https://doi.org/10.24926/24716839.1686.

10

Lene Schmidt-Nonne, "Kinder-
zeichnungen," *Bauhaus* 3, no. 3 (July–
September 1929): 13–16.

11

Hal Foster, "Blinded Insights: On the
Modernist Reception of the Art of the
Mentally Ill," *October* 97 (Summer 2001):
3n1. The term "primitive" was understood
to be "improper" as early as 1927, following Olivier Leroy's discussion of French
sociologist Lucien Lévy-Bruhl, who wrote
about the "primitive mind" in *Les fonctions
mentales dans les sociétés inférieure*s (1910),
translated as *How Natives Think*, in which
he characterized the two basic mindsets
of humankind as "the primitive" and "the
modern." See Olivier Leroy, *La raison
primitive: Essai de réfutation de la théorie du
prélogisme* (Paris: Librairie Orientaliste Paul
Geuthner, 1927), 16, and Joyce S. Cheng,
"Primitivisms," in *Neolithic Childhood:
Art in a False Present, c. 1930*, ed. Anselm
Franke and Tom Holert (Zurich: Diaphanes;
Berlin: Haus der Kulturen der Welt, 2018),
187. According to Joshua I. Cohen, "Under
scrutiny, 'primitivism' comes to appear
conspicuously limited, for its concerns
rarely exceed the confines of a Western van-
tage point. At once a tacit endorsement of
so-called primitive art and a privileging of
'primitivists,' the concept mainly coheres for
the purposes of rehearsing Western exoti-
cism and Western art history. While these
remain valid topics, 'primitivism' delimits
its subject matter as their exclusive purview,
under the pretext of historical accuracy."
Cohen, *The "Black Art" Renaissance: African
Sculpture and Modernisms across Continents*
(Oakland: University of California Press,
2020), 7. In this context, "primitivism" is
employed as a historically delimited comparative tool, albeit one weighted with significant baggage, that nevertheless allows for
a better understanding of how children's art
was positioned in the construction of certain
strains of modernism. This is especially the
case given that children's art is significantly
underanalyzed compared to primitivism,
though they were frequently equated.

12

Cheng, "Primitivisms," 185.

13

Foster, "Blinded Insights," 3.

14

Rosalind E. Krauss, "No More Play," in
*The Originality of the Avant-Garde and Other
Modernist Myths* (Cambridge, MA: MIT
Press, 1985), 52.

15

Georges-Henri Luquet, *L'Art primitif*,
Encyclopédie scientifique, Bibliothèque
d'Anthropologie (Paris: G. Doin, 1930), vol.
13, quoted in Georges Bataille, "Primitive
Art," in Bataille, *The Cradle of Humanity:
Prehistoric Art and Culture*, ed. Stuart
Kendall, trans. Michelle Kendall and Stuart
Kendall (New York: Zone Books, 2005), 35.

16

Cheng, "Primitivisms," 185.

17

Trenton Doyle Hancock, *The Trenton Doyle
Hancock Handbook* (New York: Picture
Box, 2006), 16.

18

Brooke Davis Anderson, "Vegans and
Vivian Girls: Mythology and Grand
Thinking in the Work of Trenton Doyle
Hancock and Henry Darger," in *Trenton
Doyle Hancock: Skin and Bones, 20 Years
of Drawing*, ed. Valerie Cassel Oliver
(Houston: Contemporary Arts Museum,
Houston, 2014), 27.

19

Trenton Doyle Hancock, conversation with
the author, June 16, 2021.

20
Hancock, *The Trenton Doyle Hancock
Handbook*, 16–17.

21
Brian Belott, Radcliffe Institute for
Advanced Study at Harvard University
exploratory seminar "Access Points:
Children, Artists, and Museums," October
15, 2021, transcript, 85.

22
The total number of artworks making up
the Rhoda Kellogg International Child
Art Collection is not known today, as the
complete collection was never fastidiously
maintained. Much of the collection is
housed in a storage unit in Connecticut,
while large portions are now cared for
by Belott in a dedicated studio space in
Brooklyn, New York.

23
"History: Rhoda Kellogg," Phoebe A.
Hearst Preschool Learning Center,
accessed December 12, 2021, https://
phoebehearstpreschool.org/history
/rhoda-kellogg/.

24
Belott, "Access Points," 92.

25
Belott, 89.

26
Rhoda Kellogg interview on KPFA radio,
Berkeley, date unknown. Archived at
https://soundcloud.com/jack_lawler
/rhoda-kellogg-interview-kp7a.

27
Oscar Murillo, conversation with the author,
October 19, 2021.

28
Murillo conversation.

King Malcolm

Joshua Bennett

American pimp, dope addict, slinging
Gun and saddle on pilgrimage
To his painful Mecca, where the muezzin's
Call to prayer is a heron's faint cry
In the saturnalia of a city.
Come from a frontier land where fraud
And lies worn naked for survival,
Gave honest light denied the righteous
Outside the camel's eye and safe
In our great society, his soul
Purged its own smoke from its sight;
Saw clear morning.

—from Sylvia Wynter, "Malcolm X"

I.

At the conclusion of Spike Lee's 1992 tour de force biopic *Malcolm X*—
yes, the very same one I will argue with anyone should have garnered
Denzel Washington his second Oscar in three years—there is a scene that
strikes me as one of the purest on-screen expressions of a historical phenomenon I have only just found a name for, but have been thinking about
for years. The name for this long-standing obsession is one I borrow from
the poet and scholar Michael Harper: *a continuum of consciousness.*[1] I will
say more about the contours of this concept in a moment, but the afore-
mentioned closing scene looks something like this: directly following
Ossie Davis's recitation of the eulogy he wrote for Malcolm X three
decades earlier, his resounding baritone (and accompanying historical

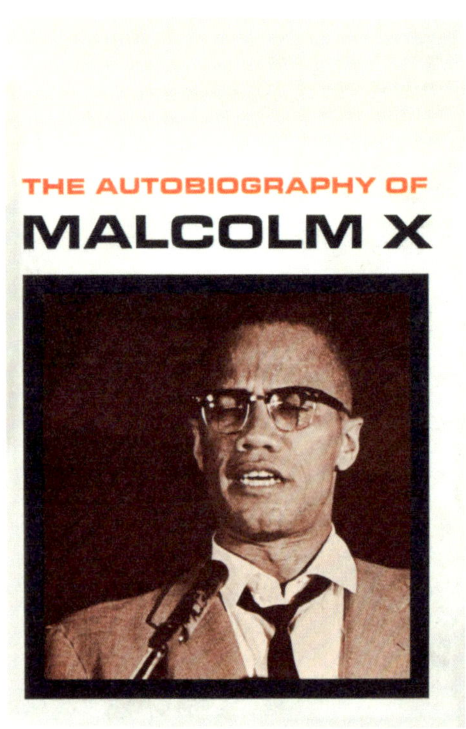

Fig. 1. Alex Haley's *The Autobiography of Malcolm X*, 1965, cover

images of Malcolm alongside black people the world over holding photographs of him in the present day) gives way to a teacher, played by Mary Alice Smith, standing at the front of a classroom. The words inscribed on the hunter-green chalkboard behind her tell us that we are in Harlem, New York, at P.S. 153 on May 19. It's Malcolm X Day. As the camera pans away from her and toward the audience, she says the following lines: "And so today, May 19th, we celebrate Malcolm X's birthday because he was a great, great Afro-American. Malcolm X is you, all of you. And you are Malcolm X." This precedes fifteen seconds of cinema as fresh in my mind as any I have ever watched. One by one, the children in the classroom stand up and declare in rapid succession, "I am Malcolm X!" The classroom in Harlem becomes a classroom in South Africa. The children standing in Harlem become the children in South Africa standing, their shared chant like a baton cast across the ocean from one child's hand to another. Nelson Mandela stands at the front of this new classroom. He cites Malcolm X directly: "As Brother Malcolm said, we declare our right on this Earth to be a man, to be a human being, to be given the rights of a human being, to be respected as a human being, in this society, on this Earth on this day, which we intend to bring into existence." The screen flashes, and it is no longer Mandela standing before us, but gray-scale footage of the man himself, El-Hajj Malik El-Shabazz, reciting what is perhaps his most well-known phrase: *by any means necessary!*"

Malcolm X was the first film I ever watched in a theater. I was seven years old. True to form, once the credits rolled, I asked my parents how I could learn more about the man at the center of its story. Though I had seen Denzel elsewhere at this point—alongside classics like *Polly* and *Sister Act*, the 1989 Civil War film *Glory* was a consistent presence in our home—his embodiment of Malcolm on-screen felt to me so vivid, so memorable, that I wanted to understand as much as I could about this martyr, this hero, whose name I had heard before but whose life I knew so little about. My parents gave me a copy of Alex Haley's *The Autobiography of Malcolm X*, which I began to delve into in the following days (fig. 1). Eventually, it became a kind of talisman. I carried it with me everywhere.

Looking back, it makes a great deal of sense that my introduction to both the world of cinema—or at least, the experience of going to a theater, which for me has become in some ways inextricable from the art form itself—and the world of *books for adults* (autobiography in particular) was through the life and times of Malcolm X. He was part of a much larger pantheon of black writers, black scientists, black teachers and orators and freedom fighters that had been with me ever since I first learned to read. The historical figures I was given by my parents in those early days—Benjamin Banneker, Mary McLeod Bethune, George Washington Carver, Lewis H. Latimer, Harriet Tubman—were introduced to me in technicolor through children's books, always with the explicit aim of teaching me history, black history, that I could use as armor in an unjust world. A world firmly set against any truthful accounting of who and what our people were, what we had built, what we were owed. But my first encounters with Malcolm were in many ways distinct from these lessons. I discovered his ideas through a set of forms that were much more elaborate than children's books and required a more honed sort of attention: a nearly three-and-a-half-hour film and a 544-page tome it took me months to work through with the help of the large red dictionary I kept next to my bed. My mother, to her credit, was never one to abide questions about what certain words meant; she enjoined me instead, at every turn, to "look it up, young man."

From Malcolm, I gained a new vocabulary for the world around me. The pages of his conversations with Alex Haley helped provide some of my first insights into mass incarceration, autodidacticism, mental health diagnoses as a weapon of the carceral state, the Nation of Islam, the black social scene of Harlem in the 1960s. The power of charisma.

The power of love, and kinship. What it means to lay down one's life for one's friends and strangers alike. I knew nothing, at the time, about the conditions under which the book was produced. But I did know something about the importance of *genre*. I regularly read the King James Bible, and the *Chronicles of Narnia*, and was consistently writing my own short stories based in part on the television shows I watched at the time (*Power Rangers*, *Transformers*, that sort of thing). What I was reading in the *Autobiography* was distinct from all that. I hadn't turned to it for moral lessons, or for an escape into a fantasy realm. I carried the book with me to learn something about myself as a black human being that I had previously understood only in part. This learning was inextricable from the way my parents spoke to me about the terror and indomitable beauty of being black in the here and now, why it was important for me to know that I came from a long legacy of people who saw value as something that was not assessed primarily in terms of what one owned or possessed, but what one gave away. What one did for other people. In giving me Malcolm—and allowing me to learn about him on my own terms, at my own pace—my parents had provided me, consciously, with an exemplar. They were teaching me something about the transformative power of literacy, collective empowerment, and the importance of living with the courage of one's convictions, even and especially *if those convictions changed*, in public, and at great cost. The lesson was not simply that I should take pride in our history, but that I should allow that history to make me brave. And in doing so, join that unbounded chorus singing that we, too, were Malcolm X. Now, and forevermore.

II.

Glenn Ligon's *Malcolm X, Sun, Frederick Douglass, Boy with Bubbles (version 2) #2* (2001; page 65) immediately evokes this much larger personal and political history for me. Though Frederick Douglass—another timeless black folk hero—is included within the frame, he is almost entirely obscured by what appears to be a child's furious scribbling in black crayon or colored pencil. Malcolm remains unmistakable. His iconic frames and his suit and tie are legible to us though his crown is likewise covered by blackness. If the sun overlaid with blood is any indication, we are in the midst of an apocalyptic event. An intergenerational gathering at the end of the world. Our heroes adorned in black, the eponymous "boy with bubbles" enrobed in royal blue. Taken together, the collision of the scribbles and drawings recalls the poet and cultural theorist Fred Moten's critical term "blur," which holds within itself, I think, a much longer theoretical lineage that is relevant here.[2]

In *Black Skin, White Masks*, Frantz Fanon deploys the term "inner kinship"[3] to describe what we might think of, *avec* W. E. B. Du Bois, Moten, and others, as a form of multiple personhood: the sense that in a moment of racialized encounter a black person is no longer reducible to themselves as a localized, individual entity but is tied, across space and time, to every black person living, as well as every black person *that has ever lived*. For Fanon, this theorization crystallizes in his encounter with a white male child and his mother on the train—which, again, gives us echoes of Du Bois's own autobiographical moment in *The Souls of Black Folk* where he historically locates the origins of "double-consciousness" in a racist childhood encounter with a classmate[4]—a moment that Fanon describes as follows: "In the train it was no longer a question of being aware of my body in the third person but in a triple person. In the train I was given not one but two, three places. . . . I was responsible at the same time for my body, for my race, for my ancestors."[5]

For Fanon, then, the fact of blackness, the lived experience of the black person, is the inescapable truth that we are never alone. To be black is to be bound to one another, linked across space by the geographic power of this irreducible beauty that we share and that the world calls terror. Blur, it seems to me, inherits this framing from Fanon. It is also tied to what the contemporary critical theorist Denise Ferreira da Silva offers in a number of her more recent writings. Nowhere more strikingly perhaps than in her 2018 essay "On Difference without Separability":

What if, instead of the Ordered World, we imaged each existant (human and more-than-human) not as separate forms relating through the mediation of forces, but rather as singular expressions of each and every other existant as well as of the entangled whole in/as which they exist? What if, instead of

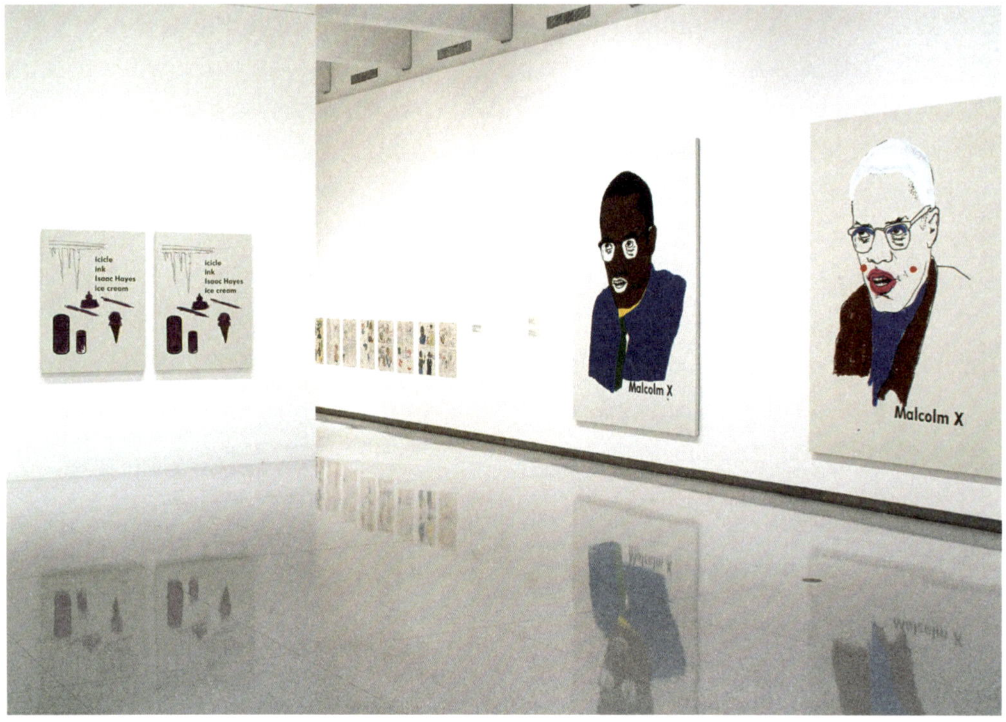

Fig. 2. Installation view, *Coloring: New Work By Glenn Ligon*, Walker Art Center, Minneapolis, 2000

looking to particle physics for models of devising more scientific or critical analysis of the social we turned to its most disturbing findings—such as nonlocality (as an epistemological principle) and virtuality (as an ontological descriptor)—as poetical descriptors, that is, as indicators of the impossibility of comprehending existence with the thinking tools that cannot but reproduce separability and its aids, namely determinacy and sequentiality?[6]

Here, Ferreira da Silva extends Fanon's vector of thought outward, utilizing black social life as the grounds for reconsidering any number of the most essential categories we have inherited from the Western philosophical tradition. Though the full breadth of her analysis takes hold of a variety of actors including but not limited to Georges Cuvier and Charles Darwin, her central objects of critique on this front are dual components of what she calls the "Kantian program"—that is, *separability* (which has less to do with the spatial distance or distinction between objects in the

                                                  Bennett

material world and more to do with Kant's thinking about the limits of the knowable world as made available through forms of intuition and understanding) and *determinacy*, the relationship between the formal constructs we assemble in order to process information and that which falls beyond the scope of our sensory powers. The core of this claim is that until we are able to imagine a sociality set free from the limitations of these twin constraints, these formalized arrangements that each and every day weaponize the distinction between self and Other, stranger and dearest kin, we shall remain unable to ameliorate the present geopolitical conflicts (over water, land, color, creed) that collectively threaten to tear the known world asunder.

Ligon's *Malcolm X, Sun, Frederick Douglass, Boy with Bubbles (version 2) #2* is bound up with a real-world instance of collaboration with young people. In 1999 the artist engineered a people-centered artist residency at the Walker Art Center Library and Archives in Minneapolis with three distinct arms. The first was a book display curated on the contents of the University of Minnesota's Archie Givens Collection of African American Literature. The other two focused explicitly on the work of young people: an art exhibition created in collaboration with the Walker Art Center Teen Arts Council, and a set of coloring sessions with daycare-aged children from around the city. This latter project would directly inspire a new series of paintings by Ligon entitled, simply, *Coloring* (fig. 2). In an interview with curators Olukemi Ilesanmi and Joan Rothfuss, he described the practice of collaborating with the children as follows:

> Everything that comes to mind when I see an image of Malcolm X—his speech on 125th St., his red hair, the trip to Mecca, how handsome he was—got mixed in my head with the way the kids colored in the image, and I made the paintings something more than I expected them to be. A friend said that this project was about borrowing someone else's unconscious to make my work. I rather liked that because it is so much in line with the strategy of quotation I have employed in the past, except that the source material is other artworks, not text. What I've done is meet the kids' drawings and images

on the coloring book pages halfway. They are not "mine," but they are not "not mine."[7]

Ligon admits at the outset of the interview that this final outcome was altogether unexpected. His original aim had been to simply color the images himself. But he found, in his own words, that those paintings "weren't any good." It was only when he began to collaborate with the children in their own space, with their teachers and friends and the crayons they use all the time, that something new emerged from his attempts to replicate their unwieldy, spontaneous invention—their renderings of Malcolm separated out from the history that Ligon describes as informing his own approach to the final version of the work. From within their own peculiar universe of colors and sounds—this unbound aesthetic that comes to us, quite literally, from the future—these children provided a previously unavailable insight into what the blank page, the blank canvas, could offer. What it could become.

Do you see? Ligon could not paint or draw *like a child*, exactly. He could only, with patience and care, approach their grand inventiveness from a distance, build what he could from the shards of the vision they allowed him to see. He could only approximate, with time and effort, what was possible for them in that instant. In this way, the circuit of knowledge as we might otherwise imagine it is reversed. It is the collective practice of children, their untamed sociality, that sets the work of art free. It is their wisdom, their expertise, that leads us. In Ligon's practice, over and against a larger web of brutally tenacious social and political arrangements the world over, black childhood is a scene set free by blur. The boy with bubbles and the great folk heroes of his tradition share space, their grand visages rendered opaque by everyday materials of experimentation and play. Crayons and pencils, stenciled outlines of historical actors on a white page, take center stage. The painting becomes a playground. The scene it depicts becomes a lens through which we can view the true scope and scale of our collective inheritance: the sun in the sky and all its stars; joy beyond the bull's-eye reach; a poetics of the untamable, indomitable soul.

1
James Randall, "Interview with Michael S. Harper," in *American Poetry Observed: Poets on Their Work*, ed. Joe David Bellamy (Urbana: University of Illinois Press, 1984), 93.

2
Fred Moten, *Black and Blur* (Durham: Duke University Press, 2017).

3
Frantz Fanon, "The Fact of Blackness," in *Black Skin, White Masks*, trans. Richard Philcox (New York: Grove Press, 2008), 95.

4
W. E. B. Du Bois, *The Souls of Black Folk* (1903; Oxford: Oxford University Press, 2007).

5
Fanon, "Fact of Blackness," 94.

6
Denise Ferreira da Silva, "On Difference without Separability," in *Incerteza Viva: 32nd Bienal de São Paulo*, ed. Jochen Volz and Júlia Rebouças (São Paulo: Fundação Bienal de São Paulo, 2016), 63–64.

7
Olukemi Ilesanmi and Joan Rothfuss, "A Conversation with Glenn Ligon," in *Coloring: New Work by Glenn Ligon* (Minneapolis: Walker Art Center, 2001), 31.

The Third Way: Seeing Childhood Agency Anew

Ruth Erickson

When I brought my first son, at the age of fifteen months, to meet my ninety-year-old grandmother, she made an offhand comment that spurred me down a path of research that led to this exhibition and book: "You modern parents sure give your kids a lot of choices." Everything I read was suffused with models of children's empowerment—from the lessons of the early pedagogues I revered, such as Maria Montesorri and Reggio Emilio, to the articles I camc across on my late-night iPhone searches. The belief is that we seek to enfranchise children as a means to build their self-worth, resilience, and criticality. This is why I asked my son if he wanted this or that for a snack, or which clothing item he would like to put on first. These were testing grounds for more nuanced questions that he would later face: questions of risk, of consent, of ethics. I felt that through choice, through some modicum of self-determination, a better and stronger, even a more empathetic, person would grow. What I did not realize is how distinct this approach was from what my grandmother had practiced on her own children half a century earlier. Except for the socioeconomic marker of education—my grandmother having finished high school and I having completed a Ph.D.—we were similar: white, cis, heterosexual women, middle class, and living in New England. Nevertheless, we were at different points in recognizing power regimes—those of race, gender, sexuality, ability, wealth, and age—and seeking to dismantle them.

Dynamics of power, both visible and invisible, conscious and unconscious, inform the experiences of children from birth. They are as blatant as child servitude and trafficking, as abuse and neglect, and as discreet as a posture, a tone of voice, a sense of unbelonging. It is easy to understand children as one of many disenfranchised groups, whom the processes of capitalization, labor, racism, and policy have left out of favor and distanced from resources. And yet children are also the bearers of immense power—through their expressions of creativity and criticality, inventiveness, capacity to learn and grow, buying power and influence, and embodiment of the future. These vast experiences of young people have meant that childhood, as an idea with its own history, is intricately intertwined with histories of power.[1]

Much of the scholarly work on childhood and power has taken place since the 1970s and especially in the 1990s, which witnessed the emergence of childhood studies.[2] A belief in children's agency has formed the backbone of that field, a reaction to the prevailing theory that children are merely products of their environment, passively shaped by the conditions of their existence. Instead, according to the paradigm outlined by the sociologists Allison James and Alan Prout in 1990, "Children are and must be seen as active in the construction and determination of their own social lives, the lives of those around them and of the societies in which they live. Children are not just the passive subjects of social structures and processes."[3] The ways that children act and express their thoughts (their agency) are contingent on a host of other factors, identity positions, and social dynamics. While accepting children as active agents, childhood studies scholars disagreed about the relationship between young people and the cultural construct of childhood. Was childhood an idea formed by adults to produce their own power? Or did the complicated lives of young people defy such abstract formulations? Following a line of thinking in Robin Bernstein's path-breaking book *Racial Innocence* (2011), children constantly receive impressions of childhood—the scripts and images of how to act or look, of what they symbolize within society, of frequently racialized ideas like innocence, freedom, and disobedience. These cultural constructions shape the lives of children, and children constantly deconstruct and reconstruct the prompts and idealizations they encounter. Bernstein identifies "the simultaneity and mutual constitution of children and childhood" and "the processes by which children and childhood give body to each other . . . coproduce each other."[4] Many scholars have argued convincingly for the coexistence of empowerment and disenfranchisement in the lives of children, and in the idea of childhood itself. Indeed, the newest areas of research in the field of childhood studies center on more expansive conceptions of agency.[5] These studies across the social sciences and humanities argue for models in which coping, caretaking, vulnerability, dependency, and collectivity are constitutive factors to agency as opposed to a model based entirely on individual power and autonomous will.

What follows is an exploration of the nuanced terrain of children's power as invoked by the diverse practices of living artists. Many of the selected artworks project a vision of childhood agency as deeply complex, even conflicted, shaped by strength and dependency, by potential and constraint, by care, harm, and fear. These works cannot be mapped into the neat binaries to which discussions of power and agency so often succumb. Instead, they open an ineffable space between artwork and receiver, between positions of power, and through them we have an opportunity to see childhood agency anew.

Reimagining Containment

One of the most iconic objects of children's safety and containment is the crib. Archaeological evidence suggests there were devices for holding children far back in human history, but the modern crib dates firmly to the mid-1800s, coinciding with the modern conception of childhood itself.[6] While crib design has changed dramatically throughout cultures and time, the fundamental goal to keep a sleeping child safe, and sleeping, has remained intact. Despite the images of soft fabrics, pale colors, and soothing rocking motions, the contemporary crib with its vertical slats and rectilinear shape also resembles other places of containment. Perhaps this is the reason that once, in my own sleep-deprived state, I suggested to my husband that we put our son "in his pen." It is a space separate from that shared with others; it is an isolating space. Adults cannot enter it. Many artists—Robert Gober, Mona Hatoum, Hugh Hayden, and Doris Salcedo, among others—have used the form of the crib to probe diverse sentiments. These have included estrangement, violence, and fear, which too often characterize the lives of children and yet go unremarked. Their sculptures speak to disquieting acts, when places of security and safety become dangerous, inaccessible, or disorienting. And while the literature about these works and even the artists themselves have spoken about the sculptures as symbolic of the powerful, dispossessing forces affecting the infant child, I would like to suggest that these crib sculptures also forecast the child's potential for agency.

Gober took up the form of the playpen in 1987, when he made three sculptures whose titles describe the modification the artist made to each enclosing cubic form. In *Open Playpen*, the fourth side is missing; in *X Playpen*, the long edges cross (fig. 1); and in *Slanted Playpen*, all four sides bend at an angle. These almost minimalist modifications—seemingly straightforward in their variations on the cube—multiply the potent symbolism of the objects' foundational form. If these distortions recall those forces at work on a very young child, whose prone body fits within these sides and who, even before walking, contends with the pressures of the family and society, they might also project the infant child who actively deconstructs this primary place of containment.

Gober referred to these as "traumatic playpens,"[7] and art historians and critics have sought to articulate the trauma. Hal Foster described them in 2000 as "cages marked with aggression—whether of the child or the other (as intuited by the child)." He continued, applying the psychoanalytic lens of his scholarship, "Rather than happy accession of the infant to representation, then, Gober evokes a socialization that is blocked or broken."[8] Writing in 2014, Hilton Als goes slightly further, describing Gober's sculptures based on domestic furniture as "the work of an absented child—absented by his difference." "Gober's cribs," he writes, "are also a continuation of the life of the absent boy in his work."[9] Foster and Als read the crib as a surrogate for the child—more specifically for the artist as a child—and thus the blockages or absences given form are those of the human psyche. They pinpoint the distortions as a manifestation of a queer child/artist unable to be himself and now making sculpture in the time of the AIDS epidemic. How differently, one might ask, would that epidemic have turned out if we had supported children in expressing and exploring their genders and sexualities freely? Would this illness, like others, then have been considered a natural part of human existence and survival? And what if in Gober's playpens we were also to summon an active child who is reimagining the first place of his containment otherwise?

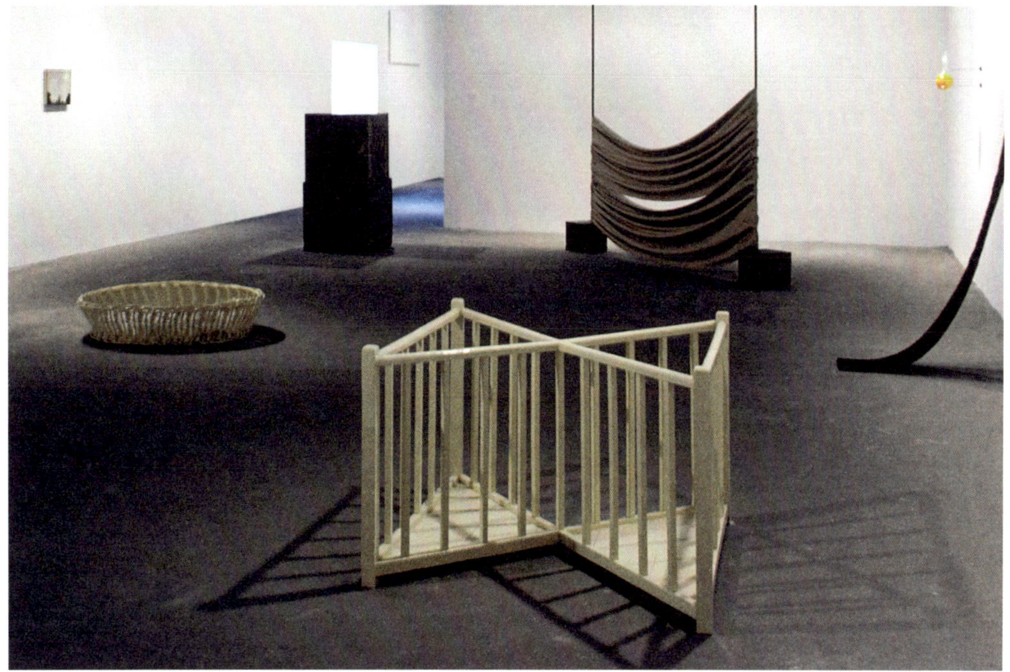

Fig. 1. Robert Gober, *X Playpen*, 1987. Installation view, *1989 Whitney Biennial*, Whitney Museum of American Art, New York, 1989

Cribs with black pipes jutting through them and with cold tiled floors would follow in the subsequent years, each offering its own rendition of quiet violence but also perturbing the *ur*-form of the house and family unit into which a child is born, or arrives. Gober's various crib sculptures powerfully concretize the traumas of a child's initial socializations, and they also reveal the inventiveness of a child in confronting and derailing the very structures of its containment and safety. These sculptures variously expose the crib/family/house as unsafe and the total containment of the child as impossible. It is in these opposing forces that the sculptures speak so strongly of childhood and the vast and individual experiences that make up its unique contours for each person.

Mona Hatoum's numerous crib sculptures, which she began in 1993, follow her uses of domestic objects to probe displacement, trauma, and systems of power, concerns that have inflected her work across multiple mediums for decades.[10] Her earliest crib work, the gray metal *Incommunicado* (1993; fig. 2), consists of a stripped-down infant's hospital cot in which Hatoum has replaced the base with a series of thin

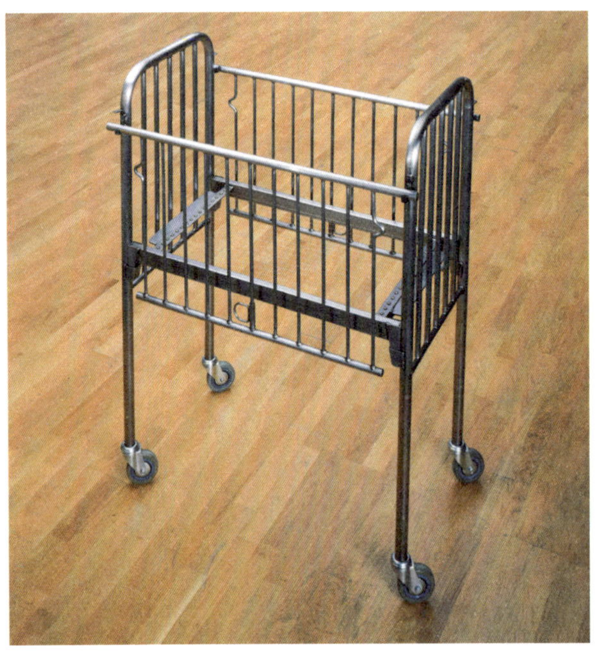

Fig. 2. Mona Hatoum, *Incommunicado*, 1993. Metal cot and wire. 49 ¾ × 22 ⅝ × 36 ¾ inches (126.4 × 57.5 × 93.4 cm). Tate, London; Purchased with funds provided by the Gytha Trust, 1995

wires stretched end to end. "It looks more like an egg-slicer," the artist explains, "and you immediately associate it with a situation of danger and abuse. I called it *Incommunicado* to associate it with prisoners in solitary confinement. But also an infant in those situations has no ability to communicate about extremes of fear or pain."[11] The work has a visceral effect, as it invites viewers to mentally project themselves into the crib, with all its violent allusions to bodily harm. In her discussion of the piece, Hatoum relates infants to prisoners—individuals under the power of someone else and suspended in a state of voicelessness, though for different reasons. While every viewer was previously an infant, very few are likely to have been in solitary confinement, and yet we might all imagine the pain and horror of being laid in *this* crib.

For *To Begin Again* Hatoum created a new work, titled *Caught-up* (page 117). For its base Hatoum used a cream-colored crib that she had purchased at a Parisian flea market and kept in her studio for over two decades.[12] The small metal crib on wheels—similar in form to the one used in *Incommunicado*—has chipped paint and likely dates to a mid-twentieth-century hospital or orphanage, where space for children was at a premium and their portability while enclosed useful. This object carries its own stories—traces left in the crib's patina and suggestive

Erickson

of use and neglect. Inside the crib, Hatoum has woven a spiderweb in small, red glass beads. The web is delicate and beautiful, evenly spun and dipping slightly between the attachment points, just as in nature. It spans the entire interior space. The linearity of the web overlapping with the diamond-pattern base of the crib as well as its vertical bars offers a dynamic visual experience, where the overlaying lines constantly change as you move around the sculpture. Unlike a cobweb in a corner, this deep red one suggests something more active. It is an elegant and industrious production. It is like a net, threatening but also potentially protective. It disallows the crib's use; it could entrap someone inside.[13] The spider spins its web to sustain its own life, and this web is a life force; its color recalls blood and veins. As in most of Hatoum's work, where domestic objects function as surrogates for the body and corporeal experiences,[14] opposing ideas or feelings enter into uneasy relation. *Caught-up* holds in tension a sense of new life and death, of care and neglect, of the found and the created.

In their uses of the everyday object of the crib, Gober and Hatoum have found a powerful symbol to evoke the infant child and to probe the psychological and physical forces internal and external to that figure. The crib recalls not just the body of the child but also social entities like family and institutions such as the hospital. Within the space of articulating the profound failures of these institutions to protect and nurture the most vulnerable among us, these works also conjure the child figure as an agent actively contending with these forces by undoing their basic forms or generating means of protection.

Representation and Self-Determination

No one is more readily photographed than children, and this massive store of images has been a source of inspiration for numerous artists. Njideka Akunyili Crosby and Deborah Roberts have created some of the most striking portraits of children in recent years. Featuring Black children between the ages of around five to twelve years, their works register the act of self-definition within and against the representations society offers. For both artists, collage techniques are a means to convey the complex matrix of identity formation and to intervene specifically into the ways Black children have been depicted. The robust literature around childhood and race has demonstrated how dominant conceptions of childhood, and especially childhood innocence, are coded white.[15] This has led to an "adultification" bias toward children of color (who are perceived as "more adult" than their white peers), among a host of other factors that radically affect Black and brown children's experiences of childhood.[16] Akunyili Crosby and Roberts create multidimensional and humanizing images of Black children and interrogate Black childhood in all its complexity.

In her series of portraits of Nigerian youth, "The Beautyful Ones," begun in 2014, Akunyili Crosby uses a photo-transfer process to incorporate found and personal photographs. The painted figures emerge from multilayered spaces composed of family photos, street scenes, historical images, and images from popular culture, and together they reflect a complex tapestry, which the child pictured is a part of and also stands apart from.[17] On top of and between the shallow photo-transfer layers (the photos appear as both background and middle ground), Akunyili Crosby paints her primary subjects with opaque color and a great attention to detail. In one portrait (page 127), a girl dressed in bright yellow stands on a bustling street surrounded by a trio of yellow vehicles; she faces forward, with arms crossed, and looks out confidently at the viewer. In another (page 129), a tall, bespectacled girl dressed in white stands elegantly within a domestic setting. The literal and symbolic spaces these Nigerian youth inhabit are reflections of our hybrid realities; they are intercultural, postcolonial, and physical. By locating her figures within a collaged pictorial space, Akunyili Crosby literalizes the idea that the individual sitter—the child—is part of a matrix of social and personal histories registered through photography; and yet by painting the figures starkly on top of this pictorial matrix, she also captures their independence and self-determination, qualities suggested through their poses and expressions. If her protagonists exude power, this position is relational to the material, social, political, and personal circumstances conveyed in the setting and the pictorial milieu surrounding them.

Roberts builds her composite figures from photographs, drawings, and painted areas, a process that underscores how each portrait is an

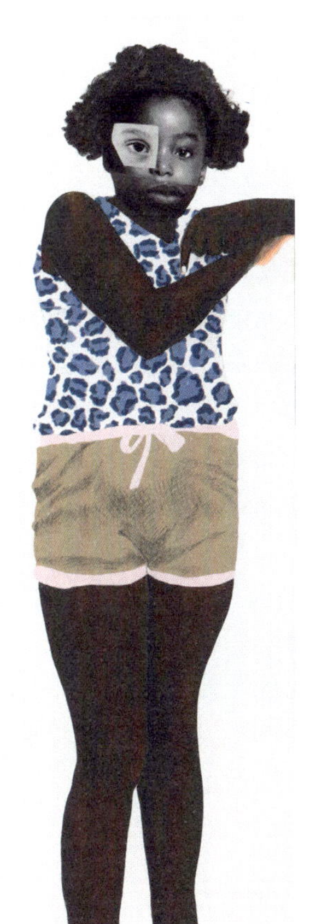

Fig. 3. Deborah Roberts, *Becoming*, 2021.
Mixed-media collage on canvas. 65 ×
45 inches (165.1 × 114.3 cm). Institute
of Contemporary Art/Boston; Promised
gift of Fotene Demoulas and Tom Coté

assemblage of images, histories, and ideals. She initially focused her
work on Black girlhood, and in a conversation with the critic and curator
Antwaun Sargent, she explained her choice of young Black female figures at the pivot from early to middle childhood: "It's about the first act
of freedom. When you are seven or eight, and you want to start to wear
different clothing or do your own hair because you are starting to enter
into your own idea of who you are, where are the examples of little black
girl beauty for you to look to?"[18] Drawn to the child's active development
of her identity, and in a critique of the narrow beauty standards and the
prevalent emotional and physical stereotyping of Black girls and women,
Roberts endeavors to reflect the multidimensionality of these girls.[19] Her
recent work *Becoming* (2021; fig. 3), which Roberts describes as a portrait
of herself around age eight, presents a single figure against a white background, her face composed of three black-and-white photographs and
the rest of her body and clothing rendered in paint and oil crayon. The

girl is set off to the right side, knees knocking together and raised arms crossing over her body. The relationship of the girl to her body, as the title suggests, is in a state of becoming, juxtaposed between the photographic and the painted, the known and the unknown, the girl and the woman. While her body evokes a degree of timidity or uncertainty, her facial expression is one of determination and resolve. Her alert eyes and resting lips suggest the figure is ready to confront what the world and adulthood throw her way. In this merging of countenance and corporeality, Roberts beautifully pictures the dynamic development of a child, especially as a Black girl contends with the pressures of external forces and defines herself.

Black boys are the focus of a series of paintings that Roberts began in 2019, which touch upon the incarceration and tragic murders of young Black males.[20] In these paintings, Roberts collages facial features from esteemed Black men, such as James Baldwin, to point to the adulthoods that were robbed of the children she references.[21] *Ulysses* (2019; page 123) shows a boy dressed in a striped shirt and standing demurely to the left of the canvas, his hands splayed, as if to clarify they are not holding anything that might be construed as a weapon. He appears to be held back, or held in place, by a white hand entering from the left side of the canvas and resting on his chest. The boy's weary eyes possess a conflicting sense of innocence and wisdom, as do many of the eyes in Roberts's prolific portraits: "I'm looking for this type of innocence that has not been touched by pop culture but maybe has been touched by tragedy," the artist has said. "I know when I find that face."[22] In interviews about her work, Roberts has referenced the adultification of Black and brown children who are often not provided the same protections as white children and experience vastly higher rates of disciplinary action and incarceration.[23] While *Ulysses* and many of Roberts's subsequent works refer to this fact, each portrait possesses a breadth of emotional and physical states, pushing against the operative narrowing of experience that white supremacist stereotypes try hard to solidify. Perhaps what defines Roberts's oeuvre and makes her paintings feel so raw, true, and original is her ability to capture both vulnerability and strength.

Through their distinct uses of collage, Roberts and Akunyili Crosby present pictures of children that include history, ancestry, and sociopolitical conditions, while allowing for the possibility of existence and self-presentation apart from these preexisting forms of representation. While on the one hand they picture the real constraints in the lives of the children they depict, on the other hand they also point to a generative potential to restructure the symbolic order. The agency intimated in their works occupies both ends of a spectrum of power, giving space to creative self-determination while acknowledging the impact of racist, patriarchal, and colonialist forces in our society.

Dependency and Survival

The above discussion approaches children as independent actors or figures within social and political structures of family and society. Such a perspective, based in Western liberal ideology, does not fully account for the inherent interdependence of children with others—parents, siblings, grandparents, friends, and even the multiple selves of a single child. In discussions of power in the lives of children, it is the role of parents, guardians, and those endowed with the legal right to make decisions on behalf of minors that comes to mind immediately. Childhood is in large part defined by dependency on adults, without a complete acknowledgment of the potential for interdependence among young people.

Depictions of mothers taking care of their young have been around for millennia, and numerous artists today continue that tradition (pages 134–41, 146–47). At the same time, contemporary artists and writers have been actively rethinking the very notion of motherhood, considering factors of race and gender, making visible the invisibility of reproductive labor, redefining traditional family structures, and expanding the scope beyond the person who gave birth.[24] Jordan Casteel and Ramiro Gomez (now Jay Lynn Gomez), for example, offer powerful tributes to the rarely pictured caretaking role of fathers and domestic workers in their large-scale paintings and practices (pages 149–51). And in a call to reimagine mothering as a collective project, a feminist one, that foregrounds the practical and intangible needs of those whose survival is most threatened in their community, Alexis Pauline Gumbs proposes that "in order to collectively figure out how to sustain and support our evolving species, in order to participate in and demand a society where people help to create each other instead of too often destroying each other, we need to look at the practice of creating, nurturing, affirming, and supporting life that we call mothering."[25] In this view, mothering is an action that anyone could adopt and practice, including children.

Depictions of care among children themselves are common in popular and fine art and yet they are rarely discussed as the expression of childhood agency. The photographs in Justine Kurland's 1997–2002 series Girl Pictures (pages 152–55) depict adolescent girls who appear to be runaways or living outside of a traditional home. The sixty-nine photographs in total possess a romantic streak of freedom, of punk rock delinquency, and of existence at the literal margins of society (scrubby woods, underpasses, and abandoned cars are recurring locations). But more than a vagabond's radical self-sufficiency, what comes across in the series is a deeply interdependent and communal sense of power and existence. Kurland shows the girls grooming one another, providing shelter, and offering a sense of safety conventionally expected of adult guardians. As the critic Johanna Fateman has described, these staged photographs "offer a vivid daydream of widespread revolt and cooperation among girls, a vision as poignant and tantalizing as ever."[26] The series reconfigures power as a force that emerges through the intimate bonds among subjects whose collaborative survival presents a menace to civil society founded upon individualism and capitalism.

We might also return to the work of Deborah Roberts, whose multifigure paintings depict relationships between children. The group of five young girls in *Sisterly Love* (2021; pages 124–25) presents a striking visual dynamic of individuality and collectivity (and is the cover of this book). Gathered on the right side of the canvas, the five figures are differentiated by their patterned clothing, painted nails, and expressions. The eyes of each figure come from different black-and-white photographic sources and meet at an angle in the center of the face; the lighter and darker papers create a visual rhythm that unites the ensemble. The overlapping of the five figures, especially the two central ones whose arms drape comfortably over each other, shores up a sense of their connection as a tight group, formed not by their blood relations but from their shared experiences. From this collectivity a sense of power emerges, and

 Erickson

grounding that strength is the individuality of each girl and the potential she finds within this group to express her voice, feelings, desires, and self. Girl Pictures and *Sisterly Love* poignantly compel a reconsideration of agency not as the outlet of individual will but as an acknowledgment of interdependence with others. By depicting caretaking among individuals other than mothers and children, these artists richly expand the notion of care and the subject positions associated with it.

Postscript

I recently called my grandmother to check in. We had not spoken in many months, and in that time, she had moved from the house where she had lived for more than forty years to stay with her daughter and son-in-law, my aunt and uncle. Her voice was unusually faint on the other end of the line. After we covered the recent weather and the well-being of my two boys, she hinted at struggling with her recent loss of independence, with the fact that someone had to help her off the couch or out of bed and ask her each morning what blouse she would like to wear. I was brought back to our encounter some seven years earlier, and to the parallels between my desire to honor the self-determination of my young son through those simple choices I gave him and the attempt of my grandmother's caretakers to meet her needs while also assuring that she retained a modicum of autonomy. After speaking with my grandmother, and sensing the complex diminishment of her agency, I reflected on how I might have rephrased my question to my toddler son. Rather than asking, "Would you like to wear this or that?," I could have included a consideration of both his competences and my own needs and those of others: "I have pulled out two shirts and will help you put one on. It would help me if you could choose one to wear so that we can move on to the next part of our day. I need to meet a friend after I drop you to school, and I don't want to be late for her." What would it mean to gesture, in that small moment, to the expansive ramifications of every choice we make? To illustrate how we are connected to others even when such ties are not immediately apparent? Could such a change begin to reshape agency not only as the operations of the self but also as a deep and collective project?

Such questions point to a third way through the thickets of power that are part of life—for me, as a mother, a white woman, a curator—where I can reimagine and celebrate agency as a strategy of collective existence.

1

See Philippe Ariès, *Centuries of Childhood: A Social History of Family Life*, trans. Robert Baldick (New York: Vintage Books, 1962).

2

A fundamental event in the history of attitudes toward childhood and power was the United Nation's Convention on the Rights of the Child (UNCRC), adopted on November 20, 1989, and ratified by all but three countries: Somalia, South Sudan, and the United States of America. This convention is the most comprehensive treaty on children's rights, and it established a model for children to have agency in determining aspects of their lives. Article 12, for example, gives children the right to participate in decisions that concern them. In the United States, arguments against ratification have centered on issues of individual freedom and states' rights—that is, that families or state governments should be able to make the best decisions for children, rather than a larger governing body. For pivotal collections of essays cementing the field of childhood studies, see Sharon Stephens, ed., *Children and the Politics of Culture* (Princeton: Princeton University Press, 1995), and Henry Jenkins, ed., *The Children's Culture Reader* (New York: New York University Press, 1998). See a discussion of the development of the field in Anna Mae Duane, ed., *Children's Table: Childhood Studies and the Humanities* (Athens: University of Georgia Press, 2013).

3

Allison James and Alan Prout, *Constructing and Reconstructing Childhood: Contemporary Issues in the Sociological Study of Childhood*, classic ed. (London: Routledge, 2015), 7.

4

Robin Bernstein, *Racial Innocence: Performing American Childhood from Slavery to Civil Rights* (New York: New York University Press, 2011), 22.

5

See David Oswell, *The Agency of Children: From Family to Global Human Rights* (Cambridge, UK: Cambridge University Press, 2013), especially "Conclusions," 263–80; and Florian Esser et al., eds., *Reconceptualising Agency and Childhood: New Perspectives in Childhood Studies* (London: Routledge, 2016).

6

Stephen Kline, "The Making of Children's Culture," in Jenkins, *Children's Culture Reader*, 96–101. See Karin Calvert, "Cradle to Crib: The Revolution in Nineteenth-Century Children's Furniture," in *A Century of Childhood, 1820–1920*, ed. Mary Lynn Stevens Heininger (Rochester, NY: Margaret Woodbury Strong Museum, 1984), 33–64.

7

Hal Foster, "An Art of Missing Parts," *October* 92 (Spring 2000): 139.

8

Foster, "An Art of Missing Parts," 139.

9

Hilton Als, "I Don't Remember," in *Robert Gober: The Heart Is Not a Metaphor*, ed. Ann Temkin (New York: Museum of Modern Art, 2014), 36, 41.

10

Michelle White, ed., *Mona Hatoum: Terra Infirma* (Houston: Menil Collection, 2017).

11

Janine Antoni, "Mona Hatoum," *Bomb Magazine* 63 (Spring 1998): 59, https://bombmagazine.org/articles/mona-hatoum/.

12

Hatoum, conversation with the author, September 7, 2021.

13

Hatoum's work with spiderwebs recalls Louise Bourgeois's long engagement with spiders and webs, which she related to the figure of her mother, a tapestry restorer, and suggesting they were protective symbols for her. See Elizabeth Manchester, "Louise Bourgeois, *Maman*, 1999," object summary, December 2009, Tate, https://www.tate.org.uk/art/artworks/bourgeois-maman-t12625.

14

"The sculptures based on furniture are very much about the body too, they encourage the viewer to mentally project themselves onto the objects." Antoni, "Mona Hatoum," 59.

15

See in particular Bernstein, *Racial Innocence*; Kyra D. Gaunt, *The Games Black Girls Play: Learning the Ropes from Double-Dutch to Hip-Hop* (New York: New York University Press, 2006); and William S. Bush, *Who Gets a Childhood? Race and Juvenile Justice in Twentieth-Century Texas* (Athens: University of Georgia Press, 2010).

16

Rebecca Epstein, Jamilia J. Blake, and Thalia González, *Girlhood Interrupted: The Erasure of Black Girls' Childhood* (Washington, DC: Georgetown Law Center on Poverty and Inequality, 2017), https://genderjusticeandopportunity.georgetown.edu/wp-content/uploads/2020/06/girlhood-interrupted.pdf; Jamilia J. Blake and Rebecca Epstein, *Listening to Black Women and Girls: Lived Experiences of Adultification Bias* (Washington, DC: Georgetown Law Center on Poverty and Inequality, 2019), https://www.law.georgetown.edu/poverty-inequality-center/wp-content/uploads/sites/14/2019/05/Listening-to-Black-Women-and-Girls.pdf.

17

The title of the series comes from the 1968 novel *The Beautyful Ones Are Not Yet Born*, by Ayi Kwei Armah, which tells the story of a man who works at a railway and struggles with the reality of a recently independent Ghana. In evoking this title, Akunyili Crosby connects to the postcolonial project of many West African countries and the linking of a newly born national identity to children, seen as the future of now self-governing nations.

18

Antwaun Sargent, "The Artist Changing the Face of Black Girlhood," *Vice*, March 6, 2018, https://www.vice.com/en_us/article/59kapb/the-artist-changing-the-face-of-black-girlhood. See also the recent catalogues *Deborah Roberts: If They Come* (London: Stephen Friedman Gallery, 2019), and *I'M* (Austin: The Contemporary Austin, 2020).

19

We should see Roberts's initial focus on Black girls as an effort to highlight this largely unseen subject position, which had been elided within dominant calls against racism and sexism. As bell hooks wrote in 1981: "White women and black men have it both ways. They can act as oppressor or be oppressed. Black men may be victimized by racism, but sexism allows them to act as exploiters and oppressors of women. White women may be victimized by sexism, but racism enables them to act as exploiters and oppressors of black people. Both groups have led liberation movements that favor their interests and support continued oppression of other groups. Black male sexism has undermined struggles to eradicate racism just as white female racism undermines feminist struggle." bell hooks, *Feminist Theory: From Margin to Center* (Cambridge, MA: South End Press, 2000), 14–15. I see Roberts's paintings as very much in line with the creative self-expressions of Black girls documented in Ruth Nicole Brown, *Hear Our Truths: The Creative Potential of Black Girlhood* (Urbana: University of Illinois Press, 2013).

20
While the literature on the phenomenon of the criminalization of Black boys and the school-to-prison pipeline is extensive, one early book deserves mention for tracing the contours of what subsequent studies and scholars would bear out to be true: Jawanza Kunjufu, *Countering the Conspiracy to Destroy Black Boys* (Chicago: African American Images, 1982).

21
Cherise Smith, essay for Roberts's exhibition *Native Sons: Many Thousands Gone*, at Vielmetter Gallery, Los Angeles, 2019, https://vielmetter.com/exhibitions /deborah-roberts-native-sons-many -thousands-gone.

22
Roberts quoted in Robin Pogrebin, "A Dream Deferred, for Now," *New York Times*, April 12, 2020.

23
Siddhartha Mitter, "Deborah Roberts Conjures Black Girl Magic," *Village Voice*, December 6, 2017, https://www .villagevoice.com/2017/12/06 /deborah-roberts-conjures-black-girl-magic/.

24
Andrea Liss, *Feminist Art and the Maternal* (Minneapolis: University of Minnesota Press, 2009); Emily Liebert and Nadiah Rivera Fellah, eds., *Picturing Motherhood Now* (Cleveland: Cleveland Museum of Art, 2021).

25
Alexis Pauline Gumbs, "Introduction," in *Revolutionary Mothering: Love on the Front Lines*, ed. Alexis Pauline Gumbs, China Martens, and Mai'a Williams (Oakland, CA: PM Press, 2016), 9.

26
Johanna Fateman, "Justine Kurland," *4Columns*, June 15, 2018, https://4columns .org/fateman-johanna/justine-kurland.

No More Innocent Signs

Anne Higonnet

At a pivot in history, *To Begin Again* asks what childhood looks like. The title reminds us that the subject of childhood is always about another start. The young of our species ensure our natural survival, but it is the meanings we make for what we call childhood that propel our history. In 2022 we restart from a global pandemic and a social justice movement. What used to be taken for granted about the image of childhood is no longer credible. The notion of an absolutely blank innocence was predicated on a social order we no longer accept without question. Many traditional power structures have proved to protect neither a majority of children nor their mothers. Yet we cling to an equation of childhood with hope, and so does our art. Even as art abandons one vision of childhood, it is gaining another. In the place of eternal verities, we see trajectories. The personally authentic is multiplied by collective experience. And the subjects of childhood and parental care, too long associated with a natural femininity, are propelled into new cultural terrain through a wide range of brilliant aesthetic tactics.

Young humans delight in making marks. Throughout the twentieth century, artists who sought to turn from a European realist standard toward abstraction believed those marks would validate their sophisticated project of modernism. With the most laudatory intentions, artists such as Paul Klee (pages 46–51) adopted the staccato traces, rough outlines, subjective scale, and arbitrary color they observed in art by children. They ignored the economic histories that allowed a small fraction of the world's children the leisure to make art for hours, months, and years, as well as the industrialization of paper, pencils, crayons, and paint that gave children access to disposable materials. Nonetheless, it was not unreasonable to assume that the very young had been making similar even if ephemeral marks since human history began. They could have used natural materials like burnt wood or colored pollen and made their marks in sand and loose dirt, or on rock walls. According to this modernist view, marks made by children are the authentic signs of the human creative impulse.

An exceptional artist like the photographer Helen Levitt might have agreed with this belief in primal mark-making. Yet rather than appropriate children's finished lines or gestures as found objects, she connects the action of children's drawing with adults' optical process of perception. Not only are children shown in the moment of drawing, but Levitt's compositions make their art seem to emanate from their whole bodies (pages 55–59). The magnification by the camera lens of their activity in the foreground of her images pours the child's creativity out toward the viewer. Clear signs of contemporary urban context, moreover, situate children's art in a social present rather than a primeval past.

In the spirit of Levitt's photographs, to draw like a child can now function as a kind of narrative device. In the work of artists like many of those in this exhibition, it no longer indicates that the maker knows nothing, or that the mark signals a primitive origin. Instead, the childlike mark has become a moment in a story, a story with many moments. The story may be about an increasing individual self-awareness or a collective identity coming into being.

Too many bankrupt variants of twentieth-century "primitivism" should make us suspect the political motives of a childlike mark conceived as a primal gesture. There have been too many instances when art by people of color was described as childlike, too many equations between the art of children and the art of the insane, the incarcerated, or the marginalized. What has been meant by any of those assertions, and what happens when they are interlaced? Too often they have reinforced spurious claims that the people who already wielded social power were the only ones who had the intellectual capacity to make significant art. The mimicry of a supposedly innocent mark was all too often a self-serving appropriation. What feels more productive now is the use of the childlike mark to reference those intersecting appropriations self-consciously.

Jacob Lawrence, like his contemporary Levitt, represents children in the act of representing (fig. 1). His point of view pulls their action far below us spatially, so we can see them within an expanse, entirely immersed in a bright, teeming world of their own invention. Yet the

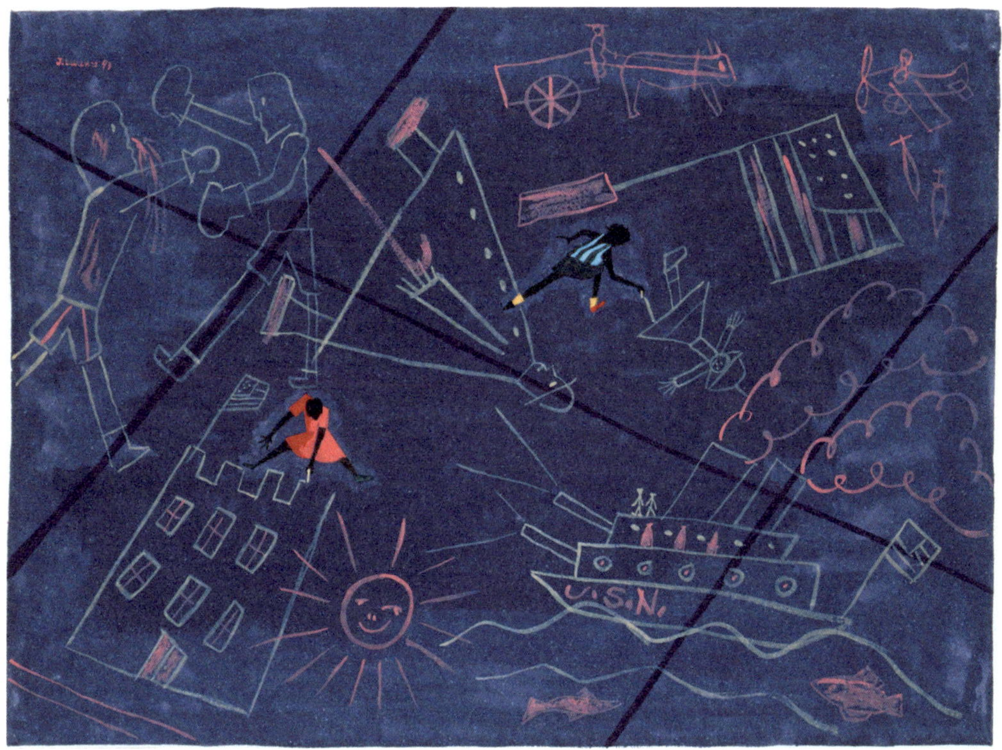

Fig. 1. Jacob Lawrence, *Sidewalk Drawings*, 1943. Gouache on paper. 22 ⅜ × 29 ½ inches (56.8. × 74.9 cm). Collection of Shahara Ahmad-Llewellyn

same point of view maps the children's marks over a grid of sidewalk cracks, which represents the reality of an actual urban location. As part of a later generation, Jean-Michel Basquiat managed to perform Klee's abstraction while invoking Lawrence's realism. At first glance, Basquiat's marks might seem childlike in their forms, but more careful attention and identification reveal their layered and complex historical meanings; an abstract stack of wobbly rectangles, for instance, turns out to be a game structured by rules and played on pavements in the Bronx and Queens neighborhoods where Basquiat lived and painted (page 61). Another step has been taken toward the idea that children are not limited to merely channeling the natural, but rather interpret what has already become social.

Or perhaps this is what I can see in older work like Levitt's or Lawrence's or Basquiat's because my eye has been retrained by contemporary work like Brian Belott's, which overtly curates art by children. Belott has helped preserve a vast collection of anonymous children's

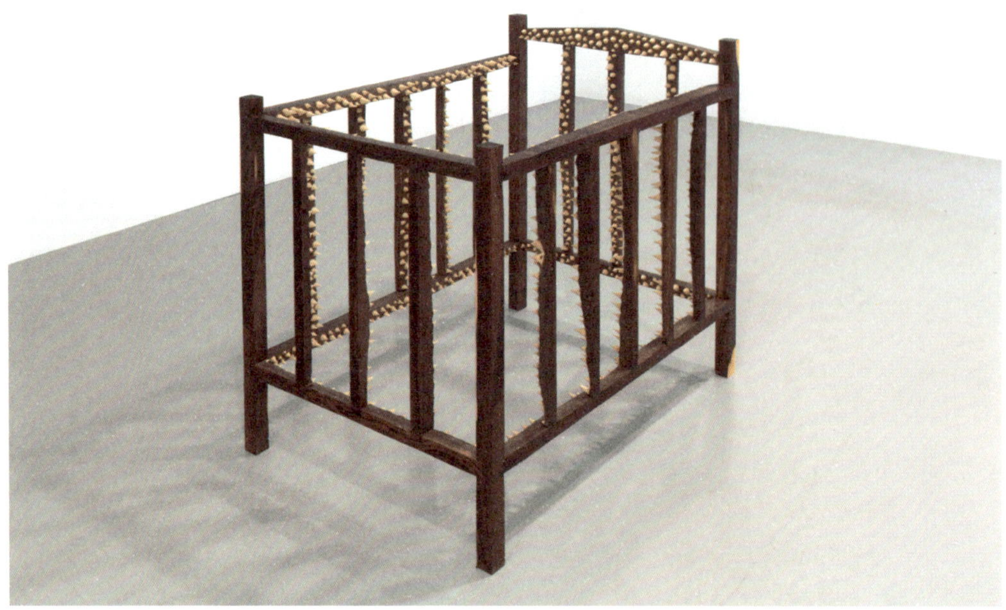

Fig. 2. Hugh Hayden, *Oreo*, 2018. Texas ebony (*Ebonopis ebano*). 36 × 37 × 26 inches (91.4 × 94 × 66 cm)

drawings and paintings originally collected by the early childhood scholar Rhoda Kellogg.[1] Among other artistic projects, Belott chooses, frames, enlarges, and composes many of these works of art by children. His homage to the marks of real children reminds us that even though all adults were children once, they are no longer. When he copies real children's work, he calls his copies "failures" or "forgeries." He leaves child and adult skills distinct from each other, even while building one on the other, in a performance of the cumulative process by which skills are acquired. Belott's artistic hand is both everywhere and discreet, organizing the whole while allowing each child-part its autonomy. He reminds us that the use of media, as well as the politics and diplomacy of institutional art worlds, is a skill, and skills are what human beings master with practice over time.

As a retort to a modernist admiration of the child's mark, detractors would often say, sometimes only half-jokingly, that a painting by Jackson Pollock could have been made by a child, or that a kindergarten painting was every bit as good as one by Joan Mitchell. But a recent systematic study has proved that even people with no professional art experience can tell the difference between the marks of a child and those of a skilled

                                                          Higonnet

adult artist.[2] The most formally elementary marks made by an adult will be perceived as intentional signs, not random scribbles. Adults' experiences, including of their own childhoods, stir purpose and reference into their representations, no matter how abstract. Even if a childlike mark is being mimicked, the conscious effort of the mimicry shows.

Anyway, there are no more innocent signs. Robert Gober (page 115), Mona Hatoum (page 117), Hugh Hayden (fig. 2), and Doris Salcedo can all take the simple rectangular shape and upright slats of a baby crib and layer them with evocations of the vise, the prison, or the torture instrument because a crib can never now be just a crib. Nor will anyone who has looked at these artists' versions of a crib ever look at a crib in the same way again.

Or take the example of a Duane Hanson sculpture in which a child appears to be innocently putting together the pieces of an ordinary puzzle of the United States (pages 30–31). But of course the puzzle itself is far from innocent, no matter how ordinary. Through the puzzle, the child is learning the outcome of a history of the United States. The very idea that the United States is a whole whose pieces fit perfectly together is a great national fiction, achieved at the price of revolution, civil war, mass migrations, and murderous campaigns to confine Indigenous peoples within reservations. To Hanson's credit, he has paused the child in the midst of putting the pieces of that fiction together, as if her own thoughts were interrupting the lessons she is consciously and unconsciously absorbing.

At the rate at which all sorts of information and images now move through our machines and our brains, we no longer can maintain an elite category of images with an exclusive claim to historical reference. Art historians and critics used to make it their business to do the exceptionally arduous job of tracking down lineages of allusion for masterpieces of oil painting, metal or stone sculpture, and architecture. The visual democracy of the Internet, which allows us to check, cross-reference, and research anything online, has recognized allusion in all media and all audiences. We find and decode clues everywhere in popular culture. Media for and about children are no longer immune to exegesis. What could be more densely layered with references and puns than the television show *The Simpsons*, despite the association of its animated cartoon medium with childhood? Episodes of *The Simpsons* have been laced with references to the poetry of Edgar Allan Poe, to 1950s television shows, to Dunkin' Donuts, and (as I write) to the luxury couture of Balenciaga. The jokes depend both on an encyclopedic range of references and on a lingering awareness of past cultural hierarchies. The challenge now is not knowing too little, but knowing too much. If all meanings are conflated, or the latest meaning devours all previous meanings, there is no more interplay among meanings, only a leaden burden. The trick now is to keep some distance between the meanings invoked. The best art of our time does that, by using distinct layers, juxtapositions, and adjacencies to keep meanings reverberating.

If only because the online circulation of images levels old hierarchies, the art world has finally allowed into its sanctums media once negatively associated with women and with crafts. Textiles, especially, inform our present artistic moment, and works made entirely with fabric are now routinely held up as cultural icons. Quilts, notably, now appear to us to have always been bearers and producers of American signs. When an artist like Faith Ringgold works in the medium of the quilt, she is no longer perceived to have marginalized herself by working in a lesser, feminine, matrilineal domain, but instead to have tapped into a fundamentally American tradition. To the extent that the content of her art, as in her works related to *Tar Beach* (page 97), tells stories of racial segregation and of children's escape from their circumstances into dream worlds, the medium of the story quilt is now understood to support her meanings, not diminish them.

Similarly, Ringgold's reproduction of her quilt work as children's book illustrations no longer suffers dismissal. If anything, her willingness to educate children with alternative narratives of race feels like an extension of her lifelong activism. With the realization of how many social lessons children absorb from the moment they are born, children's books have come under political scrutiny. Both the left and the right find some books too dangerous for children to read, and especially for them to read in schools, each side equally aware that children's books instill enduring values both negative and positive. In children's books, perhaps even more than in art for adults, the diversification of authors and imagery has come to seem necessary.

Our reckoning with the impact of book illustrations on children's imaginations is dismantling the boundary between "art" and "illustration." In 2021, for example, the Museum of Fine Arts, Boston, devoted a major exhibition to the work of the artist Ekua Holmes (pages 98–99, 101),[3] whose prestigious Caldecott award is nonetheless an award for book illustration. For Holmes's radiant collages to receive the attention they deserve, we have had to change our attitudes.

Our collective image of childhood has opened wide in twenty-first-century art practices. Though in theory this could have been accomplished by white male artists, in reality it simply wasn't. Only from experience, apparently, could images of the childhoods lived by the poor and people of color surface in art. Only from experience, apparently, could the caretaker's point of view on childhood surface in art, or a woman's point of view on the act of giving birth. What was the likelihood that in 1973 anyone other than a mother fully engaged in the care of a child would notice, let alone represent, the subject of Mierle Laderman Ukeles's *Dressing to Go Out / Undressing to Go In* (pages 140–41): the tension between love and tedium involved in dressing and undressing a small child day after day, year in and year out?

Caretaking by fathers and queer or nonbinary parents is starting to produce important images of childhood, but it is still disproportionately women who raise children. As I write, school and day-care closures caused by the COVID-19 pandemic have pushed two million U.S. women out of the public workforce to care for children at home. In September 2021 alone, three hundred thousand women dropped out, driving women's participation rate in the public workforce to its lowest level since the 1970s.[4] Needless to say, the burdens of domestic work fall most heavily on the poor, as always.

Meanwhile, however, women are accepted in the art world more than ever before. For the first time in history, therefore, our vision of childhood is being substantially formed by the people who have lived its realities. We face a more nuanced, angrier, sadder, and also more powerful range of childhoods than we used to. In some ways, Lenka Clayton's 2013 sculpture *63 Objects Taken from My Son's Mouth* (fig. 3) echoes the repetitive domestic chore subject as well as the time-measuring grid format of Ukeles's 1973 work. Yet Clayton's work expresses an

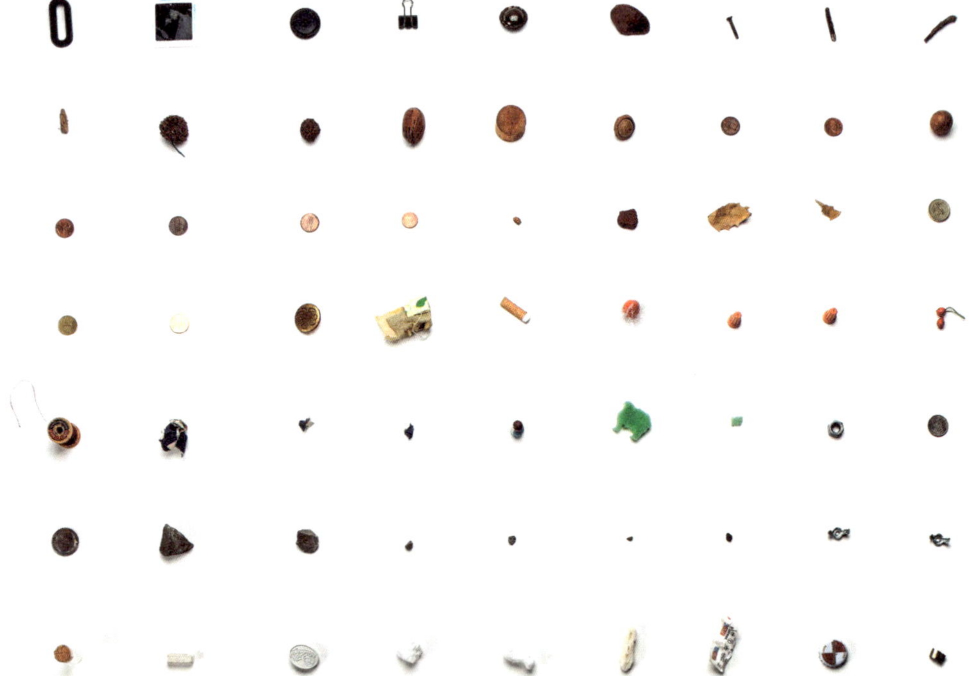

Fig. 3. Lenka Clayton, *63 Objects Taken from My Son's Mouth*, 2013. Acorn, bolt, bubblegum, buttons, carbon paper, chalk, Christmas decoration, cigarette butt, coins (GBP, USD, EURO), cotton reel, holly leaf, little wooden man, sharp metal pieces, metro ticket, nuts, plastic "O," polystyrene, rat poison (missing), seeds, slide, small rocks, specimen vial, sponge animal, sticks, teabag, wire caps, and wooden block. 40 × 40 inches (101.6 × 101.6 cm). Crystal Bridges Museum of American Art, Bentonville, Arkansas

intimacy more fiercely visceral than an earlier generation would have dared. The danger of the child choking to death, the mother's fingers inside her child's mouth, and the adamantly clinical demonstration of each threatening object's reality all extend the emotions of Ukeles's more tender image. And we are even further from the cool psychoanalysis of Mary Kelly's 1975 *Post-Partum Document* (pages 62–63), though its elegant background shadows are actually excrement stains, and her fastidious foreground charts translate a passionate obsession with her son's every utterance.

Of course there have been precursors, artists who have produced skeptical, daring, embodied, and mournful images of childhood and parenting. Among many, they include: Berthe Morisot, Paula Modersohn-Becker, Frida Kahlo, Elizabeth Catlett, Alice Neel, Sally Mann, Kerry

James Marshall, and Rineke Dijkstra. We would not be where we are now without them. All these examples might be precedents for Jordan Casteel's ongoing subway painting series (pages 150–51). Casteel updates their various experiments with impressive scale, intimate point of view, monumental figures, tautly interlocking compositions, and contemporary locations. She translates the fleeting moments of childcare and childhood, such as weary commutes on the New York City subway, into majesty. Her subjects, slumped with fatigue in their ordinary clothes, still support and embrace each other. And we are there with them, in the same packed car, placed by Casteel at a child's height.

The just demand to confront the diversity of childhoods has focused us on the content of art and on the identity of artists. But as *To Begin Again* reveals, the legacy of past work has also produced powerful forms. Exercised by its history, contemporary art about childhood flexes aesthetic muscles. Its styles are several, and equally effective.

Njideka Akunyili Crosby packs multiple registers of realism into her paintings, on an epic scale (pages 127, 129). She builds floors with terrazzo shards of newsprint imagery that might read as intricate, flat collagework, except that her massively perspectival mid-ground forms pound three-dimensional illusions of volume into her images: rows of desks, hoods of taxis, consoles, shelves. Against these competing optics, Akunyili Crosby audaciously pits her figures, themselves constructed with arresting contrasts between assertively flat color, masterfully drawn and shaded representations of fabric worn on bodies, and faces rendered with photographic realism. When the fabrics Akunyili Crosby represents are patterned, her extraordinary ability to bend and fold those patterns with the tricks of painting adds yet another force field to her images. And as if that weren't enough, the signs embedded in her representations of newspaper-print pictures and fabrics invoke social and family history, often the history of the women in her family. Containment and release have been forced to coexist. Space, color, and time yield to her art.

In a very different style, Carmen Winant has achieved something equally grand for our time. Though as I write I cannot predict what the work about childhood commissioned for *To Begin Again* will end up being, the commission summons the impact Winant has already made with her 2018 *My Birth* (see page 256). Taking the form of both an installation shown at the Museum of Modern Art, New York, and a book, *My Birth* attaches itself like a rhizome to the history of women through some two thousand small, banal, reproduced photographs, some of her own mother giving birth, but many more of anonymous women. In the installation, the photographs were attached to facing walls with deceptively casual tears of tape. Yet Winant builds the ostensible insignificance of any one image into a massive bulwark of maternal experience. Her astoundingly consistent aesthetic finds the potential in each tiny, frail element to be united through scale, tone, and internal composition into an overwhelming strength. Every element is its own individual story, and becomes an integral component of a heroic collective story. No experience of birth is like any other, and most go unsung, but Winant has orchestrated their multiplicity.

In yet another very different style, Heji Shin has expressed the shock of birth. Where Winant diffused the experience of birth into its communal social vastness, Shin's photographs concentrate on the personal experience of its brutality (pages 109–11). Her format, which crops out the mother's body so that all we see is an infant's head emerging from between thighs and held by expertly placed gloved hands, corresponds to the clinical gaze of the trained midwife or obstetrician. But the photographs are so chromatically saturated, so large, and the infant's heads are so deformed by their passage through the birth canal, so glistening with the mother's fluids, that the clinical is magically reversed into the visceral. Shin manages to flip objective observation into subjective experience. To be at the end of labor, to force a baby's head out of your body, its size at the very outer limits of evolutionary possibility to develop the brain in the protection of the womb, is to feel Shin's image. Nothing of you exists any longer except the pulverizing compression of will and pain into that push. What was invisible, once a part of your body, suddenly becomes an extrusion. At that exact moment, the baby is both born from your body and still inside you. Your body, briefly, but unforgettably, becomes a threshold. It is the moment of the mother's utmost triumph, a phenomenal feat of courage. And hope. The moment looks terrifying, and it is, as all truly sublime experiences are. Shin has represented its hideous ferocity. Her photographs violate every convention of feminine decorum. It's about time.

                                                          Higonnet

To begin again was never going to be easy. To reimagine childhood will take every ounce of conviction, purpose, and beauty we can summon. It will be worth all the trouble.

1

For more on Kellogg and her collection, see Jeffrey De Blois's essay on page 179.

2

Leslie Snapper et al., "Your Kid Could Not Have Done That: Even Untutored Observers Can Discern Intentionality and Structure in Abstract Expressionist Art," *Cognition* 137 (2015): 154–65, https://dx .doi.org/10.1016/j.cognition.2014.12.009. This study extends the findings of a previous one by Angelina Hawley-Dolan and Ellen Winner, "Seeing the Mind Behind the Art: People Can Distinguish Abstract Expressionist Paintings from Highly Similar Paintings by Children, Chimps, Monkeys, and Elephants," *Psychological Science* 22, no. 4 (April 2011): 435–41, https://doi .org/10.1177/0956797611400915.

3

Paper Stories, Layered Dreams: The Art of Ekua Holmes, July 17, 2021–January 24, 2022. Although the Morgan Library & Museum in New York has honored children's book illustrators in the past, notably Maurice Sendak and J. R. R. Tolkien, it is both an art museum and a library.

4

National Women's Law Center, cited in Kathryn Dill, "Millions of Workers Stay Home to Watch Young Children as Daycares Struggle," *Wall Street Journal*, October 24, 2021, https://www.wsj.com /articles/millions-of-workers-stay-home -to-watch-young-children-as-daycares -struggle-11635087600.

Border

Valeria Luiselli

"Why did you come to the United States?" That's the first question on the intake questionnaire for unaccompanied child migrants. The questionnaire is used in the federal immigration court in New York City where I started working as a volunteer interpreter in 2015. My task there is a simple one: I interview children, following the intake questionnaire, and then translate their stories from Spanish to English.

But nothing is ever that simple. I hear words, spoken in the mouths of children, threaded in complex narratives. They are delivered with hesitance, sometimes distrust, always with fear. I have to transform them into written words, succinct sentences, and barren terms. The children's stories are always shuffled, stuttered, always shattered beyond the repair of a narrative order. The problem with trying to tell their story is that it has no beginning, no middle, and no end.

When the intake interview with a child is over, I meet with lawyers to deliver and explain my transcription and occasional notes. The lawyers then analyze the child's responses, trying to come up with options for a viable defense against a child's deportation and the "potential relief" he or she is likely to get. The next step is to find legal representation. Once an attorney has agreed to take on a case, the real legal battle begins. If that battle is won, the child will obtain some form of immigration relief. If it is lost, they will receive a deportation order from a judge.

I watch our own children sleep in the back seat of the car as we cross the George Washington Bridge into New Jersey. I glance back now and then from the copilot's seat at my ten-year-old stepson, visiting us from Mexico, and my five-year-old daughter. Behind the wheel, my husband concentrates on the road ahead.

It is the summer of 2014. We are waiting for our green cards to be either granted or denied and, in the meantime, we decide to go on a family road trip. We will drive from Harlem, New York, to a town in Cochise County, Arizona, near the U.S.-Mexico border.

According to the slightly offensive parlance of U.S. immigration law, for the three years or so that we had lived in New York we had been "nonresident aliens." That's the term used to describe anyone from outside the United States—"alien"—whether or not they are residents. There are "nonresident aliens," "resident aliens," and even "removable aliens"—that I know of. We wanted to become "resident aliens," even though we knew what applying for green cards implied: the lawyers, the expenses, the many vaccinations and medical exams, the months of sustained uncertainty, the rather humiliating intermediate steps, such as having to wait for an "advance parole" document in order to be able to leave the country and be paroled back in, like a criminal, as well as the legal prohibition against traveling abroad, without losing immigration status, before being granted advance parole. Despite all that, we decided to apply.

When we finally sent out our applications, a few weeks before leaving for our road trip, we started feeling strange, somewhat out of place, a little circumspect—as if throwing that envelope in the blue mailbox on our street corner had changed something in us. We joked, somewhat frivolously, about the possible definitions of our new, now pending, migratory status. Were we "pending aliens," or "writers seeking status," or "alien writers," or maybe "pending Mexicans"? I suppose, deeper down, we were simply asking ourselves, perhaps for the first time, that same question I now ask children at the beginning of each intake interview: "Why did you come to the United States?"

We didn't have a clear answer. No one ever does. But the deed was done, we had filed our applications, and while we waited for an answer we were not allowed to leave the country. So, when summer arrived, we bought maps, rented a car, packed a few basics, made playlists, and left New York.

The green card application is nothing like the intake questionnaire for undocumented minors. When you apply for a green card you have to answer things like "Do you intend to practice polygamy?" and "Are you a member of the Communist Party?" and "Have you ever knowingly committed a crime of moral turpitude?" And although nothing can or should be taken lightly when you are in the fragile situation of asking for permission to live in a country that is not your own, there is something almost innocent in the green card application's preoccupations with and visions of the future and its possible threats: polyamorous debauchery, communism, weak morals! The green card questionnaire has a retro kind of candor, like the grainy Cold War films we watched on VHS. The intake questionnaire for undocumented children, on the other hand, reveals a colder, more cynical and brutal reality. It reads as if it were written in high definition, and as you make your way down its forty questions it's impossible not to feel that the world has become a much more fucked-up place than anyone could have ever imagined.

The process by which a child is asked questions during the intake interview is called screening, a term that is as cynical as it is appropriate: the child a reel of footage, the translator-interpreter an obsolete apparatus used to channel that footage, the legal system a screen, itself too worn out, too filthy and tattered to allow any clarity, any attention to detail. Stories often become generalized, distorted, appear out of focus.

Before the formal screening begins, the person conducting it has to fill in basic biographical information: the child's name, age, and country of birth, the name of a sponsor in the United States, the people with whom he or she is living at the time, and a contact number and address. All these details have to be written down at the very top of the questionnaire.

A few spaces down, right before the first formal interview question, a line floats across the page like an uncomfortable silence:

Where is the child's mother?____________ father? ____________

The interviewer has to write down whatever information the child can or will give to fill in those blanks—those two empty spaces that look a bit like badly stitched wounds. Too often, the spaces remain blank: all the children come without their fathers and mothers. And many of them do not even know where their parents are.

We are driving across Oklahoma in early July when we first hear about the wave of children arriving, alone and undocumented, at the border. On our long westbound drives we begin to follow the story on the radio. It's a sad story that hits so close to home and yet seems completely unimaginable, almost unreal: tens of thousands of children from Mexico and Central America have been detained at the border. Nothing is clear in the initial coverage of the situation—which soon becomes known, more widely, as an immigration crisis, though others will advocate for the more accurate term "refugee crisis."

Questions, speculations, and opinions flash-flood the news during the days that follow. Who are these children? What will happen to them? Where are the parents? Where will they go next? And why, why did they come to the United States?

"Why did you come to the United States?" I ask children in immigration court.

Their answers vary, but they often point to a single pull factor: reunification with a parent or another close relative who migrated to the U.S. years earlier. Other times, the answers point to push factors—the unthinkable circumstances the children are fleeing: extreme violence, persecution and coercion by gangs, mental and physical abuse, forced labor, neglect, abandonment. It is not even the American Dream that they pursue, but rather the more modest aspiration to wake up from the nightmare into which they were born.

Then comes question number two in the intake questionnaire: "When did you enter the United States?" Most children don't know the exact date. They smile and say "last year" or "a few months ago" or simply "I don't know." They've fled their towns and cities; they've walked and swum and hidden and run and mounted freight trains and trucks. They've turned themselves in to Border Patrol officers. They've come all this way looking for—for what, exactly? The questionnaire doesn't make these other inquiries. But it does ask for precise details: "When did you enter the United States?"

As we drive deeper into the country, following the enormous map I take from the glove box and study from time to time, the summer heat becomes drier, the light thinner and whiter, the roads more solitary. We start hunting down any available information about the undocumented children and the situation at the border. We collect local newspapers, which pile on the floor of our car, in front of my copilot seat. We do constant, quick online searches and tune in to the radio every time we can catch a signal.

                                                        Luiselli

More questions, speculations, and opinions flood media coverage of the crisis: some sources elaborate lucid and complex conjectures on the origin and possible causes of the sudden surge of arrivals of unaccompanied minors, others denounce the inhumane conditions and systematic maltreatment the children must endure in detention facilities near the border, and a few others endorse the spontaneous civilian protests against them.

A caption in a web publication explains an unsettling photograph of men and women waving flags, banners, and rifles in the air: "Protesters, some exercising their open-carry rights, assemble outside of the Wolverine Center in Vassar [Michigan] that would house illegal juveniles to show their dismay for the situation." In another photograph that we find on the web, an elderly couple holds signs saying "Illegal Is a Crime" and "Return to Senders." They are sitting on beach chairs, wearing sunglasses. A caption explains, "Thelma and Don Christie (C) of Tucson demonstrate against the arrival of undocumented immigrants in Oracle, Arizona. July 15, 2014." I zoom in on their faces and wonder. What passed through the minds of Thelma and Don Christie when they prepared their protest signs? Did they pencil in "protest against illegal immigrants" on their calendars, right next to "mass" and just before "bingo"? What were they thinking when they put their beach chairs inside their trunk? And what did they talk about as they drove the forty miles or so north, toward the protest in Oracle?

In varying degrees, some papers and webpages announce the arrival of undocumented children like a biblical plague. Beware the locusts! They will cover the face of the ground so that it cannot be seen—these menacing, coffee-colored boys and girls, with their obsidian hair and slant eyes. They will fall from the skies, on our cars, on our green lawns, on our heads, on our schools, on our Sundays. They will make a racket, they will bring their chaos, their sickness, their dirt, their brownness. They will cloud the pretty views, they will fill the future with bad omens, they will fill our tongues with barbarisms. And if they are allowed to stay here they will—eventually—reproduce!

We wonder if the reactions would be different were all these children of a lighter color: of better, purer breeds and nationalities. Would they be treated more like people? More like children? We read the papers, listen to the radio, see photographs, and wonder.

In a diner near Roswell, New Mexico, we overhear a conversation between a waitress and a customer. As she refills his coffee, she tells him that hundreds of migrant kids will be put on private planes—rumored to have been funded by a patriotic millionaire—and deported that same day back to Honduras, or Mexico, or somewhere. The planes full of "alien" children will leave from an airport not far from the famous UFO museum, the one our children have been set on visiting. The term "alien," which only a few weeks ago made us laugh and speculate, which we had been passing around the car as an inside family joke, is suddenly shown to us under a bleaker light. It's strange how concepts can erode so easily, how words we once used lightly can alchemize abruptly into something toxic.

The next day, driving out of Roswell, we look for news on what happened with those deportees. We find no details of the exact circumstances under which they were deported, or how many there were, and if it's true that a local millionaire financed their removal. We do, however, come across these lines in a Reuters report that read like the beginning of a cruel, absurdist story by Mikhail Bulgakov or Daniil Kharms: "Looking happy, the deported children exited the airport on an overcast and sweltering afternoon. One by one, they filed into a bus, playing with balloons they had been given." We dwell for a while on the adjective "happy" and the strangely meticulous description of the local weather in San Pedro Sula, Honduras: "an overcast and sweltering afternoon." But what we really cannot stop reproducing, somewhere in the dark back of our minds, is the uncanny image of the children holding those balloons.

In our long daily drives, to fill in the empty hours, we sometimes tell our children stories about the old American Southwest, back when it used to be part of Mexico. I tell them about Saint Patrick's Battalion, the group of Irish Catholic soldiers who joined the U.S. Army as cannon fodder during the Mexican-American War, but later changed sides to fight along with the Mexicans. I tell them about the Treaty of Guadalupe Hidalgo, signed after that war, in which Mexico lost half its territory to the United States. Their father tells them about President Andrew Jackson's Indian Removal Act, approved by Congress in 1830, and explains how it brutally exiled Native Americans to reservations. He tells them about Geronimo, Cochise, Mangas Coloradas, and the other Chiricahua Apaches: the last inhabitants of a continent to surrender to the white-eyes, after years of battle against both the U.S. Bluecoats and the Mexican Army. Those last Chiricahua resisted for many more years after the Indian Removal Act was passed. They finally surrendered in 1886 and were "removed" to the San Carlos Reservation—in southern Arizona, toward which we are now driving. It's curious, or perhaps just sinister, that the word "removal" is still used to refer to the deportation of "illegal" immigrants—those bronzed barbarians who threaten the white peace and superior values of the "Land of the Free."

When we run out of stories to tell our children, we fall silent and look out at the unbroken line of the highway, perhaps trying to put together the many pieces of the story—the unimaginable story—unfolding just outside the small and protected world of our rented car. Though all of it resists a rational explanation, we talk it over and consider its many angles. We try to answer our own children's questions about the situation as best we can. But we don't do very well. How do you explain any of this to your own children?

The third and fourth questions on the intake questionnaire are ones that our children, too, ask many times, though in their own words: "With whom did you travel to this country?" and "Did you travel with anyone you knew?" All children travel with a paid coyote. Some of them travel also with siblings, cousins, and friends.

Sometimes, when our children fall asleep again, I look back at them, or hear them breathe, and wonder if they would survive in the hands of coyotes and what would happen to them if they were deposited at the U.S. border, left either on their own or in the custody of Border Patrol officers. Were they to find themselves alone, crossing borders and countries, would my own children survive?

Conversation: Naima J. Keith, Oscar Murillo, and Sable Elyse Smith

This conversation was recorded in person in New York City on March 6, 2020, and was transcribed and edited over the fall of 2021.

Naima J. Keith: Sable, can you begin by telling us about the Coloring Book series and how you arrived at making it?

Sable Elyse Smith: In 2015 I was walking down 125th Street in Harlem, taking a break from work. At that time, I worked in the education department at the Studio Museum. I was just out on a coffee run, and I saw this coloring book on the ground, and it had a weird image on the front. There was a pigeon, and then I saw the phrase "County Court" on it. Something compelled me to pick it up. I went back to my desk and started looking through this object that had been colored by a child. And there was one page that was incredibly terrifying to me (fig. 1)—I was kind of shocked, and I thought, "Oh, there's something here, I have to keep looking through this and move it around with me." Initially I wasn't thinking about making work with it. But it was an object with images and these frightening narratives that I couldn't escape. About three years later, I started making the paintings based on it. There were so many things that were fascinating about it. One was the weird racialization of all the people in the book. And then, because it's a coloring book and an activity book, it was meant to be, in its functionality, a kind of didactic tool: to teach children something. It had a very specific audience, right? Because I also came out of this education space, I understood how early childhood development works: the implications of how things are worded, or how when you ask someone to listen and participate or engage their motor skills with it, that can entrench a certain type of idea. And so at every turn of the coloring book, there was a real foreclosure of imagination, and an incessant projection of oneself into the pages of the coloring book, and then into the system and into the narrative of having an interaction with courts.

NJK And these coloring books would appear when the child was waiting to see a parent who may be incarcerated, or they may be in some sort of court setting. . .

SES Also social service environments and nonprofits that are interacting with people. And they're given out for free. They're either in the court lobby or other touch points where a child might be dragged along by whomever they're with.

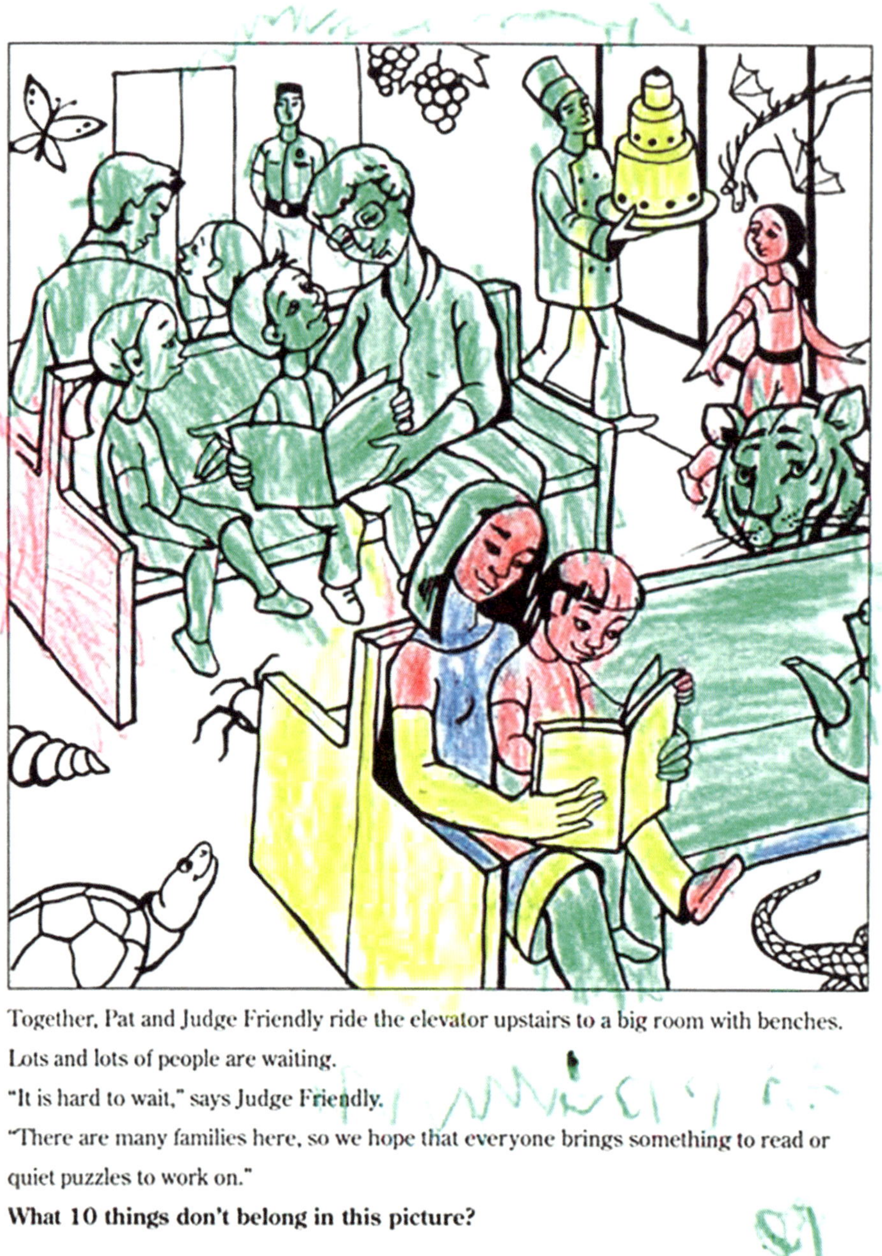

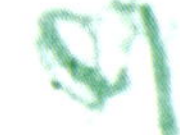

Fig. 1. Page from the coloring book Smith found on 125th Street, Harlem, New York

Keith, Murillo, Smith

NJK   It crystallizes the idea that some children are exposed to this type of material and others are not, that there's a certain innocence for kids who look a certain way or come from a certain economic background.

SES   Yeah, and just the intentionality of producing an object like this, right? It's a thing that's deemed good or helpful. But I'm always fascinated by and pay attention to language, and how the language is also incredibly oppressive and creates a limit for certain types of bodies, and there's a violence in that. This book is geared toward children. Before you even grow up, does your life lead you to some interaction with the space you're already being primed for? Are you being told that this is where you'll end up? The last page of the coloring book says, "Thank you for visiting." And there's a little pigeon waving. As if you had a choice. It feels like there's an implication, a "come back again." So there are all these really bizarre moments that I think are quite pointed. And even though maybe the institution that made the book doesn't think so (and I think there are a lot of arguments we can make there as well), it talks about how entrenched the prison system is in our society. And that it is built on the absolute necessity that people, specifically Black people, continuously circulate through it. All these biases come out in the way the book is organized. It teaches you something about syntax and the frame. And I mean that in many ways.

NJK   Oscar, how did you arrive at the *Frequencies* series in 2013? How did you choose the schools that you were going to interact with to produce the series?

Oscar Murillo: The project started around thinking about drawing and collaboration. It all started from the context of my own practice, and how I kind of gave up the idea of the purity of drawing. And through seeing myself as an already corrupted subject, as an adult who has already been indoctrinated. Throughout history, there have been attempts to unlearn, and to recognize the importance of children's drawings. So I thought, "Well, why not go to the source directly, and turn it into a collaboration?" Another influence was the Swiss artist Dieter Roth, specifically his *Tischmatten* [table mats] project, which he made throughout his life, basically by putting a sheet of cardboard on a desk (fig. 2). In that way of making seamless work, you're inviting the unconscious to be part of it. And then I thought, as an adult, I cannot do that, because I'm already too aware.

NJK   Did you feel like corruption came from school, from outside influences?

OM   I think we're all implicated in the corruption of how we maneuver, how we dress, how we move in society. It's not really about pointing at any specific individual in any given society. There's this picture of my son going to school for the first day, and he looks like he's carrying the weight of the world, like, "I don't want to be here." We all go through those kinds of initial moments of indoctrination. And by the time we're adults, it's over. Collaboration to me becomes an interesting, very rich arena in which to explore the push-and-pull relationships that are happening in institutions around the world. Another factor was that every school system around the

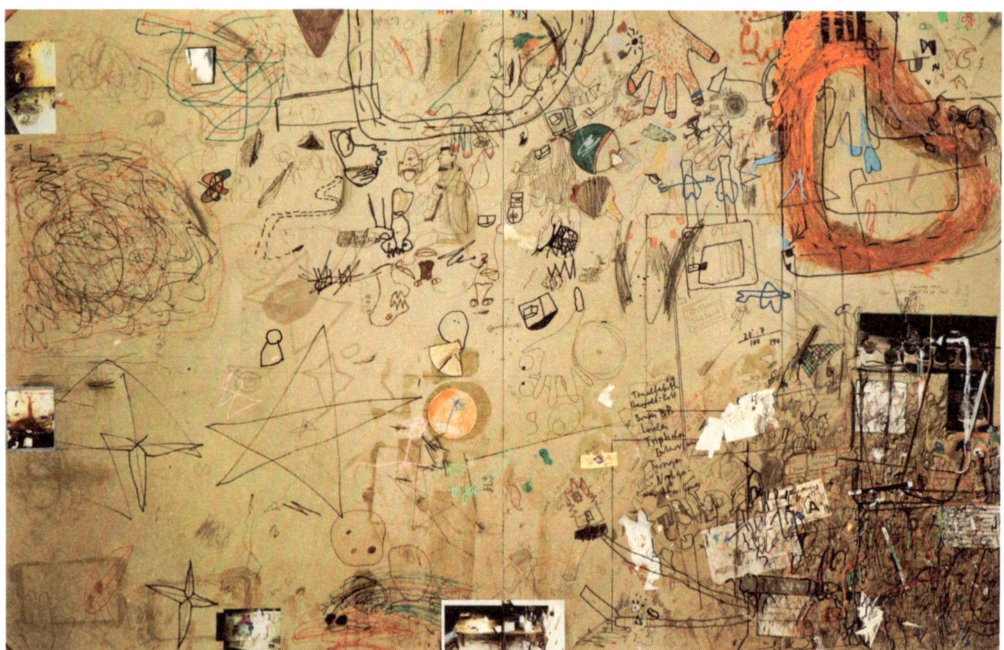

Fig. 2. Dieter Roth, *Matte vom Kaffeetisch, Bali-Mosfellsbaer*, 1996–97. Pencil, marker pen, ink, acrylic, oil, glue, and collage (color and Polaroid photographs, printed materials, nails, paper clips, plastic adhesive tape, pins, washers, staples) on chipboard, glued on plywood. 41 ¼ × 64 ½ × 1 ⅝ inches (104.8 × 163.8 × 4.1 cm)

world is different—whether you move around the classroom and go from one classroom to the next or stay in one place for the whole day. Ultimately, that child, or a multitude of children, will be in a given space long enough to interact with the varying space of the canvas wrapped around their desk. It was also important that there aren't any instructions given and that we don't provide anything in terms of writing.

NJK   So they are not even given a set of crayons or colored pencils?

OM   Exactly. Even if the child decides not to interact, just the fact that they were touching the canvas—that space—and the patina that builds up over the months are indicative of that interaction. It was with help from friends and family that I saw the possibility for the project

to become much more universal in scope, and that I could not do it alone. It needed its own system.

NJK   You essentially reached out to different schools and said, "I'm an artist, I want to do a project where I literally lay canvas on students' desks."

OM   Yeah, but it was much more organic, because it happened initially in places I knew. My school in Colombia from when I was a kid was the first one, and a very easy entry point (fig. 3). Then we did it in Berlin through friends, and then in Bogotá. And then, when [political scientist] Clara Dublanc, who's a friend and now very much a colleague, came on board in 2013, she really pushed it. I said, "Well, I want this to be something that we take outside of the Western context, outside of those confines."

Keith, Murillo, Smith

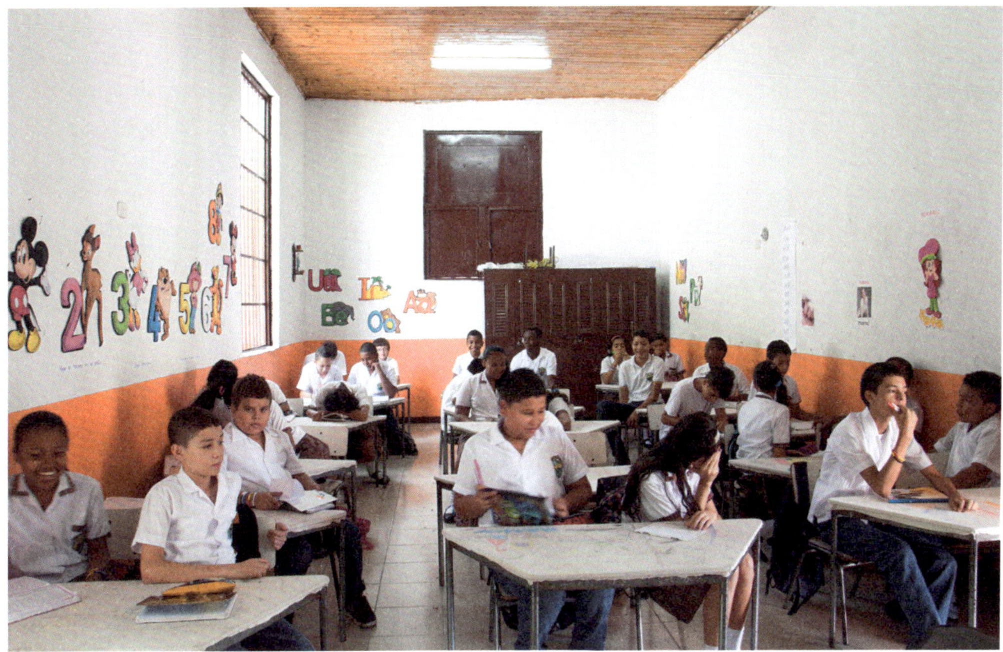

Fig. 3. Oscar Murillo, *Frequencies* project at Colegio Hernando Caicedo, La Paila, Colombia, 2013

NJK When you exhibit the works, is it important for people to know where they came from?

OM Eight years on, there is an immense amount of material. To me, it's a kind of index library, so in a way, when one is putting together a show, politics comes in. And what I mean is that, with this material, you can construct a narrative as a coauthor, or as a cooperating institution.

NJK What are the ages of the children?

OM It's usually ten to sixteen, depending on the context. To me, those years are fundamental in the shift from child to young adult, which I know from my time as a teaching assistant.

NJK Sable, do you know what ages the coloring book is targeted for?

SES It feels to me like it maxes out around eight. Just because of the simplicity of the activity and the coloring. But the actual target is a lot younger. I think someone has to read the stories, so it makes siblings perhaps interact with it. Thinking about how many people touch or interact with the book was also an interesting aspect for me to consider. Hannah Black wrote in an essay once about this series: "The coloring book is not for the child, who knows very well what a prison is, but for the adult handing it over. For the adult who supplies it, the book, with its figures blank of color, is a prop for the performance of faith in the law's terrible gravity."[1]

NJK How do these projects relate to your own childhoods, your own personal experiences, or your own relationships to ideas of innocence or outside influences in your own life?

245

SES On the one hand, I have moved through a public school system, so there are some similarities in characters, and an assumed narrative related to intention that certain institutions perpetuate. But this project is not about personal narrative or history or experience even. It's about language as a tool and how tools have been used and continue to be used. Weapons are also tools, and tools are activated, given power, by the one who wields them.

OM For me, I think it has a duality. It's both very personal and also invokes the unconscious. Personally, leaving Colombia as a ten- or eleven-year-old probably equates to the biggest trauma I've ever felt because of where I was at that age. Drawing became a therapeutic pursuit, and also a kind of escapist space. I would heavily attribute a lot of the genesis of *Frequencies* to that spirit. Knowing how all these barriers exist, barriers in terms of access, and the fact that a kid from a certain place will just never get to see another context because of their conditions. In that way, the idea of frequency becomes a reference of difference.

NJK How do your projects problematize ideas about childhood, and why are you interested in thinking about this demographic in your work?

SES There were a couple of different threads that I was interested in. On the one hand, the idea of "childhood" is extracted from an actual child, although childhood, or rather the image of a child (read: white child), has become a stand-in for the idea of innocence. Or rather our collective projection of what innocence is, which is another way to say "pure" within the foundation of our Anglo-Christian Western society. That's what makes the coloring book inside the carceral context incredibly interesting to me. The ideas of innocence and guilt are volleyed back and forth within conversations around criminal justice. But both of these terms—"criminal" and "justice"—were birthed within a carceral landscape, which was birthed from slavery, which was birthed from anti-Blackness, etc. Meaning I am not necessarily interested in childhood per se. I'm interested in investigating the Black experience in relationship to the very infrastructure of the world Blackness exists in. The systems we live in do not afford Black people access to the status of child or the state of childhood.

NJK Are you thinking of the line racially, or are you thinking around children who have interfaced with the system in some way?

SES Both. But definitely racially first, because race cannot be extracted. And all children are not seen as equal in the eyes of the state, despite the patriotic rhetoric of equality in the United States. Sometimes race is the only reason for one's exposure to the carceral system. When we close our eyes and hear the word "child," there are a number of images that might flood to the surface. We should question ourselves about those images. And we've seen over and over again, both historically and presently, that when someone encounters a young Black male child, that child is now scary or larger-than-life, or seen as an adult or a threat, or not given the same kind of leeway or space or compassion that a white child would receive.

NJK   You both have touched on this idea that there's an instance in childhood when we start to become indoctrinated. Things start happening; you become more corrupted because you're exposed to all these outside forces. In some cases, for certain families, of certain economic backgrounds, that happens a lot sooner.

Sable, with this body of work, how important was it for you to not just replicate the images, the actual coloring book pages, but to also suggest what a child could have done to them, a child of a very particular age? Why was that "childlike" mark-making important for the project and what does it mean to you?

SES   For these paintings, there are seven pages that I chose to work with from one primary coloring book and then from an additional one I researched. All of these are reproduced; they're screenprinted, so there are multiples of each page. That repetition is important; it's a part of the narrative and a part of the tension that's created. There are a couple of things I was thinking about with the mark-making, but one is that the marks also further our understanding, our perception of who might be interacting with this. In some of the paintings, there are two different styles of marks, or marks that are competing with each other. Those are things that were important to distribute and have present. But also, the way that I start working with the pages is to just try to get pigment on paper, to have something that's really performative and kind of frenetic. It's about capturing a type of intensity and energy, and then going back and making more deliberate

choices that aren't necessarily aesthetic but that point to things. There are elements that are weird and convoluted in every aspect of the coloring book page—whether it's the drawing, or how someone is racialized, or the fact that there are all these fantastical objects, or that corrections are built into how children are supposed to interact with the page. "Color inside the lines." But what does it mean not to? And then there's the language. . .

As I'm rendering these works, sometimes there are subtleties that I'm pulling up or pointing to, and I'm thinking about how the marks can function. But then also pointing to that age group. Sometimes there are a couple of materials used on them, but mostly, it's oil sticks. They have a cerebral lushness to them, especially in person. They're very seductive, right? For the viewer, when you walk into a space, you are seduced and kind of mesmerized by these drawings. They have a certain tactility and texture on top of the page, and then also the color is doing something because I'm not mixing colors. I'm just working with the saturated pigment.

NJK   I was going to ask you about the color.

SES   For the most part, I use primary colors. And then sometimes it gets a little wild with Wite-Out or graphite or other pigments. That is a methodology I use in making any object—this kind of progression from seduction to horror. So the viewer comes in and is hella seduced. They're walking into some space and it feels playful, it feels whimsical, it's bright, it's kind of beautiful. There is what seems like a simplistic narrative on the surface. There are things that are sort of playing in the composition of the balance, and then as other things start to unfold or reveal themselves, maybe because your eye is brought to the top by some kind of pop, then you're like, what is actually happening there? Or something that might not have been immediately apparent to you if you just looked at the black-and-white screenprint now registers in full focus. There are a lot of strategies that the mark-making employs, and one of them is mimicking who's interacting with the page.

NJK   Is it important for a viewer to get those nuances or the references to the correctional system? I know my daughter would be very excited to see certain types of imagery and probably would not make the association with some of the references. Because there is that seduction, are you concerned that it's going to take away from one's understanding of the complexity of what those paintings are doing?

SES   There are two speeds that the work operates at. There's a kind of durational element, or time delay, that is built in. There is the viewer actually reading the words on the page. The scale produces one kind of viewing relationship. You walk in, you're trying to take it all in, and maybe you step back and you are invited to move closer because there is something that's drawing you in— maybe it's the texture of the paint caked on the surface, or you move in to look at a detail and then you stop and read the text. And then you step back and read the image in relationship to the text, and then maybe what the activity is. So there is a kind of time built in, a slowness. Small things pop up to the surface,

and whether someone thinks about prison or not is not important to me. I'm thinking about the structure, the apparatus, the language, and the violence; those are the things that are important. And sometimes that's called prison and sometimes that's called our daily life, and sometimes that's called our political system, and sometimes that's called . . . any number of things. Honestly, the legacies and the residue of prison are all around us.

NJK   I think that speaks to what Oscar was saying about how trauma comes in many forms, and it's not necessarily just in an incarceration situation but could also happen from moving to a different place. Oscar, in terms of mark-making, it's certainly an essential part of the *Frequencies* project, but also in your work overall. Can you talk about the importance of mark-making, both in terms of what the young people are doing in this work and then how you approach it in your own practice?

OM   For me, the idea of violence is a way in to how I think about my own mark-making. There's a collision that happens that is very violent. And yet there's an unruliness in not being able to do it neatly or from a kind of pure, let's say aesthetic, perspective. In the context of my paintings without any collaboration, it's a space to off-load energy, physical energy, and intensity. With oil painting, I'm not looking, I'm just marking, and that is for my own relief as a kind of high-intensity individual. This notion of therapy still continues. Then you have the other dimension of *Frequencies*, which is the collaboration, and the seductive beauty of these drawings when they come back, and you can

Keith, Murillo, Smith

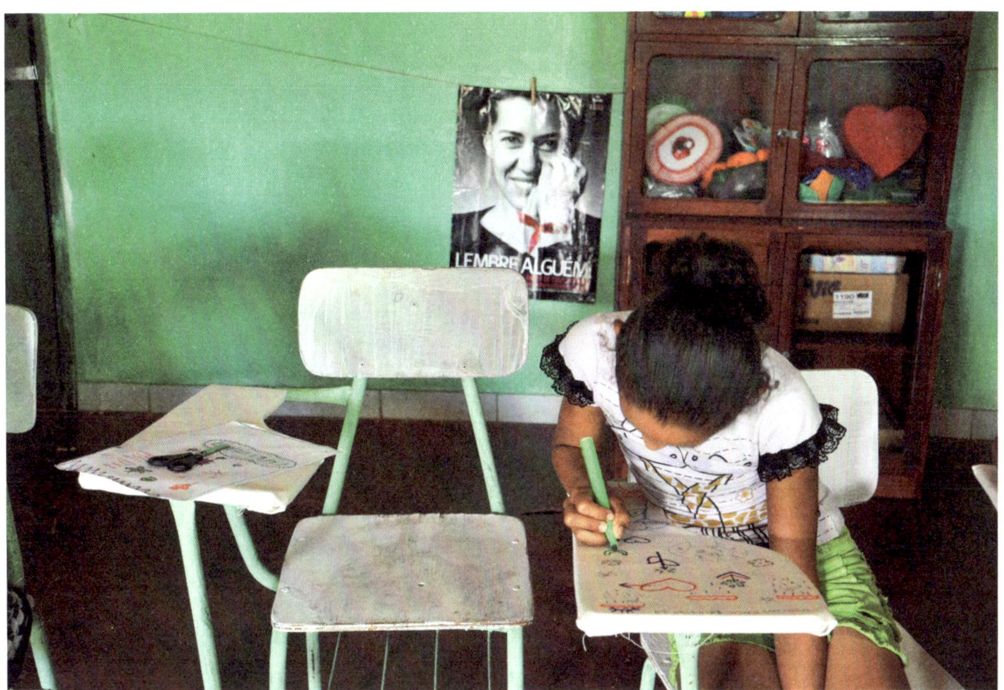

Fig. 4. Oscar Murillo, *Frequencies* project at Ai.Bi: Associação Amigos das Crianças, Brazil, 2014

dive into this world of multiple voices and people manifesting their consciousness or unconsciousness. And of course, you can get lost in that world, but in a way, that romanticism succumbs to violence again. For many years, I only saw *Frequencies* as a reference, as an index library, where it's just this amalgamation of frequency. Recently, I started to engage with them by stitching six to ten canvases together. Is it a political motive, to want to bring about this collision of two places that might never in real terms exist together?

NJK　Violence is certainly something that is touched on in both of these bodies of work. There's also a notion of control, right? On one level, childhood is associated with innocence and freedom, yet there are mechanisms of control that enter at all these different points. How

docs control enter into each of your projects?

SES　I think it's something I saw as being present in the actual object as it exists and functions out in the world, and so that was a thing to highlight—how these ideas and assumptions about how one might interact with the space or go and interact with the world are sort of controlled and shaped and also confined. And correction is a part of it, even if this wasn't a coloring book that talks specifically about the court space. But then once it's placed on top of this narrative that is about a very specific system and the child is projected into it, what do all these layers on top of each other do? I was interested in figuring out ways to highlight that even more. To highlight the assumption that this is how it's supposed to be, that this is how we interact

249

with this thing, and just kind of accept it, right? Even the things that feel very subtle, and feel like they don't have an impact, they do have a larger impact. It's about bringing to light those smaller or more invisible things that can go unnoticed or be perceived as something else.

OM　　Another thing that's important to say is that children, too, have their dark side. In a way, it's not just this very simple transition. When you have a chance to see these canvases, it's kind of frightening. I've seen a swastika, guns, and so on.

NJK　　I'm glad you're talking about this, because I was curious. I'm sure you've seen just about everything on these canvases.

OM　　Yeah, and in a way that enhances the need to have somebody who wants to be a collaborator, for there to be a space for that kind of engagement. But also, in that space, I see the canvases as recording devices (fig. 4). And the recording happens when the kid reflects how society is evolving; they offload information onto the canvas. Do they live with both parents or just one, how do they exist on a daily basis, and what relationship do they have to their desk or school? Each canvas then has a certain kind of strength to it, in defining both the kids' engagement and also what structures that engagement. The more we have pursued the project, the more it has continued to evolve, and the more we are able to introduce certain measures.

1

Hannah Black, "Universal Gravitation: Sable Elyse Smith," in the exhibition brochure for *MOOD: Studio Museum Artists in Residence*, 2018–19, MoMA PS1, New York, 2019.

Keith, Murillo, Smith

Conversation:
Mierle Laderman Ukeles
and Carmen Winant

This conversation took place over Zoom on June 10, 2021, and was transcribed and edited over the summer and fall of 2021.

Mierle Laderman Ukeles: We have never met in real life, but I feel like I've known you my whole life.

Carmen Winant: The feeling's mutual.

MLU   I think you contacted me first about "practice." We had this hysterical phone conversation about the artist's practice. That was in 2017, correct?

CW   Yes. I was pregnant with my second son; he was born in early 2018, so it must have been the summer of 2017. I was working on a long-form essay that I'm still plugging away on, all these years later, punctuated by kids and work. And I had a fantastical idea that I would speak with you for the project, a person I had never met before, a heroine to me. I can't remember how I got in touch with you, but I thought, she'll never reach back, why would she reach back? You called me a few days later, and we talked for about an hour and a half. I remember laughing hysterically during that phone call. I recorded and transcribed the conversation, and it is still sitting in this book project I'm working on. So it's still ongoing, Mierle, all these years later. I have faith that we'll meet in person one day.

MLU   You sent me, and I don't know if I was expecting this, a beautifully handwritten letter that's dated September 1, 2019.

CW   I sent you a letter because I couldn't help myself. It was a little bit like calling you. I felt pulled in your direction, and had a hundred questions that it seemed only you could answer. So I wrote you this letter and mailed it across the Atlantic Ocean. I worried that I was being invasive into your life, first with the phone call and then with the letter.

MLU   Well, I found that I was quite intimidated by the letter, actually, because I didn't know how to begin to respond. It took me several months to respond, but I finally did. It was amazing to me that you handwrote this thing. I handwrite a lot of notes, but I don't handwrite long documents. But I figured, the hell with it, and I just sent you an email a few months later.

CW   I think the central question of my letter to you was: "How was your consciousness formed?" No small question. No wonder you felt intimidated by it! I suppose that was a way in for me

to think about your life's work, to try
and crack something open for myself.
Looking at the dates of your early and
seminal works —1969, 1973, and so
forth—it's impossible not to note that
you were making revolutionary work
before the feminist revolution unfolded.
You were making meaningful connections between public maintenance and
private maintenance workers, between
the homeworker and the homemaker,
the mother worker and the maintenance worker. I have always been really
interested in how one "finds" feminist
consciousness, how it enters our bodies,
speaks to and for us. How and when
does that happen? I was putting that
question to you. You seemed like the
right person to ask.

MLU   I was a fanatic about the notion
of freedom, always. Freedom. So the
notion that art equals freedom has been
the driving force for me as far back as
I can remember. As an undergraduate
majoring in international relations, I
wrote my thesis about the development
of the independence movement of the
Tanganyika African National Union
movement toward freedom, toward
independence. It's just been in me.

After being in a bunch of schools, I
was at NYU in a new master's program called Creative Experiences in
Interrelated Arts. One of my teachers
was a very famous sculptor, and I was
his best student. I became pregnant and
was continuing to work. I came to class,
and it was obvious that I was pregnant
by then. He was at the other end of this
big studio, and when he saw me—I
still remember it, to this day—across
this entire studio space he said, "Well,
I guess now you can't be an artist."

I should have walked up to him and
smacked him. I really should have. I
didn't. I went silent, and it was actually
deep, deep in me, a fury. Furious. So,
that was one thing.

And then I had this baby; we were very
thrilled with this baby. I didn't know
what the hell I was doing. I was very
rigid about everything. Like early femi-
nists—not too humorous and rigid. For
example, we lived in Greenwich Village,
and during the day I would walk her
around Washington Square Park in her
carriage. There was a playground there,
and there were a lot of young women in
the playground, nannies and mothers.
And I said to myself, if you cross that
threshold, you're never going to come
out. I was so rigid. I never stepped inside
that playground. I bet I could have had
a good time there. Instead, I walked
her around and around and around,
and it was very lonely. I mean, it's so
ideological.

Then when the baby was two months
old, I went back to work. I got a
babysitter, and I would go to work two
or three days a week. When I closed the
door, I would stand out in the hall listening if the baby was being murdered
inside. That began this whole thing of
when I was with the baby, I would be
thinking, "I'm going to lose it. I'm going
to lose it. How am I going to keep going
with my work? I won't be an artist."
Hearing that voice in the back of my
head. I was also so tired. Nobody even
knows how tired you can get with little
babies. It's beyond comprehension. So,
finally, I got the babysitter and went to
work. There I was. Okay, now you're at
work. Now work. Now make art. And
I'm thinking to myself, "Is she paying

attention to her? Is she really paying attention to her?"

This split became my life. I felt like two separate people. There was very little support out there. I felt like I was just falling, falling. I felt that each one was me. I felt so privileged that I could be a part of this incredible discovery that makes up the life of the baby. They don't come with a manual. Like, how do you sit up? How do you talk? They invent everything and, as an artist, I was fully aware of this extraordinary level of creativity in the human, in the human child, inventing everything, falling down, getting up, trying it again, experimenting with this, experimenting with that. I did what I had to do to enable her to have that maximum effort or freedom to do what she was doing. She was doing great things. But hardly anybody was interested in this experience I was having. I mean, Jack was interested. My relatives were interested. But artists and other people I knew didn't ask, "What? What is this?" They didn't ask me any questions.

The other phrase, besides "Now you can't be an artist," is "Do you do anything?" I'm splitting myself down the middle trying to keep my work going and to be a good mother, and people who knew me only as a mother would say, "Do you do anything?" Those two sentences, they made me so pissed off that they have fueled my work ever since. When I arrived in the New York City Sanitation Department eleven years later and heard them saying, "People think we're part of the garbage," and saw how pissed off they were that they weren't seen, I was on very firm ground in that we were joined in

this pissed-offness. How stupid. Such a waste. The doors not opening, not expanding. So I ended up writing this manifesto. I had an epiphany. I really did have one. I was in such a crisis about being two separate people that it just came to me in my state of being so pissed off. This is what suddenly became crystal clear: If I am the boss of my freedom, then I can say, "This is art. All of this is art." And you're going to have to work it out, you people who define art, because now there's a new kind of art out there. I say what's art because I'm an artist. That's what I do. That's my job. And I say maintenance is art, as contradictory as that is. What is culture? What is art? You have to begin again. That's who we are. This is a revolution and a new world because, people, we're here. We're not going away. We are not going away. Work it out. Just work it out.

CW   It moves me to hear you talk about this. It has me thinking about the sheer power and the authority that it takes to say, "I am an artist. Let me insist on it not once but every day." That feels to me like such an engine for everything. It helps me begin to understand what it took, the fortitude.

I also want to linger on the point that nobody asked you any questions after you gave birth and into young motherhood. I remember reading an interview you gave in 2016, just a few weeks after I'd given birth to my first son, in which you made a similar statement. I teared up reading those words. My baby was sleeping on my chest; I felt immense joy, exhaustion, isolation. Most of all, I felt I'd had this revelatory experience—ecstatic and agonizing—particularly in relation to birth. People would occasionally come over, and they would say, "How are you sleeping? How's the baby eating?" You know, questions that demonstrated support. But nobody said, "How did it feel to become an animal? How did it feel to lose language? How did it feel to shit in front of other people? How did it feel to sense your body rip open? How did it feel to make an organ and then pass that organ?" I was really stunned that nobody asked me about that experience, or those that followed, in any frank way.

Of course, birth can be a very private experience. But to a greater extent, I think, we just don't want to talk about it, you know? It's deemed less serious, less worthy of creative and critical intervention. It's deemed gross or grotesque or shameful. We don't have the words because we don't want the words. And, Mierle, from across an ocean and on the page, you helped me understand that. You helped me find freedom—to use your word—in naming the work I was already doing as meaningful and rejoining my selves. I'd long admired your work, but thinking back on it now, I am certain that is one reason I felt so compelled to really know you.

MLU   Imagine that. Imagine a world and a culture where that's true, what you're saying. Imagine what was shut down—windows closed, doors shut. It's a glimpse of what was wrong with Western culture right there.

CW   I came to realize how many images of birth—in my mind, absorbed from culture—were either of the mother monster or the mother martyr. Reading those words from you, that put a fine point on it. I was like, all right, here's

somebody—and what year was that, 1968, 1969?—who had been insisting on this complicated, nuanced work. You made it urgent. I wanted to do the same. To not only pay attention to labor but give it language. And I took that up as a charge, both in the work that is directly about motherhood and in the work that is more focused on family making in all its forms, and I've never let go of it.

I also want to say that, with both of my boys, I went back to work six weeks after I'd given birth. Six unpaid weeks. My vagina was still bleeding. I was pumping in a public bathroom stall, changing my blood-soaked pads. It was really horrible. That was my capital "W" work that I needed to return to, not like my lowercase "w" work that was happening over here with my children. It was made so clear to me which work was ascribed "value" and which was to be done entirely out of sight. It was no longer a cause or a metaphor. It was my life.

I remember showing your work *Dressing to Go Out / Undressing to Go In* [1973] to my graduate seminar around that time. I think about it often as it relates to this project of repetition and insistence.

MLU   As for that work, Lucy [Lippard] had invited me to be in *c. 7,500* [1973–74] and I was making things, doing maintenance tasks—doing the laundry, changing the baby's diaper—and I needed someone to photograph them (fig. 1). I knew a guy who was a good photographer, not a professional photographer, but he would work cheap, do me a favor, and take these pictures. You could see the children looking at him like, "Who are you?" You could see their ambivalence.

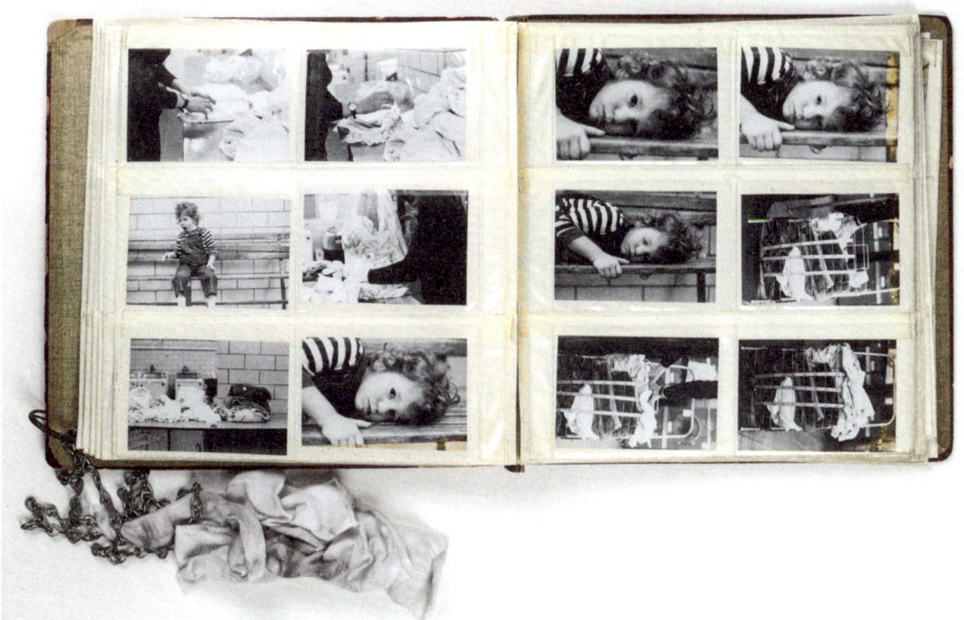

Fig. 1. Mierle Laderman Ukeles, *Maintenance Art Tasks*, 1973. Photographs by Joshua Siderowitz, album, chain, and rag. 13 × 12 ½ × 1 ¾ inches (33 × 31.8 × 4.4 cm), closed

The older child, Yael, was showing the camera that she was very proud of her accomplishments, of how she put on and took off her outdoor clothes. And Raquel, two and a half years younger, although she proceeded by demonstrating very fine small muscle control, was a little more like, "Who are you? Why are you taking these pictures?" It was very important to me to let the child do whatever the child was able to do, and I wanted to capture that. If they needed me to come in and help them with something, I would do that. So you see the mother entering and exiting, in, out, in, out, all these different gestures of expertise that they were conquering. There was a third baby in there. You just see a little glimpse of this baby screaming his head off because we're not paying any attention to him.

I was so blown away by your piece at MoMA [*My Birth*, 2018] (fig. 2), on so many different levels. There's the work, which is mind-blowing, and the fact that you taped it with temporary blue tape. At first, I got so worried that people would take the photographs away. But they ruffled, and it made me more alert to the precarity of these images. And I could see you sticking them up, moving them over, like that.

The response of people was hysterical. There were quite a few visitors when I was there who put their head down, or looked sideways, and then got the hell out of there. I think it terrified a lot of people. Others were moving into the photographs. The choreography of the audience was amazing. Standing back, talking, coming in close. I think the coming in was wonderful. That was the

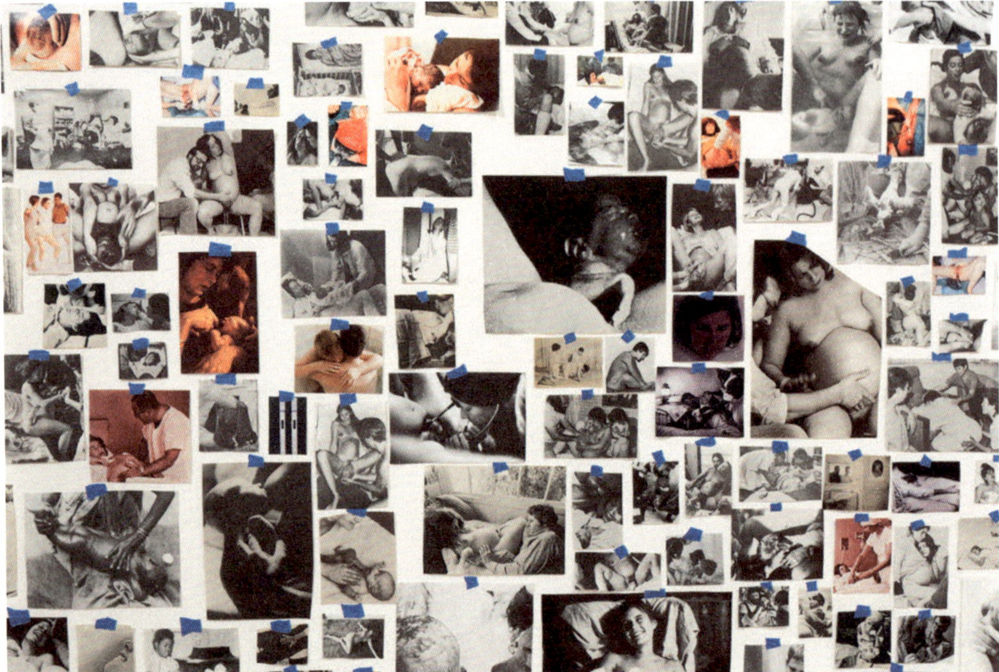

Fig. 2. Carmen Winant, *My Birth*, 2018. Found images and tape. Installation view, *Being: New Photography 2018*, Museum of Modern Art, New York, 2018

height of what you were offering people. When I read that you used to take photographs yourself, and now you use images photographed by others and create the collection of images in relation to your ideas, concepts, attitudes, I wrote, "Carmen and mongo." Do you know what mongo is?

CW   No. Tell me more.

MLU   Mongo is a sanitation word. Mongo is when you're behind the truck—this was many years ago—and if you see something like copper wire, certain metals, you reach in and you take it out and you sell it on the side. Completely illegal, but the sanitation workers said, "This is so stupid. I'm not letting this go to waste. I can make some money." The garbage belongs to the city, so you're not allowed to take it

for yourself. However, more important, mongo is insistence on seeing value in an object no matter that someone threw it out: that act of reaching into the hopper and selecting, as the artist does, taking it out and changing its context. There were famous garages in New York with a thousand pieces of mongo hung up, like a huge exhibition.

CW   What were they?

MLU   They saved art. I saw the worst art that people had thrown out, which the sanitation workers wouldn't allow to go into the hopper. Religious figures, statues, little religious objects. They saved boots, images, pictures, all sorts of stuff that was personal. But this hand reaching into the flux of material flow and then moving items, reorganizing them—I said, "That's what Carmen

Ukeles, Winant

does also. That's what she does. She puts her hands into the belly of the culture and reorganizes it."

There's another statement by you that I'm going to read: "I want artwork—at least the work I make, and the work I love—to feel as if it has exhausted every end. I want to see the labor on the surface of the work, as the work. I want the artist to present as a self-made expert, and I want to sense that process of self-making in the thing they do."[1] I thought, oh my God, she's talking about me, that's what I do.

CW   That's why we are in relation to each other; it is why we are here! Our shared affinity and charge. Well, where do I begin? It feels to me like the ultimate compliment that you would think of me in relation to that work of finding and resuscitating. The work, and the pleasure, of mongo.

MLU   It has an outlaw aspect that the artist always has.

CW   That makes me smile, hearing that from you. I mean, really, what does it take to sift through one's life—one's so-called trash—and find it beautiful, interesting, worthwhile? What social position engenders a proximity to trash in the first place? I love the idea of declaring oneself an expert on the mess—of finding meaning and beauty in the mess—and determining one's own rules in that process.

I keep thinking about you as a figure inside of the work. About how you hired a photographer to follow you around while you were making *Touch Sanitation*, the *Work Ballets*, *Dressing to Go Out /*

Undressing to Go In, and so on. For that reason, you are in most of those pictures; you're on the record. This has an outlaw aspect too, doesn't it? I take thousands of pictures of my kids a year on my phone and, classically, I am in almost none of them. I wanted to put the mother back in the picture in *My Birth*, thousands of times. I wanted to position her as the protagonist and subject, not only the vessel.

Though I had never thought about it in these terms before, as mongo. But of course, that is what it is. And that is why it feels like such a fugitive act: reaching into the depths of what people discard as trivial or used up and, without too much intervention, making it seen and impossible to dispose of. That is the real intervention, I suppose. Thank you for seeing it and thinking about it in that way.

MLU   There's something that comes into my mind: with *Touch Sanitation*, where I insisted on going everywhere and seeing all the workers, the whole system, I felt that if I didn't do the whole system, then I couldn't crash the stupidity of what was going on. It had to be total. It was set up with consciously inviting TV press at the beginning, and other people who came along during the course of this eleven-month performance work. And also, when I was walking behind the truck for so many months throughout this year, I felt that I was making the case that this should not be invisible: here we are, right out in public, we're right here. Look at the workers. For the first time, articles were written in the paper. That was a miracle to a lot of sanitation workers. Nobody ever did that before. That's what they would say. But it was the same with me. As I said, I'm a feminist artist. I'm a mother, a maintenance worker, and when people didn't value my work, I was so upset. I would put out, "Why am I here? Who am I that you're looking at?"

CW   What a job, to render yourself invisible. To state the obvious, the maintenance worker, the mother . . . they are only really foregrounded when some sticky drink has spilled or when a kid is throwing a tantrum or whatever the case may be. We necessitate our own erasure by virtue of existing, by virtue of doing our jobs "well"; it's dehumanizing. And it reminds me of something else you've said, in critiquing the minimalism of some of your contemporaries: that they make work without the workers.

There are some interesting parallels here with kids as subjects too, who after all are also deemed less serious or knowing, who are also told to fade into to background—for whom behaving well is a kind of voiding of the self. My sons are three and five now. They really want to be seen. What does it mean to do that, to take them seriously as subjects, even as collaborators? In what ways is that an outlaw strategy? Serious is maybe the wrong word, because that sounds like it precludes playfulness. Maybe there's a better word for it, that might center them as full human beings, if developing, thrashing, complicated ones.

And so my work as a mother-artist is complicated in this way. I want to insist on the mother as a central figure, and one who doesn't recede in the face of her children. But I also want to see my children—in life and in art—as meaningful subjects who are allied with their mother

for all the ways mothers, too, are told to stay silent and still.

I was just rereading Adrienne Rich's chapter on mothers and sons from her book *Of Woman Born: Motherhood as Experience and Institution* [1976]. I am paraphrasing here, but she concludes that brilliant essay, now almost fifty years old, by writing something along the lines of: "To ask what we want for our children is to ask what we want for ourselves." What she is asking, really, is what does it mean to self-actualize? How do we circumnavigate the force of patriarchy, which seeps in everywhere? A particularly pertinent question, I think, as it comes to the relationship between mothers and their boys. And, of course, as it relates to care. . .

MLU   In my "Manifesto for Maintenance Art 1969!," the other half of the title is "Proposal for an Exhibition 'CARE.'" That was 1969, when care was not up there in people's thinking or attention. I pictured this exhibition that would become a world of maintenance. I pictured it in the old Whitney Museum. I would take over the whole museum, and the exhibition would have three elements. First is personal maintenance. I would live in the museum; I'd sweep, clean, cook, take care of the whole deal. The second is societal maintenance. How do you keep going? How do you maintain yourself? How do you survive? And what happens to your freedom if you have to do this work that eats up your soul? What's left? Then the third part is earth maintenance. Degraded materials, garbage, polluted air, polluted river water would come into the museum and be transformed in some way and be returned to the city healthy. So that the museum would be seen as this world of care. Sound is important: a person sweeping, voices of spectators making those questions their own, and the raucous materials being transformed—these sounds would flow from one floor into another, tumbling, rolling throughout the space. And the most important thing to me is what we're talking about, that it has so much to offer for the whole culture. It flows from the mother often making herself invisible in order to care and then moves into the whole society, care of the society, care of the planet. The whole thing comes from care.

1

"Labor and Delivery: Carmen Winant Interviewed by Jen Schwarting," *BOMB*, August 7, 2018, https://bombmagazine.org /articles/labor-and-delivery-carmen -winant-interviewed/.

Acknowledgments

Analogies of gestation and birth are often invoked when speaking about the long process of organizing an exhibition or writing a book. When *To Begin Again: Artists and Childhood* opens at the ICA/Boston in October 2022, when this book is in the hands of readers, this "child" will already be six and finishing kindergarten. From the very beginning, the impetus for this project was a commitment to the remarkable lessons that children and childhood teach to those astute enough to pay close attention. Artists have long been uniquely attuned to the creative possibilities inherent in childhood, perhaps more acutely than others. Is it that artists have felt in children a kindred spirit of unbridled creativity, of being ungovernable, of resisting, of needing? Is it that "every child is an artist," as Pablo Picasso would have it, or simply that every artist was once a child? Is it that childhood, shrouded as it is in memory and the twists and turns of a developing mind, is indeed a wellspring of inspiration? What do the things artists make reveal about childhood? This exhibition and catalogue map these and other generative points of contact between artists, children, and ideas of childhood, and none of this would have been possible without the generosity and input of countless individuals.

To Begin Again: Artists and Childhood is the culmination of many people's insights, hard work, and commitment. We are grateful to Jill Medvedow, Ellen Matilda Poss Director, for believing in this project from the beginning, and to Eva Respini, Deputy Director for Curatorial Affairs and Barbara Lee Chief Curator, for her guidance throughout its development. We extend our heartfelt appreciation to the ICA's Board of Trustees and Advisory Board members for their continued support of the museum's work, and we are deeply beholden to the generous sponsors of this exhibition, and thank each of them for making all of this possible: First Republic Bank, Kate and Chuck Brizius, Paul and Katie Buttenwieser, Marina Kalb and David Feinberg, Andree LeBoeuf Foundation, Kristen and Kent Lucken, Tristin and Martin Mannion, Erica and Ted Pappendick, and Cynthia and John Reed.

Innumerable colleagues, scholars, artists, registrars, students, and strangers advanced the research for this project with their insights and references, which have filled numerous notebooks cover to cover. While listing names always risks leaving someone out, we want to attempt to account for the many individuals who have given their time and energy to this endeavor. We must begin by thanking Anne Higonnet, whom we initially approached because of her own important book *Pictures of Innocence: The History and Crisis of Ideal Childhood*, and who quickly became more deeply involved, contributing to this book, co-organizing an exploratory seminar at Harvard's Radcliffe Institute for Advanced Study, and teaching a seminar on the subject at Barnard College. Her unflagging enthusiasm has been contagious. We have been fortunate to have the immense support of an excellent group of interns and fellows over the years, including Sami Hopkins, Juan Omar Rodriguez, Catherine Huang, Rachel Tang, Phillippa Pitts, and Anni Pullagura (before joining ICA staff). The project has been much improved thanks to their efforts.

We are grateful for the camaraderie of numerous fellow curators, especially Samuel Adams, Ian Alteveer, Claire Barliant, Kelly Baum, Layla Bermeo, Dan Byers, Tyler Cann, Eric Crosby, Dina Deitsch, Jonathan Fineberg, Michelle Millar Fisher, Patricia Hickson, Katherine Jentleson, Beth Kantrowitz, Juliet Kinchin, Chaédria LaBouvier, Ethan Lasser, Thomas J. Lax, Amy Rosenblum Martin, Kate McNamara, Janine Mileaf, Al Miner, Helen Molesworth, Liz Munsell, Heather Pesanti, Jenelle Porter, Jennifer Roberts, Meg Rotzel, Ben Sloat, Susan Stoops, Jordan Troeller, Emily Watlington, and Maja Wismer, who listened to many iterations of this project, pointed us in the direction of interesting artists and artworks, and offered sage advice. Scholars with deep knowledge of childhood and training in fields far from our own were generous with their unique insights, and we thank each of them: Sarah Archino, Associate Professor of Art History, Furman University; Robin Bernstein, Dillon Professor of American History, Harvard University; Allison Curseen, Assistant Professor of English, Boston College; Clara Dublanc, Director, Itinerant Works; Marah Gubar, Associate Professor of Literature, MIT; Melissa Kibbe, Associate Professor of Psychological and Brain Sciences, Boston University; Laura Koenig, Team Leader for Children's Services at the Central Library of the Boston Public Library; Francie Latour, writer, editor, and cofounder of Wee the People; Robin Meisner, Senior Director of Child Development at Boston Children's Museum; Wangui Muigai, Assistant Professor in African and African American Studies and History, Brandeis University; Camille Owens, Junior Fellow, Harvard Society of Fellows; Liz Phipps-Soeiro, Director of Boston Public School Libraries; Vivian Poey, Professor of Photography, Lesley University; Siddhartha V. Shah, Director of Education and Civic Engagement, Curator of South Asian Art, Peabody Essex Museum; Vita Weinstein, author; and Ellen Winner, Professor of Psychology, Boston College. Many of these individuals joined an exploratory seminar supported by the Radcliffe Institute for Advanced Study at Harvard University and co-organized with Higonnet in October of 2021, and participated in advisory group meetings to consider the access points between the exhibition and its visitors, especially children.

We celebrate the incredible work of the exhibiting artists, many of whom have explored childhood as a subject for a long time and have been in dialogue with us for years. They have opened up our minds to new directions and lines of inquiry, and their enthusiastic collaboration ultimately shaped the exhibition and catalogue. We are so appreciative of their amazing studio assistants and managers as well as the incredible gallery staff whose support often makes their work possible. In addition to those included in the exhibition, many artists were generous with their time during studio visits and in meaningful conversations driven by a shared fascination with the subject. A special thanks to

Acknowledgments

artists Betsy Cameron, Sari Carel, Anna Craycroft, Mark Dion, Britt Hatzius, Julian Hoeber, Eva Kot'átková, Liz Magic Laser, Roberta Paul, Tabitha Soren, and Tavares Strachan.

Our deep appreciation goes to the exhibition lenders (listed on page 276), who agreed to part with their artworks and share them with museum visitors. Over the course of securing these loans, we had the chance to visit many collections and storerooms, and we wish to especially thank Indira Abiskaroon, formerly of the Solomon R. Guggenheim Museum; Fabienne Eggelhöfer at Zentrum Paul Klee; the late Marvin Hoshino; Karan Rinaldo at the Metropolitan Museum of Art; and Valérie Rousseau at the American Folk Art Museum.

We are grateful to our devoted colleagues at the ICA/Boston, many of whom played a direct role in this exhibition and catalogue. We want to thank, in particular: Megan Des Jardin, Associate Registrar, for navigating complicated loans and shipping while being in steady communication with us; Kate Herlihy, Director of Exhibitions, for her able oversight of budgets, contracts, schedules, and myriad logistical details; Tim Obetz, Chief Preparator, and Toru Nakanishi, Preparator, for their expertise, reliable advice, and problem solving; and the incredible staff across the entire museum in the Development, Education, External Relations, Membership, Special Events, Facilities and Security, Finance and Operations, Information Technology, Performing Arts, and Retail departments. Former ICA staff members Abigail Newbold and Carrie Van Horn also made significant contributions to this project at critical junctures.

We are proud of this catalogue and hope that it will be an inspiration and a resource for many years to come. We express our sincere thanks to our contributors for their insightful texts and conversations: Joshua Bennett, Anna Craycroft, Anne Higonnet, Naima J. Keith, Valeria Luiselli, Oscar Murillo, Sable Elyse Smith, Mierle Laderman Ukeles, and Carmen Winant. Our editor, Michelle Piranio, greatly improved each text and worked tirelessly to make a more coherent and fluid publication. This book is as beautiful as it is thanks to the collaboration and expert design of Mark Owens. We are very fortunate to have DelMonico Books as the copublisher of this volume and we thank Mary DelMonico and her team for their enthusiasm and collaboration.

Having had children at various phases of this project, we were able to measure our ideas against the litmus test of real life. Our work would not have been possible without our families, especially our incredibly supportive spouses Catriona Wilkey and Sahir Kalim and our children Jan-Pieter and Alida De Blois and Julian and Cassidy Kalim. Without the network of family members, caretakers, nannies, and teachers who took such great care of our children, we would not have been able to do this work.

Jeffrey De Blois,
Associate Curator and
Publications Manager

Ruth Erickson,
Mannion Family Senior Curator

Works in the Exhibition

Ann Agee
Born 1959, Philadelphia
Nursing Bra Madonna, 2019
Glazed porcelain with red
overglaze enamel
17 ¼ × 4 × 5 ¾ inches
(43.8 × 10.2 × 14.6 cm)
Courtesy the artist and
P.P.O.W., New York

Raised Curtain Madonna, 2020
Glazed porcelain with matte blue glaze
14 ¾ × 10 ¼ × 8 ½ inches
(37.5 × 26 × 21.6 cm)
Courtesy the artist and
P.P.O.W., New York

Green Pleated Shift Madonna, 2021
Glazed earthenware with slip
30 × 15 × 14 inches
(76.2 × 38.1 × 35.6 cm)
Courtesy the artist and
P.P.O.W., New York

*Sideways Plaid Madonna
with Drawer*, 2021
Earthenware with glaze and underglaze
26 ½ × 14 ⅞ × 6 ⅞ inches
(67.3 × 37.8 × 17.5 cm)
Collection of Roxanne Ingoe, New York

Spandex Madonna with a Ball, 2021
Earthenware with colored slips
35 ½ × 13 × 12 inches
(90.2 × 33 × 30.5 cm)
Private collection, New York

John Ahearn and Rigoberto Torres
Born 1952, Binghampton, New York;
Born 1960, Aguadilla, Puerto Rico
*Homage to the People of the Bronx:
Double Dutch at Kelly Street—La Freeda,
Jevette, Towana, Staice*, 1981–82
Oil on fiberglass
54 × 154 × 12 inches
(137.2 × 391.2 × 30.5 cm)
The Broad Art Foundation, Los Angeles

Njideka Akunyili Crosby
Born 1983, Enugu, Nigeria
"The Beautyful Ones" Series #1b, 2014
Acrylic, colored pencil, and
transfers on paper
60 × 52 inches
(152.4 × 132.1 cm)
Collection of Kehinde Wiley, New York

"The Beautyful Ones" Series #7, 2018
Acrylic, colored pencil,
and transfers on paper
59 ⅞ × 42 ½ inches
(152.1 × 108 cm)
Institute of Contemporary Art/Boston;
Acquired through the generosity of
Fotene Demoulas and Tom Coté, in
honor of Eva Respini

Francis Alÿs
Born 1959, Antwerp, Belgium
*Children's Game #1: Caracoles
(Mexico City, Mexico)*, 1999
Video (color, sound; 4:34 minutes)
In collaboration with Julien Devaux
Courtesy the artist and David Zwirner

*Children's Game #6: Sandcastles
(Knokke-Le-Zoute, Belgium)*, 2009
Video (color, sound; 6:04 minutes)
In collaboration with Julien Devaux,
Cristian Manzutto, and Félix Blume
Courtesy the artist and David Zwirner

*Children's Game #16: Hopscotch
(Sharya Refugee Camp, Iraq)*, 2016
Video (color, sound; 4:02 minutes)
In collaboration with Julien Devaux
and Félix Blume
Courtesy the artist and David Zwirner

Jean-Michel Basquiat
Born 1960, Brooklyn;
died 1988, New York
Untitled, 1981
Acrylic and spray paint on canvas
80 × 80 inches (203 × 203 cm)
Princeton University Art Museum,
Lent by Herbert Schorr, Graduate
School Class of 1963, and Lenore Schorr

Brian Belott
Born 1973, East Orange, New Jersey
Dr. Kid President Jr., 2022
Wall-based installation, including
paintings and wallpaper, with drawings
from the Rhoda Kellogg International
Child Art Collection, San Francisco
Courtesy Barbara Bablinsky Labs, New
York, and Golden Gate Kindergarten
Association, San Francisco

Jordan Casteel
Born 1989, Denver
Lean, 2018
Oil on canvas
72 × 56 inches (182.9 × 142.2 cm)
Collection of Matt and Yasmine
Johnson, Los Angeles

Twins (Subway), 2018
Oil on canvas
56 × 72 inches (142.2 × 182.9 cm)
Collection of Kimberly and Elliot Perry,
Memphis, Tennessee

**Child from the class
of Hans-Friedrich Geist**
Lübeck, Germany
*Ohne Titel (Schiff mit drei Figuren und
Steuermann* (Untitled [ship with three
figures and helmsman]), ca. 1930
Pencil and watercolor on paper
13 ⅜ × 15 ¾ inches (34 × 40 cm)
Private collection, Switzerland, on
permanent loan to the Zentrum Paul
Klee, Bern, Switzerland

Lenka Clayton
Born 1977, Cornwall, United Kingdom
*The Distance I Can Be from My
Son (Back Alley)*, 2013
Video (color, sound; 1:53 minutes)
Courtesy the artist and Catharine
Clark Gallery, San Francisco

*The Distance I Can Be from My
Son (Park)*, 2013
Video (color, sound; 1:43 minutes)
Courtesy the artist and Catharine Clark
Gallery, San Francisco

*The Distance I Can Be from My
Son (Supermarket)*, 2013
Video (color, sound; 00:52 minutes)
Courtesy the artist and Catharine Clark
Gallery, San Francisco

Allan Rohan Crite
Born 1910, North Plainfield,
New Jersey; died 2007, Boston
Tire Jumping in Front of My Window,
1936–47
Oil on canvas board
23 ½ × 17 ½ inches
(59.7 × 44.5 cm)
Museum of Fine Arts, Boston;
Charles H. Bayley Picture and Painting
Fund and The Heritage Fund for a
Diverse Collection

Henry Darger
Born 1892, Chicago; died 1973, Chicago
*6 Episode 3 Place Not Mentioned.
Escape during violent storm, still
fighting though persed for long
distance*, mid-20th century
Double-sided watercolor, pencil, and
carbon tracing on pieced paper
24 × 74 ¾ inches
(61 × 189.9 cm)
American Folk Art Museum, New York;
Gift of Nathan and Kiyoko Lerner

Karon Davis
Born 1977, Reno, Nevada
Pattycakes, 2022
Plaster bandages, steel, glass eyes, and
chicken wire
31 × 56 ½ × 25 inches
(78.7 × 143.5 × 63.5 cm)
Private collection, West Palm
Beach, Florida

Robert Gober
Born 1954, Wallingford, Connecticut
Untitled, 2006–7
Wood and enamel paint
27 × 39 ⅛ × 39 ⅛ inches
(69 × 99 × 99 cm)
Collection of the artist; Courtesy
Matthew Marks Gallery, New York

**Ramiro Gomez
(now Jay Lynn Gomez)**
Born 1986, San Bernardino, California
*Nanny and Child
(Madison Square Park)*, 2018
Mixed media on canvas
72 × 72 inches
(182.9 × 182.9)
Collection of Joel Braslow, New York

Trenton Doyle Hancock
Born 1974, Oklahoma City
Torpedoboy Fights a Bear, 1984
Graphite on notebook paper
7 ¾ × 10 ½ inches
(19.7 × 26.7 cm)
Courtesy the artist and James
Cohan, New York

Torpedoboy Fights Aliens, 1984
Graphite on notebook paper
7 ¾ × 10 ½ inches
(19.7 × 26.7 cm)
Courtesy the artist and James
Cohan, New York

Torpedoboy Flying, 1984
Graphite on notebook paper
7 ¾ × 10 ½ inches
(19.7 × 26.7 cm)
Courtesy the artist and James
Cohan, New York

Torpedoboy vs. A Giant, 1984
Graphite on notebook paper
7 ¾ × 10 ½ inches
(19.7 × 26.7 cm)
Courtesy the artist and James
Cohan, New York

  Works in the Exhibition

*8 Back Icon Series: Torpedoboy—
Protector of the Mounds, No. 5185*, 2016
Acrylic and mixed media on canvas
66 × 38 inches
(167.6 × 96.5 cm)
Courtesy the artist and James
Cohan, New York

*Torpedoboy, Moundverse
Infants Doll*, 2018
Vinyl, factory-applied paint,
artist-designed packaging, and
Risograph booklet
16 × 7 ½ × 5 ½ inches
(40.6 × 19.1 × 14 cm)
Courtesy the artist and James
Cohan, New York

Duane Hanson
Born 1925, Alexandria, Minnesota;
died 1996, Boca Raton, Florida
Child with Puzzle, 1978
Polyvinyl, polychromed in oil,
and mixed media with accessories
24 × 61 × 32 inches
(61 × 154.9 × 81.3 cm)
The Estate of Duane Hanson and
Gagosian Gallery

Mona Hatoum
Born 1952, Beirut
Caught-up, 2022
Painted metal, wood,
glass beads, and wire
47 ⅛ × 33 ¼ × 18 ⅞ inches
(119.5 × 84.5 × 48 cm)
Courtesy the artist and
White Cube, London

Sharon Hayes
Born 1970, Baltimore
Ricerche: one, 2019
Two-channel HD video
(color, sound; 28:00 minutes)
Courtesy the artist and
Tanya Leighton Gallery, Berlin
and Los Angeles

Ekua Holmes
Born 1955, Roxbury, Massachusetts
Precarious, 2017
Collage on board
24 ½ × 18 inches (62.2 × 45.7 cm)
Collection of Kamil and Jake Shields,
Washington, DC

Bold Beirut, 2021
From *Hope Is an Arrow*, 2022
Paper and acrylic on paper
12 × 20 inches (30.5 × 50.8 cm)
Courtesy the artist

Boston, 2021
From *Hope Is an Arrow*, 2022
Paper, fabric, and acrylic on paper
12 × 20 inches (30.5 × 50.8 cm)
Courtesy the artist

Crashing Winds, 2021
From *Hope Is an Arrow*, 2022
Paper and acrylic on paper
12 × 20 inches (30.5 × 50.8 cm)
Courtesy the artist

Inspiration, 2021
From *Hope Is an Arrow*, 2022
Paper and acrylic on paper
12 × 13 ½ inches (30.5 × 34.3 cm)
Courtesy the artist

Oceanality, 2021
From *Hope Is an Arrow*, 2022
Paper and acrylic on paper
12 × 20 inches (30.5 × 50.8 cm)
Courtesy the artist

The Prophet, 2021
From *Hope Is an Arrow*, 2022
Paper and acrylic on paper
12 × 14 inches (30.5 × 35.6 cm)
Courtesy the artist

Winged Spirits, 2021
From *Hope Is an Arrow*, 2022
Paper and acrylic on paper
12 × 20 inches (30.5 × 50.8 cm)
Courtesy the artist

Mary Kelly
Born 1941, Fort Dodge, Iowa
*Post-Partum Document: Documentation
III Analysed Markings and Diary
Perspective Schema*, 1975
Works on paper, graphite, crayon,
chalk, and printed diagrams, mounted
on paper
Thirteen parts, each 11 ¼ × 14 ¼ × 1 ⅜
inches (28.6 × 36.1 × 3.5 cm)
Tate, London

Paul Klee
Born 1879, Münchenbuchsee, Switzer-
land; died 1940, Muralto, Switzerland
Man, ?, Chair, Hare, 1884
Pencil and chalk on paper on cardboard
4 ⅞ × 6 ⅞ inches
(12.3 × 17.3 cm)
Zentrum Paul Klee, Bern, Switzerland,
and Ann-Marie Klee-Coll, Klee-
Nachlassverwaltung, Hinterkappelen

Untitled (Self-Portrait), 1922
Hand puppet
14 ½ × 9 × 5 ½ inches
(37 × 23 × 14 cm)
Zentrum Paul Klee, Bern, Switzerland,
and Ann-Marie Klee-Coll, Klee-
Nachlassverwaltung, Hinterkappelen

Untitled (Electrical Spook), 1923
Hand puppet
14 ¼ × 6 × 3 ½ inches
(36 × 15 × 9 cm)
Zentrum Paul Klee, Bern, Switzerland,
and Ann-Marie Klee-Coll, Klee-
Nachlassverwaltung, Hinterkappelen

Untitled (Big-Eared Clown), 1925
Hand puppet
19 ⅞ × 6 ¼ × 2 ¼ inches
(48 × 16 × 7 cm)
Zentrum Paul Klee, Bern, Switzerland,
and Ann-Marie Klee-Coll, Klee-
Nachlassverwaltung, Hinterkappelen

Hot Pursuit, 1939
Colored paste and oil on paper on jute
19 × 25 ½ inches
(48.3 × 64.8 cm)
Harvard Art Museums/Fogg Museum;
Gift of Mr. and Mrs. Alfred Jaretzki, Jr.

Justine Kurland
Born 1969, Warsaw, New York
Girls Curled Up, 1997
Chromogenic color print
24 × 36 inches (61 × 91.4 cm)
Courtesy the artist and Higher Pictures
Generation, New York

　　　　　　　　　Works in the Exhibition

Blood Sisters, 2000
Chromogenic color print
24 × 30 inches (61 × 76.2 cm)
Courtesy the artist and Higher Pictures
Generation, New York

Feminine Hygiene, 2000
Chromogenic color print
24 × 30 inches (61 × 76.2 cm)
Courtesy the artist and Higher Pictures
Generation, New York

Broadway (Joy), 2001
Chromogenic color print
24 × 30 inches (61 × 76.2 cm)
Courtesy the artist and Higher Pictures
Generation, New York

Helen Levitt
Born 1913, Brooklyn;
died 2009, New York
N.Y., ca. 1939
Gelatin silver print
8 ¼ × 10 ¼ inches (20.8 × 26.1 cm)
Courtesy Galerie Thomas Zander,
Cologne, Germany

N.Y., ca. 1939
Gelatin silver print
7 × 10 inches (17.8 × 25.4 cm)
Courtesy Galerie Thomas Zander,
Cologne, Germany

N.Y., ca. 1940
Gelatin silver print
8 × 10 ¾ inches (20.3 × 27.2 cm)
Courtesy Galerie Thomas Zander,
Cologne, Germany

N.Y., ca. 1940
Gelatin silver print
10 ¼ × 8 ¼ inches (26.1 × 20.8 cm)
Courtesy Galerie Thomas Zander,
Cologne, Germany

N.Y., ca. 1940
Gelatin silver print
10 ¼ × 8 ¼ inches (26.1 × 20.8 cm)
Courtesy Galerie Thomas Zander,
Cologne, Germany

Tau Lewis
Born 1993, Toronto
Untitled (play dumb to catch wise), 2017
Hand-sewn fabrics, wire, polyester
stuffing, plaster, acrylic paint, human
hair, and stones
24 × 20 × 33 inches
(61 × 50.8 × 83.8 cm)
Courtesy the artist and Night Gallery,
Los Angeles

Glenn Ligon
Born 1960, New York
*Malcolm X, Sun, Frederick Douglass,
Boy with Bubbles (version 2) #2*, 2001
Silkscreen and oil crayon on
primed canvas
96 × 72 inches
(243.8 × 182.9 cm)
Solomon R. Guggenheim Museum, New
York; Gift, The Bohen Foundation, 2001

Oscar Murillo
Born 1986, Valle del Cauca, Colombia
Frequencies, 2013–ongoing
Installation featuring wallpaper,
canvases, and video (color, silent;
duration variable)
Dimensions variable
Courtesy the artist

Rivane Neuenschwander
Born 1967, Belo Horizonte, Brazil
Cabra-Cega / Blind Man's Bluff, 2016
Four-channel animated projection
(black-and-white, sound; 2:31 minutes)
based on original drawings by Thomas
N. Maciel Baron, sound by Arto Lindsay
Dimensions variable
Courtesy the artist and Tanya Bonakdar
Gallery, New York / Los Angeles, Fortes
D'Aloia & Gabriel, Brazil, and Stephen
Friedman Gallery, London

Berenice Olmedo
Born 1987, Oaxaca, Mexico
Olga, 2018
Hard plastic leg prostheses,
steel rods and joint screws, aluminum
box, electrical motor, and CPU-
controlled hardware
29 ⅞ × 15 × 12 ⅝ inches
(76 × 38 × 32 cm)
Collection Köser, Cologne, Germany;
Courtesy Jan Kaps, Cologne, Germany

Charles Ray
Born 1953, Chicago
School Play, 2014
Solid stainless steel
76 × 23 × 15 ½ inches
(193 × 59 × 40 cm)
Collection of Glenn and Amanda
Fuhrman, New York; Courtesy the
FLAG Art Foundation

Faith Ringgold
Born 1930, Harlem
Tar Beach #2, 1990–92
Silkscreen on silk
60 × 59 inches
(152.4 × 149.9 cm)
Courtesy the artist and ACA
Galleries, New York

Deborah Roberts
Born 1962, Austin, Texas
Ulysses, 2019
Mixed media and collage on linen
65 × 45 inches
(165 × 114.3 cm)
Institute of Contemporary Art/Boston;
Promised gift of Fotene Demoulas
and Tom Coté

Sisterly Love, 2021
Acrylic and collage on canvas
65 × 125 inches
(165.1 × 317.5 cm)
Private collection, Detroit

Tim Rollins and K.O.S.
Born 1955, Pittsfield, Maine;
died 2017, New York
The Interior of the Heart, 1987–88
Acrylic, watercolor, and charcoal on
book pages on linen
90 × 102 inches
(228.6 × 259.1 cm)
Rose Art Museum at Brandeis
University; Gift of Sandra and Gerald
Fineberg, Boston

Rachel Rose
Born 1986, New York
Lake Valley, 2016
Single-channel video
(color, sound; 8:25 minutes)
Courtesy the artist, Gladstone Gallery,
New York and Brussels, and Pilar
Corrias, London

   Works in the Exhibition

Heji Shin
Born 1983, Seoul
Baby 6, 2016
Inkjet print
31 ¼ × 23 ¼ inches
(79.5 × 59 cm)
Courtesy the artist and Galerie
Buchholz, Berlin, Cologne, and
New York

Baby 7, 2016
Inkjet print
31 ¼ × 23 ¼ inches
(79.5 × 59 cm)
Courtesy the artist and Galerie
Buchholz, Berlin, Cologne, and
New York

Baby 10, 2017
Inkjet print
23 ¼ × 31 ¼ inches
(59 × 79.5 cm)
Courtesy the artist and Galerie
Buchholz, Berlin, Cologne, and
New York

Sable Elyse Smith
Born 1986, Los Angeles
Coloring Book 37, 2019
Screen-printing ink and
oil stick on paper
60 × 100 inches
(152.4 × 254 cm)
Collection of Michael Sherman,
Los Angeles

Coloring Book 76, 2021
Screen-printing ink, oil pastel, and
oil stick on paper
60 × 50 inches
(152.4 × 127 cm)
Institute of Contemporary Art/
Boston; Promised gift of Steve Corkin
and Dan Maddalena

Becky Suss
Born 1980, Philadelphia
8 Greenwood Place (1985–88), 2021
Oil on canvas
84 × 60 × 1 ½ inches
(213.4 × 152.4 × 3.8 cm)
Institute of Contemporary Art/Boston;
Promised gift of Fotene Demoulas
and Tom Coté

Mierle Laderman Ukeles
Born 1939, Denver
*Dressing to Go Out /
Undressing to Go In*, 1973
Gelatin silver prints mounted on foam-
core with chain and dust rag
57 ¼ × 44 ⅜ × ¾ inches
(145.6 × 112.9 × 2.1 cm)
Collection of Frayda and Ronald
Feldman; Courtesy Ronald Feldman
Gallery, New York

Cathy Wilkes
Born 1966, Belfast, Northern Ireland
Untitled, 2012
Mixed media
Overall dimensions variable
Museum of Modern Art, New York; Gift
of the Speyer Family Foundation and
Mrs. Saidie A. May (by exchange)

Carmen Winant
Born 1983, San Francisco
What it is like to be, 2022
Found books
Dimensions variable
Courtesy the artist, Patron Gallery,
Chicago, and Fortnight Institute,
New York

Works in the exhibition
as of July 8, 2022

Contributors

Joshua Bennett is a writer and Professor of English and Creative Writing at Dartmouth College. Bennett is the author of *The Sobbing School* (Penguin, 2016), which was a National Poetry Series selection and a finalist for an NAACP Image Award. He is also the author of *Being Property Once Myself* (Harvard University Press, 2020); *Owed* (Penguin, 2020); *The Study of Human Life* (Penguin, 2022); and *Spoken Word: A Cultural History* (forthcoming from Knopf). He has received fellowships and awards from the Guggenheim Foundation, the Whiting Foundation, the National Endowment for the Arts, and the Society of Fellows at Harvard University. Bennett's recent writing, especially on the work of Deborah Roberts and on Black childhood more generally, inspired his contribution to this volume. He is a father to his son.

Anna Craycroft is a multidisciplinary artist based in New York. Her work frequently considers subjects related to childhood, from *Childhood Is an Endless Frontier for New Social Imaginaries* (2014–ongoing), an illustrated narrative lecture that draws together artworks that use childhood as their proxy, to her exhibition and book *The Agency of the Orphan* (2008), exploring the trope of the orphan in popular culture. Craycroft is the author of *Developing Patterns* (2011), a five-volume set of children's-style board books expanding on the ideas of the nineteenth-century pedagogue Friedrich Fröbel. Her work has been exhibited widely, including at the New Museum, New York; Portland Institute for Contemporary Art, Oregon; Ben Maltz Gallery, Otis College of Art and Design, Los Angeles; Blanton Museum of Art, Austin; and deCordova Sculpture Park and Museum, Lincoln, Massachusetts. Her writing has been published in *Art Journal* and in museum catalogues for Serpentine Galleries and ICA/Boston, among others. Craycroft's singular and multifocal dedication to childhood as a subject led to the artwork imagined for these pages. She is a mother to her son, Bayard.

Jeffrey De Blois is Associate Curator and Publications Manager at the Institute of Contemporary Art/Boston. At the ICA, he has organized exhibitions of the work of Carolina Caycedo, Raúl de Nieves, Napoleon Jones-Henderson, William Kentridge, Caitlin Keogh, and Eva LeWitt, among others. His writing has appeared in numerous publications, including *Marlon Forrester: If Black Saints Could Fly 23* (2021); *Sterling Ruby: A Relief Lashed + A Still Pose* (2020); *Sterling Ruby* (2020); *Art in the Age of the Internet, 1989 to Today* (2018); *Caitlin Keogh: Headless Woman with Parrot* (2017); and *The Artist's Museum* (2016). De Blois was previously curatorial fellow at MIT List Visual Arts Center. He holds an M.A. in the History of Art & Architecture from Boston University. His interest in childhood as a multifaceted subject intensified after becoming a parent. He is a father to his son and daughter.

Ruth Erickson is Mannion Family Senior Curator at the Institute of Contemporary Art/Boston. At the ICA, she has organized more than a dozen exhibitions, including solo projects with Kevin Beasley, Mark Dion, Wangechi Mutu, and Vivian Suter, among others, as well as group exhibitions on Black Mountain College, contemporary art and migration, and new modes of figurative painting. Her exhibitions reflect her interest in interdisciplinary practices and the ways artists mine diverse cultural material in the creation of art. Her writing has appeared in numerous publications, including *France and the Visual Arts since 1945: Remapping European Postwar and Contemporary Art* (2018); *Mark Dion: Misadventures of a 21st-Century Naturalist* (2017); *Leap Before You Look: Black Mountain College 1933–1957* (2015); *Critical Landscapes: Art, Space, Politics* (2015); and *Take It or Leave It: Institution, Image, Ideology* (2014). She received her Ph.D. from the University of Pennsylvania in 2014. That same year, she became a parent, as did many of her friends and colleagues, spurring her interest in childhood as a subject of study. With her husband, Sahir, she is a mother to her two sons in Cambridge, Massachusetts.

Anne Higonnet is Professor of Art History at Barnard College of Columbia University. Her work is focused on art since 1650, on childhood, and on collecting. She received her B.A. from Harvard University and her Ph.D. from Yale University. She has published many essays, books, and two book-scale digital projects, is a prize-winning teacher, and lectures widely, including in the Live Arts program of the Metropolitan Museum of Art. Her work has been supported by Getty, Guggenheim, and Social Science Research Council fellowships, as well as by grants from the Mellon, Howard, and Kress Foundations. Higonnet's influential book *Pictures of Innocence: The History and Crisis of Ideal Childhood* (Thames & Hudson, 1998) traces a visual history of the ideal of childhood innocence in modern Western culture. A key interlocutor in the development of the exhibition, Higonnet is a mother to her two children.

Naima J. Keith is a curator and Vice President of Education and Public Programs at Los Angeles County Museum of Art, where she oversees all aspects of LACMA's exhibition-driven educational programming. Before joining LACMA, Keith worked as Deputy Director and Chief Curator at California African American Museum, and as Associate Curator at the Studio Museum in Harlem. She has organized exhibitions of the work of Genevieve Gaignard, Charles Gaines, Kenyatta A. C. Hinkle, Rodney McMillian, Robert Pruitt, and Gary Simmons, among others. Keith was co-artistic director of Prospect.5, New Orleans, in 2021. She holds degrees from Spelman College and the University of California, Los Angeles. A mother to her daughter and son, Keith is committed to exposing her children to culture, art, and history, and to accessibility to museum visitors of all ages.

Valeria Luiselli is an acclaimed writer of both fiction and nonfiction. She is the author of *Sidewalks*, *Faces in the Crowd*, *The Story of My Teeth*, *Tell Me How It Ends: An Essay in Forty Questions*, and *Lost Children Archive*. Her numerous awards include a 2019 MacArthur Fellowship, a DUBLIN Literary Award, two Los Angeles Times Book Prizes, the Carnegie Medal, and an American Book Award; she has been nominated for the National Book Critics Circle Award, the Kirkus Prize, and the Booker Prize. Her work has appeared in the *New Yorker*, the *New York Times*, *Granta*, and *McSweeney*'s, among other publications, and has been translated into more than twenty languages. She is a writer in residence at Bard College. Luiselli's powerful book-length essay *Tell Me How It Ends*, a damning confrontation between the American Dream and the reality of undocumented children seeking a new life in the United States, is excerpted in this volume.

Oscar Murillo is an artist working between various locations. His wide-ranging and restless artistic practice includes paintings, works on paper, sculptures, installations, actions, collaborative projects, videos, and more. Taken together, Murillo's works hinge on an ongoing interest in cultural exchange and the ways in which materials, ideas, and language circulate and constantly take on new meanings as they move. For Murillo's project *Frequencies*, begun in 2013 and created in collaboration with members of his family and studio team, canvases are temporarily affixed to classroom desks in selected schools across the globe, encouraging students aged ten to sixteen to create any kind of mark. To date, it has amassed an archive of forty thousand canvases. Murillo earned degrees from the University of Westminster, London, and the Royal College of Art, London. His investment in childhood as a subject of global significance influenced the exhibition's purview. He is a father to his daughter.

Sable Elyse Smith is an interdisciplinary artist, writer, and educator based in New York, where she is Assistant Professor of Visual Arts at Columbia University. Smith employs video, sculpture, photography, and text to make legible quotidian forms of violence that are largely unseen. Her work has been featured at MoMA PS1, the New Museum, the Studio Museum in Harlem, and Recess Assembly, New York; Yerba Buena Center for the Arts and Artist Television Access, San Francisco; and Birkbeck Cinema in collaboration with the Serpentine Galleries, London. Her writing has been published in *Radical Teacher*, *Studio Magazine*, and *Affidavit*, and she is currently working on her first book, in addition to publishing numerous artist's books. Smith has received awards from Creative Capital, Fine Arts Work Center, the Queens Museum, Skowhegan School of Painting and Sculpture, Rema Hort Mann Foundation, the Franklin Furnace Fund, and Art Matters. She is an artist-educator with unique experience within and outside of museums, and her work considering the ways that children interface with the carceral system influenced her inclusion in the exhibition and this volume.

Mierle Laderman Ukeles is a ground-breaking artist based in Israel. Her 1969 "Manifesto for Maintenance Art 1969! Proposal for an Exhibition 'CARE,'" a widely influential text, was written, she says, as "a call for revolution" and also as an exhibition proposal. It conceptualized the possibility of maintenance as a creative strategy. Through works in both the public and the private domains, Ukeles has fostered an artistic practice that foregrounds labor and care as well as a commitment to maintenance as a collaborative endeavor aimed at preservation, repair, and survival. Her work in a range of media, including performance, video, digital animation, light and sound, photography, and social sculpture, has been exhibited internationally. Ukeles holds degrees in international relations from Barnard College and in interrelated arts from New York University. For forty-four years, she has been the unsalaried official artist in residence for the New York City Department of Sanitation. Her "Manifesto for Maintenance Art" is a primary text for this exhibition and catalogue. She is a mother to her three children and a recent grandmother.

Carmen Winant is an artist and Associate Professor in the Department of Art at the Ohio State University, where she is the Roy Lichtenstein Chair of Studio Art, and an unaffiliated member of the faculty. Winant's work utilizes installation and collage strategies to examine feminist modes of survival and revolt. Her recent projects have been shown at the Museum of Modern Art and SculptureCenter, New York; and the Columbus Museum of Art and Wexner Center of the Arts, Columbus. In 2019, as part of the CONTACT Photography Festival, twenty-six of her billboards were mounted across Canada. Her recent artist's books include *My Birth* (2018) and *Notes on Fundamental Joy* (2019). Winant was a key interlocutor in the development of the exhibition whose long-standing engagement with childhood as a subject begins with her articulated position as a mother and an artist. She is a mother to her two sons, Carlo and Rafa, whom she shares with her partner, Luke Stettner.

Lenders to the Exhibition

ACA Galleries, New York
Ann Agee, New York
Francis Alÿs, Mexico City
American Folk Art Museum, New York
Barbara Bablinsky Labs, New York
Tanya Bonakdar Gallery, New York/Los
    Angeles
Joel Braslow, New York
The Broad Art Foundation, Los Angeles
Galerie Buchholz, Berlin, Cologne, and
    New York
Catharine Clark Gallery, San Francisco
Lenka Clayton, Pittsburgh
James Cohan, New York
Steve Corkin and Dan Maddalena, Boston
Pilar Corrias, London
Karon Davis, Los Angeles
Fotene Demoulas and Tom Coté, Boston
Frayda and Ronald Feldman, New York
Ronald Feldman Gallery, New York
Fortes D'Aloia & Gabriel, Brazil
Fortnight Institute, New York
Stephen Friedman Gallery, London
Gagosian Gallery
Gladstone Gallery, New York and Brussels
Robert Gober, New York
Golden Gate Kindergarten Association,
    San Francisco
Solomon R. Guggenheim Museum,
    New York
Trenton Doyle Hancock, Houston
Estate of Duane Hanson
Harvard Art Museums, Cambridge,
    Massachusetts
Mona Hatoum, London
Sharon Hayes, Philadelphia
Higher Pictures Generation, New York
Ekua Holmes, Roxbury, Massachusetts
Roxanne Ingoe, New York
Matt and Yasmine Johnson,
    Los Angeles

Jan Kaps, Cologne, Germany
Collection Köser, Cologne, Germany
Justine Kurland, New York
Tanya Leighton Gallery, Berlin and
    Los Angeles
Tau Lewis, New York
Matthew Marks Gallery, New York
Oscar Murillo
Museum of Fine Arts, Boston
The Museum of Modern Art, New York
Rivane Neuenschwander, São Paulo
Night Gallery, Los Angeles
Kimberly and Elliot Perry, Memphis,
    Tennessee
Patron Gallery, Chicago
P.P.O.W., New York
Princeton University Art Museum,
    New Jersey
Private collection, Detroit
Private collection, New York
Private collection, Switzerland
Charles Ray, Los Angeles
Faith Ringgold, New York
Rachel Rose, New York
Rose Art Museum at Brandeis University,
    Waltham, Massachusetts
Herbert and Lenore Schorr, New Jersey
Michael Sherman, Los Angeles
Kamil and Jake Shields, Washington, DC
Heji Shin, Berlin
Tate, London
White Cube, London
Wilding Cran Gallery, Los Angeles
Kehinde Wiley, New York
Carmen Winant, Columbus, Ohio
Galerie Thomas Zander, Cologne,
    Germany
Zentrum Paul Klee, Bern, Switzerland
David Zwirner

Reproduction Credits

Among Children, pp. 26–41
pp. 30–31: Courtesy the Estate of Duane Hanson and Gagosian Gallery. © 2021 Estate of Duane Hanson / Licensed by VAGA at Artists Rights Society (ARS), NY); p. 33: Courtesy Alexander and Bonin, New York. Photo by Joerg Lohse. © John Ahearn; pp. 34–35: Courtesy the artist and Wilding Cran Gallery, Los Angeles. Photos by Jeff McLane. © Karon Davis; pp. 36–37: Courtesy the artist and Jan Kaps, Cologne, Germany. © Berenice Olmedo; pp. 38–39: Courtesy the artist and Night Gallery, Los Angeles. © Tau Lewis; p. 41: Courtesy the artist and Matthew Marks Gallery, New York. © Charles Ray.

Draw Like a Child, pp. 42–75
pp. 46 and 49–51: Courtesy Zentrum Paul Klee image archive. © 2022 Artists Rights Society (ARS), New York; p. 47: Photo © President and Fellows of Harvard College. © Artists Rights Society (ARS), New York; p. 53: © Estate of Allan Rohan Crite; pp. 55–59: © Film Documents LLC, Courtesy Galerie Thomas Zander, Cologne, Germany; p. 61: Image courtesy Princeton University Art Museum. © Estate of Jean-Michel Basquiat. Licensed by Artestar, New York; pp. 62–63: © Tate, London / Art Resource, NY. © 2021 Artists Rights Society (ARS), New York / IVARO, Dublin; p. 65: Image courtesy Solomon R. Guggenheim Museum, New York. © Glenn Ligon; Courtesy the artist, Hauser & Wirth, New York, Regen Projects, Los Angeles, Thomas Dane Gallery, London and Chantal Crousel, Paris; pp. 66–69: Courtesy the artist and Tanya Bonakdar Gallery, New York / Los Angeles, Fortes D'Aloia & Gabriel, Brazil, Stephen Friedman Gallery, London. © Rivane Neuenschwander; pp. 70–71: Courtesy the artist; pp. 72–75: Used by permission of the Golden Gate Kindergarten Association, San Francisco.

The Page Is a World, pp. 76–103
pp. 80–83: Photo by Gavin Ashworth. © American Folk Art Museum / Art Resource, NY. © 2021 Kiyoko Lerner / Artists Rights Society (ARS), New York; pp. 84–91: Courtesy the artist and James Cohan, New York. © Trenton Doyle Hancock; pp. 92–93: Courtesy the artist, Gladstone Gallery, New York and Brussels, and Pilar Corrias, London. Photo: Andrea Rossetti; pp. 94–95: Courtesy the artist, Gladstone Gallery, New York and Brussels, and Pilar Corrias, London. © Rachel Rose; p. 97: Courtesy the artist and ACA Galleries, New York. © Faith Ringgold / Artists Rights Society (ARS), New York; pp. 98–99, 101: Courtesy the artist. © Ekua Holmes; pp. 102–3: Courtesy the artist and Jack Shainman Gallery, New York. © Becky Suss.

Born into Being, pp. 104–29
pp. 109–11: Courtesy the artist and Galerie Buchholz, Berlin, Cologne, and New York. © Heji Shin; p. 112: Photo by Gunter Lepkowski; pp. 112–13: Courtesy the artist and Tanya Leighton Gallery, Berlin and Los Angeles. © Sharon Hayes; p. 115: Courtesy the artist and Matthew Marks Gallery, New York. © Robert Gober; pp. 116–17: Courtesy the artist and White Cube, London. Photo © White Cube (Theo Christelis). © Mona Hatoum; pp. 118–19: Courtesy the artist, JTT, New York, Carlos/Ishikawa, London, and Regen Projects, Los Angeles. © Sable Elyse Smith; pp. 120–21: Courtesy the artist, JTT, New York, Carlos/Ishikawa, London, and Regen Projects, Los Angeles. Photo by Charles Benton. © Sable Elyse Smith; pp. 123–25: Courtesy the artist and Vielmetter, Los Angeles. © Deborah Roberts; pp. 126–29: Courtesy the artist, Victoria Miro, and David Zwirner. © Njideka Akunyili Crosby.

Gestures of Care, pp. 130–55
pp. 134–39: Courtesy the artist and P.P.O.W.,
New York. © Ann Agee; pp. 140–41:
Courtesy the artist and Ronald Feldman
Gallery, New York. © Mierle Laderman
Ukeles; pp. 142–45: Courtesy the artist and
Catharine Clark Gallery, San Francisco.
© Lenka Clayton; pp. 146–47: Digital Image
© The Museum of Modern Art/Licensed
by SCALA / Art Resource, NY. © Cathy
Wilkes; p. 149: Courtesy the artist and
P.P.O.W., New York. © Jay Lynn Gomez;
pp. 150–51: Courtesy the artist and Casey
Kaplan Gallery, New York. © Jordan
Casteel; pp. 152–55: Courtesy the artist and
Higher Pictures Generation, New York.
© Justine Kurland.

After School, pp. 156–75
p. 161: Courtesy Rose Art Museum at
Brandeis University, Photo by Charles
Mayer; pp. 162–65: Photos by Luke Stettner.
© Carmen Winant; pp. 166–67: Courtesy
the artist and PinchukArtCentre, Kyiv,
Ukraine. Photo by Sergey Illin; pp. 168–
71: Photos by Tim Bowditch and Reinis
Lismanis. Courtesy the artist; pp. 172–75:
Courtesy the artist and David Zwirner.
© Francis Alÿs.

**De Blois, "Slightly Closer to the Heart of
Creation than Usual, but Still Not Close
Enough," pp. 179–91**
p. 181, left: Courtesy Unterwegs Antiquariat
M.-L. Surek-Becker, Berlin; p. 181, right:
Courtesy Zentrum Paul Klee image archive;
p. 185: Rhoda Kellogg International Child
Art Collection. Used with permission of the
Golden Gate Kindergarten Association,
San Francisco; p. 186: Courtesy the artist.

Bennett, "King Malcolm," pp. 193–201
p. 198: Courtesy Walker Art Center,
Minneapolis.

Erickson, "The Third Way," pp. 203–18
p. 207: Photo by Geoffrey Clements. Digital
image © Whitney Museum of American
Art / Licensed by Scala / Art Resource,
New York; p. 208: Courtesy Tate, London.
© Mona Hatoum; p. 211: Photo by Jeff
McLane. Courtesy the artist and Vielmetter,
Los Angeles. © Deborah Roberts.

**Higonnet, "No More Innocent Signs,"
pp. 221–31**
p. 223: © 2021 The Jacob and Gwendolyn
Knight Lawrence Foundation, Seattle /
Artists Rights Society (ARS), New York; p.
224: Courtesy the artist and Lisson Gallery.
© Hugh Hayden; p. 228: Courtesy the artist
and Catharine Clark Gallery, San Francisco.
© Lenka Clayton.

**Conversation: Naima J. Keith, Oscar
Murillo, and Sable Elyse Smith, pp.
241–50**
p. 242: Courtesy Sable Elyse Smith, JTT,
New York, Carlos/Ishikawa, London,
and Regen Projects, Los Angeles; p. 244:
Courtesy Hauser & Wirth. © Dieter Roth
Estate; pp. 245, 249: Courtesy Frequencies
Institute.

**Conversation: Mierle Laderman Ukeles
and Carmen Winant, pp. 251–59**
p. 255: Courtesy the artist and Ronald
Feldman Gallery, New York. © Mierle
Laderman Ukeles; p. 256: Courtesy the
artist. © 2018 The Museum of Modern Art.
Photo: Kurt Heumiller.

Every reasonable attempt has been made
to identify owners of copyright. Errors or
omissions will be corrected in subsequent
editions.

Reproduction Credits

This book is published on the occasion of:

To Begin Again: Artists and Childhood

Organized by Ruth Erickson,
Mannion Family Senior Curator, with
Jeffrey De Blois, Associate Curator
and Publications Manager,
Institute of Contemporary Art/Boston

October 6, 2022–February 26, 2023

Support for *To Begin Again:
Artists and Childhood* is provided
by First Republic Bank.

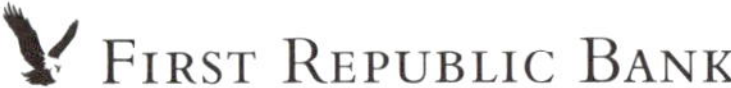
FIRST REPUBLIC BANK

Additional supoort is generously provid-
ed by Kate and Chuck Brizius, Paul and
Katie Buttenwieser, Marina Kalb and David
Feinberg, Andree LeBoeuf Foundation,
Kristen and Kent Lucken, Tristin and Martin
Mannion, Erica and Ted Pappendick, and
Cynthia and John Reed.

Published in 2022 by the Institute
of Contemporary Art/Boston and
DelMonico Books • D.A.P.

Institute of Contemporary Art/Boston
25 Harbor Shore Drive
Boston, MA 02210
www.icaboston.org

DelMonico Books
Available through ARTBOOK | D.A.P.
75 Broad Street, Suite 630
New York, NY 10004
artbook.com
delmonicobooks.com

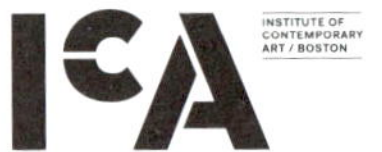

Library of Congress Control Number:
2022910175

ISBN: 978-1-63681-070-6

A CIP catalogue record for this book
is available from the British Library.

Editors: Jeffrey De Blois and Ruth Erickson
Copyeditor: Michelle Piranio
Proofreader: Bruno George
Designer: Mark Owens
Printing: die Keure

Type: ABC Walter Neue (Dinamo)
and OPS Blok (Our Polite Society)

Printed and bound in Belgium

Front cover: Deborah Roberts, *Sisterly Love*
(detail), 2021. Acrylic and collage on canvas.
65 × 125 inches (165.1 × 317.5 cm)

Enpapers: Brian Belott, *Dr. Kid President Jr.*
(detail), 2022. Wall-based installation, including paintings and wallpaper, with drawings
from the Rhoda Kellogg International Child
Art Collection, San Francisco

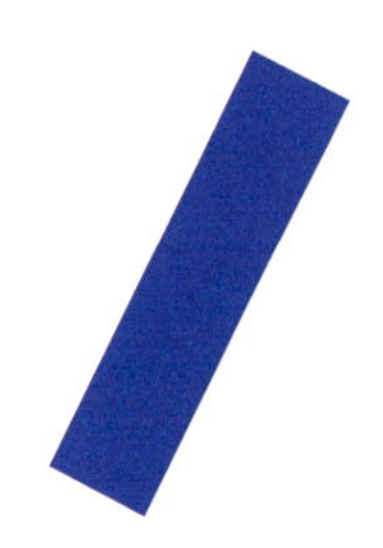

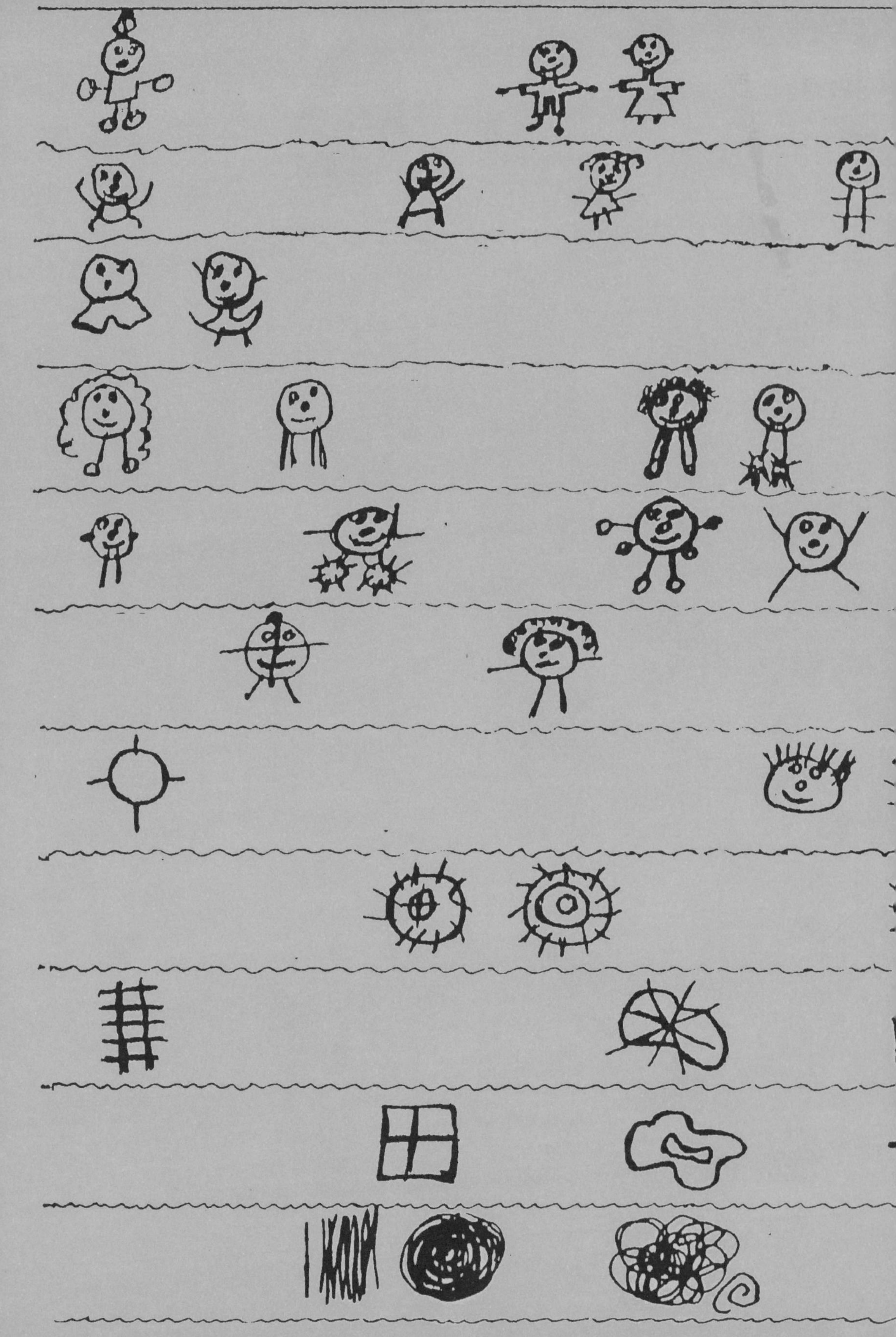